Creative Writer's Handbook

SECOND EDITION

PHILIP K. JASON
ALLAN B. LEFCOWITZ

United States Naval Academy

PRENTICE HALL, Englewood Cliffs, NJ 07632

Library of Congress Cataloging-in-Publication Data

Jason, Philip K.
  Creative writer's handbook / Philip K. Jason, Allan B. Lefcowitz.
  —2nd ed.
      p.   cm.
  Includes bibliographical references and index
  ISBN 0-13-709099-4 (pbk.)
    1. Authorship.   2. Creative writing.   I. Lefcowitz, Allan B.
  II. Title
  PN145.J37   1994
  808'.02—dc20   93-7757
                                                            CIP

To our students—
Past, present, and future

Acquisitions editor: Alison Reeves
Editorial/production supervision and interior design: Margaret Antonini
Cover design: Bruce Kenselaar
Production coordinators: Herb Klein, Tricia Kenny
Assistant editor: Kara Hado

Pages 373–377 constitutes an extension of the copyright page.

Printed in the United States of America
10   9   8   7   6   5   4   3   2   1

ISBN   0-13-709099-X

Prentice-Hall International (UK) Limited, *London*
Prentice-Hall of Australia Pty. Limited, *Sydney*
Prentice-Hall Canada Inc., *Toronto*
Prentice-Hall Hispanoamericana, S.A., *Mexico*
Prentice-Hall India Private Limited, *New Delhi*
Prentice-Hall of Japan, Inc., *Tokyo*
Simon & Schuster Asia Pte Ltd., *Singapore*
Editora Prentice-Hall do Brasil, Ltda., *Rio de Janeiro*

Contents

ANTHOLOGY OF POEMS

Because the many illustrative poems in this text are not found in a single chapter, we provide the following list for convenience.

See also excerpts from works by Robert Browning, John Ciardi, Margaret Gibson, Richard Hugo, Philip Levine, Andrew Marvell, Marianne Moore, Alexander Pope, Wyatt Prunty, John W. Saxe, William Shakespeare, Dave Smith, Andrien Stoutenburg, Dylan Thomas, and many student poets (page references in index).

Preface

The *Creative Writer's Handbook* is designed to help beginners. While creativity itself cannot be taught, our premise is that you can learn to tap and shape your creative energies. We do not hold with that popular image of the creative artist as a solitary, inspired soul who spins out a sublime work without sweat and labor. Paradoxically, you need to be "practical" about creative writing.

Just as people with physical gifts can be coached so that these gifts are perfected, people with creative imaginations can be led to exercise and develop that creativity. They can be "coached" in the intricacies of language and literary structure. Though abilities will differ, our experience with hundreds of students in creative writing classes and workshops has shown us that most people have more creative talent than they realize. When they first begin to practice the craft, however, they need some direction about conventions, forms, and procedures. Each writer does not need to invent the game for him or herself.

This book began because we felt that the texts available to us, though admirable, were too advanced *for beginners.* They were like calculus to those who need algebra. We wanted a text that responded to the issues we faced in the classroom and the workshop with novice writers who needed to know everything from the rules of the game, to the proper formats, to the professional lingo. We had in mind a text that students could refer to for specific information and help on basic issues and problems.

In each chapter, we have combined the most useful theory, practical advice, and examples. The many questions and exercises are designed to involve you in the issues and practice of literary craft. Some of them may even spark results worth developing into poems, stories, or plays.

Although your creative energies can be directed to produce successful results, not every writer can or deserves to make it into print, just as not every athlete can make it to the Olympics. Still, with hard work in a sport, craft, or art, you can improve, learn from experience and from authority, and find ways of making any such activity pleasurable and useful. Our first premise is rooted in the idea that doing creative writing is valuable in itself, if only to increase one's understanding of just how hard it is to write successfully.

Another premise is that *any* successful writing is finally the result of rigorous editing. As important as it is to get something down on paper in the first place—and we have given that problem much of our attention—it is even more important to learn how to shape and reshape, how to spot your problems, and how to work out your solutions. Every writer must learn how to take and use criticism and, at some point, every successful writer must take on the role of self-editor.

In the *Creative Writer's Handbook* we have provided a series of occasions for you to think, read, investigate, write, write again, and rewrite—and also to imitate, invent, respond, discover, and surprise yourself. However, even though we have given the order of presentation considerable thought, there can be as many paths through the book as there are readers. While this text is aimed at the student in the creative writing course, we have kept in mind the needs of the writer who wants to go at it solo.

The five chapters of "Part I: A Writer's Concerns" take up issues of importance to every creative writer; the next nine chapters—Parts II, III, and IV—focus on specific issues in the major genres; the final two chapters, Part V, contain reference materials for writers.

Chapter 1 provides an opportunity for you to assess your motives and attitudes as a student of writing. We suggest ways that will help you to become assertive, disciplined, and ready for work. We encourage you to be serious, but not sour. Once you are "Working Like a Writer," you have a fighting chance of doing the work of a writer.

Chapter 2, "Keeping a Journal," aims to show one way that a writer forces commitment. Writers write. We provide a full box of suggestions to keep you working, but the goal is for you to strike off on your own. The journal is your lab, your practice field, where you can make false starts, mistakes, and discoveries.

Chapter 3 contains the broad, somewhat technical subject of "Point of View." In the journal, a person very close to the intimate "I" does almost all of the recording. Literary creations, however, often involve a less literally autobiographical "I." Who is the speaker in the story or poem? What difference does it make? Exploring these key questions requires careful reading and a number of exercises—occasions—to help you become confident in handling this complex, unavoidable issue.

In Chapter 4, "Language Is Your Medium," you have an opportunity to exercise all the muscles in the body of words you need to command, and to get them working in harmony. You don't expect a landscape painter to succeed without knowing anything about lines, shapes, and colors, and about brushes, pigments, and canvas. The writer too must master the materials, in this case the materials of language. Most of us take language for granted—it's something we're born to. Remember, however, that just as the demands put upon your language skills are now heightened, your concern for language must be similarly heightened. We think you will enjoy these jumping jacks, push-ups, and other language calisthenics.

Chapter 5 takes up the interplay between imagination and fact. In "Invention and Research" we share ideas and techniques, collected in many places over many years, that will enable you to access your creative energies. This chapter includes suggestions on how to find the facts you need to build the worlds your imagination will create. It also provides exercises that show how to use facts to stimulate creativity. In these exercises we show how writers can create their own games.

These first five chapters are grounded in general issues, so you can come to understand the ways in which any writing task can be "creative." In the next nine chapters, you will explore the specific conventions and special concerns of the major genres: poetry, prose fiction, and drama. These chapters, the next three parts of the book, are, of course, the heart of the book; they are substantially more detailed than the preliminary chapters and require a slower pace.

The genre chapters combine information, examples, and exercises and contain both professional and student work to show various levels of achievement. We have isolated the major problems that beginners have and examined the nature and causes of those problems. Often we suggest solutions. We are convinced that effective creative writing is a network of solved problems.

Each of the three parts devoted to genre exploration begins with a chapter focusing on the conventions through which that genre defines itself. Our bias here is that without coming to grips with the conventions, you cannot reach an audience, nor can you ever become effectively unconventional.

In this book, "conventional" refers to the customs or protocols of a literary type. Just as religious groups have set patterns of observance, just as a meeting of foreign ministers has its established courtesies, just as a formal meeting has its way of getting things done (following, for instance, Robert's Rules of Order), so literary types have their conventional—customary—methods of expression. Conventions enable everyone to start off with an agreement about the ground rules, and so, it is *through* these conventions, not *despite* them, that creative expression takes place. Through them, you meet the audience halfway.

Part Five provides a writer's tool box. Chapter 15, "from Revision to Submission," aims at further development of editorial skills. It also explains and illustrates the conventions of manuscript form and discusses strategies for submitting work to editors. The lists in "Tools and Resources," Chapter 16, are not meant to be definitive but suggestive, illustrating the kinds of books a creative writer wants to know about or own. The book concludes with a glossary of key terms.

As much as possible we have followed our own classroom practice. We have tried to provide occasions for writing. Our approach is more like that of editors and writers than of critics. We have tried to give a realistic picture of the processes, demands, and rewards of the game. We cannot, of course, touch on everything. You will need someone—a teacher, workshop leader, or editor—to deal with the exceptions and complications.

For a Teacher or Workshop Leader

We have included many more examples and exercises than anyone could use, even in a year-long course or workshop, so that both you and your students might have a variety from which to choose.

We invite you, as we do all our readers, to send us the results of these exercises for possible inclusion in future editions, as well as exercises of your own. We would also like to hear about aspects of craft you would like to see treated more fully. On the other hand, where do you think we could cut back? Remembering that this text is for beginning creative writers, please let us know what elements we missed completely. As editor out in the field, you become our best source for improving the book.

Philip K. Jason
Allan B. Lefcowitz

Preface to Second Edition

This new edition emphasizes more consistently the interweave of techniques among poetry, fiction, and drama. Throughout, we have made minor revisions to tighten and improve exercises. Benefitting from the suggestions of teachers who used the first edition and in response to student users, we have added brief sections on style and on long fiction (the novel). We have added new illustrative material on journal keeping, brainstorming with researched material, and poetic forms.

We have deleted the chapter on the creative writer and word processing that seemed a useful feature several years ago, but we have absorbed some of that material into other chapters: our second edition retains a high consciousness about how word processing affects the writing process.

We have replaced our major illustrative play, *The Browning Version* by Terence Rattigan, with the briefer and somewhat more accessible *Trifles* by Susan Glaspell. This substitution, of course, brings with it a new discussion and set of exercises. We think we have covered the essential ground on playwriting more efficiently and more attractively.

Finally, we have updated the "Tools and Resources" chapter and refined the Glossary.

Once again, we invite you to share your experiences in using this text so that we continue to improve it.

PKJ
ABL

1

Working Like a Writer

ATTITUDES

The mere *desire* to be a writer is not sufficient. You need to train yourself in certain habits of mind and work, develop the attitudes, that can help carry you from the desire to the reality. This chapter focuses on one attitude in particular—*taking a professional stance* toward your work, your audience, and your editor.

While you can have many motives for writing, usually the reader has only one motive for reading: to experience writing that pleases both in its shape and subject. Of course, both experts and students in a field—let's say nuclear physics—might slug their way through poorly expressed prose to get information they need in order to understand the Big Bang—but most of us would not. To satisfy the readers' desire for writing that pleases, you have to be aware of their needs and then take pains to satisfy them. In fact, 90 percent of what is "creative" in creative writing grows from a professional attitude toward taking pains over what the amateur thinks of as mere details.

For most of us, the *mature* stance toward writing that we are talking about here does not simply happen.

Good creative writing is good writing. In all good writing, the conventions of English mechanics and usage (grammar, punctuation, spelling, word order) remain relevant. These conventions ought not be looked at as a block to creativity; in fact, they are the very things that allow others to share in your creativity. For example, conventional spelling allows you and the reader to share a way of recognizing a word. Mispell to meny wurds and sea how rapidly the goodwill of your reader disappears.

Of course, you may take license with these conventions for special purposes. For example, you may have a character who speaks in ungrammatical ways, or you may decide not to use capitals or punctuation for particular effects (as did e e cummings, the poet). These are purposeful decisions you make from your knowledge and control of the language system. However, flawed prose does not become good poetry. Carelessness, slovenliness, and ignorance do not become virtues just because you are doing "creative" writing.

A professional writer is not satisfied with mere self-expression. If you write only for yourself, you have severely restricted your audience. In any case, your writing will become more effective when you are aware that you must please, involve, awaken, provoke, excite, move—other people. The sense of a potential audience should create in you both energy and a feeling of obligation. Unless you make something happen to a reader, you are not doing anything worthwhile *as a writer*. (There are therapeutic uses of writing, of course, but those are not concerns of this book.)

How can you determine your success? One way is by being in a course or workshop that will provide feedback from the instructor and the other participants. They are your sounding boards, to be replaced at some point by editors and by your own developed editorial capabilities. Learning to invite and make positive use of this feedback—even of harshly negative commentary—is essential to your growth as a writer.

Listen carefully, take notes, and keep an open mind. Of course, you can't write and revise merely to satisfy others. You are the boss. However, you shut your ears to such responses at your peril. The reactions of your teacher and your fellow writers help you develop a consciousness of audience, and your responses to their efforts can sharpen your own editorial skill.

Being a writer means being a reader in a new way—being more conscious of how the game is played. Almost without exception, great athletes are fans of their sport, artists visit galleries and museums, musicians attend concerts. It is reasonable for writers to read, both for pleasure and for professional development. You don't have to reinvent everything about writing to be creative. Existing stories, plays, and poems are the essential context for new work in each genre. As a writer, you must have a knowledge of genre conventions, the scope of literature, and the contemporary literary environment. If you have aspirations to poetry, you should be constantly reading poetry. You need to read your contemporaries as well as the major voices of each literary period. Read, analyze, ponder, imitate, and record your impressions.

As you read, keep your eyes open for blunders you think the writer has made and work out how you might have handled the problem differently. Look for techniques that you can borrow and apply to your own writing. Imagine your own variations on another writer's characters, images, themes, or premises. Writing is a response to other writing just as much as it is a response to life.

Don't expect miracles. Part of being professional is having patience. Successful writing comes through a mixture of talent, learned skills, and commitment over a period of time. About commitment we have little to say—except that it is indispensable.

A DIGRESSION FOR THE CLASSROOM USER

All we have said until this point assumes that you are serious about becoming a published writer. However, there are many other reasons for reading a book or taking a course in creative writing. Let us discuss some of the possibilities.

- ◆ You always wanted to try writing something, so you thought you would take this course. A good enough reason. Your desire to experiment, to try something new, should be given an outlet. Take maximum advantage of this pleasant fact: your school has made this opportunity available to you. Though you may never go further with your writing than this course, you will have satisfied your curiosity. Certainly, you will come away with some sense of the demands placed upon a creative writer, and your appreciation of literature should only be enhanced by your having faced the series of complex problems that a successful writer must solve.

- ◆ You always had trouble with writing in other courses, so you thought you would take a course that focuses on writing. A good motive, but maybe this is the wrong course. A creative writing course is neither a remedial course nor a review of grammar and mechanics; successful creative writing builds on a firm control over the basic conventions of the written language. On the other hand, if you write correctly but not *effectively,* a creative writing course can help you. The attention to writing strategies, diction, organization, figurative language, and other issues can benefit any writer. All writing becomes creative when it escapes being bland, meandering, and impersonal. So, yes, your efforts in imaginative literature will make a positive contribution to your general writing ability—though only if the fundamentals are well in hand.

- ◆ You needed to fulfill a distribution requirement and this was the only humanities course that fit your schedule. A practical reason, certainly, but not an impressive one. The key to what happens now is your attitude. Others are in the course for more urgent, personal reasons. As a matter of respect for them, you have to agree to be serious about this endeavor. Be positive. Get the most out of the situation. You will meet some interesting people, and you will have fun reading their work as well as the work of accomplished, published writers. Remember also that everyone can benefit from the kind of engagement with language and human issues that this course will afford.

On Being Unprofessional

You will have a productive, professional attitude when you no longer offer defenses for unsatisfactory work. Here is a small sampling of unprofessional stances toward criticism of one's writing:

1. "That's how I felt" or "that's what I believe," when somebody points to a writing problem in a work. This "defense" confuses the issue. If the criticism is about fuzzy diction, for example, by defending the legitimacy of our feelings or belief, we are avoiding the issue of the *effectiveness* of our writing. What often happens is that the writer has only managed to state an emotion or idea and hasn't made it live for the reader. Moreover, the excuse assumes that the reader cares about the "I" or that a record of personal experience or belief, in and of itself, has merit. The writer's job is to create experience through language. Of course, we always know (or do we?) what *we're* talking about, so that as readers of our own work we are privileged in ways that make us poor critics of it. The reader doesn't care how the writer feels. The real question is: Has the writer made the *reader* feel?

2. "But it really happened like that." This excuse focuses on events rather than feelings. We mistake a certain kind of accuracy in rendering events that are our source experiences with the needs of the work at hand. The mere fact that something really happened does not justify placing it in a story, play, or narrative poem. The writer's job is to use experience, not be used by it. If it is important *to the story* that the gas tank was one-quarter full or that early Beatles tunes were being played on the radio or that the predicted thunderstorm did not come, then give the reader such information. Remember that the demands of the story are not *necessarily* what happened, especially if what happened is downright tedious. Your job is to convince the reader that the event *happened in the story,* not that you saw it happen in the streets. Of course, if something is important to the story and did not happen, put it in.

3. "Doesn't 'creative' mean I can do what I want?" This is almost a meaningless question. It's similar to saying, "doesn't 'freedom' mean I can do what I want?" Both questions reveal frivolous attitudes. The

freedoms we have are a result of our agreements to limit ourselves; we have responsibilities to others. Similarly, there are limitations—conventions of language and genre—that you must master as part of your responsibility to readers. We know we've said this before. We'll no doubt say it again.

4. "What are the formulae?" While we do have to work with and through conventions of the language system and of the genre, creative writing is not the same as mathematics. Trial and error are just as often the means to success as is a clear, logical plan. A writer cannot be the slave of prescriptions or categories. Formula writing produces some kinds of popular literature and some superficially pleasing work, but nothing significant gets done by plugging material into formulas. The answers are always inside the writer, never outside. Your job is to make thinking in the conventions second nature so that you draw on them spontaneously rather than reach for them like so many cookie cutters. There are no easy answers.

5. "Isn't it just a matter of taste?" Certainly, it is a matter of taste whether someone likes avant-garde writing; it is a matter of taste whether one likes mystery stories; it is a matter of taste whether one likes long, elaborate sentences. Many aspects of writing, however, are also matters of knowledge about usable traditions. Someone may know these traditions better than you and know better how to manipulate them. Someone else may have read more widely than you. Still someone else's taste may have more weight than yours right now because that person has greater experience. You ignore such judgment at your peril. However, if you feel strongly about something, from a detail to an entire work, stick to your guns. Just be willing to pay the price your confidence may cost. That price ranges from turning off a reader to being rejected by an editor.

6. "In his recent bestseller, Clancy Steiningway did the same thing you criticized me for. If he can get away with it, why can't I?" Sometimes poor writing gets published and sells well; sometimes famous writers get by on their reputations; sometimes other elements in a work are so effectively handled or the subject matter is so engrossing that stretches of poor writing or violations of useful conventions are overlooked. That such things happen is not an excuse for shoddy practice, and your instructor cannot in good conscience encourage bad habits. If Steiningway has gotten away with chaotic plotting, inconsistent characters, or leaden dialogue, rest assured that his work wasn't published *because* of these traits. Also, when the novice writer claims a parallel or precedent in the work of an accomplished (or honored) professional that similarity is often quite superficial. Did you *really* do the same thing? Or perhaps Steiningway has managed to pull off

something quite risky while the beginner has failed miserably. The point then is not to misunderstand the instructor's criticism: usually such strategies, devices, or styles don't work. Until you have Steiningway's skills, perhaps you should avoid such practices.

WORKING HABITS

Discipline is part of the professional attitude. Newspaper columnist Colman McCarthy offered his students these ten guidelines:

1. Work in a location safe from noise and interruptions.
2. Begin with a definite goal of how long your writing period will last. If five minutes, fine. If five hours, fine. Just know. Then regularize. Gandhi, who wrote more than 10 million words in his lifetime, put down 500 words every day for fifty years.
3. Learn new words. Have a vocabulary program. Add a new word a day, a week, a month, whatever. Keep adding, that's all. Master the one- and two-syllable Anglo-Saxon words. Five- and six-syllable Latin-Greek derivations are for show-offs. Study idioms.
4. Spray disinfectant on clichés, slogans, bromides. Eliminate useless words such as *very, nice, quite, rather, presently, brilliant.* Go over each piece word by word and cut each that doesn't work.
5. Never begin a piece of writing with *the.* Writers who do so are yawning in print, at you.
6. If you are not in the mood to write, write anyway. Writing is more sweat than sweetness, more fidelity than feelings. If you need to be in the mood to write, the only topic you'll ever master is "moods."
7. When not writing, don't bore people by quoting yourself. Don't boast, even covertly, about where you've just been published. And don't quiz friends on whether they have (a) read your latest literary effort, (b) caught its "full meaning," (c) taped it on the refrigerator door.
8. Comfort other writers. Read their latest efforts, strive to catch its "full meaning," and make room among the recipes and kids' drawing on the refrigerator door.
9. Spend as much time reading as writing, but read only writers who know Samuel Johnson's edict, "What is written without effort is in general read without pleasure." Skip hacks.
10. Be a fanatical reviser. Remember Paul Engle's line: writing is rewriting what you have rewritten. Never trust a first draft. Never be satisfied with a second. Never think a third is your best. Never hope that a last draft is a final draft. Come back in ten years for revision.

These suggestions (reported in the *Washington Post*, January 2, 1987) make pretty good sense to us. Here are some additional observations about writing that McCarthy quotes:

"A work of art is first of all work."

Paul Engle

"I spent all morning putting in a comma and all afternoon taking it out."

Oscar Wilde

"Real seriousness in regard to writing is one of the two absolute necessities. The other, unfortunately, is talent."

Ernest Hemingway

"My family can always tell when I'm well into a novel because the meals get very crummy."

Anne Tyler

"Without devotion, writing is secretarial work."

Colman McCarthy

We have a few additional suggestions, expansions on McCarthy's points, that should help you get your work as a writer done as efficiently as possible.

First, ideally you want a large, clear working surface so that you don't need to stack materials on top of one another. Have the materials you need available at your work space. Paper, card files, pens and pencils, and resources such as dictionaries, handbooks, and style manuals should all be handy. You don't want to interrupt your work because something you need isn't there. If you compose on the computer, take advantage of the accessory software packages that serve the same ends as these desk references. Have your word processor's reference manual handy. Keep plenty of formatted disks on hand for backing up your files. Stock extra printer ribbons. In short, set up your space and equipment so you can get down to work with as few distractions as possible.

Second, commit regular periods of time to writing. Writing, like everything else of importance, needs its established time as well as its place. Reinforce your working procedures so they become working habits. Then, when it's "time to write" and you are in your writing environment, getting your work done will become just a bit easier.

Third, even when you are running hot on a piece of writing, a moment will come when you feel that your inspiration or energy is about to run dry. Rather than continue writing until you have squeezed all the juices from that session, stop in the middle of a sentence, or scene, or line that you are fairly sure you know how to finish. In your next writing session you will have some work that you can complete easily—a running start.

Fourth, don't talk about your work too much to friends, family, or teachers. Telling your story over a brandy to a fascinated lover has one doubtful benefit attached to two certain drawbacks. Talking out your idea does get you immediate feedback. If the feedback pumps you up, however, it also removes that inner urge to do the communication the hard way—in writing. And if the feedback is negative, you might abandon an idea that is in fact a good one but just doesn't "sound" good in a crowded bar. Your job is not to talk about but to write about.

Fifth, don't keep yourself from moving onward in a piece of writing by looking for an ideal beginning, ideal phrasing, or ideal structure. The answer to the question "Where should I begin?" is the same answer you give to the question "Where does a 500-pound gorilla sleep?" In fact, not only can you can begin writing your poem or story or play any place you want to, but also you need not be concerned about the conventions, coherence, logic, or any other responsibility to the reader—just so long as you are drafting.

This paradox is only apparent, not real. It makes no difference where you begin or by what fits and starts you proceed. What counts is *where you decide— finally—to have your reader begin and proceed.* In other words, what counts is the final draft. Don't try to be perfectly polished as you go along, thinking you can avoid rewriting. Remember the fate of Grande, a character in Camus's *The Plague*, who believed he would write the perfect novel if only he could find the ideal opening sentence. He never got beyond the first sentence. So don't be afraid of letting the material flow undisturbed. In later drafts your editor-self can take over from your writer-self and channel the flow in useful directions.

Finally, you must set high standards and be ready for disappointment. As coaches say about exercise, "No pain, no gain." We are not suggesting that writing is a form of self-punishment, but it is a constant struggle. Still, just as athletes can find great pleasure in preparing for the game, you can find as many pleasures in the process of writing as in the results. Think of the analogy to an athlete again. If only the results—the winning or losing—matter to you, you can find them in something as unimportant as tossing a coin.

Something else must be at the heart of the endeavor to invest so much love and caring in, let us say, hours of exercise for one minute on a balance beam. There must be satisfactions in the exercise itself—the doing. What we do as writers is practice, plan, and engage ourselves in the intricate pressures of choosing well, tearing apart, rediscovering, rebuilding—in short, recognizing that literary works *become.*

There are few accomplishments as ultimately rewarding and meaningful as creating a literary work through which visions of the human experience are shared or, at a more modest level, people are entertained and diverted for a moment. When that sharing happens, the world is a better place—if only because it's a little less lonely. These are lofty but distant goals. On a day-to-day basis writers learn to find pleasure in the pains of creation.

A WORD ABOUT INTENTIONS

Eudora Welty said: "It was not my intention—it never was—to invent a character who should speak for me, the author, the person. A character is in a story to fill a role there, and the character's life is defined by that surrounding—indeed is created by his own story" (from *One Writer's Beginnings*, Harvard University Press, 1984). The implication of Welty's statement is that her writing isn't a disguise for something she wishes to hide in her fiction, a kind of sugar coating for what she would like us to swallow about morality, politics, or the ultimate purposes and significance of almost anything. Although any character in a play or story, any speaker in a poem, is a partial revelation of the writer, the *intention* to reveal one's self or sell one's views is not a necessary or useful approach to the art.

The truth is that you can't help but reveal yourself when you write honestly. Your worldview is the lens through which you look at experience, choose plots, characters, images, and settings. The conscious pressure of trying to make a point—of sending a message—can block the flow and distort the final shape of any literary work. An artwork, when it goes well, has a life of its own, its own demands. Sometimes *it* has something to say, and you need to let the writing process make such discoveries.

To quote Welty again, "If somewhere in its course your work seems to you to have come into a life of its own, and you can stand back from it and leave it be, you are looking then at your own subject—I feel."

Aside from thematic or moralistic intentions, we often find ourselves highly motivated by aesthetic ones—we want to put the demonstration of craft before anything else. We act like the tennis player who falls down after every difficult shot to punctuate its difficulty. "Look how clever I am" or "look how hard I am trying" such an attitude appears to say. However, no one enjoys reading a collection of skill exhibitions—not even creative writing teachers. Writings that only call attention to their author's virtuosity are rarely successful. What you learn about the craft of writing should serve your own efforts; it should not be the subject—even the hidden agenda—of what you do.

Nor should you approach your work as if preparing a treasure hunt. Don't put yourself in the position of having to explain that you have purposely buried "hidden meanings" for the reader to dig out. Writing is not like a jigsaw puzzle that the reader puts together after searching out the missing pieces.

In the best writing, themes often emerge while the writer keeps struggling with language and following the characters around. Though it is convenient to begin with an idea, an image or a situation is a better starting point.

Trust yourself, trust the reader, and trust the writing process. Don't ask, "How am I going to get across to my reader that our involvement in Southeast Asia was the result of economic forces?" Ask, "What would my character do next?" "How does he or she feel about these circumstances?" "What words will resonate with the words I have just put down?" Only in the late stages of revision, when a work has announced its purpose—*its* intention—can we allow ourselves some calculating decisions, and then only to be true to the work we have come to understand.

Does this mean that writers proceed with blind ignorance about where they are going? Sometimes yes and sometimes no. That's not the issue. Writing needs an attitude of openness and flexibility even within a plan. A writer's intentions are not what finally matters, and holding on to intentions too fiercely or justifying a work in terms of intentions is a more serious blindness than writing without a clear direction.

In spite of what we have just said, we are not partisans of the idea that art is an end in itself. There is no reason for literature except to communicate something about what it means to be human. What Cynthia Ozick calls "a corona of moral purpose" (in "Innovation and Redemption: What Literature Means") surrounds every significant work of literary art.

This is different, however, from saying that literature must be narrowly or explicitly didactic. We each have our own way of knowing that literature affirms our ability to choose. In writing, we are choosing—asserting our freedom, our capacity to grow and to change. When we do this for ourselves, we do this for others as well: we do it for everyone. This, as Ozick points out, is the essential, implicit moral of creative acts.

FEIFFER®

FEIFFER © 1987 Jules Feiffer. Reprinted with permission of Universal Press Syndicate. All rights reserved.

2

Keeping a Journal

WHY KEEP A JOURNAL?

As you've probably noticed, we have decided to use sports metaphors and analogies in this book. We are not simply trying to jazz up the presentation. We truly believe that writing (some might say all art) satisfies a basic human impulse—the need to play. Actually, we are perhaps never so serious or intent as when we are playing. Just look at the face of someone about to make a billiard shot. Watch a diver prepare for a difficult dive. See how a defensive back in a football game has no other reality than the unfolding play.

This chapter is about one way that writers prepare for playing the game well. We say "one way" because a successful writer's practices cannot be reduced to a formula. On the other hand, it makes good sense to imitate the stance and gestures of those who have made it to the major leagues. What worked for them might just work for you.

Almost all writers keep a journal. Some keep several different journals or notebooks:

- *A working journal* in which they practice writing and work out parts or whole drafts of a poem or story or play.
- *A journal of ideas* for future writing.

♦ *A commonplace book* in which they jot down quotations from their reading, along with their reactions, as models or for inspiration.

Most writers keep a single journal to serve all of these purposes.

What follows is an excerpt from a real journal that contains aspects of all three. The Greek poet George Seferis is reading to get himself started on his writing; he is reacting to his daily experience; he is free-associating; and, finally, he is starting to develop a poem.

> Tuesday Morning, October 8, 1946
>
> I have been working on Cavafy again since last Saturday afternoon. I am reading articles about the poet written in the past and more recently. They bore me. Too much "literature," too much padding in all of them; very few noteworthy observations. I don't yet know if I'm in Cavafy's ambience. A thought put aside for the moment: *I am trying to return to the habit of working.* [Italics added]
>
> I'll read every morning—I started yesterday—about a hundred lines of the *Iliad*.
>
> Yesterday and today were superb days, too much for me; they distract me; I feel terribly lost. As in a ruined house, I have to put many things in order. I don't know if I'll ever be able to reconstruct it.
>
> After swimming: the light is such that it absorbs you as blotter does ink; it absorbs the personality.
>
>> Days are stones. Flintstones
>> that accidentally found each other and made two or three sparks,
>> stones on the threshing floor, struck by horseshoes,
>>   and crushing many people.
>> pebbles in the water with ephemeral rings,
>> wet and multicolored little stones at the seashore,
>> or lekythoi, gravestones that sometimes stop the passerby
>> or bas-reliefs with the rider who went far out to sea
>> or Marsyas or Priapus, groups of phallus-bearers.
>> Days are stones; they crumble one on top of the other.
>
> from *A Poet's Journal*

Journal keeping can get even more elaborate than we have described. Some writers keep separate journals for all aspects of their work: drafts, exercises, dreams, ideas, quotations, newspaper clippings, and so on. We even know one writer who keeps a separate journal for submissions to publications and payments for manuscripts. Most of us are hardly so organized or need to be, and so we recommend much less elaborate journal keeping for you.

The point is to keep a journal. It makes writing a regular part of your life. Many would-be writers hope that an occasional stab at a short story or a poem when the mood strikes them will produce significant results. That attitude is something like expecting to play a par round of golf by playing only once a month. Writing takes practice and preparation.

Let us put the matter less kindly. You should take an armchair writer about as seriously as you take an armchair athlete. Writers write; posers talk about writing. The journal is one place for you to be a writer.

YOUR JOURNAL

Go out now and buy yourself a journal. We suggest that it be either a ruled composition book with a hard cover (approximately 81/2 by 11 inches) or, if you want something more portable, a hardcover "record book" (5 by 8 inches) with ruled lines. The essential idea is to keep your journal in a form that ensures permanence. Avoid loose-leaf notebooks or spiral notebooks from which you can inadvertently rip pages. Tiny flip notebooks don't give you enough room to jot down more than a few words. (Many writers, however, do carry around some kind of small notebook for ideas that come to them in the middle of a workday or a dance.) If you carry your journal around with you, be sure to write your name, address, and phone number at the beginning along with the statement that, in case of loss, you will reward the returner.

Now that portable computers are affordable, the last practical obstacle to keeping an electronic journal has been removed. And, if your journal keeping tends to be a desk-bound activity anyway, why not perform this task with your preferred word processor? The choice of recording technology is yours; see what works best for you and take advantage of it.

Once you have your journal, you need to make it part of your daily routine. At first you probably will need a conscious strategy for keeping it up. Pick a time of day that you promise *always* to write in it. The time you choose should be one that works for you, but it makes sense to choose one in which you are not likely to be interrupted by a phone call or the meter reader.

If you can't keep your writer's notebook every day, then set up an appointment with it for at least three times a week. If you're having discipline problems, find some way to reward yourself for keeping it or to punish yourself when you don't. Here's a trick: tell a friend that you are keeping a writer's journal and say that he or she is to ask you every other day if you have been writing in it—and if you haven't, promise to give your friend a dollar. You may have to modify your behavior to develop the journal-keeping habit, but once you have developed the habit, you will no more think of not writing in your journal than you would think of not brushing your teeth.

It won't do simply to greet the blank page with "Hello, dear journal, I've got nothing to write. Goodbye." That's like doing one push-up and feeling that you have exercised. You have to give the journal enough time so that you can work up a sweat—twenty to thirty minutes a session minimum, enough to get you beyond simply saying "hello" and into the rhythm of writing. Put it another way: you have to run more than a block to get into running.

Journal keeping has nothing to do with feeling inspired. You write in it because you are or want to be a writer. And even when INSPIRATION has deserted you, you write on to prepare yourself for her—or his—return.

WHAT TO WRITE IN THE JOURNAL

It's your journal. What you stuff it with depends on your way of looking at and reacting to what you see, learn, and remember. In brief, you write what you want to write. We will, however, offer you some basic principles that can make your journal more useful over the short and long run. Unless your classroom instructor asks to see your journal as part of your course work, the journal is the writing place in which you have no commitment to anyone but yourself.

In some writers' journals, you might find:

what they did that day
lists of books to read
drafts of letters
quotations
columns of words
bits of dialogue
dreams
ramblings about events and people
memories
anticipations
story possibilities
descriptions
lists of intriguing words and phrases

. . . in short, anything.

Some of this material simply keeps them working as a writer. Some of it is the record of their mind, a place to hold and look at their past self at some future time. Some of it will end up in writing meant for other eyes.

John Steinbeck kept a journal in which he blended observations about his daily life with reminders to himself about the ongoing challenges of his work-in-progress, *Grapes of Wrath*. Here is an excerpt:

> Early start this morning. Can't ever tell. Worked long and slowly yesterday. Don't know whether it was good, but it was a satisfactory way to work and I wish it would be that way every day. I've lost this

rushed feeling finally and can get back to the easy method of day by day—which is as it should be. Got the iron gate for an autograph. That is a bargain. Today I shall work slowly and try to get that good feeling again. It must be. Just a little bit every day. A little bit every day. And then it will be through. And the story is coming to me fast now. And it will be fast from now on. Movement fast but the detail slow as always. I seem to be delaying pretty badly today. Half an hour gone already and I don't care because the little details are coming, are getting clearer all the time. So the more I wait, the more of this book will get written. How about the jail. Today, the preacher and Tom and the raid on the tent and the killing of the preacher. Tom's escape. Kills. Goes back to the camp to hide. Tom—half bitterness, half humane. Escapes in the night. Hunted, hunted. Over the last pages Tom hangs like a spirit around the camp. And in the water brings stolen food. Must get to work now. The thing speeds up.

Though anything goes in the journal, you do have a responsibility to yourself as a writer. Imagine, for example, that you have written the following sample journal entries:

September 6. I met a strange man on a train and was he interesting. He told me about his life. He might make an interesting story.

1975. The mountains in the north of Italy are simply tremendous. So big and with such lovely names.

April. I really feel low today. It's the lowest I've felt in years. He disappointed me in the worst way.

Friday the 13th. A good idea for a story about a future world based on an incurable disease. I wonder what would happen?

Suppose today you decide to look back over your old journals because your mind is sluggish and you want some ideas for a story or some precise information about an event in the past that has come up in a poem. These old journal entries would leave you few triggering images with which to recapture the past, let alone your past feelings. The entries lack alertness, an awareness of the senses, discrimination, contemplation, or imagination. They indicate that you had worked neither at seeing nor at reporting.

Before we make additional suggestions, it may be worthwhile to say something about the relationship between the journal and the growth of the writer's imagination. The very effort put into keeping a journal over a period of time starts to sharpen both memory and awareness, both within and without the journal. Because you know you are keeping a journal, you start to become more conscious of your surroundings, more sensitive to the flow of your experience, your thinking, and your reading. You are more aware precisely because you know you are going to write, and as you write, you become more conscious of what you need to be aware of next time. The cycle is continuous, a whirlpool that sucks you deeper into both the world and yourself—that is, your material as a writer.

The journal entries just cited have little value as a library of memories, feelings, ideas, or pictures. They have no value as writing because they are stylistically flaccid. You need to run a bit of a game on yourself. Since you will be a different person when you read it, write the journal for that different self. Think of each entry as a time capsule you have sent to you. The following entry should make the principles clear.

> September 6, 1967. Today sat next to a lawyer on the metroliner to N.Y.C. (Going to see my agent about the paperback rights to Forever Never) He was a large man, rather rumpled—his clothes, his face, his body. He saw I was reading Williams' book about famous negligence cases. Told me had worked for Williams and before that Nizer. Spent the whole trip telling me that he was the one who planned the jury trials. Then started to tell me about cases he had won but they all sounded like cases I had read about in books on famous legal events. Said he was going up to New York to assist on the Yukonsky case but, of course, he would be kept out of the limelight. While he was telling me all this garbage I realized that he believed it—or at least believed it while he was telling it. Good potential character. Perhaps a metaphor of the writer. We believe it when we tell it. I asked for his card. "Sorry, I'm having them printed up now," he said when we left the train and he was back into rumpled reality. My god, did I really write "rumpled reality"? And now I just made it worst. He was wearing a worsted wursted suit.

When you compare this entry to the earlier ones, some principles of journal keeping should be clear:

1. Date each entry fully and precisely.
2. Make your journal entry as specific as you can.
3. Start trying to find the hard nouns and verbs that capture the feel of the situation.
4. If you are being flabby, tell yourself to straighten up. Talk to yourself in your journal. And play with the material. Start thinking about it. Let yourself go.
5. Look for associations in your past or in literature—anything that will help you recapture the emotion and feel of the event at some future time.

All this work in your journal hones skills you will need when you sit down to begin constructing something for an audience.

GETTING STARTED

Open your journal.

An effective first entry might be your autobiography, a brief overview of your life. Hit the most memorable points, especially the turning points when, had events or choices been different, you think your life might have been different. Don't try to be complete at this point. Leave yourself material for the entries that will come as you work into the journal-keeping habit. In later sessions start adding:

1. Your likes and dislikes.
2. Detailed sketches of people who are important to you—parents, brothers and sisters, friends and relatives, enemies, and so on. (See Anaïs Nin's sketch of her dance teacher later in this chapter.)
3. Memory portraits of homes, rooms, toys.
4. The truth about your weaknesses (it's permissible to write about what you think are your strengths too), your fears and anxieties.

What you are engaged in is self-exploration, the writer's archaeological dig. Even a writer who is writing in a naturalistic tradition filters the world through his or her own mind, a mind shaped by memories and experiences.

Write spontaneously—a suggestion easier to recommend than to follow. Try the technique used in this passage:

> June 5, 1986. One of my earliest memories.
> I am five years old and I am sitting on my red tricycle on the slate sidewalks in Scranton, Pa. Behind me is our house, an attached house. Did it have a front porch? I must ask Dad. I know I am not supposed to cross the street but I want to play with a friend who lives in the house opposite. For some reason, perhaps she is busy baking or with my baby sister, I cannot ask my mother. It is August and I hear a humming sound. I now know it is the cicadas but I think it is the sound of people talking over the telephone wires. I do not remember having talked on the phone but I had heard my father talking to Uncle Joe about business and my mother talking to Aunt Syl. It is so hot I can smell the asphalt. My friend's house is green. I want to cross that street. Why not? There are no cars and no people. Suddenly I am aware that I am I and that my parents are other people. I have this deep sense of me. It comes as such a surprise that thinking about this new thing I forget that I want to cross the street.

Notice that the sentences are in the present tense. The writer is trying to capture the names, feel, smell, sound, color . . . the moment. Because we invented this journal entry, we can also tell you another fact; because we couldn't remember everything, we put in elements that felt as if they should have been there. Where did we get those elements? From other past experiences. We lied about the precise experience to capture for ourselves the true feel of the experience. Put the earliest memories you have into your journal. Why are they important to you?

Spontaneity does not mean sloppiness, and by "sloppiness" we are not referring to handwriting (though an unreadable journal entry is useless for future exploration and to your biographer). Even though you wish to keep the material flowing, try different ways of saying it, look for the precise word, and keep a running commentary to yourself on exact information you will need later to make the journal entry complete.

The family, with its experiences and stories, is important material for your journal. It is the stuff out of which you can build completely imagined scenes, even in stories having nothing to do with your family. And it may be the stuff of the stories and poems and plays you wish to write. Who are the characters in your family tree, what happened to them, and what do they mean to you? Because celebrations, dislocations, operations, vacations, maturations, and more are the stuff of life, they are the stuff of literature. In your journal start practicing your recreation of them: your first birthday party, moving to a new house, getting your driver's license, realizing that one of your parents had a specific fault.

KEEPING UP

What we have suggested to this point are ways to build the journal-keeping habit through the subjects you know the best. In fact, you will probably return again and again to these same subjects as events in your life shake out more memories. However, your life will flow on, and in your journal you will paste more word snapshots of daily events, ideas, character sketches, and pieces of your reading.

Copy short passages from your reading that appeal to you and then analyze the reasons for this appeal. What strikes you in your reading tells you something about yourself as a writer-in-the-making. Be alert to other writers' techniques and comment on them, even imitate and parody them. For example, if J. D. Salinger is one of your favorites, copy a paragraph that you think is representative of his work and then model a paragraph of your own on his sequence of sentences, saving even the shape of the sentences: introduce new characters, nouns, verbs, and modifiers. Doing this is a way of involving yourself in the world of words and making from your journal a laboratory in which you experiment with your medium—language.

As a writer you will of course keep reading, and your reading is always a source for journal keeping, even on those days you feel wiped out, empty of anything to say. It is those days that test your mettle and mental as a writer. Keep going.

1. Write a letter in your journal—to your parents (the letter you always should have written), to someone you want to curse out, to an author you admire.
2. Open a dictionary at random and look at a page of words. Jot down a few that interest you because they are strange or suggestive. Play with them.
3. Try to recapture in detail the last moment you felt pleased with yourself.
4. Retell the plot of a book—even one from your childhood.
5. Turn on some music and freeassociate: just write anything that captures your emotional response to the music.
6. If your word processor shows page breaks automatically, turn this feature off and see what difference it makes to draft without "page consciousness."
7. Freewriting is often hampered by our paying too much attention to the accumulating product. Try freewriting on the word processor *with the screen turned off*, allowing yourself to read what you have written only after the writing session is over. After practicing this technique for a while, evaluate the results.

Nothing much may come of all this except keeping to your discipline, but that is no small matter. And we know that it is easier to write "discipline" than it is to summon reserves for running that last mile when your legs are leaden. Sometimes you won't; sometimes you will. What separates the writers from the pretenders is that most times the writers keep going.

WHAT WILL YOU DO WITH IT ALL?

In most of your journal writing you will practice your craft and discover yourself. In fact, some people can fall so in love with journal keeping itself that it becomes all their writing. Interesting books, such as the *Diary of John Evelyn*, have actually come from dedicated journal keepers:

> 29th June 1678. Returned with my Lord by Hounslow Heath, where we saw the new-raised army encamped, designed against France, in pretence, at least; but which gave umbrage to the Parliament. His

Majesty and a world of company were in the field, and the whole army in battalia; a very glorious sight. Now were brought into service a new sort of soldiers called *Grenadiers*, who were dexterous in flinging hand grenados, every one having a pouch full; they had furred caps with coped crowns like Janizaries, which made them look very fierce, and some had long hoods hanging down behind, as we picture fools. Their clothing being likewise piebald, yellow and red.

We are grateful to Evelyn because he has left us a detailed picture of his time. You will notice that his journal entry, even though he had no intention to create a work for public consumption, has many of the virtues of journal writing that we have suggested, all of which can be summed up in one expression: "a sense of detail."

As fine and useful as a journal like Evelyn's is, we assume your motive is to produce writing that will be read during your lifetime—to do some public good, for fame and approbation, for money, for revenge . . . for any or all of the motives that drive writers. The danger in journal writing is that you get immediate satisfaction from your most approving audience, yourself, and so may stop at the starting line.

Your journal is a *resource* for the writing that you hope will be published. Most of the time, of course, nothing transfers exactly from the journal into your public writing. Read and compare the following entry from Hawthorne's journal with the passage that actually occurs in his *The Blithedale Romance*.

> In a bar-room, a large oval basin let into the counter, with a brass tube rising from the centre, out of which gushes continually a miniature fountain, and descends in a soft, gentle, never ceasing rain into the basin, where swim a company of gold fishes. Some of them gleam brightly in their golden armor; others have a dull white aspect, going through some process of transmutation. One would think that the atmosphere, continually filled with tobacco-smoke, might impregnate the water unpleasantly for the scaly people; but then it is continually flowing away, and being renewed. And what if some toper should be seized with the freak of emptying his glass of gin or brandy into the basin? Would the fishes die, or merely get jolly?
>
> Journal entry for May 16, 1850

> The prettiest object in the saloon was a tiny fountain, which threw up its feathery jet, through the counter, and sparkled down again into an oval basin, or lakelet, containing several gold-fishes. There was a bed of bright sand, at the bottom, strewn with coral and rock-work; and the fishes went gleaming about, now turning up the sheen of a golden side, and now vanishing into the shadows of the water, like the fanciful thoughts that coquet with a poet in his dream. Never before, I imagine, did a company of water-drinkers remain so entirely uncontaminated by

the bad example around them; nor could I help wondering that it had not occurred to any freakish inebriate, to empty a glass of liquor into their lakelet. What a delightful idea! Who would not be a fish, if he could inhale jollity with the essential element of his existence.

Passage from *The Blithedale Romance*

Some material disappears, such as the tobacco-smoke, and some material is added, such as the detailed description of the sand. Most interesting of all is the shift from an abstract narrator in the journal to the first-person narrator of the novel. The material in the journal is the seedling that Hawthorne nurses into a full passage, pruning and adding as he needs to. Still, he had a seedling.

Study the following extended journal entry from *The Diary of Anaïs Nin, 1931–1934:*

October, 1933

The death of Antonio Francisco Miralles in a hotel room, alone, of asthma. Miralles, my Spanish dancing teacher.

Whenever I stepped off the bus at Montmartre, I could hear the music of the merry-go-rounds at the fair, and I would feel my mood, my walk, my whole body transformed by its gaiety. I walked to a side street, knocked on a dark doorway opened by a disheveled concierge, and ran down the stairway to a vast room below street level, a vast cellar room with its walls covered with mirrors. It was the place where the little girls from the Opéra Ballet rehearsed. When I came down the stairway I could hear the piano, feet stamping, and the ballet master's voice. When the piano stopped, there was always his voice scolding, and the whispering of smaller voices. As I entered, the class was dissolving and a flurry of little girls brushed by me in their moth ballet costumes, laughing and whispering, fluttering like moths on their dusty ballet slippers, flurries of snow in the darkness of the vast room, with drops of dew from exertion. I went down with them along the corridors to the dressing rooms. These looked like gardens, with so many ballet skirts, Spanish costumes hanging on pegs. It overflowed with the smell of cold cream, face powder, cheap cologne.

While they dressed for the street, I dressed for my Spanish dances. Miralles would already be rehearsing his own castanets. The piano, slightly out of tune, was beginning the dance of Granados. The floor was beginning to vibrate as other Spanish dancers tried out their heel work. Tap tap tap tap tap. Miralles was about forty, slender, erect, not handsome in face but graceful when dancing. His face was undefined, his features blurred.

I was the favorite.

He was like a gentle Svengali, and by his eyes, his voice, his hands, he had the power to make me dance as well as by his ordinary lessons. He ruled my body with a magnetic rule, master of my dancing.

One day he waited for me at the door, neat and trim. "Will you come and sit at the café with me?"

I followed him. Not far from there was the Place Clichy, always animated, but more so now, as the site of a permanent fair. The merry-go-rounds were turning swiftly. The gypsies were reading fortunes in little booths hung with Arabian rugs. Workmen were shooting clay pigeons and winning cut glass for their wives. The prostitutes were enjoying their loitering, and the men were watching them.

My dancing teacher was saying to me: "Anaïs, I am a simple man. My parents were shoemakers in a little village in the south of Spain. I was put to work in an iron factory where I handled heavy things and was on the way to becoming deformed by big muscles. But during my lunch hour, I danced. I wanted to be a dancer and I practiced every day, every night. At night I went to the gypsies' caverns, and learned from them. I began to dance in cabarets. And today, look!" He took out a cigarette case engraved with the names of all the famous Spanish dancers. "Today I have been the partner of all these women. If you would come with me, we could be happy. I am a simple man, but we could dance in all the cities of Europe. I am no longer young but I have a lot of dancing in me yet. We could be happy."

The merry-go-round turned and sang, and I imagined myself embarking on a dancing career with Miralles, dancing, which was so much like flying, from city to city, receiving bouquets, praise in newspapers, with joyous music at the center always, pleasure as colorful as the Spanish dresses, all red, orange, black and gold, gold and purple, and red and white.

Imagining . . . like amnesia. Forgetting who I was, and where I was, and why I could not do it. Not knowing how to answer so I would not hurt him, I said, "I am not strong enough."

"That's what I thought when I first saw you. I thought you couldn't take the discipline of a dancer's life. But it isn't so. You look fragile and all that, but you're healthy. I can tell healthy women by their skin. Yours is shining and clear. No, I don't think you have the strength of a horse, you're what we call a *petite nature*. But you have energy and guts. And we'll take it easy on the road."

Many afternoons, after hard work, we sat at this little café and imagined what a dancer's life might be.

Miralles and I danced in several places together, at a *haute couture* opening, at a millionaire Brazilian's open house, at a night club; but when I auditioned for the Opéra, *Amor Brujo*, and was accepted and would have traveled all over the world, I gave up dancing [1928].

And Miralles died alone in his hotel room, of asthma. He had been saving his money to retire to his home town, Valencia. He was good, homely, and would say to me: "You know, I have no vices like the others. I would be good to you." Just because I listened to his gaudy stories of a gaudy past, he glowed,

he went at his dancing with renewed vigor, he was rejuvenated, he bought himself a new suit.

For a while, it was as if I had lived in his shabby hotel room, with photographs of Spanish dancers pinned to the walls. I knew how it was in
Russia, in music halls all over the world. The odor of the dancers, of dressing rooms, the pungent atmosphere of rehearsals. Lola, Alma Viva,
L'Argentinita. I would wear bedroom slippers and flowered kimonos, big
Spanish flowered cottons. I would open the door and my father would be
standing there, saying: "Have you forgotten who you are? You are my
daughter, you have forgotten your class, your name, your true stature in
life."

One day I awakened from my amnesia. No longer a dancer. Miralles
turned ashen and grey, was snuffed out. He became again an old, weary dancing teacher.

from *The Diary of Anaïs Nin*, 1931–1934

We can observe that this entry is much more than a recording of the
day's events and that it wasn't tossed off to meet a deadline. Nin's impulse
is to fashion material as she recalls it, a sure sign of someone who is already
practicing the art of storytelling. Not only does this memory portrait collect fine details of place and atmosphere, but it also pretends to record conversation. Since this entry was written five years after Nin gave up dancing,
the dialogue she attributes to herself and to Miralles could not actually be
remembered. Nin is *telling a story* based on the force of her memories as
they well up. Notice how she strategically employs the merry-go-round
image: you are not yet likely to have developed such a sure sense of how an
image can link memories and provide a structure for the entry. Nin is at this
time working toward the stories and novellas that will reach an audience in
a few years. Her diary, begun in childhood, has become a writer's workbook.

The following entries are from the diaries that James Boswell kept.
Though he probably did not realize it yet, he was gathering material for his *Life
of Johnson*, one of the world's great biographies, and was learning to become a
writer. The entries we have selected cover a three-week period (July 16 to
August 3, 1763) just after Boswell met Johnson and began the journal.
Though these selections represent less than 20 percent of the total journal writing Boswell did during this period, they illustrate, among other things, how
through time a journal can reveal the patterns of one's own life. Boswell's
entries, while not as consciously literary as Nin's, show him becoming the master of details that are the life of all effective writing. His way of moving from
description to reporting to contemplation, his other- and self-directed observations—this very jumping from topic to topic—is the way most writers are likely
to proceed. You may find that Boswell's model is the one you want to follow.

SATURDAY 16 JULY. . . . [Dr. Johnson] advised me to keep a journal of my life, fair and undisguised. He said it would be a very good exercise, and would yield me infinite satisfaction when the ideas were faded from my remembrance. I told him that I had done so ever since I left Scotland. He said he was very happy that I pursued so good a plan. And now, O my journal! art thou not highly dignified? Shalt thou not flourish tenfold? No former solicitations or censures could tempt me to lay thee aside; and now is there any argument which can outweigh the sanction of Mr. Samuel Johnson? He said indeed that I should keep it private, and that I might surely have a friend who would burn it in case of my death. For my own part, I have at present such an affection for this my journal that it shocks me to think of burning it. I rather encourage the idea of having it carefully laid up among the archives of Auchinleck. However, I cannot judge fairly of it now. Some years hence I may, I told Mr. Johnson that I put down all sorts of little incidents in it. "Sir," said he, "there is nothing too little for so little a creature as man. It is by studying little things that we attain the great knowledge of having as little misery and as much happiness as possible."

❦

At present we have an old woman called Mrs. Legge for a laundress, who has breakfast set every morning, washes our linen, cleans the chambers, wipes our shoes, and, in short, does everything in the world that we can require of an old woman. She is perhaps as curious an animal as has appeared in human shape. She presents a strong idea of one of the frightful witches in *Macbeth;* and yet the beldame boasts that she was once as handsome a girl as you could clap your eyes upon, and withal exceedingly virtuous; in so much that she refused £500 from the late Lord Hervey. She was servant in many great families, and then she married for love a tall strapping fellow who died. She then owns that she married Mr. Legge for money. He is a little queer round creature; and claiming kindred with Baron Legge, he generally goes by the name of *The Baron,* and fine fun we have with him. He serves as porter when we have any message to send at a distance.

To give a specimen of Mrs. Legge, who is a prodigious prater. She said to Bob this morning, "Ay, ay, Master Robert, you may talk. But we knows what you young men are. Just cock-sparrows. You can't stand it out. But the Baron! O Lord! the Baron is a staunch man. Ay, ay, did you never hear that GOD never made a little man but he made it up to him in something else? Yes, yes, the Baron is a good man, an able man. He laid a married woman upon the floor while he sent the maid out for a pint of porter. But he was discovered, and so I come to know of it."

MONDAY 18 JULY. At the head of St. James's Street I observed three Turks staring about in a strange manner. I spoke a little of English, French, and Latin to them, neither of which they understood a word of. They showed me a pass from a captain of a ship declaring that they were Algerines who had been taken by the Spaniards and made slaves. That they made their escape, got to Lisbon, and from thence were brought to England. I carried them with me to a French house, where I got a man who spoke a little Spanish to one of them, and learnt that they wanted to see the Ambassador from Tripoli, who though not from the same division of territory, is yet under the Grand Signior, as they are. I accordingly went with him to the Ambassador's house, where I found a Turk who could speak English and interpret what they said; and he told me that they had landed that morning and had already been with the Ambassador begging that he would get liberty for them from the Lords of the Admiralty; and that he had ordered them victuals. I gave them half a crown. They were very thankful, and my Turkish friend who spoke English said, "GOD reward you. The same God make the Turk that make the Christian. But the English have the tender heart. The Turk have not the tender heart."

WEDNESDAY 20 JULY. Dempster argued on Rousseau's plan, that the goods of fortune and advantages of rank were nothing to a wise man, who ought only to value internal merit. Replied Johnson: "If man were a savage living in the woods by himself, this might be true. But in civilized society we all depend upon each other, and our happiness is very much owing to the good opinion of others. Now, Sir, in civilized society, external advantages make us more respected by individuals. A man who has a good coat upon his back meets with a better reception than he who has a bad one.

"Go to the street and give one man a lecture of morality and another a shilling, and see who will respect you most. Sir, I was once a great arguer for the advantages of poverty, but I was at the same time very discontented. Sir, the great deal of arguing which we hear to represent poverty as no evil shows it to be evidently a great one. You never knew people labouring to convince you that you might live very happily upon a plentiful fortune. In the same way, you hear people talking how miserable a king must be. And yet every one of them would wish to have his place."

THURSDAY 21 JULY. I remember nothing that happened worth relating this day. How many such days does mortal man pass!

FRIDAY 22 JULY. Mr. Johnson said that Mr. Hume and all other sceptical innovators were vain men; and finding mankind already in possession of truth, they could not gratify their vanity by supporting her; and so they have taken to error. "Sir," said he, "Truth is a cow which will yield such people no more milk, and so they are gone to milk the bull."

He maintained that a boy at school was the happiest being. I maintained that a man was more so. He said a boy's having his backside flogged was not so severe as a man's having the hiss of the world against him. He talked of the anxiety which men have for fame; and how the greater it is, the more afraid are they of losing it. I considered how wonderful it must be if even the great Mr. Johnson did not think himself secure.

TUESDAY 26 JULY. I called upon Mr. Johnson.

We talked of the education of children and what was best to teach them first. "Sir," said he, "there is no matter what you teach them first, any more than what leg you shall put into your breeches first. Sir, you may stand disputing which is best to put in first, but in the mean time your backside is bare. Sir, while you are considering which of two things you should teach your child first, another boy has learnt 'em both."

THURSDAY 28 JULY. I sat up all last night writing letters and bringing up my lagging journal, which, like a stone to be rolled up a hill, must be kept constantly going.

SATURDAY 30 JULY. Mr. Johnson and I took a boat and sailed down the silver Thames.

We landed at the Old Swan and walked to Billingsgate, where we took oars and moved smoothly along the river. We were entertained with the immense number and variety of ships that were lying at anchor. It was a pleasant day, and when we got clear out into the country, we were charmed with the beautiful fields on each side of the river.

We talked of preaching, and of the great success that the Methodists have. He said that was owing to their preaching in a plain, vulgar manner, which was the only way to do good to common people, and which men of learning and genius ought to do, as their duty; and for which they would be praised by men of sense.

When we got to Greenwich, I felt great pleasure in being at the place which Mr. Johnson celebrates in his *London: a Poem*. I had the poem in my pocket, and read the passage on the banks of the Thames, and literally "kissed the consecrated earth."

We supped at the Turk's Head. Mr. Johnson said, "I must see thee go; I will go down with you to Harwich." This prodigious mark of his affection filled me with gratitude and vanity. I gave him an account of the family of Auchinleck, and of the Place. He said, "I must be there, and we will live in the Old Castle; and if there is no room remaining, we will build one." This was the most pleasing idea that I could possibly have: to think of seeing this great man at the venerable seat of my ancestors. I had been up all last night yet was not sleepy.

SUNDAY 31 JULY. In the forenoon I was at a Quakers' meeting in Lombard Street, and in the afternoon at St. Paul's, where I was very devout and very happy. After service, I stood in the center and took leave of the church, bowing to every quarter. I cannot help having a reverence for it. Mr. Johnson says the same. Mr. Johnson said today that a woman's preaching was like a dog's walking on his hinder legs. It was not done well, but you were surprised to find it done at all.

Johnson said that he always felt an inclination to do nothing. I said it was strange to think that the most indolent man in Britain had written the most laborious work, *The English Dictionary.* He said he took ten years to do it; but that if he had applied properly, he might have done it in three. . . .

WEDNESDAY 3 AUGUST. I should have mentioned that on Monday night, coming up the Strand, I was tapped on the shoulder by a fine fresh lass. I went home with her. She was an officer's daughter, and born at Gibraltar. I could not resist indulging myself with the enjoyment of her. Surely, in such a situation, when the woman is already abandoned, the crime must be alleviated, though in strict morality, illicit love is always wrong.

from The Heart of Boswell

Here are some entries from the journal of novelist and short story master John Cheever. While in the first two entries Cheever addresses the business of writing, in the extended ones he sets down observations that could find their way into fictional works. Note Cheever's mix of precise detail and thematic pointing.

The first page of a new journal, and I hope to report here soon that the middle section of the Wapshots has fallen into shape. I expect that I will continue to report here that I drink too much.

The O'Hara book—he is a pro, a gifted man. There is the sense of life being translated, but I think also an extraordinary vein of morbid sexual anxiety. I would like "The Scandal" to be clear of this. I think the difference is between a fascinated horror of life and a vision of life. He is good and rough and not so lacy as me, but I hope to come to better terms.

The firemen's bazaar. Seven o'clock. A July night. A rusted and battered backstop stands behind the circle of trucks and booths turned in against the gathering darkness like a circle of covered wagons. Parents and children hasten along the roads that lead to the bazaar as if it might all be over before they got there, although in fact they will get there before it has begun. The sumptuary revolution makes me feel old. Both the boys and the girls are wearing skintight pants, and there are many cases of ungainly and sometimes painful tightness. And in the crowd there are reminders of the fact that there are still some farms outside the village limits. I see a red-faced man, a little drunk, followed by an over-worked woman who has cut her own hair as well as the hair of the four shabby children that follow. These are the poor; these are the ones who live upstairs over the shoe store, who live in the cottage down by the dump, who can be seen fanning themselves at their windows in the heat. When you leave at six to catch an early plane, these are the ones that you see at dawn, waiting by the bus stop with their sandwiches in a paper bag. But it is the children I enjoy most, watching them ride in mechanical pony carts and airplanes, suspended by chains from a pylon. Their brilliance, this raw material of human goodness. A very plain woman in the last months of pregnancy, who looks out at the scene calmly and with great pride in this proof of the fact that someone has taken her in his arms. Many of the girls have their hair in rollers half concealed by scarves. Like primitive headdresses and, in the darkness, like crowns.

All Hallows' Eve. Some set piece about the community giving a pri-mordial shudder, scattering the mercies of piety, charity, and mental health and exposing, briefly, the realities of evil and the hosts of the vengeful and unquiet dead. I see how frail the pumpkin lanterns are that we light on our doorsteps to protect our houses from the powers of darkness. I see the little boy, dressed as a devil, rattling a can and ask-ing pennies for UNICEF. How thin the voice of reason sounds tonight! Does my mother fly through the air? My father, my fishing compan-ions? Have mercy upon us; grant us thy peace! Although there seemed to be no connection, it was always at this season that, in the less well-heeled neighborhoods of the village, "For Sale" signs would appear, as abundant as chrysanthemums. Most of them seemed to have been printed by children, and they were stuck into car windshields, nailed to trees, and attached to the bows of cabin cruisers and other boats, rest-ing on trailers in the side yard. Everything seemed to be for sale—pianos, vacant lots, Rototillers, and chain saws, as if the coming of winter provoked some psychic upheaval involving the fear of loss. But as the last of the leaves fell, glittering like money, the "For Sale" signs vanished with them. Had everyone got a raise, a mortgage, a loan, or an infusion of hopefulness? It happened every year.

SUGGESTIONS FOR JOURNAL WORK

1. Write a character sketch that incorporates an anecdote modeled on Boswell's treatment of Mrs. Legge.

2. Report a conversation in your journal, capturing the personal style of one of the participants as accurately as Boswell has captured Dr. Johnson's.

3. After you have been keeping a journal for a while, reread it to see if any patterns have begun to develop. Note, for example, Boswell's concern with controlled and uncontrolled sexual passion.

4. Holidays and special events provide opportunities for catching individual behavior within group behavior and custom. Prepare entries like Cheever's sketches of the firemen's bazaar and Halloween.

After a time—and we would not say what that time might be—your journal will become a resource both for passages such as those in this chapter and for whole works. Often you will find that ideas or impulses appearing over a period of time in your journal start to form a pattern that sparks or confirms a story, poem, or play. Our space being limited, we cannot give an example of such a development in operation. You will simply have to trust that in time the exercise does help in the game.

Reread Boswell's entry of 28 July!

3

Point of View

WHAT IS IT?

In common speech *point of view* means either (1) the position from which we look at something or (2) the consequences of looking at something from a particular position, that is, the opinions, judgments, or attitudes that we form. This metaphor grows from our experience: a house that looks good to us from a distance, on close inspection may seem poorly maintained. Our changed perspective may bring a change in our feelings or judgment about whether or not to buy it—though the realtor will probably "see" it quite differently. In fact, it looks different to different people viewing it from the same physical perspective: a painting contractor, a ten-year-old who has lived there since birth, a neighbor who doesn't like the present owners. "Point of view" is such a powerful metaphor that we use it to describe how people judge all kinds of physical, social, and psychological events: "From my point of view, it's all . . ." or "That's your point of view."

In writing, the phrase has its common meaning plus a specialized meaning having to do with grammatical person. For example, a story may be told in the "first person," that is, from the "I" perspective. Because of its fundamental nature, this complex concern affects everything else the writer does. It is the key to the structure of the work and to the reader's response.

WHO WILL DO THE TELLING?

We began this book with a point of view.

That point of view involves both decisions we made before we began writing and decisions we made, consciously or unconsciously, as we were writing and revising. Though the aims of this book are different from the aims of a story, poem, or play, the essential point-of-view question is the same: who is going to do the telling? As you will see, deciding who "who" will be is not merely a matter of deciding if the speaker will be first, second, or third person and if the "voice" will be omniscient, limited, the voice of someone who has been directly involved, or that of an onlooker (see "The Range of Perspectives" later in this chapter). Who the narrator will be concerns viewpoint to the world and the audience. Point of view is, then, partly about how to tell.

In planning and writing this book, for example, we had to decide whether to pretend we were authorities delivering the gospel from a distance or, at the other end of the spectrum, whether to act as close friends at a table discussing writing processes and problems. We finally decided to take a position somewhere between authority and collegiality. Our decision about viewpoint derived from what we believed our audience already knew and what it needed to know, as well as our premise that while ideally all matters are open to discussion, some rules are helpful when you are starting to play the game. In this sense, choosing a point of view is closely related to searching for a tone or style that would communicate just where we stand about the writing process. Point of view, considered this way, is a process that is closely connected with *what* to tell.

Our point of view was not a settled matter. It evolved as we tried to grapple with the subject, as we talked with and explained things to each other, and as we reviewed the notes we kept during our meetings (a version of the writer's notebook). It also developed from what we already knew, consciously and unconsciously, about writing and editing, as well as from what we found out along the way.

In shaping what and how we tell, point of view determines our audience's response. For example, if we chose to communicate to you in magisterial formulations, we might say, "Point of view is implicated in every decision the writer makes, including diction. Structure your point of view to maximize effects." We suspect that one of your reactions would be to see the statement as a RULE and the writers as rule makers. Since we actually feel that writing involves process and decision and because we personally do not care for the platform and the bureaucratic, we are more likely to say, "Point of view affects everything you do in your writing, including your choice of words. To put it another way, once you have decided to have your say, choose a viewpoint that will guide your reader's understanding and reactions." So, we haven't just decided to speak in the first-person plural (we) and to address the second person (you) reader. We have created a narrator with an attitude toward the material and toward the reader.

Let us look at how these concerns operate in Shelley's "Ozymandias." After you read the **sonnet,**[*] go back over it and try to isolate the various points of view it incorporates. Make a list outlining (1) whose mind is being reflected and (2) what attitude is revealed in each case. Then read the commentary that follows.

> I met a traveller from an antique land
> Who said: Two vast and trunkless legs of stone
> Stand in the desert . . . Near them, on the sand,
> Half sunk, a shattered visage lies, whose frown,
> And wrinkled lip, and sneer of cold command,
> Tell that its sculptor well those passions read
> Which yet survive, stamped on these lifeless things,
> The hand that mocked them, and the heart that fed;
> And on the pedestal these words appear:
> 'My name is Ozymandias, king of kings:
> Look on my works, ye Mighty, and despair!'
> Nothing beside remains. Round the decay
> Of that colossal wreck, boundless and bare
> The lone and level sands stretch far away.
>
> 1817

Immediately, we are told that the "narrator" or "speaker" heard a story. But that's only the beginning of point-of-view complications. The remainder of the poem is the speaker's report of the traveler's experience. We can't be sure if Shelley's **persona** is quoting the traveler or merely paraphrasing what the traveler told him.

Let us construct a fiction of what happened in the writing process that may have led to this decision about point of view:

1. Shelley hated tyrants and believed that the poet's task was to challenge tyranny in preparation for the creation of more perfect societies. Let's not worry about how he came to this position.

2. In a book, in a dream, from a friend—somehow—an image came to him of a tyrant whose monument stands in a wasted land. He jots the image down in his journal, perhaps even first imagining that the statue is intact. Maybe he launches into the poem immediately. Maybe he writes a first draft in his journal and, coming across it years later, is moved to complete it. No matter.

---

[*]Boldface terms are defined in the glossary.

3. At some point, Shelley had to decide who would tell the story. The most obvious person is himself, or, rather, the voice he creates to tell the story of Ozymandias's statue. Shelley could have cast the traveler as the persona and saved the extra step of narrating through someone who encountered the traveler. Perhaps Shelley feared that his message would be discounted by readers who would identify such a speaker with the poet, who was known to hate tyrants. Locating the story in another's experience can be a way of increasing the reader's readiness to accept it. At the same time, Shelley's surrogate (our secondhand narrator) hears the tale and passes it on to us, and if we know Shelley's attitude (point of view) toward tyrants we can quickly catch his point. The poem is not, finally, addressing the haughtiness and transient stature of Ozymandias, but of all tyrants—especially those of Shelley's own day.

4. Looking further, we can see that the poem contains no less than four points of view: what Ozymandias thought of himself (the inscription still visible on the pedestal); what the sculptor thought of Ozymandias (through capturing his inner nature in stone); what the traveler records of his own experience; what the persona retells upon hearing the traveler's story. At some point, Shelley found that this layered perspective projected his feeling about tyranny most effectively. The character of Ozymandias —of tyranny—becomes a shared understanding of sculptor, traveler, conveyor-poet, and reader. Only the king himself is left out, his haughty words—actually blasphemous words—shown to be absurd.

Though some of our speculations are fictive, this exploration tells something about point of view. Point of view involves a series of finely adjusted decisions. Many of them you will have to make as you discover the needs of your story; nevertheless, you will save yourself a good deal of grief if you start working them out before you write. We know one writer who plunged into a novel told in the first person and on page 110 found out that the narrator had to die. The writer then had to figure out how a dead person could be talking and who was going to tell the rest of the novel. Could he rewrite all 110 pages with a deadline just two months off? Not to leave you wondering, the novelist invented a second narrator to find the dead narrator's tape recording. What do you think of this solution?

Now that you've had a chance to think about point of view for a while, do the following exercise in your journal:

OZYMANDIAS EXERCISE

1. What kind of person is the traveler in Shelley's poem? How do you know?

2. Do you think Shelley's narrator is paraphrasing or quoting the traveler? How do you support your position? What difference does your position make on how the poem works?

3. Compose a description that takes a different attitude toward this statue and its subject.

4. Imagine that the traveler (or a traveler of your own invention) had stumbled across a crumbling, isolated monument that we are all familiar with—the Statue of Liberty, or the Lincoln Memorial, or something else that you choose. Write a description that makes your point through what the traveler has told you of his (or her) experience.

EXERCISE

We said earlier that the point of view you choose affects many other aspects of writing. Because point of view touches on attitude and personality, it can affect the words you choose and even the sentence patterns with which you string them together. Examine the following passages and jot down what you think about each narrator. We've commented at the end.

> 1. In the fall the war was always there, but we did not go to it any more. It was cold in the fall in Milan and the dark came very early. Then the electric lights came on, and it was pleasant along the streets looking in the windows.
>
> Ernest Hemingway, "In Another Country"

> 2. There was music from my neighbor's house through the summer nights. In his blue gardens men and girls came and went like moths among the whisperings and the champagne and the stars. At high tide in the afternoon I watched his guests diving from the tower of his raft, or taking the sun on the hot sand of his beach while his two motorboats slit the waters of the Sound, drawing aquaplanes over cataracts of foam.
>
> F. Scott Fitzgerald, *The Great Gatsby*

> 3. Joseph, who whilst he was speaking had continued in one attitude, with his head reclining on one side, and his eyes cast on the ground, no sooner perceived, on looking up, the position of Adams, who was stretched on his back, and snored louder than the usual braying of the animal with long ears, then he turned towards Fanny, and, taking her by the hand began a daliance, which, though consistent with the purest innocence and decency, neither he would have attempted nor she permitted before any witness.
>
> Henry Fielding, *Joseph Andrews*

4. I went along up the bank with one eye out for pap and 'tother one out for what the rise might fetch along. Well, all at once, here comes a canoe; just a beauty, too, about thirteen or fourteen foot long, riding high like a duck. I shot head first off the bank, like a frog, clothes and all on, and struck out for the canoe. I just expected there'd be somebody laying down in it, because people often done that to fool folks, and when a chap had pulled a skiff out most to it they'd raise up and laughed at him. But it warn't so this time.

Mark Twain, *Huckleberry Finn*

5. The fact was that his perception of the young man's identity—so absolutely checked for a minute—had been quite one of the sensations that count in life; he certainly had never known one that had acted, as he might have said, with more of a crowded rush. And the rush, though both vague and multitudinous, had lasted a long time, protected, as it were, yet at the same time aggravated, by the circumstance of its coinciding with a stretch of decorous silence.

Henry James, *The Ambassadors*

Our reactions: (1) Understated, matter of fact, direct—as if told at a bar. A person whose emotions are masked. (2) A wistful fellow with a romantic imagination. Slightly adolescent, but polished too. (3) An entertainer, self-conscious effect-maker. He revels in his circumlocutions and false delicacies. An ironist. (4) An unlettered youngster; impetuous, observant, worldly wise. (5) Finicky, fastidious, constantly qualifying and interjecting. Concerned with nuances (as it were).

The Decision and Its Consequences

Granted, some of the preceding examples may indeed be close to the author's voice rather than a persona created especially for the work; however, from our point of view as readers, we can hear the story only through the narrator's voice, which shapes our response to that story. Consciously or unconsciously the writer has the following decisions to make. He or she must:

1. Choose a narrator, usually first or third person.
2. Decide what the narrator's attitude will be.
3. Decide how the reader should respond to the narrator and how to make the narrator create that response.

Let us further explore the decisions involved in number 2.

Imagine: a baseball game. Nine players are on the field. A batter is at the plate. Perhaps there are one or more base runners. Umpires are at their positions. So are coaches. Each manager is in a dugout along with his assistants and the other players—some of the players are also out in the bullpen. Ball and bat-boys (or girls) are doing their jobs. Fans are in the stands, along with vendors of snacks, drinks, and souvenirs. Security guards patrol the area. In the press box, sports journalists are hard at work. Mini-studios hold members of the radio and television broadcast crews.

Think of all the people who are involved in the scene, all the potential stories. But perhaps there is just one story to tell: the simple story of the game.

Who should tell it?

As soon as we attempt to answer this question, we see that there is an intimate connection between the telling and what is told. The shortstop's story can never be the same as the ball-girl's or the visiting manager's. Which story holds the truth? Which truth? The decision about who tells the story (even if the "story" is about someone's feelings as expressed in a poem) makes the story take on certain contours. No convincing narrator is totally objective, and the subjective perceptions and needs of the storyteller make the story come out the way it does.

Umpires are neutral, but the umpire's story is about calling the game, not playing in it. A journalist may not favor either team yet his love for the game itself—or for his job, or his wife, or his lunch—can affect how he reports what he sees. And *his* story is, at bottom, about reporting.

Consider the rookie's wife. She sits in the stands behind home plate. She is seven months pregnant, worried about her husband's future in baseball and their future together. What does she see on the playing field? Does the umpire block her view of the pitch that her husband doesn't swing at? Does a memory of their first meeting distract her? Does the pitcher care about this? Does he even notice her? What is the pitcher's story—a fable of blisters and beer?

By this time the point about point of view should be clear. Decisions regarding point of view involve as many combinations and possibilities as a baseball game. It is one of those concerns that has endless reverberations.

Let's dig into point of view a bit more.

Imagine: a multilevel house built of flagstone and redwood with large expanses of glass. The house is sprawled out along the side of a mountain. To the right is a small vineyard, where a young woman sits on a weathered bench, reading. Near her an Irish setter sleeps in the shade. A narrow gravel road winds around the side of the mountain, and branching off from it a dirt driveway leads to the house. It is late afternoon, and, though the low sun shines brightly, there are signs that it has rained within the hour.

Now imagine two men. One is hiking through a valley below the mountain. He looks up at the house. What could he see? Given his position, how would he describe it? The other man is driving past it on the narrow mountain road. Does he see what the hiker sees?

One meaning of point of view has to do with the physical perspective a viewer can have on the subject. The hiker, far below the house, can see it in less detail. From his perspective and distance he may not be able to make out the materials of the house; perhaps he won't see the woman or the dog. If so, both might as well not be there. What the man in the car will see depends upon how fast he is driving and how long he can risk taking his eyes off the road. If he comes to a stop, he will be able to take in far more detail than the hiker down below.

EXERCISE

Choose a place—perhaps your workplace or a building at your school—and describe it from different physical and psychological vantage points. (For example, how might a French chef see a McDonald's?)

Going back to our two men and the mountain house, let us do some more imagining. We need to give the men identities. Suppose the hiker, let's call him Chick, is a stranger to this part of the country who has come here to flee a complex life in Chicago. He is tired and thirsty, soaked from his exertion, the humidity, and the wet grasses he has tramped through. How does this circumstance affect what he sees when he looks up at the house? How will his situation color his perception? Now imagine that the hiker is the woman's husband. They have lived together in the house for three years and he has worked on every inch of it. Each day he walks to the valley to pick up mail and food at the general store. He then climbs the mountain again and joins his wife for wine and cheese in the vineyard. He raised the setter from a pup. What does *this* hiker see when he looks up at the house?

If we imagine each of these hikers as the narrator of a story in which looking up at the house from the valley triggers an important scene, we can readily understand the importance of point of view. Each narrator will see the house at that moment through a unique lens because he relates to the house differently and has different expectations. Let's see what might happen with Chick, who, at this point in the story, a third-person narrator wishes us to know a bit better:

> Chick saw the tangled geometry of a rambling house halfway up the mountainside. To the right, a splash of color told him someone was home—someone who might offer a bit of hospitality if he could just manage to push himself up the slope. The house swam in a flux of long shadows and little mirrored explosions of the sun, reminding Chick that he'd better start moving before it got dark. He doubted they got many strangers stopping in such an isolated spot, particularly strangers carrying $100,000 in their knapsacks. He'd have to be careful.

Now it's your turn. Imagine the driver. Is he a lover? A detective? As he slows to swing onto the access road, what does he see? What does he think? Perhaps the house is for sale and he has come to examine it. Put the situation in motion. Just when does the noise of the car wake the dog? When is the central consciousness—the driver—aware of the dog?

Now let's turn the game around. A young woman has been sitting on a bench in the arbor alongside her elaborate mountain home. She puts down her book (what is she reading?), stands, stretches, and faces the valley. She is pretty sure that she can make out someone just reaching the bottom of the mountain slope. Then she becomes aware of a car slowing to turn into her driveway. Freeze the frame: what does she see in this frozen moment? Now roll the camera: follow her consciousness of what's going on in the world around her.

One more, final, wrinkle. Make the character who waits in the arbor a man and make the other characters women.

As we have seen, the term *point of view* covers a wide range of results that come from a writer's decisions. Deciding to tell a story in the first or third person is merely the first decision. The usefulness of information readers receive depends upon how the writer has filtered the material through a narrator's consciousness and what coloring that consciousness has given to the information. For example, we get the information about what has happened in Emily Brontë's *Wuthering Heights* from Lockwood as reported to him by Nelly Dean, and much of her information is secondhand. In Daniel Defoe's *Moll Flanders* we learn all that happens from Moll, but the whole experience happens to her directly. Though both novels are written in the first person, there are far more differences than similarities. In F. Scott Fitzgerald's *The Great Gatsby* a character who is not at the center of the action tells the story; in Camus's *The Plague* we receive, without knowing it until near the end, all of our information from a first-person narrator who hides his identity and presents the story clinically. Technically, all these works are first person but, from the writer's point of view, both the possibilities and limitations are infinite.

THE RANGE OF PERSPECTIVES

Third Person

The third-person narrator speaks from outside of the story as an onlooker or reporter rather than as a participant. The degree to which the narrator is given access to external and internal information and the degree to which the narrator is allowed to express judgments about that information determine more precisely the narrative stance. Within the broad third-person category, the narrator has three options:

Full Omniscience.   The fully omniscient narrator accesses the minds, feelings, and dreams of all the characters in the work. Thus the author, through the narrator, can shift focus along the way, giving the reader a variety of perspectives. This kind of omniscient narrator also shifts back and forth between subjective and objective approaches, sometimes becoming engaged in explaining, interpreting, assessing, and moralizing on the events and characters. The narrator may at times comment extensively, a technique we call *editorializing*. The absence of any limitation on the narrator's information (and presence) can create havoc for an inexperienced writer. The tendency is to lose focus, to bully the reader, and to subjugate the story and characters to thematic concerns in unattractive ways.

Limited Omniscience.   The limited omniscient narrator stands behind the shoulder of one character, usually the major character, and conveys to the reader only what that character experiences, knows, and feels. Other characters are treated objectively: what they say and do is recorded. However, what the central character thinks about them is an important ingredient. Sometimes, on top of this limited omniscience, the narrator is allowed a bit of knowledge or speculation beyond what the central character knows. This is important in order for the reader to gain perspective on that character, to get outside of the main character's head. Most successful stories and novels use some variation of the limited omniscient point of view.

Objective Limitation.   The objective limitation point of view is most like that of the dramatist. Setting, action, and dialogue are the only tools the author allows the narrator-self. Readers are given no direct access to the minds of the characters and are left to form judgments on their own. This perspective is as difficult, in its own way, as unlimited omniscience.

First Person

In first-person point of view the narrator is one of the characters in the story or novel, either a witness to the events or a participant. The narrator's relationship to the events and to the other characters determines what can be convincingly revealed from the chosen perspective. The first-person narrator does not have access to the minds of others (unless the narrator is a psychiatrist revealing professionally gained knowledge—a cute trick). At every moment of the story's progress, the first-person narrator is being characterized by the way he or she thinks and speaks.

Central Character.   When the narrator is the central character, the fiction is borrowing the appeal of autobiography. The author has to be careful to restrain this kind of narrator. It is easy to sacrifice the developmental lines of the story to the narrator's ego. Often first-person narration is an exploration of how memory works and how a person comes to understand, with the passage of time, the meaning of events that happened years earlier.

Minor Character/Witness.   "I was there" can be almost as compelling as "It happened to me." This kind of narrator has to be a true personality, not merely a convenient reporter of events. The reader must be able to gauge the degree of emotional interest—bias—of this narrator as well as of the central character narrator. Why is it important *to the teller* to relate these events?

As you can see, there are places where these categories overlap. Certain kinds of third-person narration come very close to first-person witness, but more than pronoun choice should separate these perspectives. The third-person narrator, even if given a personality as in Henry Fielding's *Joseph Andrews*, is primarily there to tell the story. The first-person minor character is *involved* in some way, even if not in terms of the main action. Of course, in works like those by Arthur Conan Doyle, Dr. Watson works with Sherlock Holmes, he doesn't just know about him or see him from afar.

EXERCISES

1. Describe an object:
    a. as if you secretly desired it.
    b. as if you weere trying to, but could not quite, conceal your contempt for it.
    c. as if you had never seen anything like it before (you are from Alpha Centaurus).
    d. as a child of ten might describe it.
    e. as your roommate, mother, father, sister, or brother might describe it.
    f. as someone who is blind might describe it.

2. Look at some full-page newspaper or magazine advertisements. What, besides the product itself, is being "sold" in each case? What is the point of view of the ad copy? What kind of "speaker" is presented in each case? Write some ad copy for an object you own, but first imagine a person (or type of person) to whom you are trying to sell the object.

3. Here is a passage from "The Dead," a story from James Joyce's *Dubliners* in which Gabriel Conroy is the major character. After studying the paragraph, rewrite it in the first person, making Gabriel the narrator. Then, after making your own comparison of the two versions, read the commentary that follows the excerpt:

Gabriel could not listen while Mary Jane was playing her Academy piece, full of runs and difficult passages, to the hushed drawing-room. He liked music but the piece she was playing had no melody for him and he doubted whether it had any melody for the other listeners, though they had begged Mary Jane to play something. Four young men, who had come from the refreshment-room to stand in the doorway at the sound of the piano, had gone away quietly in couples after a few minutes. The only persons who seemed to follow the music were Mary Jane herself, her hands racing along the keyboard or lifted from it at the pauses like those of a priestess in momentary imprecation, and Aunt Kate standing at her elbow to turn the page.

As Joyce has written it, Gabriel's consciousness is part of a larger scene, some of which he is probably not paying attention to. If he became specifically aware of the other people and their attentiveness to Mary Jane's performance, some of his self-centered insularity would be lost. Gabriel is part of a social situation that is under Joyce's satiric scrutiny. For *Gabriel* to say Mary Jane's playing is "like . . . a priestess's" would give him too much distance from what is going on. Changing "Gabriel" and third-person pronoun references to first person will only bring about a mechanical difference.

Rewrite the paragraph, this time from Mary Jane's point of view. Now try Aunt Kate's. Each time, pay attention to how many other elements of the story can change when you change perspective. In some of your refashionings, allow yourself to revise the order of the material, the language, the implications. Try writing a similar paragraph in which someone is preparing a meal while another character, perhaps your main character, reacts to what he or she sees in such a way that we learn about both characters.

4. Though point of view is usually—and properly—treated as a concern of prose fiction (the identification of the narrator), it is also a legitimate concern of the poet. This is especially true when the speaker is clearly identified and characterized. Often we are asked to understand how the truth of what is being perceived depends upon who is doing the perceiving. This theme is one thread in Myra Sklarew's "Leaving." After reading the poem, respond to the questions and tasks that follow it.

His Song

I go out foraging against
the molten core rising
rising daily inside me

against the voice saying
What did you mean to be in your life?

against the slow thought
that would come

when I drove out
on a Sunday

Ways I could change my life

But this other
this danger is too compelling
I tell you I'd die for it
The threat
of that man
with his sack of evidence
with his knife out after me
in the dark
slashing my tires
to keep me
from running off
with his wife

It doesn't matter now
It's what I want

My whole life is back there
leaning against the porch rail
thinking itself down
along the narrow edge
of the years

But it's not strong enough
to keep back
what's broken through
that part of me I set onto another
never quite fitting

It's something I can't do without
that friction to raise up a feeling
against the questions
that won't leave me
against the answer
out there in front of me

Her Song

After he left
I posted innocence
at my door

When he spoke
of his reason for leaving
I knew my own part in it

but I never said a word

At first it was good
filling up the boxes
with his books of naked girls
putting them
by the front door

But then
there was the empty closet
a white pill
on the floor
in the corner
the familiar smell

At night
innocence
like the book beside me
brings no comfort at all

nor the thin legs
of self-righteousness

nor the stem and leaf
of selfhood

Why is it
in my dream
it seems perfectly natural
to be taking off my clothes
in front of two men
who are naked

Perfectly natural for one
of the men to enter me
until I become aware
of someone else
standing in the corner
of that room

from *The Science of Goodbyes*

In this poem, the author attends to both the husband's and wife's point of view about a broken relationship. "His Song" and "Her Song" step into the consciousness of two people who now share only the legacy of their failed marriage.

a. How does each view the past and the present?
b. Is each point of view handled convincingly?

   c. Rewrite the poem so the man tries to express the woman's attitude and the woman tries to express the man's.

   d. Rewrite the poem from a third-person perspective. Do more than merely changing the "I" to "he" or "she."

   e. Imagine that the couple has a child who is now about fifteen years old. Rewrite the poem (in prose if you wish) from the child's perspective.

   f. Imagine another conflict between two people: father and son, jail guard and criminal, hostess and gate-crasher. Present the contrasting points of view in a two-part poem in which each mind is entered (as in Sklarew's) or in a piece of dialogue.

   g. Now, in prose, recast this conflict from an outside perspective: first try third-person omniscient, then objective.

5. In "Rhody's Path," William Goyen chooses an unusual point of view, that of an unnamed minor character. As you read the story, look for answers to the following questions:

   a. Can you tell the approximate age of the narrator at the time of the events? How? Is there a distance in time or maturity established between the events and the telling?

   b. Is the narrator male or female?

   c. Why does Goyen have the narrator refer to "we" rather than "I"? Can you think of other circumstances in which such use of the first-person plural would be appropriate?

   d. Does Goyen create an authentic "voice" for his narrator? What are its characteristics?

   e. How would you describe the personality of the narrator? Why does the narrator seem so self-effacing?

   f. In what ways would the story be different if Rhody told it? If Mama or Idalou told it? If a third-person narrator told it?

   g. Prepare an overall assessment of the relationship between Goyen's point-of-view decision and the theme of individual versus family identity.

Rhody's Path

William Goyen

Sometimes several sudden events will happen together so as to make you believe they have a single meaning if 'twould only come clear. Surely happenings are lowered down upon us after a pattern of the Lord above.

'Twas in the summer of one year; the time the Second Coming was prophesied over the land and the Revivalist came to Bailey's pasture to prove it; and the year of two memorable events. First was the plague of grasshoppers ('twas the driest year in many an old memory, in East Texas); second was the Revival in the pasture across from the house.

Just even to mention the pestilence of hoppers makes you want to scratch all over. They came from over toward Grapeland like a promise of Revelations—all counted to the last as even the hairs of our head are numbered, so says the Bible and so said the Revivalist—making the driest noise in the world, if you have ever heard them. There were so many that they were all clusted together, just one working mass of living insects, wild with appetite and cutting down so fast you could not believe your eyes a whole field of crops. They hid the sun like a curtain and twas half-daylight all that day, the trees were alive with them and shredded of their leaves. We humans were locked in our houses, but the earth was the grasshopper's, he took over the world. It did truly seem a punishment, like the end of the world was upon us, as was prophesied.

Who should choose to come home to us that end of summer but Rhody, to visit, after a long time gone. She had been in New Orleans as well as in Dallas and up in Shreveport too, first married to her third husband in New Orleans, then in Dallas to run away from him in spite, and lastly in Shreveport to write him to go to the Devil and never lay eye on her again. We all think he was real ready to follow the law of that note. Then she come on home to tell us all this, and to rest.

Rhody arrived in a fuss and a fit, the way she is eternally, a born fidget, on the heels of the plague of hoppers. They had not been gone a day when she swept in like the scourge of pestilence. She came into our wasteland, scarce a leaf on a tree and crops just stalks, dust in the air. So had the Revivalist—as if they had arranged it together in Louisiana and the preacher had gone so far as to prophesy the Second Coming in Texas for Rhody's sake. She could make a man do such.

Already in the pasture across the railroad tracks and in front of the house, the Revivalist was raising his tent. We were all sitting on the front porch to watch, when we saw what we couldn't believe our eyes were telling us at first, but knew soon after by her same old walk, Rhody crossing the pasture with her grip in her hand. We watched her stop and set on her suitcase to pass conversation with the Revivalist—she never met a stranger in her life—and his helpers, and we waited for her to come on home across the tracks and through the gate. Mama and Papa and Idalou and some of the children stood at the gate and waited for her; but the bird dog Sam sat on the porch and waited there, barking. He was too old—Idalou said he was eighteen—to waste breath running to the gate to meet Rhody.

The hooded flagpole sitter was a part of it all. He had come in advance as an agent for the Revival and sat on the Mercantile building as an advertisement for the Revival. He had been up there for three days when the grasshoppers come. Twas harder for him than for anyone, we all imagined. The old-timers said he had brought in the plague of hoppers as part of prophesy. They raised up to him a little tent and he sat under that; but it must have been terrible for him. Most thought he would volunteer to come on down, in the face of such adversity, but no sir, he stayed, and was admired for it. He couldn't sail down his leaflets that advertised the Revival, for the grasshoppers would have eaten those as fast as if they had been green leaves from a tree. But the town had already had leaflets enough that read, "The Day of Judgment Is at Hand, Repent of Your Sins for the Lord Cometh . . ."

The first night he was up twas a hot starry night. We all sat on the porch till late at night rocking and fanning and watching him. There he was over the town, a black statue that hardly seemed real.

When the Revivalist first appeared at the house to ask us for cool water, we invited him in on the back porch. He was a young man to be so stern a preacher, lean and nervous and full of his sermon. His bushy eyebrows met together—for jealousy, Idalou told us after he was gone, and uttered a warning against eyebrows that run together. He started right out to speak of our salvation as if it might earn him a drink of water, and of his own past sinful life in cities before he was redeemed. He wanted our redemption, the way he went on sermonizing, more than a cool drink of water; but water was easiest to provide him with and best at hand, as Aunt Idalou said after he had gone. He was a man ready to speak of his own frailties and Mama praised him for this. He wanted to make us all free and purged of man's wickedness, he said, and his black eyes burned under his joined eyebrows when he spoke of this. When he had left, one of the children—Son—helped him carry the pail of well water to the pasture, and then we all broke into sides about who would go to the Revival the next night and who would watch it from the front porch.

When Son came back he was trembling and told that the Revivalist had two diamond rattlesnakes in a cage, right in Bailey's pasture, and that he had shown him the snakes. Then he told us that the preacher was going to show how the Lord would cure him of snakebite as a demonstration of faith. He had converted and saved thousands through this example of the healing power of the Lord, saying his famous prayer as he was struck by this rattling spear, "Hand of God, reach down and help antidote the poison of the diamond rattler of Sin."

Rhody added that she had already found out all this when she came through the pasture and stopped to converse with Bro. Peters—she already knew his name where we hadn't. Then she added that the Revivalist and his company—a lady pianist and three men who were his stewards and helpers—were going to camp in Bailey's pasture during their three-day stay in town and that at the last meeting, the flagpole sitter himself was going to come down and give a testimonial. She further informed us that she had taken upon herself the courtesy to invite Bro. Peters and his lady pianist to eat supper with us that night. We were all both excited and scared. But Mama and Idalou began at once to plan the supper and went in to make the fire in the stove to cook it with.

Rhody was not much changed—a person like Rhody could never change, just add on—as she was burdened by something we could not name. We all noticed a limp in her right leg, and then she confessed she had arthritis in it, from the dampness of New Orleans, she said. Her face was the same beautiful one; she had always been the prettiest in the family, taking after Granny who had been, it was a legend that had photographic proof right on the wall, a very beautiful young woman. But Rhody's face was as if seen through a glass darkly, as the Bible says. More had happened to Rhody during the years away than she would ever tell us. "Some of the fandango is danced out in her," Aunt Idalou said, and now we would all see the change in Rhody that we all hoped and prayed for.

Rhody was thrilled by the sight of the flagpole sitter. She said she was just dying to meet him. She told us that this town had more excitement in it than any city she had been in—and that included several—and she was glad she had come on home. She unpacked her grip and took out some expensive things of pure silk her husbands had bought for her, and there were presents for us all. Then she put her grip in the pantry as though she was going to stay for a long time but no one asked her for how long. In the early days, Rhody had come and left so often that her feet had trod out her own little path through Bailey's pasture and we had named it Rhody's Path. It ran alongside the main path that cut straight through to town. We never used it, left it for her; but if she was gone a long time, Mama would say to one of us who was going to town, "Use Rhody's Path, the bitterweeds are taking it over, maybe that'll bring her home," the way mothers keep up their hopes for their children's return, though the weeds grow over and their beds are unused. Mama kept Rhody's room the way Rhody had it before she left for the first time, and the same counterpane was always on the bed, fresh and clean, the big painted chalk figure of a collie was on the dresser, the fringed pillow a beau had given her with "Sweetheart" on it, and the framed picture of Mary Pickford autographed by her, "America's Sweetheart." "She's got sweetheart on the brain," Mama used to say. She carried sweetheart too far.

Anyway, the Revivalist took Rhody's Path to come to supper on. Around suppertime here came Bro. Peters and the lady pianist across Bailey's pasture on Rhody's Path, he tall and fast-walking, the little pianist trotting behind him like a little spitz to keep up with him. They came through the gate and onto the front porch where we all greeted them, and Rhody was putting on a few airs of city ways that made Idalou look at her as if she could stomp her toe. We were introduced to the pianist whose name was Elsie Wade, a little spinster type with freckled hands and birdlike movements of head. Miss Wade asked the Lord to bless this house and said that good Christians always gathered easily as if they were blood kin, which they were, Bro. Peters added; and we all went in the house, through the hall and onto the back porch. It was a late summer evening and the vines strung across the screen of the porch were nothing but strings after the grasshoppers had devoured them, but through the latticework of string we could see the distant figure of the flagpole sitter that the setting sun set aglow. Rhody kept wanting to talk about him. She said she thought he looked keen up there. Bro. Peters told that the flagpole sitter had been a drinking man, wild and in trouble in every county of Texas and Louisiana, until he was saved by a chance Revival Meeting in Diboll where he was sitting on the County Seat flagpole as a stunt for something or other. The night he came down to give himself to the Lord at the meeting brought wagonloads of people from far and wide, across creeks and gulleys to hear and see him, and many were saved. From that time on he gave his services to the Lord by way of the difficult and lonely task of sitting on a flagpole for three days and nights as a herald of the coming Revival. The flagpole sitter and the diamond rattlers were the most powerful agents of the Gospel and redemption from sin and literally brought thousands of converts into the fold, Bro. Peters told. Rhody said she was dying to meet him and Bro. Peters assured her he would make the introduction personally on the last night of the Revival.

We sat down to a big supper for summertime: cold baking-powder biscuits, cold kidney beans, onions and beets in vinegar, sweet milk and buttermilk, fried chicken—there was nothing green in the garden left after the grasshoppers had taken their fill. Idalou told Bro. Peters and Miss Elsie Wade that she had fed the Devil with some good squash that she had rescued from the grasshoppers but burnt to a mash on the stove; and Bro. Peters said that the Devil liked good summer squash and if he couldn't acquire it through his agents of pestilence he would come by it on a too-hot stove—but that he was glad the Devil left the chicken; and all laughed, Rhody loudest of all.

Afterwards we went to the porch and while Idalou played the piano Son sang some solos, "Drink to Me Only," etc. But Rhody spoiled the singing by talking incessantly to the Revivalist. Then Elsie Wade applied her rolling Revival technique to the old piano that no one could talk over, not even Rhody, and made it sound like a different instrument, playing some rousing hymns which we all sang faintly because of our astonishment at the way such a slight little thing as she manhandled the piano as if it was a bull plow.

In the middle of one of the songs there was somebody at the front door, and when Idalou went she found it to be a man from Bro. Peters' outfit over in the pasture. He was anxious to speak to Bro. Peters. Idalou asked him in, but Bro. Peters, hearing the man's voice, was already in the hallway by the time the man entered. "Brother Peters!" he called. "One of the diamond rattlers is aloose from the cage." Bro. Peters ran out and Elsie Wade seemed very nervous, inventing a few furbelows on the treble keys as she looked back over her shoulder with a stiff pencil-like neck at the conversation at the front door. Her eyes were so small and glittering at that moment that she seemed like a fierce little bird that might peck a loose snake to death. Idalou invited her to wait in the house, though. "The diamond rattler is our most valuable property," Elsie Wade said, "next to the flagpole sitter."

All night long they were searching for the diamond rattler with their flashlights. We locked all the doors and stayed indoors and watched the lights from the windows. We started a bonfire in the front yard. There were fires in many places in the pasture. The bird dog Sam was astonished that we brought him in the house, but he would not stop barking; and Idalou said he would die of a heart attack before daylight if they didn't catch the valuable property of the viper, he was so old. It was a sinister night. At a certain hour we heard that the flagpole sitter had come down to help find the scourge of Sin. And then suddenly like a shot out of the blue Rhody jumped up and said she couldn't stand it any longer, that she was going out to help the poor Revivalist in his search for the diamond rattler. Everybody objected and Aunt Idalou said over her dead body, that Rhody's arthritis would hinder her if she had to run; but Rhody, being Rhody, went anyway. So there was that anxiousness added.

We all watched from the parlor window. In the light of the bonfire's flame we could see the eerie posse, darting here, kicking there, and we saw that the Revivalist carried a shotgun. The flagpole sitter had arrived in such a hurry and was so excited that he had not had time to take off his long black robe and hood that he wore on the flagpole, and his priestlike shape in the light of the fires was the most nightmarish of all. On went the search through the dark hours after midnight, and it seemed the Revivalist was looking for his Sin, like some penance, a dark hunter in the night searching for evil. And now Rhody was by his side to help him, as if it could be her sin, her evil, too. They seemed to search together.

We never knew, nor will, exactly what happened. When we heard the shot and saw flashlights centered on one spot, we knew they had found the snake; and when we saw them coming on Rhody's Path toward the house, the Revivalist carrying in his arms something like a drowned person, we knew it was Rhody. They came up on the porch, the Revivalist saying sternly, "Call the doctor, she was bitten on the hip by the diamond rattler and has fainted." He bit her bad leg.

They laid Rhody on the bed and Bro. Peters began saying his famous prayer asking the Lord to reach down and pluck the poison from his child. "The snake is killed—the flagpole sitter shot him," one of the men said.

It was Aunt Idalou who scarified the snakebite with a paring knife and saved the life of Rhody until the doctor got there. Though she did it without open prayer, she prayed to herself as she worked on Rhody and used solid practical ways of salvation—including leaves of Spanish dagger plant in the front yard which Son ran and got, and hog lard. When the doctor got there he marveled at the cure and said there was little more to do except for Rhody to rest and lie prone for a few days. Idalou said she could count Rhody's prone days on one hand and Rhody commented that at least the snake had the common sense to strike her bad leg.

When the commotion was over and danger was passed, someone asked where the Revivalist was. He was nowhere to be found. In the early morning light, just breaking, we saw the pasture empty. There was no sign of anybody or anything except the guttering black remains of the bonfires. The flagpole on the Mercantile Building had nothing sitting on it. The whole Revival company had vanished like a dream . . . and had it all been one, the kind Rhody could bring down upon a place?

We hoped that would teach Rhody a lesson, but Aunt Idalou doubted it seriously. Anyway, Rhody stayed on with us till the very end of summer. Then one day there was that familiar scrambling in the pantry and it was Rhody getting her grip out. There was a mouse's nest in it. She packed it, saying she was going to Austin, to get her a job or take a beauty course she had seen advertised. When she had finished it, she told us, she might come back to Charity and open her a beauty parlor. We all doubted that, knowing she couldn't stay put for long in any one place, beauty or none.

We all kissed her good-bye and Aunt Idalou cried and asked the plain air what had branded her youngest child with some sign of restless wandering and when would she settle down to make a household as woman should; and we watched Rhody go on off, on the path across the pasture with her grip in her hand, going off to what, we all wondered.

"Well," Mama said, "she'll pull a fandango wherever she goes. But through some miracle or just plain common sense of somebody always around to protect her, with hog lard, or just good plain prayer, she'll survive and outlast us all who'll worry ourselves into our graves that Rhody will come to put flowers on, alive as ever." Rhody went out and took the world's risks and chances, but simple remedies of home and homefolks rescued and cured her, time and time again. She always had to touch home, set her wild foot on the path across the pasture that led back to the doorstep of the house, bringing to it across the pasture, from the great confused and mysterious world on the farther side, some sign of what had lately happened to her to lay it on the doorstep of home.

But with the world changing so fast and all old-time word and way paying so quickly away, she will have to correct *herself* in the world she errs in and by its means; or, in some way, by her own, on her own path, in the midst of her traveling. Surely we knew she needed all of us and had to touch us there, living on endurable and permanent, she thought, in that indestructible house where everything was always the way it had forever been and would never change, she imagined; where all, for her, was redeemed and put aright. Then, when she got something straight—what it was no one but Rhody ever knew—she'd gather her things and go off again.

"The sad thing is," Idalou said, rocking on the front porch looking at the empty pasture and the sad-looking path that Rhody took, "that years pass and all grow old and pass away, and this house will be slowly emptied of its tenants." Had Rhody ever considered this? And what would she do when all had gone and none to come home to?

But surely all of us who were listening to Idalou were thinking together that the path would remain, grown over and hidden by time, but drawn on the earth, the pasture was engraved with it like an indelible line; and Rhody's feet would be on it, time immemorial, coming and going, coming and going, child of the path in the pasture between home and homelessness, redemption and error. That was the way she had to go.

As you continue experimenting with point of view, you will become more and more aware of its ramifications. Selecting the appropriate narrator or persona for a story or poem has a lot to do with the shape of the work: what information, in what order, with what coloring, reaches the reader. Once you have made—or remade—this fundamental decision, you must follow out its logical consequences.

4

Language Is Your Medium

There Is No Such Thing as a Synonym

Although everything is important in writing, obviously words come first. They are the writer's nuts and bolts, nails, screws, and bricks. Just as cabinetmakers develop an acute sense of the limits and purposes of materials—the strengths, lengths, thicknesses, and the infinite other properties of bolts, glues, and woods—so do writers develop a heightened awareness of the infinite properties of words. A cabinetmaker knows that you don't use a tenpenny nail when you need a brad, or a hacksaw when you need a coping saw.

The writer must learn to make analogous judgments: when to use an adjective, when to use a Latinate word, a complex sentence, a nickname, a noun instead of a pronoun, a quiet word rather than a noisy one. Your first job as a writer is to master the medium of your trade—language itself. This is not as simple a task as you may think.

You should already be using your journal as a place to exercise your awareness of what words function best in particular circumstances. However, it is not only when writers are writing that they are sensitive to words. Just as painters are aware of colors whenever they open their eyes, just as composers are alert to sounds even when they aren't writing music, so too are writers aware of words whenever words are near. Writers are always on a busman's holiday, listening to people use words and, in their reading, testing the choices of other writers.

Our purpose in this chapter is (1) to get you thinking about ways to hone your word sense, (2) to introduce the complex decision making that goes into finding the right words to nail your meaning to the reader's mind, (3) to change some mistaken notions you may have about effective word choice (diction).

We offer one basic principle:

For a writer, there is no such thing as a synonym.

This principle may come as a surprise if you have spent years doing synonym exercises in English classes or if you have been repeatedly warned against repeating and advised to replace a word with a synonym. Such exercises and warnings were offered in the name of vocabulary building. The writer's ideal, however, is to find the exact word or phrase for the job. We assume there is always a best choice. For a *best* choice, there is no substitute.

It is more important to know how approximate words differ than how they overlap. For example, "diaphanous," "transparent," and "see-through" refer to the same quality of a material object. Given that you can use only one of the words in a particular circumstance, you must choose the one that will have not only the correct *denotation,* but also carry the *connotation* you desire. The criteria for choosing are easy to enumerate, less easy to apply. Your choice must be

1. accurate
2. precise
3. concrete (unless an abstract term is clearly necessary)
4. appropriate
5. idiomatic

As you can see, these criteria for word choice are the same for "creative" writing as they are for "ordinary" writing. One of the bits of misinformation that hampers beginners is the idea that they must learn a special language. Actually, what they must do is learn the only language we have as well as they can. Creativity is not measured by the difficulty or sophistication of your words. Nor is it a sign of creativity to foil the reader's expectation at every turn by choosing words for their puzzle quotient. Finally, creativity does not license the misuse of language. Only a responsible, caring attitude toward language makes for good writing of any kind.

For the following passage, choose one of the alternatives—"diaphanous," "see-through," or "transparent"—to fill in the blank. Which criteria governed your choice?

> After she dismissed her ladies-in-waiting, the queen snuffed all but one of the candles. She slipped off the heavy flannel nightgown and put on a _____ gown before opening the secret door that led to the tower where Tristram waited.

Most writers would choose "diaphanous" because it feels right for a queen and for the world of secret doors and towers. The word is accurate in that it literally means what the writer intends it to mean. It is precise in that the *range* of meaning is properly limited. It is as concrete as something filmy can be—that is, it gives us an image. Most important here, the choice is appropriate to its context: "diaphanous" carries with it the sense of delicacy and romance that makes it fit the queen's seductive intent. By comparison, "see-through" seems crass, and "transparent" seems almost scientific ("having the property of transmitting rays of light through its substance"). Is "diaphanous" used idiomatically? Although it isn't the kind of word we use every day, it is consistent with a special style—the conventional *idiom* for historical romance writing.

The sense of what a word connotes, either alone or in a particular context, may differ slightly from person to person, depending upon one's experiences with life and language. There are no rules, since connotations are in the ear of the listener; the point here is that you must be aware of all the fine adjustments that may be necessary.

EXERCISES

1. A woman is preparing to meet a man. Write a brief passage in which "see-through" would be appropriate. Rewrite so that "transparent" would be the best choice.

2. Write a brief scene for each word in these triplets:

a. eat/dine/consume
b. sole/single/individual
c. whiskey/liquor/booze
d. but/conversely/on the other hand
e. single/one-base hit/one-bagger
f. sexpot/seductress/temptress
g. teacher/mentor/professor
h. frugal/cheap/economical
i. morning/ dawn/daybreak
j. fraud/hoax/deceit
k. caviar/roe/fish eggs

3. Explain the difference between having "know-how" and "skill." A "fear" and a "dread." A "job" and an "occupation." A "helper" and an "assistant." "Work" and "labor."

One way of sharpening your language skills is to practice and then evaluate word substitutions while you are reading already published works. In writing, however, we recommend a very sparing and qualified use of the thesaurus. A word chosen from a list simply because it is on the list is not likely to be an effective choice. The thesaurus can be a good memory jogger; it can provide you with a range of possibilities from which to make choices. However, once you abandon the belief in synonyms, the choosing becomes more complex, more exciting, and more professional. Thesaurus mentality assumes that any word on the list will do. The genuine writer knows that only one of them is best. Moreover, the person who relies on the synonym list assumes that the best choice is on the list to begin with.

CHOOSING WELL

Now let's take a closer look at the criteria listed earlier.

Accuracy

When a word choice is accurate, it is free from error. It is "correct" in the sense that its accepted meaning is the meaning the author intends. Unless a word choice is accurate, it has no chance of being effective. Here are some examples of inaccuracy in diction:

1. In his valedictory speech, Brad made *illusions* to Hollywood stars. [The writer has confused "illusion" and "allusion."]
2. Brad had won far *lesser* awards than his father. [The writer has confused "fewer" and "lesser." Unintentionally, the writer has addressed the significance of the awards rather than the number of them.]
3. Another significant factor was her *leapfrogging* suspicion that graduate school was not, nor would it be, her *dispensation*. [Two words don't mean what the writer hopes they mean.]
4. Once, after a particularly bitter loss—the Oilers beat the Bears by a *dropkick*—Dad patted my shoulder and said, "Son, I feel bad, too." [Dropkicks went out of the game before the Oilers came into it. The writer means "field goal."]

5. I tried to light the half-smoked Camel, but my fingers were shaking and I lit it twice. Finally, the *stogie* ignited. [A "stogie" refers to a cigar, not a cigarette.]

Precision

The meanings of words have greater and lesser ranges. It is just as accurate to call Mr. Rockwell the *spouse* of Mrs. Rockwell as it is to call him her *husband*. However, while "husband" is the more sharply defined term and thus the more precise, some occasions will dictate "spouse" as the better choice. Also we might say that "spouse" is precise in a legal context but not in other contexts. Here are some examples of damaging imprecision:

1. The small town *loomed* in the distance. [In the broad sense, "loomed" is accurate; however, its normal and expected usage has to do with figures, states, or images of impending doom or magnitude. A "small town" would be far less likely to loom than a mountain.]

2. The microwave time buzzed and the smoky aroma of cooking meat penetrated her consciousness causing her stomach to lurch. [Many problems here. Did the *time* buzz, or the microwave? "Aroma" is accurate but not precise because we associate "aroma" with a pleasant smell, not one that turns your stomach. Is the ready-made phrase "penetrated her consciousness" accurate? precise? Concrete? Appropriate? Idiomatic? Do we need to be told that the meat is "cooking"?]

3. The airline crash dominated the headlines: "Thirty dead, sixty-eight *wounded*." [We would expect "injured" in such a situation, even if the people have suffered wounds. As worded, the passage suggests a battlefield statistic rather than an accidental catastrophe.]

4. The club was *quite nice*. It *clearly* catered to an upper-class, upwardly mobile clientele. It was filled with twenty- and thirty-year-olds who had skipped lunch for the *healthy* pursuit of fitness. [In addition to using the weasel-word "quite," and the nonword "nice," this writer has shoved in the unnecessary word "clearly" and the self-evident word "healthy." When words are meaningless or useless, your diction is not precise. We see here a connection between being **pre**cise and being **con**cise.]

5. He clutched a long wooden staff with ornate carvings *inscribed* on it. [The probable redundancy and definite wordiness causes imprecision and fuzziness. How about ending after "carvings"? How about ". . . staff ornately carved" or "with ornate inscriptions"? At any rate, the carvings wouldn't be inscribed, the "designs" or "figures"—wreaths, snakes, legends—would be.]

Concreteness

Concrete diction is usually preferred over abstract or general diction. Concrete diction evokes images, bits of sensory experience. (See the "Imagery" section in Chapter 6, "The Elements of Poetry.") Compare the impact of these three statements:

> John exhibited emotional hostility.
> John was angry.
> John fumed.

The first is formal and abstract, though perhaps appropriate for a case study. The second is abstract, but at least it is clear and direct. The third is concrete: it gives us, by way of metaphor, a vivid picture that conveys the meaning more forcefully, more economically, and more memorably than the other two.

It would be foolish to argue that abstract language must be eliminated from all writing. We need words that point to concepts and feelings as well as those that refer directly to sensory experience. However, it is always dangerous to depend too much on words that *tell* rather than *show*.

Writers need to choose language that creates a sensory world for the reader's imagination to enter. As they struggle with their craft, writers learn the fine balance between abstract and concrete formulations. However, as a rule of thumb we argue: when in doubt, make it concrete. (**Figurative language,** discussed later in this chapter, often expresses the abstract in concrete terms.)

Concreteness—specificity of sensation—is a relative matter. Even terms that are not abstract can be made more concrete by being made more specific. In the sentences that follow, the italicized general terms are followed by more specific alternatives in parentheses:

1. The *girl* (child, toddler, daughter, princess, Alice) *cried* (wailed, sobbed, whimpered).
2. *He* (the student, Edgar) *got* (asked for, ordered, bought, demanded) *food* (Italian food, pizza, pepperoni pizza).

EXERCISE

Revise the following for greater concreteness:

1. The man walked down the street.

2. An emotional condition was manifest in her appearance.

3. The building seemed imposing.

4. Jane put on her clothes and ate some food.

The general principle of concreteness is that you call things by the most specific name you can and you describe actions with the most specific verbs you can, leaving minimal work to be done by modifiers. Of course, to be concrete you have to either be observant or know enough to appear so. Most of us know that a forest is made of trees, but few of us are in the habit of thinking about what types of trees. The accomplished writer knows how to find and when to use the concrete word.

Appropriateness

In creative writing you have to please two masters when you choose your words. First, you need to consider how appropriate your diction may be for the audience you have chosen to address. Second, you have to consider how appropriate your diction may be for your genre, your speaker, and the set of circumstances, including the overall language context within which your decisions take place. Compare the diction in the following three sentences.

> The patient manifests the delusion that his *siblings* are poisoning his food. [psychiatric case history]

> Henry called in the private eye because he believed his *siblings* were putting curare in his pasta. [fiction narration]

> "I tell ya Doc, my *siblings* is out to get me." [speech of illiterate character]

Since you are part of an audience yourself, and since you will probably write for people like yourself, you already have a sense of what diction is inappropriate because it will offend. You don't use street language in a poem for a religious periodical. Similarly, common sense will lead you to consider the age, experience, and knowledge of the audience you wish to address. If you have any doubts regarding audience appropriateness, simply study the kinds of things your intended audience already reads.

Here is an example of choosing appropriate diction for audience and character. Let us say you are writing for eight to twelve-year-olds:

> Tom arranged with Becky for a rendezvous at her house.

Your editorial self (or editor) tells you that your audience is not likely to know "rendezvous," and you know how looking up a word interrupts the flow of your reading. So you agree to do the dictionary work for your young reader:

Tom arranged with Becky for a rendezvous (a meeting) at her house.

You soon realize, or your editor does, that this solution won't do because the new version reads like an essay. You try some substitutions:

Tom arranged with Becky for a meeting at her house.

Tom made an agreement with Becky to present himself at her house.

The second try sounds like something corporate lawyers might say. The first is easily accessible for your audience, but the romantic overtones of "rendezvous" and your sense of Tom's show-off character (*he* might use such a word) are lost. And, while the thesaurus might tempt you with a word like "assignation," this temptation would have to be resisted on grounds already mentioned.

Tom told Becky that he'd be at her house that evening.

Too bland.

What about turning the problem with "rendezvous" into the solution? Suppose Tom does know the word—or almost knows it—but neither the reader nor Becky does.

"Let's rendezvous at your house," Tom said.
"I don't think my parents would like that and I'm not sure 1 would either," said Becky, tossing her head.
"We meet at your house all the time."
"Oh, is that all?"

You can see where one might go from here. In this case, a bit of inventiveness allowed you to teach a new word and to show Tom's character. The words that reach your audience must convey more than surface information; thus they must be appropriate to many purposes simultaneously.

Consider the following passage:

The death of a famous actress is the signal, as a rule, for a great deal of maudlin excitement. The world that knew her rushes up on that last stage where she lies with her eyes sincerely closed and joins, as it were, in her death scene, posturing and poetizing around her bier like a pack of amateur mummers. For a few days everyone who knew her is a road company Mark Antony burying her with bad oratory. The stage is a respectable and important institution, what with its enormous real estate holdings, but we still patronize an actress, particularly a dead one.

from Ben Hecht, "Actor's Blood"

The narrator of this passage is not simply reporting the fact of someone's death. We can tell that the narrator is familiar with the world of acting ("scene," "mummers," "road company," "Mark Antony"). Moreover, the writer has chosen words to reveal a contemptuous or ironic attitude about Hollywood.

EXERCISE

1. Locate and describe the word choices in the preceding passage that reveal the narrator's attitude. Consider accuracy, precision, concreteness, and especially appropriateness.

2. Answer the questions that follow this passage, intended for a historical novel about fifteenth-century England:

> With sword or lance or any kind of sidearm Alex was a deadly practitioner. As a hand-to-hand blood spiller he was second to none. He knew a thousand songs, most of them dirty. He was a royster, a rogue, a ruffian, a fornicator, and a basterlycullion, but otherwise and in all other respects the best man in the world.

   a. Is the overall impact of this passage aided or hindered by words we might have difficulty understanding?

   b. Which words contribute to the historical flavoring?

   c. Given your understanding of the writer's purpose, do any of the word choices misfire? Why? What changes do you suggest?

3. Here is a passage from a story intended to be a *naturalistic* look at a contemporary problem. Can you find language in it that is more properly associated with escapist romance fiction? What is the consequence of this diction clash? (Regina is considering artificial insemination.)

> Regina nodded, mute, hugging the sheet around her neck. She wanted to ask him what her chances were, whether he thought it would work, how many babies were conceived this way. But part of her was tired of statistics and percentages, and the other part of her was just tired. So she pushed her fears down into a deep, secret place in her heart and forced a "brave girl" smile.

4. What's wrong with the following passage from a Thanksgiving story?

> The family deployed themselves around the table, ready to devour the stuffed cadaver before them.

Appropriate diction, as we have seen, means many things. In a given context, any word or word combination can be appropriate. The writer's job requires an understanding of all the ways in which word choices can be appropriate or inappropriate.

Idiomatic Usage

An idiomatic usage is one that has a unique grammatical construction or a meaning that cannot be logically derived from its combined parts. When we say "the kettle is boiling" we are speaking idiomatically (and probably putting words together in an untranslatable way). After all, the kettle is *not* boiling, the water inside it is. Many of us, because we confuse idiomatic expressions with trite expressions, have been frightened away from using standard English idioms. While it is true that triteness is to be avoided, the rich idiomatic resources of our language should be employed whenever they are appropriate—and they almost always are appropriate.

The following sentences contain trite expressions:

1. He was *as handsome as a prince.*
2. She had a *devilish twinkle* in her eyes which, at times, would *flash with anger.*
3. Their marriage started out *all lovey-dovey.*
4. Whenever they went out for pizza, they would *travel down memory lane,* recalling the *long lost images of their youths.*

The following contain serviceable idioms:

1. Despite Elliot's good looks, Buffy could not *work up* any interest in him.
2. Elliot *ducked out* the back door rather than *face up* to Buffy's anger.
3. Buffy was Elliot's *dream.*

Idioms tend to be metaphoric and therefore colorful. Most of all, they are *natural,* and the natural is rarely misleading or ineffective. Trite expressions, on the other hand, signal their tiredness to an alert reader who will sense that the writer has *plugged in* the first available *off-the-rack* phrase. These are constructions whose impact has been worn away through overuse. Of course, what might be trite in one circumstance can actually accomplish the writer's purpose:

> Priscilla had always thought Jeffrey as handsome as a prince—in fact, a character in the romances she read by the hour.

In this example, the author used the trite expression to characterize Priscilla's way of thinking as "trite."

Generally speaking, then, you want to avoid the trite, but *not at the expense of the natural.* Examine these alternative passages:

1. In spite of the statistical probability that the situation would eventuate negatively, and half-wondering if she wanted it to, she perpetrated a fraudulent optimism upon herself and aimed her countenance in the direction of the inevitable harsh resolution.

2. Hoping against hope, she faced the music.

Neither of these renderings is effective. However, the first is so clotted, tortured, and *unnatural* that, if we had to choose, we'd select the trite yet smooth and spontaneous movement of the second.

In brief, you will usually want to work at a natural, idiomatic diction that captures the quality of friendly rather than academic or professional talk. There are exceptions, of course. Writers of historical fiction might appropriately use a more formal or archaic diction in order to suggest the past.

EXERCISE

1. Match the phrase in the left column with the idiomatic form on the right:

-withdraw his assertion	bank on
-expect to receive	tune in
-not the route usually taken	shortcut
-adopt a different attitude	pay off
-redeem a loan or note	back down
-adjust for sharper reception	change one's tune

2. Write two short scenes, the first using any three items from column "A" and the next using the parallel items from column "B." Now examine the differences.

A	**B**
wait for a favorable opportunity	— bide one's time
inspect	— look over
think of a thing unexpectedly	— hit upon
yield to (as in an argument)	— to cave in
accept an offer	— bite at
look for an implied meaning	— read between the lines
extort all one's money	— bleed white

disclaim further responsibility	—	wash one's hands of
spent money foolishly	—	blew
exclude	—	rule out
reserve a . . . in advance	—	book a . . .
malfunction	—	break down
prevent from happening	—	call a halt to
perform	—	carry out
suited to	—	cut out for
to eat greedily	—	wolf down

Like any other language tool, idioms can be misused or inappropriately used. Still, we encourage you to use idioms rather than to go out of your way to avoid them and end up with stuffy or overwritten prose. Here are some guidelines:

1. Prefer a common idiom to eccentric diction: Buffy felt that he had *no call* to *jump down her throat* simply because she forgot the mustard.
2. Prefer nothing to trite diction: He was handsome (*not* "as handsome as a prince"). Buffy felt a mess (*not* "as if she had been through a meat grinder").
3. Prefer something you may think is trite to a forced expression: When they walked by without saying hello, Buffy felt that she had been given the cold shoulder (*not* "as chilled as a lobster in a freezer").

SOME DICTION PROBLEMS

Many novice writers have the mistaken notion that they should "write writing." That is, they believe effective writing consists of verbal prestidigitation and pyrotechnics. They believe not that the words need to be chosen for specific tasks but rather that the words chosen need to sound important and weighty. Some beginners were actually taught to worship words for words' sake; some simply pile word upon words as a substitute for thinking. The end result of believing in this false god is twofold: (1) the writing becomes padded and/or inflated; (2) problems in effective word choice are actually disguised. But even before that happens, the false god leads the writer to put enormous efforts into the wrong type of work: the work of impressing rather than convincing the reader.

We might have discussed the various guises in which padded and inflated diction choices appear under one or another of our major headings: accuracy, precision, concreteness, appropriateness, and idiomatic naturalness. However, the following strivings after quick effects appear often enough to merit a separate section. They are not positive criteria for emulation, but negative habits to be avoided.

Overwriting

Many of the subclasses discussed elsewhere in this section could be placed into this category. You *overwrite* when you pad your language without adding meaning or impact, as in the following example from the beginning of a story:

> It's funny how certain things, the biggest moments and the smallest *passing thoughts alike, how they* can *both* become your sweetest memories later on. And, *years later,* when the places and the people who gave you these tender times are gone, their memories become *starbright* highlight colors for the tapestry of your life.

The problems in this passage cannot be solved only by removing the obvious overwriting (in italics). Taking out such overblown adjectives as "starbright" is only the first step. One still needs to deal with the padding sewn tightly to the rather obvious, even silly, thought that both the big and little occurrences can become sweet memories. This type of overwriting can disguise paucity of thought even from the writer. (Of course, the passage might work if it revealed a rather foolish character's habitual style.)

One type of overwriting grows from a virtue, the virtue of presenting precise detail for the reader. This virtue becomes a problem when the writer becomes too ambitious and gives us too many details to absorb. In the following passage, which describes someone the major character sees once and never again, the writer's purpose is to describe a representative character in a subway crowd.

> He was dressed in the standard Washington attorney uniform—conservative suit, solid color shirt, Ivy League tie, tan raincoat, Irish walking hat. Yet behind his Yuppiestyle glasses, his face had a devilish twinkle accented by a dimple you could dangle barefoot in and brown hair that strayed past the regulation length, curling at least an inch down his collar.

Since there is no reason in the story to give us all this detail, the elaboration becomes a distraction. In fact, when we look carefully at exactly what the narrator has told us, we wonder—as we did in the former case—if the words are attached to any authentic observations. Do faces "twinkle"?

Overmodification

This kind of overwriting comes from the admirable attempt to be concrete. However, the piling up of adjectives, adverbs, and especially prepositional phrases is a signal that something is wrong. Often the muscle of sentence structure and meaning gets covered over by the modifying fat. Sometimes choosing a more specific noun or verb is the solution. In the following cases, the modification is unnecessary because its meaning so overlaps the meaning of the modified word.

> A faded *woven tapestry* hung from the *lintel of the door.* [Most tapestries are woven; "lintel" is the part of the door from which one would assume something as large as a tapestry would be hung.]

> Her lungs felt as if someone had stabbed her *with a knife.* [Here a trite simile is automatically continued to its predictable end. Without the unnecessary final phrase, the expression is sharper.]

What modifying words can be cut or phrases reduced from the following passage?

> "A sad saint is not a saint," she often said, one of her many expressions from a seemingly endless tape. These quotes poured out from her with force or tenderness as the situation demanded. In a less energetic person, remarks such as these would bore, but Bridget's desire to serve gave her ebullient Christian advice a distinctive palatable flavor.

Saying It Twice

Redundancy is a common problem and has many causes, some of which we have already addressed. In the example that follows, the writer refused to pay attention to what her words were saying, or were supposed to say.

> Directly in front of me, a modern glass and steel tower, *illumination provided by lights* in its occupied rooms, sparkled like a monolithic crystal. [There is some nonsense in the closing simile; can you detect it?]

Excessive Variation

This problem used to go by the name of "elegant variation," but the issue has less to do with elegance than with a learned fear of repeating key words and phrases. With or without the "help" of the thesaurus, many writers act as if repetition were a deadly sin. While repetition *can* become deadly, often the means taken to avoid it create even worse problems for the reader. In the following passage, the student writer seems to be driven by a misguided but honest desire to avoid repeating his key noun.

> As Jim entered the turn, the *motorcycle* seemed to sink into the ground. He could feel the shocks being compressed as the force of the turn

pushed him and his *machine* to a lower center of gravity. As he leaned into the turn, he stuck out his knee for balance. It was hard to remain in control, but Jim calmly, smoothly, lifted his head, twisted the *vehicle* upright, and pulled back with his right wrist. Instantly, the *bike* shot forward, its front wheel once again coming off the ground. Already entering the next turn, Jim shifted his weight forward and braked hard. Slowing to 100 miles per hour, he leaned the *Kawasaki* once more over to the left. Passing by the pits, he could see David and Georgetti keeping track of his time while Rhonda displayed it on the leader board for him to see. At the end of the first session, Jim pulled his *trusty mount* back into the pit.

The result is a scattered effect, and some uncertainty about whether or not the writer is always referring to the same thing.

Latinate Diction

Linking up a series of polysyllabic words from Latin roots makes your writing self-consciously learned and unpleasantly pretentious. It also slows the reader down, as the following sentence illustrates:

> Jane held to her assertion despite Bill's remonstrance to the contrary. [Can you put this into plain English?]

Archaic Diction

This habit usually springs from a misguided notion about how to sound "literary" or "poetic." We no longer believe that such words or expressions as "yore," "thee," "o'er," or "finny prey" (for "fish") confer a poetic or dignified quality to writing. In fact, the convention of our day is that effective writing demands the words and rhythms of everyday speech. "Alas" and "ill tidings" sound like attempts to impose emotions rather than create them.

Sonic Boom

Sometimes intentionally, sometimes not, a writer allows the sounds to drown out meaning by calling too much attention to themselves, as the following case demonstrates:

> The blustery day threatened to batter the delicate blossoms that had drawn *gaggles* of *gawking* tourists to the nation's capital. [One might argue that the alliteration on "b" has a positive effect, but certainly the italicized words make too much noise.]

If, as we have suggested, all successful writing comes from editing and rewriting, then every good writer must become a word detective, hunting down the criminal elements in early drafts and taking them out of circulation.

Breaking bad habits is only part of the job, however. A writer must develop a positive working sense of what makes for effective diction—accuracy, precision, concreteness, appropriateness, and idiomatic usage. A writer must understand what it means to live without the comfort of synonyms.

EXERCISE

Locate and describe the diction problems in the following passages; then provide improvements.

1. I entered the office promptly at seven o'clock as usual, the nostalgic noises of the small-town daily reverberating against my ears, transmitting a sense of urgency. I liked my work; it gave me an opportunity to keep my thumb on the pulse of the mainstream of the city's affairs.

2. Rosa stormed from the room. I could hear her heels tiptip in harmony down the steps. The slamming door sent a thud throughout the whole empty club that I could feel even upstairs. I mentally surveyed the damage I'd just done.

3. A little past ten in the morning and I'd already brought two star-crossed kids together for who knows how much future happiness.

4. She had never mentioned the incident to anyone, not even Mark, and tried to avoid Cooper whenever possible. If only she'd come up with a clever, gentle put-down, she thought, she could have curtailed the problem without this awkwardness between them. As it was, she spoke to him from a cool distance. [The incident is an attempted rape.]

5. If Brault played him loose, he scored from outside. When he played him tight he drove by him, or, once in a while, threw a jump shot.

6. As I spoke, I felt exhilarated as I watched the sea of eager eyes and scribbling hands intently following my words. Stimulating young minds athirst for knowledge and open to new ideas was spiritual in a way, certainly far more uplifting than listening to a priest.

7. His voice so filled the bathroom that for a moment I felt his red-veined eyes on me. I could even smell the odor of sawdust and beer he always emitted.

8. I couldn't lose this chance. Not when I was getting nearer to finding the murderer. Maybe this call would give me the clue that was keeping me from solving the case.

9. With a cold gleam in her eye, Katherine swung again and struck him hard in the ribs and across the stomach. An audible gasp of air escaped from the man's bloodied lips.

10. Well, things change as time passes, he told himself. He then dismissed these thoughts with the hope that perhaps if he just let things sort themselves out, they might just come to a suitable conclusion.

11. The chance that he might lose her caused him evident stress, and to help the situation, she lowered some of her defenses and began to open up.

12. My uncle looked sadly at me. Thoughtfully, he patted down the gray lateral hairs spread thinly across his tanned veined distinguished head.

13. "I told you not to go!" shouted the angered captain as the sound of his voice drifted out of focus.

14. The battalion was split into respective companies and each platoon was assigned to a specific berthing area.

FUN WITH WORDS

Word play is an important activity. It can help you build an active vocabulary, sharpen your diction, and freshen your word combinations. In his poem "Because I Never Learned the Names of Flowers," Rod Jellema shows us the sheer fun of word play and the power of expectation. Even though the tone and technique are playful, any reader can recognize the genuine emotion in this love poem.

Because I Never Learned the Names of Flowers

it is moonlight and white where
I slink away from my cat-quiet blue rubber truck
and motion myself to back it up to your ear.
I peel back the doors of the van and begin
to hushload into your sleep
the whole damn botanical cargo of Spring.

Sleeper, I whisk you
Trivia and Illium, Sweet Peristalsis, Flowering Delirium.

Sprigs of purple persiflage and Lovers' Leap, slips
of Hysteria stick in my hair. I gather clumps of Timex,
handfuls of Buttertongues, Belly buttons, and Bluelets.

I come with Trailing Nebula, I come with Late-Blooming
Paradox, with Creeping Pyromania, Pink Apoplex,
and Climbing Solar Plexis,

whispering: Needlenose,
Juice Cup, Godstem, Nexus, Sex-us, Condominium.

from *The Eighth Day: New & Selected Poems*

Part of the fun of Jellema's poem is to discover the strange tension between what we expect (names of flowers) and the actual words and phrases the poet has put in their places. To most novices, and perhaps even to some experts, there is something almost convincing about these new "names." Some of this has to do with the Latinate formulations that sound like those used in botany. This love poem, of course, is filled with physical passion and a grand madness. Still, one could almost draw a picture of each imaginary flower.

EXERCISE

1. Look up each word that you don't know in Jellema's poem. How is the meaning of each appropriate, ironic, or fanciful? Which words overlap in meaning? How does this overlapping influence the effect of the overall poem?

2. Rewrite or extend Jellema's poem with "flowers" of your own.

3. Make a specialized word list. Perhaps you know or can find out something about computers, astronomy, chess, film editing, or even flowers. Now work this list into a surprising yet revealing context—an apparent nonsense that makes a kind of sense.

4. Rename the components of a sport or game and see what happens when you describe the game with these new words. Example: (for baseball) bat = stem, base = pillow, ball = gourd, and so on.

5. Copy the recipes for some bar drinks (a Tom Collins, Martini, Pink Lady, or White Russian, for example). Now introduce abstract words (rage, loss, enthusiasm) in place of the original ingredients. Concoct a love potion, a youth potion, a drink that will increase your intelligence.

Exercises like these help waken your sense of language. Remember, however, that liberties you can take in exercises sometimes exceed those you can take in works intended for publication. Word play helps you go beyond your concern for diction that is *literally* accurate, precise, concrete, appropriate, and idiomatic. It allows you to enter the world of *figurative language,* a world you must explore in order to make your writing lively.

FIGURES OF SPEECH

Writers achieve economy and vividness of expression through figures of speech, those complex ways of perceiving and phrasing comparisons and contrasts. At bottom, metaphors, similes, and other figures of speech are not literary devices; they are the ways in which our minds try to make sense of experience. Everyday language is filled with these constructions. When we speak of "the head of a pin," "the teeth of a gear," "the shoulder of a road," or "a dead-end street," we are speaking figuratively. To call someone "spineless" is not to make a literal statement, but a figurative one. Colloquial expressions like "get off my back" attest to the figurative habits of mind that generate new ways of communicating our ideas and feelings.

Some of the most successful figures eventually turn into clichés—dead metaphors that have lost their imaginative punch. Let's explore a few of these.

What genius first came up with the expression "he's (or she's) a brick" to make a point about a friend's solid dependability? A brick is a building block of reliable dimension and durability. A brick is kind of square. How do these physical traits relate to character traits? Does the image of the brick come to mind when the expression is used? Do we any longer enjoy the particular areas of overlap between two relatively unlike things—a human personality and a construction material? Once we stop seeing the brick, the metaphor is dead and may have become a cliché, an expression to be avoided unless selected for special, limited purposes (to make fun of it, for instance).

In the following poem by William Matthews, the cliché "it's a tough nut to crack" becomes resuscitated by its context:

Hope

Beautiful floors and a lively
daughter were all he'd wanted, and then—
that the dear piñata of her head

not loose its bounty, the girl's
father scored the soles of her new shoes
with a pocketknife, that she not slide

nor skid nor turn finally upside-
down on the oak floors he'd sanded
and buffed slick long before she first

gurgled from her crib. Now he's dead
and she's eighty. That's how time
works: it's a tough nut to crack

and then a sapling, then a tree, and
then somebody else's floor long
after we ourselves are planted.

from *Foreseeable Futures*

Matthews has given us back the reality of the nut, the literal truth from which the metaphorical use springs. The nut holds the seeds that become the sapling, the tree, and finally the floor. Also, "planted" appropriately suggests a renewal that follows burial.

Here is a passage that contains another dead metaphor: "After the leader worked his way over the log that bridged the chasm, the others *followed suit*." Though we would no longer stop to enjoy the buried picture of card players playing out the same suit that had been led, we know what the phrase means: it seems like a *literal* statement to us now and not a *figurative* one.

We don't have to avoid every expression that we recognize as a dead metaphor. In fact, we can't. As we insisted earlier, many of these formulations are simply available idiomatic expressions that work far better than outlandish alternatives some writers invent to avoid sounding trite.

Figurative expressions are literal lies. In the equation of **metaphor**, two unlike things (events, traits, or objects) are asserted to be identical: A = B. "The moon is a ghostly galleon tossed up on silvery seas." Well, the moon is no such thing, but claiming that it is—discovering an area of overlap between the way this particular moon looked and the appearance of a certain ship under certain circumstances—allows the writer to tell us much about the way things felt, not just the way they looked.

Examine the metaphor closely. What phase of the moon is suggested? Is the sky clear or cloudy? Is the work from which this passage is taken one of hard-boiled cynicism or romantic adventure? How do you know?

Direct statements of identity, "X is Y," are not the only constructions that release metaphor. The ways in which parts of speech unexpectedly relate can release subdued metaphors. The passage "Each footstep puffed a plume of dust" contains two metaphors. In the second, we are asked to see a relationship between the particular shape the dust took and a plume or feather. Of course, dust and feathers often go together, but not in this way. To give a footstep breath with which to puff likens that action to animal or even human behavior. This special kind of metaphorical expression is called **personification**.

Examine the student poem by K. D. Goeser that follows. The first stanza contains two personifications, the second contains a metaphor, the third a **simile**—a figurative linking in which A is explicitly likened to B.

Sometimes, Driving
Towards Dusk

you notice dark telephone poles
one by one lift themselves
out of a fence line
and slowly invade the sky.

Darkness drifts down
on picked cornfields,
on black trees,
into the wheelruts of combines
and the cracked prints of boots.

> Driving towards Chicago,
> I see lights in barns
> and bare trees held rigid
> like fierce men on their deathbeds.

Telephone poles can't actually "lift themselves" or "invade." Saying so attributes human characteristics to them. "Darkness" does not literally "drift" into anything because it has no substance. The poet's imagination has suggested that darkness is acting like something else—dust, perhaps. The comparative formulation that closes the poem—"bare trees held rigid/like fierce men on their deathbeds"—tells us about the trees in a striking way. *Rigidity* is the characteristic the poet wants to enhance. His simile makes these trees unforgettably rigid. He has taken two unlike things, found a linking aspect, and exploited it to the hilt. Whoops!

In the examples just given, a literal lie made something not only vivid, not only fresh in expression, but clear as well. Though it seems paradoxical, effective figures of speech do just that—lie to make things clear. Without this heightened clarity, figurative language is no better than muddy language of any kind. The writer of the following passage probably felt proud of the way in which he made an abstraction concrete—one of the goals of much figurative expression. We wonder, however, if the meaning is clear: "Time is like a trail cut through the woods that we crawl down with our noses in the dirt."

What can anyone learn about time or about human nature here? Nothing. What has gone wrong? For one thing, the writer has lost sight of his original intention. The simile, which begins with an attempt to characterize *time* through images of distance and motion, abruptly shifts to concerns that have no clear relevance to time. However, if the time under discussion was the time spent humbling ourselves before authority, the extended simile just might work.

Why are these more effective?

> Branches of class lecture brush against me, then retreat back into the grayness.

> A thicket of black hair.

The following poem is an exercise constructed almost entirely out of similes. What is the effect of each one individually? Of the entire catalog?

Anatomy of Melancholy

> The blue tears stain my cheeks
>   Like a leaky fountain pen
> Spurting its juice on white paper,
>   Like a ripe blueberry
> Bursting upon a milk-white tablecloth.

A droopy head hangs low
  Like the daisies knocked down by
Blowing gusts of wind,
  Like the signpost ran into
By the drunk kid in the red Corvette.

The thin lips pressed to viseful grip,
  Like a sad clown's inverted grin

Stamped on white facepaint,
  Like the crescent moon hanging
Upside down in the darkening sky.

A saggy flesh drapes the frame
  Like the Auschwitz inhabitants doomed
To the fuming chloride showers,
  Like the jowls of the bulldog
Standing guard at the house next door.

Like any tool at our disposal, similes and other figures of speech can be overused or go haywire. In the preceding case, while many of the expressions are successful, the parts are not subordinated to the whole. After a while, the reader ceases to be in touch with what the poem is about; the piling up of similes becomes an end in itself rather than the means to an end.

One more point about similes. They are not simply comparisons using *like* or *as*. The phrase "Jane looks like her sister" is a literal comparison (it is actually true) rather than a figurative one. Remember, it is the discovery of an area of likeness or overlap between two essentially different terms that is the basis for a figurative expression.

FIGURATIVE LANGUAGE EXERCISE

1. Expand each of the following statements: first with a literal comparison, next with a metaphor or simile, last with an **analogy**—the resemblance in a number of particulars of two things otherwise unlike. In doing these exercises, don't worry about saving all the words from the statement. The goal is vivid communication that is both clear and suggestive.

Example: My Model T takes off rapidly.

> **Literal comparison:** My Pinto accelerates almost as rapidly as
> a new Geo.
> **Figure of speech:** My Pinto takes off like a bullet.
> **Analogy:** My Pinto reminds me of a well-preserved old
> athlete. Like him, it isn't as young as it once was, but it too

has been kept in top condition through proper care and exercise. Just as that athlete can still hold his own among the youngsters, so my old car continues to show up well in competition with the newer cars.

   a. A Boy Scout knife is a handy tool.
   b. My dog is very affectionate.
   c. The exam was extremely difficult.
   d. Lisa has a lovely complexion.
   e. Israel is a new nation.
   f. Urbanites exist in a state of fear.
   g. Erosion of the shoreline is ruining the beach resorts.
   h. When I came home, my parents were up waiting for me.
   i. News of violent crime dominates the front page.
   j. The grass is already turning brown.

2. Complete the following sentences using or creating vivid figurative expressions:

   a. When he smiled, . . .
   b. The sun . . . through the trees and . . . whatever it touched.
   c. When I heard the tailpipe clatter on the road, . . .
   d. They shook hands carefully, like . . .
   e. She drew deeply on her cigarette, . . .

Two special kinds of metaphor are synecdoche and metonymy. In **synecdoche**, a part stands for the whole, as when we call a detective a "private eye." **Metonymy** works differently; an item is used in place of something associated with it, as in "the pentagon announced." Obviously, the building didn't announce anything. In practice, the two devices are often indistinguishable. See if you can sort them out in this poem by James Shirley, a British poet of the seventeenth century. What other figures of speech are in this poem?

The Glories of Our Blood and State

The glories of our blood and state
Are shadows, not substantial things;
There is no armor against fate;
Death lays his icy hand on kings.
  Scepter and crown
  Must tumble down
And in the dust be equal made
With the poor crooked scythe and spade.

Some men with swords may reap the field
And plant fresh laurels where they kill,
But their strong nerves at last must yield;
They tame but one another still.

Early or late
They stoop to fate
And must give up their murmuring breath,
When they, pale captives, creep to death.

The garlands wither on your brow,
Then boast no more your mighty deeds;
Upon death's purple altar now
See where the victor-victim bleeds.
Your heads must come
To the cold tomb;
Only the actions of the just
Smell sweet and blossom in their dust.

Though we have been giving examples from poetry, figurative language is part of all kinds of writing. So, too, are the problems that emerge when figures of speech go berserk. Metaphors and similes can be so farfetched, so forced, that readers will either tune out or be so dazzled by the writer's ingenuity that they will miss the point. More often, the problem is that elements in the metaphor are in conflict with one another. We call such a construction a mixed metaphor. The writer who puts down "My spirit, like my blood, slowly drips from my body, white feathers now turned crimson" has lost hold of effective figurative logic. It would seem that the spirit is being likened to white feathers, but it is also likened to blood. Once it is blood, it can't drip on itself, turning itself crimson; it must have been crimson to begin with. **Mixed metaphors** often come from overwriting, allowing needless complexity and elaboration to ruin a workable insight.

When we use images suggestively, they turn out to be more than descriptive. They may involve the sort of figurative comparisons discussed earlier in which one term is equated or related to another in a special way. Sometimes images generate associations in which the second term is not named, but still understood. When an image represents something other than or beyond itself, it is being used as a **symbol**.

Many symbols are conventional: their meanings are shared by a community or culture. Our flag is one such symbol; the cross is another. Traditionally, the color white is a symbol of purity, red of passion, purple of royalty. No one can refer to a snake or serpent without suggesting the meanings developed in the story of Adam and Eve. We use symbols of this sort all the time, often without even thinking about them.

In our own writing, we can also generate meanings in a particular work through local symbols. For example, in the following poem by A. E. Housman, "London" is used to suggest all that is opposed to gentleness, innocence, and inexperience. It becomes a symbol for a worldly toughness and a worldly style.

From the wash the laundress sends
My collars home with ravelled ends;

> I must fit, now these are frayed,
> My neck with new ones, London-made.
>
> Homespun collars, homespun hearts,
> Wear to rags in foreign parts.
> Mine at least's as good as done,
> And I must get a London one.

Often there is little distance between symbolism and synecdoche or metonymy. You could say here that "collars" symbolizes all of the person's clothing, style, and way of life. If you think the reference is only on the concrete level, you might say that "collars" is the part that stands for all of the speaker's garments (synecdoche). Housman's reference to "hearts" is the conventional one in which the vital organ represents the center of emotion.

EXERCISE

Evaluate the diction in the following passage from James Agee's *The Morning Watch*. How does Agee make his diction accurate? precise? Concrete? Appropriate? Idiomatic? Where does he use figurative language? How much does he depend on modifiers? Is this dependence justified?

At the far end of the break in the woods along the far side of the track they saw the weathered oak tower and soon, walking more briskly along the ties, the relics of machinery and the dead cones, putty-colored sand and the wrinkled sandstone and, at length, the sullen water itself, untouched in all these cold months. There were black slits along the sides of the tower where planks had fallen during the winter. The water was motionless and almost black. The whole place, familiar as it was, was deadly still, and seemed not at all to welcome them. As they left the track to round the near end of the Sand Cut there was a scuttling among the reddened brambles but although they went as fast as they could on their soft feet and threw rocks where the brambles twitched with noise they got no glimpse of whatever it was, and soon the scuttling stopped.

A FEW WORDS ABOUT STYLE

If personal "style" is the result of a host of conscious and unconscious choices in everything from dress to speech, we might conclude that a writer (or artist) doesn't have to worry about "style" since it is a given and, no matter what you do, your writing will have style. And that is, as a matter of fact, a correct conclusion.

Just as in dress, style in writing is likely to be a combination of ready-mades: diction choices, idioms, sentence structures, rhythms, figures of speech, and even sounds. As a developing writer, you do not need to create the language from scratch. You need to find a style or styles that fit your needs for a variety of circumstances and avoid habits or styles that are not suitable for fiction, poetry, and drama. One way to improve style is to recognize that different audiences expect different styles. Compare, for example, the following:

I: Also passed by Congress was legislation which prohibits the use of appropriated funds to influence the awarding of federal grants, contracts, and loans, and requires that an applicant for a federal grant, contract, or loan disclose any payments made with nonappropriated funds that would have been prohibited if made with appropriated funds.

II: The new law that Congress passed states that you can't use money from one government grant, contract, or loan to get another one. Also, the law requires you to disclose any money you spend to get government money.

III: What's the world coming to? Now Congress has passed a law that stops self-respecting lobbyists and gun makers from using money from one government dole to wheedle another government dole. And, get this, even if you use your own money to lobby for some government largess, you have to tell about it. There go the general's free tickets for Redskin games.

You would have little difficulty in describing these styles—cool legalese, abstract reportorial, sarcastic editorial—and understanding them as special versions of the three basic style categories: formal, informal, and colloquial.

Beyond discovering and honing your general-purpose style, you will need to develop an ability to invent styles for specific projects and purposes. If you use Latinate diction combined with long, highly subordinated sentences, your style might sound like that of a professional or bureaucrat who is trying to communicate laws, ideas, abstractions, or summations. Use simpler words and shorter sentences for a style that appears to be a simple reporting of actions and thoughts. Use many adjectives and adverbs and you give the impression of being ornate (lavish, gushy, generous). Avoid adjectives and your style becomes plain (curt, Spartan, stingy). Similes and metaphors, like decorative rocks in the lawnmower's path, can slow the pace of your prose. Short sentences speed it up.

None of these generalizations are always true. Some philosophers express quite complex ideas in relatively simple, jargon-free sentences. Some prose that is highly adjectival moves rapidly.

Experiment with a variety of styles and consciously imitate writers you admire as part of your writing apprenticeship. And read diligently, with an eye to discovering the relationships between stylistic causes and their effects.

Consistency in style (within a work) is almost always a virtue.

EXERCISE

1. Look back at the passage by Agee. What are the effects of the long opening and closing sentences? How do these serve to set off the shorter sentences in the middle of the paragraph, especially the shortest, central one? Compare this strategy of sentence relationships to that used in William Matthews's poem (p. 70).

2. Reread William Goyen's "Rhody's Path" (Chapter 3) and see if you can find stylistic features that evoke regional culture.

3. We began this discussion by noting that style is, in part, a function of personality. What elements of style reveal the narrative voices in passages presented on pages 34–35? Contrast the literalness of Hemingway's diction with the figurative richness of Fitzgerald's. Why does Fielding's narrator say "the animal with long ears" instead of "ass"? Is a genuine decorum at work here? Or just an allusion to decorum? What does this decision have to do with the fact that Fielding considers his work mock-epic? Many of James's structures involve interruptions of subject from verb, verb from object. What are the consequences of this stylistic manner?

4. Compare and contrast the styles employed in two of the short stories found in Chapter 11.

Language is your medium. Coming to a mastery of the medium is a lifelong pursuit. Through alertness, careful analytical reading, conscientious vocabulary building, imagination, dedicated work in your journal, and the responsible attitude that every decision is important, you can develop into an effective creative writer. Once you believe, as we do, that there is no such thing as a synonym, you are on your way.

5

---◆---

Invention and Research

The Original

*Origin*ally, the word *original* meant the source, the starting point, the cause of a series of effects. The spring is the origin of the river; the poet of the poem. In this sense, the term only describes; it does not evaluate. In time, it came to mean the primary instance of something after which only copies or imitations were possible. Because we tend to value a copy at less worth than its original, we can be led to an irritable striving after originality in everything—as if the only valuable creation is one in which the creator has done everything in a totally new way. But even the Mona Lisa would fail this test. The feeling that imitation is always bad and that originality means uniqueness can be a trap for the beginning writer.

Don't fall into it.

In the first sense of the word, you can't help but be original—you are *originating*—causing something to come into being that wouldn't occur without your effort. To accept the present, all-or-nothing sense of the word dooms you to failure because you have set an impossible goal: to invent materials and shapes that have no precedents.

The search for this type of total originality can develop into mere eccentricity—one of the archaic meanings of original. The reader can easily grow weary of three kinds of works:

1. Those that strive after unique effects without any justification.
2. Those that result from believing that "creative" means anything goes—poor logic, faulty mechanics, and factual inaccuracy.
3. Those that have no relationship to any shared world, natural or artistic. These works, almost by definition, will have no audience.

The false notion that the "original" is somehow independent of anything else can grow into the equally false notion that creativity is the result of brilliant flashes of the never-before-seen rather than the result of the more mundane but realistic ability-to-take-pains.

As you will see, the ability to think and act independently as a writer involves the ability to develop a mature work ethic.

ORIGINALITY AND THE EVERYDAY

While originality in writing, as in other arts, is sometimes connected with the freaky, most often truly original writing is steeped in the usual—the everyday. Even contemporary horror stories, for example, create their effects by focusing on the lives of ordinary people into which the unusual enters. The chilling effect of such tales grows, in part, from the very fact that the werewolf is the local barber who loves apple pie and Saturday night bowling. As a writer, then, you should not put yourself under *unreasonable* pressure to come up with startling ideas, exotic settings, tic-filled characters, and constantly surprising twists of plot.

Successful writing keeps a grip on probability and on universal human nature. If the writer can't present the ordinary in a vital way, the reader will never believe in what may be extraordinary in the work. And if the reader doesn't recognize the human truth of the writer's fabrications, then the work will be quickly set aside in favor of something else.

This is not to say that there is no room for invention. Indeed, there is always a great demand for it. However, invention is a means to an end, not an end in itself. Readers have expectations based on their experiences with other literary and dramatic writing, and those expectations are based on a familiarity with the conventions of language and genre. There is no baseball game until everyone is ready to play by the rules, and there is no positive effect on a reader who is confused, frustrated, or insulted. While it is possible to invent a game—or a world—in which the runners go clockwise, you need a good reason to do so.

Originality has more to do with the way in which familiar materials are combined than with a new way to say something that no one else has ever said before. Your fresh vision in a poem, story, or play will come from the unique combination that is you, but only so long as you have studied, thought deeply about, and responded honestly to your material. The great masters of litera-ture—Jane Austen, William Faulkner, William Butler Yeats, and Eugene

O'Neill, for example—are intriguing first of all because they are believable. Granted, often they get us to believe something during our experience that we would not believe in another context. Perhaps we should say that they hold their visions with such conviction and record them so powerfully that the reader can't help but believe. And, even though these writers stay in touch with the world they know—which shares a great deal with the world we know—each is strikingly original. You are unlikely ever to confuse their visions with anyone else's.

To create a world of values, assumptions, social styles, issues, speech styles, and material setting that is unmistakable and therefore original is the writer's task. Though such worlds are based on what authors see around them, *they exist only in the pages of their books.* The London of Dickens, the Georgia of Flannery O'Connor, the Chicago of Saul Bellow, the Pequod of Herman Melville, and even the Dune of Frank Herbert are truthful inventions imagined, ordered, and recorded for the very first time to serve important purposes in the work of each writer.

We should realize, too, that the fantasy worlds of Jonathan Swift's *Gulliver's Travels,* George Orwell's *1984,* and J. R. R. Tolkien's *Lord of the Rings* are not greater acts of invention than the eastern towns set down by John Updike or the semi-imaginary Wessex in which many of Thomas Hardy's novels are placed. The land of tiny people Gulliver visits are real to him, and he is real to us, and that is what finally matters. Making your hometown real to a reader, or making the reader believe in the place you see only in your imagination or in a travel guide, calls for the same faculties of invention and originality.

THE RELATIONSHIP BETWEEN INVENTION AND RESEARCH

The root meaning of *invent* is "to come upon" or to find. In this sense it is related to *discover.* The origin of the word tells us that what we are after already exists, though perhaps only somewhere inside of the writer. The meaning also suggests a seemingly paradoxical relationship between invention and research. Many of the masterpieces of our literary culture, the "great originals" of our most individualistic writers, are the result of voluminous research. Melville's *Moby Dick* is such a work. Critics have discovered the many sources on whales and whaling that Melville used to help him create this vast, imagined world. His reliance on research, however, does not diminish Melville's achievement. In fact, in some ways the marvel of what he accomplished is only enhanced by the discovery of his methods, including his dependence on facts.

In the introduction to her novel *Passenger to Frankfurt,* Agatha Christie has some advice for writers that is worth repeating. She raises the novice's question, "How shall you get full information [for people, places, and events to give your work verisimilitude] apart from the evidence of your own eyes and ears? The answer," Christie maintains, "is frighteningly simple."

It is what the press brings to you every day, served up in your morning paper under the general heading of News. Collect it from the front page. What is going on in the world today? What is everyone saying, thinking, doing? Hold up a mirror to 1970 [when Christie's book was published] in England [or the United States, or your county seat].

Look at that front page every day for a month, make notes, consider and classify.

Every day there is a killing.

A girl is strangled.

Elderly woman attacked and robbed of her meager savings.

Young men or boys—attacking or attacked.

Buildings and telephone kiosks smashed and gutted.

Drug smuggling.

Robbery and assault.

Children missing and children's murdered bodies found not far from their homes.

Can this be England? Is England *really* like this? One feels—no—not yet, *but it could be.*

And yet one knows—of one's own knowledge—how much goodness there is in this world of ours—the kindnesses done, the goodness of the heart, the acts of compassion, the kindness of neighbor to neighbor, the helpful actions of girls and boys. Then why this fantastic atmosphere of daily news—of things that happen—that are actual *facts*? To write a story in this year . . . you must come to terms with your background. If the background is fantastic, then the story must accept its background.

Christie's point is that we must do all we can to feel the pulse of the world around us, to be engaged, to look outward as well as inward, and to make our personal sense out of the cascade of facts that rushes past, selecting what we need for our work.

Agatha Christie's imagination and inventiveness were remarkable, but her writing comes alive because she created a world that her readers and characters can live in together. Like most successful writers, she knew the value of research—of finding the facts that she needed to stimulate her imagination and to weave into the fabric of her work.

Take Miss Christie's advice and make one of your journal practices the kind of newspaper reading (or research) that she suggests: *Scan the front page every day for a month, make notes, consider, and classify.* You'll find that imagination and facts are inseparable, that invention and research are parts of the same process.

Newspaper headlines bring us in touch, quickly and succinctly, not only with what's going on in the world but also with stuff for the imagination. Can you imagine any writer involved in a project that required an excavation, a graveyard scene, time travel, or some means of preservation who would ignore the following headline?

Florida Bog Reveals 8,000-Year-Old Secrets
Well-Preserved Brain Found Inside Prehistoric Woman's Skull

What other types of works-in-progress might benefit from the information this headline promises?

Do you think it was a conscious irony on the part of the person who laid out the page for the October 26, 1986, *Washington Post* that this headline was juxtaposed to a reminder about setting clocks back for daylight-saving time?

Consider what these two pieces of information have in common. Make a list of ways in which these two instances of going backward in time can be exploited in a piece of imaginative literature. What are the causes and consequences of setting clocks back—or ahead? How might these connect with the secrets of the Florida bog?

The following is an adaptation of the news article. Which of its facts do you find most provocative? What kind of opportunities for exercising your own originality are lurking in this information? Where could you do further research on this topic?

Florida Bog Reveals 8,000-Year-Old Secrets
Well-Preserved Brain Found Inside Prehistoric Woman's Skull

Titusville, Fla.—For nearly 8,000 years the old woman's body had rested in its burial place in the soft peat of a central Florida bog before giving up its secret last week.

Time and the wet peat's mild acid had removed all sign of flesh by the time Billie Barton delicately pushed her wooden chisel, actually a whittled chopstick, along the smooth skull to remove bits of clinging peat.

When Barton noticed that the old woman's skull was broken, she carefully lifted up a piece of bone from the skull's right side and peered into the cranial vault.

Inside was a human brain—shrunken slightly as if partly dried out—but clearly a human brain of the correct shape and with all

DAYLIGHT-SAVING TIME

YOU SHOULD HAVE MOVED YOUR CLOCK *BACK* ONE HOUR AT 2 A.M. TODAY

the convolutions of the living organ that once contained a prehistoric human being's perceptions, thoughts, emotions and memories.

Barton, an archeologist digging with a Florida State University team at the Windover Archeological Research project here, was astounded. Some two dozen other human brains had been found at Windover in the past three years, several as the result of her own digging, but none was as large, as perfectly formed and as well preserved as this one.

"Oh, God. It's a miracle," David N. Dickel exclaimed as he bent over the skull. Dickel, the Windover project's co-director and "brain specialist," had been called over to lift out the organ. "This is so beautiful."

Barton had spent three days in a pit, removing reddish brown peat from the skeleton. It was the 82nd "burial" found in the last three years in a now-drained bog that served ancient Americans as a cemetery. The Windover site contains more burials than have been found at any site of comparable age in North America. . . .

To remove the wet, brownish-gray brain, Dickel had to break away more of the skull. Then he scooped the organ into a Tupperware container for later analysis. Glen H. Doran, director of the Windover project, poked a hose from a nitrogen tank into the container to blow air out and replace it with inert nitrogen gas. This would exclude oxygen that might chemically alter the brain. Until minutes before, the organ had been sealed by the wet peat in an oxygen-free environment.

The cemetery, the cloth and some other finds at the site, including the skeleton of a teenager with a severe birth defect, are leading some archeologists to rethink some old ideas about how early Americans lived. Far from being rude savages struggling to survive, the prehistoric Floridians apparently led lives of comparative ease with time to develop skilled crafts and to care for seriously handicapped people.

The site was a three-foot-deep pond fringed with saw grass and palmetto in the middle of a new suburban subdivision.

As Agatha Christie insisted, such reports from the papers are among the great sources for the ongoing research that a writer needs to be doing even without a specific project in mind. Of course, when you do have a project underway, relevant items will leap out at you once you're in the habit of being on the alert for anything you can use.

SEARCHING AND IMAGINING

New information is often liberating and stimulating, especially for the writer whose imagination can take a few fresh facts and combine them in a way that gives them new meaning. On a more sophisticated level many writers have created their most important work out of intense, prolonged periods of learning. Gary Snyder has combined his formal Zen training and his explorations of American Indian culture into highly personal yet universally acclaimed poems. Writers who do a great deal of translation, like Robert Bly, are in fact "researching" into language itself and into the sensibilities of writers whose poems grow out of another culture.

Fiction writers especially need to establish an authentic sense of place and time in a story or novel through research. How did people dress in 1944? What were hairstyles like? What songs were popular? What were new parents in a certain part of the country naming their children? What is a likely Parisian neighborhood for an American cultural attaché to live in today? How can one effectively suggest this place? How would this person get to work? To the theater? What do the Japanese call a wrench?

Writers need to know how to answer questions like these and how to involve their imaginations in the new information that their fictions require. Of course, staying close to home and to one's personal experience minimizes this kind of research, but it doesn't eliminate it. A twenty-five-year-old writer trying to recapture what her hometown was like when she was twelve may have a great deal of work to do.

The answers to a lot of these questions about people and places can be found in unexpected sources, such as high school and college yearbooks. Almost everyone you know has saved such treasures, and schools and colleges usually keep complete sets of these annual publications. Any writer attempting to create the illusion of a time and place in twentieth-century America will find the yearbook a fascinating research tool. One's own yearbooks are great memory joggers, and yearbooks outline, both in words and pictures, the values of a culture as recorded by and for students. In their pages one can see a whole range of individuals, from the most popular to the most obscure. One can discover the common interests (clubs, sports teams, school events) that formed the bases for relationships. In most yearbooks the faculty and administration are portrayed, and the final pages often carry advertisements from local merchants. It is not difficult to build on the "facts" found in this source, a source readily available and waiting to be mined.

The 1955 issue of *Corral,* the yearbook of Calvin Coolidge High School in Washington, D.C., reveals many features of 1950s culture. For example, running a bank within a school was fairly common. The bank managed savings accounts, collected dues and fees, ordered government savings bonds, cashed checks, and sold tickets to student events. Business students received practical training in banking operations, while all students were encouraged to take an interest in their personal finances. Such high school activities are rare in the 1990s. A person looking through the *Corral* will find that Calvin Coolidge had a large Latin Club, a Junior Red Cross, and a new chapter of the Future Homemakers of America. The school population, to judge by the pictures and names, was almost exclusively white and heavily Jewish. Today Calvin Coolidge High School is in the heart of what, for a generation, has been a middle-class black neighborhood. A researcher comparing *Corral* yearbooks at five-year intervals would see changes in educational philosophy and cultural values as well as demographic changes in the school's neighborhood.

EXERCISE

Research, through yearbooks, the character and environment of high school life in your hometown or your present location at five-year intervals over a twenty-five-year period. Make a list of significant changes. Look for ideas, images, characters, and situations that you could use in a creative work. For example, consider two high school friends who haven't seen each other for many years meeting again at the funeral of one of their classmates.

CLASSROOM EXERCISES WITH YEARBOOKS

1. Single out two or three individuals in a group portrait and record the thoughts each has about the others. How does each feel about sitting for this photograph?

2. Turn to a page of names in the middle of the alphabet. Describe, as carefully as you can, what each person looks like. Imagine each five years later, ten years later. What are these people doing now? How do you know? How have the additional years altered appearances?

3. Which teachers or administrators receive special recognition? Can you tell why? Do their appearances fit their jobs or specialties? Explain.

4. Create an extra page in the yearbook for each of the following:

   a. A special interest club that didn't exist.
   b. A sport that you've just made up.
   c. A school event that would have been unlikely then.
   d. A group portrait for those who were absent when yearbook pictures were taken.

5. Outline plans for a high school yearbook (or equivalent) for a society of the future, one with different values.

Other tools for this kind of research include picture magazines, *Look* and *Life* in particular, as well as newsmagazines like *Time* and *Newsweek*. Convenient summaries of contemporary events and issues are useful sources for plot ideas, background, or just occasional realistic detail that will make a work authoritative and lively. Local publications—regional travel magazines, newspapers, almanacs, Chamber of Commerce brochures, metropolitan entertainment guides, and "shoppers"—are obvious places for a writer to discover information with which to be original in the best sense.

When you need compact sources for developing settings that will depend almost entirely on research, travel guides are indispensable, and so are detailed maps. Don't make the mistake, however, of using a current travel guide to help you develop a sense of Los Angeles in 1933. The American Guide Series published under the Federal Writers' project during the late 1930s is a major resource. In addition, many small towns and counties have historical associations and archives.

The interaction between research and invention is twofold: (1) you search because you need facts to fill your imagined world; (2) facts themselves, whether sought or randomly discovered, stimulate your imagination. Moreover, factual accuracy contributes to **verisimilitude** (see pp. 220–23).

BEGINNING WITH FACTS

One problem of the beginning writer, as well as the experienced one, is confronting the blank page. Finding the thing (issue, experience, memory, feeling, person, wish) to write about is an endless problem, and, paradoxically, not a very important one *if* we admit that much of what we do as writers is practice or warming up. The journal is always available as a safe place for false starts or as a source of inspiration. What's important for a writer who is blocked is simply to get started, not to find the germ of an idea that will surely lead to a masterpiece. Hard facts are good places to begin. You can research your way into a creative effort that will give you satisfaction and confidence in your ability to break through the block next time. Perhaps research is too heavy a word; *search* is the main issue here.

The following poem by Charles Ghigna was inspired by an article that appeared in a 1976 issue of *The Birmingham News* about a boy who was struck and killed by lightning as he attempted to drive his father's tractor out of the rain and back to the barn.

An Alabama August

The deep steel of our field machine
opens red earth wounds
under a darkening sky
where James rides.

The ground gathers clouds to her breast
as a thunderbolt breaks the hidden drums

of sparrow ears
and turns my brother black.

In the morning
I find the burned machine,
the sunken footprints of my father.

from *The Southern Poetry Review*

The news article sent the poet's imagination soaring. The facts he appropriated are colored and transformed by a search into his own emotions. The "I" who tells the story is an invention of the poet, a way, perhaps, of getting close to the tragedy.

Many of the poems and plays of Robert Peters begin with research on the subject characters, into whom he breathes new life: his own. Research and invention have resulted in such original works as *Hawker,* based on the writings of a nineteenth-century Cornish clergyman, *Picnic in the Snow,* about Ludwig II of Bavaria, and *Kane,* about the great Arctic explorer.

Various sources must have nourished the poems of Adrien Stoutenburg, a writer whose works are filled with information about nature and history. Here is a brief excerpt from her sequence poem *A Short History of the Fur Trade.*

In summer, even chiefs went bare,
though seldom without the pointed jewels
of claws strung into necklaces,
of clacking halos of dead teeth
strung through their black and dancing hair.

Beaten hides of bison kept out the cold,
and their swift horns, headgear for warriors,
blazed like new moons turned into bone,
or served as flagons for an antelope's blood,
while the cosmetic bear, crowded with fat,
supplied his oozing brilliantine
to blaze on scalps and in a stone lamp's
rancid flame.

from *Land of Superior Mirages*

Of course, Stoutenburg's poem is no mere listing of facts. She has transformed her material into a highly personal, emotional statement. Her originality is in her selection of material, the freshness of her imagery, the connotative charge of her language. Nevertheless, a passage like the one just quoted is rooted in facts that the author had to master about the fur trade and Indian culture.

Imagine that something you are working on requires meteorological information. You need to describe the approach of a hurricane, or you want to use increasing wind velocities metaphorically to address an emotion—a rage—building in one of your characters. The scale Sir Francis Beaufort devised—a "found poem" in itself—is just what you need. Reproductions of this scale are found in most dictionaries.

Now go ahead and build a descriptive paragraph or a short poem out of this "research" material.

The material you have researched for one purpose can jostle your imagination in other ways. For example, you might try to make your own version of such a scale. How about a scale that rates men's clothing styles by the effect they have on women? How about a scale that deals with the effects of different kinds of speakers (or jokes) on the listeners? Be true to the terse, efficient nature of the *Beaufort Scale*. Keep your language similarly flat—objective in tone.

BEAUFORT SCALE

BEAUFORT NUMBER	NAME	MILES PER HOUR	DESCRIPTION
0	calm	less than 1	calm; smoke rises vertically
1	light air	1–3	direction of wind shown by smoke but not by wind vanes
2	light breeze	4–7	wind felt on face; leaves rustle; ordinary vane moved by wind
3	gentle breeze	8–12	leaves and small twigs in constant motion; wind extends light flag
4	moderate breeze	13–18	raises dust and loose paper; small branches are moved
5	fresh breeze	19–24	small trees in leaf begin to sway; crested wavelets form on inland water
6	strong breeze	25–31	large branches in motion; telegraph wires whistle; umbrellas used with difficulty
7	moderate gale (*or* near gale)	32–38	whole trees in motion; inconvenience in walking against wind
8	fresh gale (*or* gale)	39–46	breaks twigs off trees; generally impedes progress
9	strong gale	47–54	slight structural damage occurs; chimney pots and slates removed
10	whole gale (*or* storm)	55–63	trees uprooted; considerable structural damage occurs
11	storm (*or* violent storm)	64–72	very rarely experienced; accompanied by widespread damage
12	hurricane*	73–136	devastation occurs

*The U.S. uses 74 statute mph as the speed criterion for hurricane.

EXERCISES

1. From a travel guide (book, magazine, etc.), research material for a description of a place you've never been. Develop a sketch that could be used as a setting or scene for a short story.

2. Gather a few provocative human interest stories from the newspaper. Building on the facts, develop a story sketch or a draft for a poem.

3. See if it's possible to generate material from a combination of details from two or more of the news clippings.

4. Use your imagination to build a story sketch from an ad in the classified section of the newspaper. Here are some that we found:

- ◆ CHAIRS 4 cane bottom chairs. $75 total. Need Work.
- ◆ *Itek Quadritek 1201* 2 disc drive, RS232, good cond.
- ◆ Bushwacker, Sears, $70. BMX boy's bike, $40. Rocker, contemporary ladder back, $30.

5. Place a character you know within a well-known painting or photograph. Describe the character's situation from a first-person perspective and then in the third person. Try "The Last Supper" or "The Boating Party."

6. Research some historical material: a battle, a "first" in sports, a mechanical invention, a geographical discovery. Now build on your source imaginatively.

7. Have others (classmates) help you gather a library of high school and college yearbooks. Use them to develop character sketches, relationships, community portraits, and whatever else comes to mind.

8. Plan a few pages of a guidebook for a fictional town in a fictional country. It is the year 2030.

9. Draw or build a model for the "scene of the crime" of a detective story. Use sources like *Metropolitan Home* magazine or *Better Homes and Gardens* to give you some ideas. Now write a detailed description of the scene. *Note:* Does this place suggest wealth? Region? Taste? Age of owners or inhabitants? Keep the details reasonably consistent.

10. Furnish an "interior" room—the room inside you (or inside another person). Let a reader know about the intangible qualities of your character from the way in which you describe this metaphorical space (soul, heart, complex of emotions). Again, use decorating magazines as a source.

11. Do some research on the tools necessary to perform certain specialized tasks: shoe a horse, build a model plane, tune a car, hook a rug, cut a diamond.

Now invent a story sketch or a poem that enlivens the old expression "a poor workman always blames his tools."

12. Scan the *Yellow Pages*. Study the entries under "Restaurants" or some other equally large category. Base a description of the town on your research, or sketch a series of characters in terms of their dining-out preferences.

13. In a microfilm reading room or other library source, find a newspaper for the date of your birth. Write a short narrative placing the fact of your birth in the context of local, national, and international events.

MIND EXPANDERS

1. Examine the palm of your hand. Use your observations to develop a map of a place that has never before existed. Give your reader a guided tour.

2. Closely observe a cloud formation, a cluster of tree roots, or some other suggestive natural phenomenon. Do fifteen minutes of freewriting in which you allow the images to generate a train of associations. (Research the names of clouds and use this vocabulary as the core of a few quick character sketches.)

3. How are building nails sized? Use this information imaginatively.

4. Investigate the holdings of a desk drawer, a wallet, or a pocketbook. Build a character sketch from this inventory.

5. Take the dictionary definition for a word and expand what you find into a story or poem. Try *rust* or *palm*.

6. Ask a classmate to tell you a personal or family story in no more than ten minutes. Take notes on the story; then, in twenty minutes, work up a version of the story incorporating characters drawn from your own experience.

FIELD WORK

The following prose sketches by Sharon Spencer, taken from her book *Ellis Island: Then and Now* (and originally published in the 1984–1985 issue of *Paintbrush*), are responses to a visit she made to Ellis Island accompanied by Dennis Toner, a photographer. Her visit to this set of abandoned buildings was research. Her interest in finding the voices of those who had come through this gateway to the United States required an act of imagination, an act stimulated by the visit itself, by Toner's photographs, and by Spencer's knowledge of the immigrant experience.

After studying Spencer's work, make a visit to an abandoned or out-of-use or radically altered location. Respond to the present situation and find out about how this place used to be. Let your imagination create a dialogue between voices of the past and the present, or allow the ghosts of the past to revisit their old territory. If you can, bring along a friend who enjoys photography and share your perceptions of place. Try working with the photographs as well as with your own impressions.

ELLIS ISLAND: THEN AND NOW

SHARON SPENCER

During the first quarter of the century immigrants entering the United States from Europe were examined in an enormous room in a massive red brick building on a small island situated between New York and New Jersey. It is called Ellis Island. Half of us Americans of European ancestry are descendants of at least one person who was examined in this room by immigration inspectors. The newcomers had to prove that they were in good physical and mental health, that they were capable of earning a living and that they were neither prostitutes nor anarchists. Many people, it is unclear just how many, were unable to prove these things. Refused entry, they were forced to endure the return voyage by steamship. This meant a second period of eight weeks in steerage, the dirty, badly ventilated and often dangerous part of the ship below the water line. Many immigrants died on the journey to America. Who can know how many more perished on the return trip? There was another group, too, the people who were afflicted with serious diseases: they were quarantined on Ellis island.

Today Ellis Island has been abandoned. It is "surplus government property." The only inhabitants are birds, primarily seagulls, and about two hundred thousand rats. . . .

Looking In, Looking Out

So this is America? A big empty room. It must have been beautiful once. A palace in ruins. Where are the people now?

Oooooh, it's so damp! I shouldn't have wandered away from the group. Ivan thought I'd enjoy this so much. His treat. But I feel feverish, chilled. It's so damp!

Where am I now? Here, looking in. Yes, but where are the others? I shouldn't have gone off by myself. Ivan will worry.

Oh look! There's Mamma. A big fireplace. Mamma, I can see you. "By the Fireplace." "*U Kamina.*" Remember that lovely song? It's so cold out here in the garden. No, not cold. Damp. It's autumn. Wet, misty, clouded over. But you, Mamma, are inside by the warm fire. "*U Kamina,*" Mamma:

> Alone, you sit by the fireplace
> And watch the fire go out.
> At times the flames flare up
> But then die down again.

You put her head between your hands, rock back and forth in your chair and silently curse the letter carrier. He has brought you nothing, not even one card from your daughter, who's run away to America, leaving you to sit alone by the fireplace.

> Love is like the fireplace
> Where dreams turn to ashes
> And your heart is chilled.

Mamma, I feel like a ghost. There is nothing here in America. Just this one big empty room that was once grand, loved and cared for, just as I once loved and looked after you, Mamma.

Oooooh, the wind feels cold! Weeds are growing inside the house. Mamma, speak to me. Say something. Just a word or two. Something. Mamma, I feel so sick, so cold. So confused. I don't know if I can find my way back to you.

"Darling Katya,

"I sit here by the fireplace writing to you. Through the window I watch the rain fall on the apple trees and, Darling, though I am inside by the fireplace, I can smell the apples, and I can see your father as he was before the war. Imagine! We were married only eight months before he was killed. And you, Katya, eight months inside my belly, waiting to become the love, the only love that life brought me after I grew up.

"Forget the man who has left you, dear Katya. You still think of him, I know, and you will always think of him. It is inevitable, now that you have decided to let his baby stay alive inside of you. That man was ashamed of you, and he would be ashamed of your child too. So, Katya dear, it is better that you find for your child another father over there in America.

"Choose well, my darling.

"When I was your age, I didn't even suspect that life would be so long. For an old woman it is enough to sit by the fire in a small sod house and know that the garden will always grow enough for me to eat, enough to find my only happiness in the smell of ripe apples and a song remembered from the time long ago when I was loved by a man."

Mamma, I hear your voice. You're calling me: "Come inside, Katya dear. Come in and sit here with me beside the fireplace. We will warm ourselves while we listen to the sound of the rain falling on the apple trees." Oh, Mamma, I can hear your voice! "Come inside," you call, "Katya, come to me and we will sing '*U Kamina*' together."

I want to come in. Oh so badly! But how can I get inside? Oh, there's a long stick. It looks strong. The windows are broken. Maybe I can knock out some more panes of glass. I can climb inside where it's warm and safe. I'll just knock out one or two more. There! Now I can climb inside and sit by the fire. I will drink hot tea. I will rest against Mamma's knee. I will go to sleep, finally, sleep . . .

"Hey, Mother! What're you doing with that stick?"

It's Ivan. He looks upset. "Oh, nothing. I just thought I'd . . ."

"Mother, that's called 'breaking and entering.' You can't do that."

"Oh! I'm sorry. I didn't mean to hurt anything . . . anyone. I just wanted to climb inside where it's warm."

"That's all right, Mother. It's my fault. I shouldn't have let you wander off. Let's go back to the ferry slip. The group's going back to Manhattan now. Shall we have some coffee? Maybe you'd rather have tea."

"Oh, Ivan. You're such a good boy. I'm so glad you're here. Tea. That sounds very nice now. Yes, I'd like to have some tea."

"You don't need that stick any more."

"Oh no. Of course I don't. For heaven's sakes, what was I doing with it in the first place?"

Fatima

There is a crash. The sound of glass shattering. A woman's voice, at first low, then a flow of words, high and sharp. The words stop. There is the sound of short regular screams, evenly paced, mechanical. A shrill calliope of terror. Two immigration inspectors are standing in a wide corridor filled with light.

"What's going on in there?" one asks, jerking his head toward the door marked WOMEN.

"Locked herself in. On the way over she went crazy. No one can control her. Not even her husband."

"Is that him?"

A man is walking up and down in the bay area in front of the large bright windows. He is young, dark, bearded. He is wearing a black suit. On his head is a white turban, around his throat a red and gold scarf. Head lowered, he walks up and down, clasping and unclasping his hands. He does not seem to notice the immigration inspectors.

A calliope of terror. The short sharp screams continue to pierce the morning. Then there is a heavy thud. A flow of words, high and sharp. A scream, prolonged.

The pacing man lifts his head, covers his face with his hands, groans.

"Who's handling this?" asks one of the inspectors. "Allen. She's Allen's case."

"So it's back to Damascus for this one, right?" The screams continue. Then a sustained flow of sharp words. The pacing man stops, crouches, his elbows on his knees, face in cupped hands. He murmurs swift urgent-sounding words into his hands.

"What's he doing? Praying?"

"Beats me!"

Four men wearing white uniforms come hurrying down the corridor. One holds a ring of keys, another, a hypodermic needle.

The crouching husband throws them a swift glance. "Say, did you see that woman before she locked herself in the restroom?"

"No."

"She was some sight! Tall and wild looking. Wearing those white robes they like. Black and red scarves. Lots of jewelry. Tense as she was, she still looked like a queen!"

"What'll he do if they send her back?" "Who knows? He can go back with her. He can stay here. Or he can send home for another wife. Maybe he already has another wife. They do that, you know."

The Ones Who Stayed Behind

When Buster walks through Building Three, making rounds, checking for dead birds and other debris, he often stops and gazes through the broken windows across the strip of water to Liberty Island where she stands, the lady, our lady, lady of the harbor. And at such times, especially on melancholy autumn afternoons he just closes his eyes, that's all, and the voices begin to talk, usually, at least in these rooms in the Contagious Disease Ward, the voices talk about the ones who stayed behind.

"Hammid, who do you miss the most? Someone who stayed behind?"

"Oh, Affifa! I loved her. But I could not marry her. Affifa was a dancer. A Guedra dancer of Goulimine. It's almost sacred. Oh, it's useless to try to explain to you! A Guedra dancer is so loved, so respected, she'd never leave home!"

"And you, Angelo, is there someone you miss who stayed behind?"

"My sister Gina. She wore her black braids like a crown around her head. When she was twelve Gina married a man from Controguerra. Up north. She went to live in a village near an old fortress. Povera Gina! She would have loved America."

"Teddy, tell me, was there someone you left behind." "Yes, my yes. My older sister Nora. She was nine years older than me, babied me, you know. And I loved her. But Nora crossed the North Sea to Liverpool. She worked in a hospital, doing I don't know what. And she married a guy for Cork. After that, I don't know. Nora stopped writing to us. She and I used to walk down the hill to the town pump. Then we'd trudge back up the hill, sharing the weight of the bucket between us, Nora was a love, all right. Oh, I hope that guy from Cork treats her all right."

"Magdalena, it's your turn. Was there someone you cared for, someone who stayed behind?"

"'Lena,' please. Call me 'Lena.' My village was a bowl of dirt dumped on a rocky hill. Miserable, winter and summer, summer, winter, spring, fall and all other times, it was miserable. The people were so beat by the sun, they were mean. Everyone I loved died before I was thirteen years old. I don't miss no one from back there. It was a shit hole and I'm glad to be out of it. That's the truth. No one can understand who hasn't tried to live there. Starved there. Shivered there. A shit hole!"

"Now, Buster, it's your turn. You've been asking us who we miss from the ones who stayed at home. What about you?"

Buster shakes his head, fiddles with the buckles on his yellow slicker, and wonders how that Lena got the guts to turn around and ask him a question.

He raises his hand, traces the bubbly glass, stares at the wet leaves. "I guess . . . Well, there was Aunt May. She married a man who made her black and blue nearly every pay day. She had a son who was always in trouble with the cops. Her daughter married a steelworker . . ."

Buster breaks off, tugs at the end of the vinyl garbage bag in his hand, then goes on: "Well, Lena, all her life Aunt May was a cleaning lady. She cleaned office buildings in downtown Detroit. When Aunt May died, her daughter—she was named Crystal, she took Aunt May to Hawaii for a vacation. And do you know what happened in Hawaii?"

"No, Buster, I've got a lousy imagination. What happened?" "In Hawaii Aunt May had a stroke and died." Buster rubs his eyes with his fist. He jerks the vinyl bag several times and walks out of the Contagious Disease Ward, dragging his feet.

~✘~

THE TIME CAPSULE GAME

On special occasions, societies have attempted to communicate with the future by sending a time capsule, a sealed container holding artifacts, statements, aspirations, images of the present. The time capsule buried at the New York

World's Fair of 1939–1940 is a well-known example. The makers of time capsules might be thought of as inverted archeologists, scientifically burying a culture instead of digging it up. Into the fair's time capsule went copies of popular magazines, mail-order catalogs, card-game rules, airline timetables, newsreels, comic strips, coins, watches (one with a Mickey Mouse face), a compact, and other items.

1. List items for your hometown's time capsule to be opened in 200 years.
2. List items for your school's time capsule.
3. Research a community of 100 or more years ago and list items for its time capsule to be opened now.
4. List time capsule items for a society that you invent. Now exchange lists with a classmate and describe the society suggested by your classmate's list.
5. Characterize someone by what he or she would put in a personal time capsule.
6. Draft a time capsule poem.
7. Write a glossary of contemporary slang to put in a time capsule.
8. Imagine a situation in which unexpected changes create unintended impressions on those who open a time capsule.
9. Is the time capsule an act of vanity or humility? Write a sketch about someone who buries a personal time capsule.

THE WORLD'S FAIR GAME

As E. L. Doctorow discovered, the World's Fair is a marvelous backdrop for a work of fiction. An event as monumental as a world's fair has all kinds of potential for creative transformation.

After you read the following extracts from the *Official Guide Book of the New York World's Fair* of 1939, make a list of ideas for stories, poems, plays, movies, and television shows that take advantage of the World's Fair setting. After each idea, jot down what further information you would need in order to get your project rolling. Where would you look for it? Then read the draft proposal that follows the *Official Guide Book* material.

The Site

Originally known, in popular parlance, as the "Corona Dumps"—1216 1/2 acres of primeval bog, spongy marshland, and the accumulated debris and ashes of many years–the site is located in New York City in the borough of

Queens not far from the geographical and population centers of the great metropolis. The area extends almost three and one-half miles southeastward from Flushing Bay to Union Turnpike in Kew Gardens, and is more than a mile wide between Lawrence and 111th Streets. Eager for the reclamation and transformation of one of the city's most conspicuous sore spots, the City of New York acquired the tract at a cost of more than seven million dollars, officially designated it Flushing Meadow Park and leased the ground to the Fair Corporation for the duration of the exposition. Ground breaking ceremonies were held on June 29th, 1936, and the colossal task of transformation soon began. The appearance of the site was enough to daunt many of the most optimistic of the officials who fought their way to the ceremonies through the accumulated junk of many decades. It once presented a scene of stagnant pools and muddy runlets, a source of evil odors that threatened asphyxiation to the distressed inhabitants for miles around. Mountains of ashes rose to a height of 100 feet; the topmost peak, waggishly named "Mount Corona," dominated the dismal panorama. A creek called Flushing River meandered through the bog, virtually undisturbed since President Washington crossed it in 1790 to Flushing Bay.

Architecture of the Fair

There was no attempt to create a pattern of uniform design in the architecture but only to control scale, color, and relationships. There was an absolute conviction that buildings must be made to look what they are—temporary exhibit structures. No imitations either of historic architecture or imitations of permanent materials were permitted, with one exception only, namely—in the sector devoted to exhibits of the States. Here various traditional architectural forms were used, each related to the current architecture of the period of the particular State's colonization.

In view of the proximity of the Fair site to New York City with its towering skyscrapers, it was deemed absurd to build a "skyscraper" Fair. By way of contrast a "flat" Exposition, consisting largely of one-story structures, was constructed. There are no windows in Fair-built buildings, for the most part, except in entrance halls, because of the great amount of space that would be "lost" as exhibit space in the buildings if windows were installed. Another factor to be considered was that huge areas of glass in buildings in this climate would render them insufferably hot in the summertime. Virtually all Fair-erected buildings are artificially illuminated and ventilated.

Characteristics which best fit the functions of the exhibits in the various buildings were determined before the structures themselves were designed—for example, the prow-line façade of the Hall of Marine

nozzles, 400 gas nozzles, and numerous fireworks containers, vast jets of water, flame, and pyrotechnics shower the darkness with unique designs— reds, greens, yellows, blues, and sparkling silver against the background of the night. Still more extensive—some have said, staggering—is the "inferno" over Fountain Lake. Searchlights play upon captive balloons; titanium tetrachloride produces the smoke of conflict; time bombs add thunderous realism to the sound amplifications.

Theme and Purpose

The basic statement issued by the Committee on Theme declared that "The New York World's Fair is planned to be 'everyman's fair'—to show the way toward the improvement of all the factors contributing to human welfare. We are convinced that the potential assets, material and spiritual, of our country are such that if rightly used they will make for a general public good such as has never before been known. In order to make its contribution toward this process the Fair will show the most promising developments of production, service and social factors of the present day in relation to their bearing on the life of the great mass of the people. The plain American citizen will be able to see here what he could attain for his community and himself by intelligent coordinated effort and will be made to realize the interdependence of every contributing form of life and work."

The Theme Center—Democracity

For miles around and from every point on the side, your attention is arrested by the towering Theme Center (Harrison & Fouilhoux, architects; Henry Dreyfus, designer). Piercing the sky 700 feet above the earth like some giant three-sided obelisk, *the Trylon,* symbol of the Fair's lofty purpose, adjoins a huge hollow globe, 200 feet in diameter—*the Perisphere.*

Never before in history has man undertaken to build a globe of such tremendous proportions. Eighteen stories high, it is as broad as a city block, its interior more than twice the size of Radio City Music Hall. Plans prepared by the architects represented the final distillation of more than one thousand preliminary sketches, the use of the sphere and triangle (geometry's simplest and most fundamental forms) resulting from a determination to strike a new note in design, yet one simple in form and structurally sound. To describe these structures, new words were coined: Trylon, from "tri," the three sides of the structure, and "pylon," indicating its use as the monumental gateway to the

Theme Building; and Perisphere, from "peri," meaning "beyond, all around, about."

As the interior is revealed, you see in the hollow beneath the sky, "Democracity"—symbol of a perfectly integrated, futuristic metropolis pulsing with life and rhythm and music. The daylight panorama stretches off to the horizon on all sides. Here is a city of a million people with a working population of 250,000, whose homes are located beyond the city-proper, in five satellite towns. Like great arteries, broad highways traverse expansive areas of vivid green countryside, connecting outlying industrial towns with the city's heart.

After you have gazed at the model for two minutes, dusk slowly shadows the scene. The light fails, and the celestial concave gleams with myriad stars. To the accompaniment of a symphonic poem, a chorus of a thousand voices reaches out of the heavens, and there at ten equi-distant points in the purple dome loom marching men—farmers, stamped by their garb; mechanics, with their tools of trade. As the marchers approach they are seen to represent the various groups in modern society—all the elements which must work together to make possible the better life which would flourish in such a city as lies below. The symphony rises to diapasonal volume, the figures assume mammoth size; the music subsides, the groups vanish behind slowly drifting clouds, and suddenly a blaze of polaroid light climaxes the show.

Zoning the Fair

The Fair is divided into seven geographic and thematic zones. Two of the Zones, Amusement and Government, do not have Focal Exhibits; there are also two Focal Exhibits which, because their related exhibits are housed in but a single building, do not have any corresponding zones. The zones and focal exhibits, in alphabetical order, are: Amusement, Communications and Business Systems, Community Interests, Food, Government, Medical and Public Health, Production and Distribution, Science and Education, and Transportation. For each of them there is a separate editorial section. The reader may observe, after an examination of the list, that there are many important aspects of life in modern society that seem to have been neglected. But the Fair *has* included exhibits of many of the other important interests of modern man. Lack of the necessary space in the proper zone has sometimes caused an exhibit to be placed in a zone to which it has little thematic relationship. This has not been frequent. The official exhibits of the Swedish and Turkish governments are in buildings which they have erected in the Food Zone; the great exhibit of the State of Florida is on the west side of Fountain Lake in the Amusement Area; the extensive exhibition of "Masterpieces of Art" is in the Communication and Business Systems Zone. But these are some of the few exceptions to the general zoning plan in the Fair. The Exhibition of Contemporary American Art is in the Community Interests Zone, as is the Temple of Religion. The editorial treatment of each exhibit is found in the text on the zone where it has its physical location; otherwise appropriate cross-references are supplied.

Laffland

The facade of the building is embellished with spectacular lighting effects, color and action. Here a spiral tower of light surmounts an overhanging porch, the front of which is paneled with grotesque scenes—a mechanical laughing man, a mechanical musician, dancing ghosts, climbing frogs and monkeys. In the interior, a stage with four terraces sloping toward the audience is used for a procession of fantastic and amusing figures. Stunts by clowns and employees are supplemented by the actions of the flying phantom ghost. A mechanical barking dog with a tin can tied to its tail runs across the stage. Here is an electric drinking fountain, controlled by a photo-electric cell. Other features are a theatre auditorium with electrically operated trick seats, each seat fitted with compressed air for emergencies, a walk-thru, trick zoo, special rooms and a house of mystery.

Live Monsters

In a building whose exterior is covered with bamboo, Clif Wilson's show exhibits ten or more giant pythons, from 18 to 30 feet in length, and approximately 150 smaller specimens of various rare snakes—cobras, kraits, mambas, lizards, etc. The specimens are contained in tanks, pits, cages and glass cases, and the visitor can view them with the utmost safety.

Living Magazine Covers

Jack Sheridan's eight-minute show presents beautiful girls in person, whom the artists for magazine covers have made nationally famous. The show is accompanied by music and trick lighting. Titles identify the magazines represented.

Merrie England

Here is a faithful reproduction of an old English Village, its exterior wall simulating the Tower of London, its main entrance resembling that of Hampton Court. Occupying more than an acre of ground on the shore of Fountain Lake immediately to the left of the Amphitheatre, the village consists of crooked streets, village greens, quaint inns, grim castles, and picturesque people. Reproductions of Shakespeare's House, the Cheshire Cheese, the Jolly Mermaid, the Old Curiosity Shop, and the John Harvard House, furnish an authentic background representative of Merrie Old England. And here you may enjoy historical pageants, Punch and Judy shows, Welsh Choral singing, and entertainment on the village green. Condensed versions of Shakespearian plays are given in a replica of the Globe Theatre, where they were originally produced. Numerous shops offer souvenirs, novelties, and merchandise for sale. Eating and drinking places include "pubs" and inns.

Mexico

Located on Presidential Row South, the Exhibit contains displays of historical relics reminiscent of the glorious past civilizations of Mexico. Collections of exquisite carvings and decorated ornaments, produced by native artisans, show the type of handicraft for which Mexico has long been famous. Exhibits emphasizing present day achievements include photographs of improved irrigation lands and up-to-date schools. Recent social and industrial reforms are depicted by means of drawings and charts. Displays of industrial products, Mexican glassware, pottery, silver and fabrics are also presented. The aim of the entire Exhibit is to give Fair visitors a clearer and more sympathetic understanding of the Mexican people.

Netherlands

On Continental Avenue, the Exhibit presents a comprehensive survey of the economic and cultural importance of the three parts of Her Majesty's empire—the Kingdom in Europe, the Dutch East Indies, and the territories Suriname and Curaçao in South America. In the reception hall a huge painting on glass visualizes the solidarity of the kingdom and its overseas territories.

A large animated relief map of Holland demonstrates the age-old struggle by which the land was wrested from the sea. Among other subjects the Exhibit deals with the products of the soil; the aid that science gives agriculture by warring against diseases of plants and beasts; city planning, slum clearance, social welfare; the fight against infant mortality, vocational diseases, unemployment; and the various other phases of Government endeavors to spread the boons that modern science has made available to all classes of society.

In sections devoted to overseas territories, murals and dioramas set forth the grandeur of tropical scenery. And here are the music and the theatre of Java; the art of Bali, the irrigation system of its terraced rice fields; native education and tropical hygiene; and the cultivation of various crops. A major attraction is a model in bas-relief of the Borobudur, greatest of Java's Buddhist monuments.

Some 65,000 tulips blooming in a garden about the pavilion add their color to the million tulips which the Netherlands donated to the Fair Corporation. The Exhibit is completed by displays in the Hall of Nations.

Elgin National Watch Company

The Elgin National Watch Company Building on Commerce Circle consists of a semicircular Exhibition Hall and an inner structure designed in the shape of a circle. The historical significance of time is portrayed by a large mural in oils, and here a display of ancient and modern timepieces may be found. The inner structure is a typical astronomical observatory. At the end of a cascade of water near the Observatory, stands a representation of one of the most ancient of timepieces—the water clock. In a nearby hall various exhibits show some of the technical phases of watch manufacturing. Here visitors can have their own watches rated free of charge.

General Electric Company

Bordering the Plaza of Light, the Building (Voorhees, Walker, Smith & Foley, architects) is distinguished by a huge stainless steel lightning bolt which sets the mood for the Exhibit—the taming of the savage natural forces of electricity to serve the needs of men. The copper-paneled structure comprises three sections: In Steinmetz Hall—vivid lightning, thunderous noise, ten million volts flashing over a 30-foot arc. In the House of Magic—great whirling discs, synchronized with light; a metal carpet floating in space; a large sun motor driven by sunlight; a shadow that comes and goes independently of the person who casts it. In the Exhibits Hall—a huge mural (Rockwell Kent), depicting the development of electricity throughout the ages; a complete television studio; a model electric appliance store, showing a full line of G.E. products for the home; and the General Electric X-Ray Corporation's exhibit of a 2700-year-old mummy from the Chicago Museum.

WORLD'S FAIR PROPOSAL

The New York World's Fair stood at a crossroads in time. The fair was built in the last years of the Depression and opened in the last year of peace. The fair's theme was "The World of Tomorrow," and it showed at least part of what was coming in that world: television, atomic energy, sleeker automobiles. But hidden in the brave new world of predicted tomorrow were signs that something was going to go wrong.

The drama of the fair is that hardly anyone noticed the signs.

There was a moment when the fair and America entered tomorrow, but at that moment the fair and the nation were still innocent. The moment came on the afternoon of the Fourth of July, 1940, when a bomb, removed from the British Pavilion, exploded behind the Polish Pavilion. It was, the *New York Times* reported in words of such innocent detachment, a "scene reminiscent in small scale of the more vivid accounts of war areas in Europe."

As a screenplay or novel, the World's Fair becomes the stage for a story that illumines an era. Like the Nashville of *Nashville* or the Hollywood of *Chinatown* and *The Day of the Locust*, the World's Fair is the reality that seems like make-believe.

We [the authors] would concentrate on a three-week period, in the summer of 1940, when the United States was becoming aware of a world at war but did not yet fully realize that this country soon would be in it. The fair becomes a setting for a detective story—the tracking down of a potential bomber—at the same time the fair is a setting for a crossover in time: on Japan Day, the Japanese ambassador assures his audience that his country and the United States can remain at peace. On the day that France falls, the French Pavilion is staging a waiters' walking race. War planes are rolled into the U.S. government exhibit. On the Fourth of July a mother gets into a fight with judges who did not select her son to be Superboy. It is Superman Day at the fair when someone in the British Pavilion picks up a canvas bag with something ticking in it, carries it through the crowded pavilion, takes it into the room where the Magna Carta is on display, finally gets in touch with police, who decide to take it outside . . .

Every celebrity of the era walks the fair's stage: FDR and Eleanor, Mayor LaGuardia (and his young secretary, David Rockefeller), Einstein, who opened the fair with a cosmic ray stunt, Howard Hughes, Shirley Temple. Every event in the coming decade is foreshadowed—often wrongly: Joseph P. Kennedy visits the fair with the son he hopes will be president someday; but Joseph P. Kennedy, Jr., will die in World War II. Under pressure from such powers as the president of the borough of Queens and the American Legion, the U.S.S.R. dismantles its Heroic Worker statue (nicknamed Big Joe) and pulls out of the fair. Queens declares a school holiday. The Fair turns down Thomas Mann's suggestion for an Old Germany Pavilion—such action might offend Nazi Germany.

The bomb is in the canvas overnight bag. The eight-day clock is ticking. A detective from the newly organized bomb squad tears away a strip from the side of the bag. He sees the dynamite inside and says, "This looks like the real goods . . ."

The fair was absurd as well as monumental. It was a fair where there were a few laughs: a bicyclist pedals to the fair from Florida, chained to his bike; the key to the padlock and the publicity stunt is somewhere in the mails. About 3,000 people attend a party for Elektro, robot, who celebrates with a metal cake that is frosted. Fair officials dicker with the parents of the Dionne Quintuplets to get them as an exhibit. Wild animals, stalked by press agents, keep wandering out of Frank Buck's "Bring 'Em Back Alive" show. A couple is married on the Parachute Jump. The Living Statues, an artistic show in the Amusement Area, can be nude as long as they do not move; policemen frequently drop into the show to watch for violations.

The bomb explodes. The World's Fair is over, though it will go on for a while. And the world that the fair had known is over, though it will take a while for people to notice.

Finding that moment in *our* time is the theme of this remembrance of the World's Fair.

EXERCISE

Populate, plot, focus an episode for this proposal. Use some of the "research material" in your draft. Do additional research in newspaper and magazine files.

As you have now discovered, invention and research go hand in hand in writing just as they do in other creative processes. No scientist ever made a major breakthrough without gathering information and exploring various approaches to the problem at hand. The original thinker in any field is a person who keeps at least one foot on the ground. Though we have said nothing in this chapter directly about writing, we are convinced that the discovery and amplification of raw material for creative works is a creative act in itself.

6

The Elements of Poetry

THE NATURE OF POETRY

Of all the literary forms, poetry focuses most intensely on language itself. Like other writers, poets tell stories, create characters, and formulate ideas, but these activities do not give poetry its special distinction. A display of language, an exploration of language, is always a special part of what poetry offers. Of course, no writer is unconscious of the impact of words in themselves; still, poets give the most concentrated attention to their medium: language.

Poetry distinguishes itself in other ways as well. First of all, it looks different on the page from other kinds of writing. We recognize a poem by its ragged right-hand margin and its relatively narrow blocks or columns of type. The right margin is uneven because where and how lines end is a defining element in poetry. While all writers compose in sentences and paragraphs, poets have this other unit—the line. The line itself can be defined in many ways, as we shall see. In almost every significant work, the line is not only poetry's visual signal, its garment, but also its basic unit of expression.

Poets are alert to and exploit the *physical* aspects of language far more than writers in the other genres. The fact that language is made out of sounds and rhythms has always been a special truth for poets. Indeed, poetry's origins are oral. The transmission of story, chronicle, and experience from one generation to another was the driving motive of the earliest poetry. Voice to ear. Patterns of sound and rhythm were at first memory aids. In a way, they have never lost that function, though over the generations other functions have become even more important, including emphasis and organization.

Poetry has other distinguishing characteristics. It is the form that most intensely conveys emotion. In fact, poetry is often called the language of emotion. Poets put a high premium on language loaded with sensory materials (images) in order to recreate emotions in us as we read. Poetry stirs us through its mysterious economy that communicates more than the words would seem to allow.

Because of these special considerations, writing poetry can be fun and yet frustrating. We want to say so much and to say it so well that our goals seem unattainable. Our tools are so various and interdependent that it is difficult to make everything work in harmony. Nevertheless, as in any other endeavor, practice coupled with knowledge and determination will carry any writer a long way toward success. It's important not to expect to get there all at once.

In this chapter we invite you to explore the many possibilities, demands, and satisfactions of writing poetry. We begin with a basic introduction to poetry's conventions. Since these conventions are fairly specialized and jargon-filled, some of you will find our review demanding. Stay with us. You wouldn't want to whittle without some wood and a knife. In Chapter 7, we provide a series of exercises that will keep you busy creating poems. Chapter 8 reviews student problems and illustrates the revision process.

THE LINE

The line and the various strategies of line break are fundamental concerns of poetic craft. At the very outset, the shape on the printed page announces the work as a poem. Consider these lines from "Fog Township" by Brendan Galvin:

> It's that delicate time
> when things could spill
> any way, when fog
> rides into the hollows,
> making bays, and Cathedral
> and Round Hills are
> high islands. Brooks
> have already churned back
> into their beds to trickle
> their own placid names
> again, and cloud shadows
> have drawn across

the landscape's lightest
movements. Now I begin
to hear something trying
to come through, a message
tapped on twigs out there:

Galvin has chosen relatively short lines to project both his descriptions of a place and his reactions to that place. The flow of images, the fog itself, and the short but regularly **run-on** lines (lines ending without punctuation) keep us moving from one unit to the next. No set number of syllables or accents are repeated—just a limited *range* that the reader's eye and ear get used to.

Consider these variations of Galvin's first sentence:

1. It's that delicate time when things could spill
   any way,
   when fog rides into the hollows, making bays,
   and Cathedral and Round Hills are high islands.

2. It's that delicate time when things
   could spill any way, when fog rides
   into the hollows, making bays,
   and Cathedral and Round Hills
   are high islands.

3. It's that delicate
   time when things
   could spill any
   way, when fog rides
   into the hollows,
   making bays,
   and Cathedral and Round Hills are high islands.

Although the language of the poem does not change, our experience does. One reason for this change is that the differing line constructions send different pieces of the developing message; that is, the rate at which we absorb the material and the ways in which the materials relate differ in each case. These differences occur because the white space around each line acts as a temporary frame, and as we read we add frame to frame, often overriding or suspending the logic of **syntax**. Decisions about lines and line break become decisions about the poem as an *experience* or a sequence of experiences.

As you can see, line length and line break are devices that control emphasis. For example, isolating "making bays" in version 3 gives that phenomenon more emphasis than it has in the other versions. Moreover, the contrast between that line and the considerably longer line that follows heightens our awareness of just how short the earlier line is. It also forces us to consider why the last line is so extended. What difference does it make? This is the question we must ask over and over again as alert readers and adventuring writers.

Notice, for example, that the last lines of variation 1 and variation 3 are identical but their impact is quite different because the preceding line is of equal length in one case and much shorter in the other. Obviously, the effect—the expressiveness—of a given line length is a function of its context, the environment of other lines that surrounds it.

But that's not all.

The position of a word on a line influences the emphasis it receives. Generally speaking, what's at the end of a line receives the greatest emphasis, what's at the beginning of a line receives secondary emphasis, and the material in the middle gets the least emphasis. At the beginning of Galvin's poem, "time," "spill," "fog," and "hollows" receive the greatest emphasis. Their placement gives the first full syntactical unit (sentence) a different flavor than is projected by the three variations. Galvin's decision to split a line between the words "fog" and "rides" gives each word relatively equal emphasis and impact. Compare the effect in the original with that in the variations.

QUESTIONS

1. What is the effect of keeping the words "high" and "islands" together, with "high" at the beginning of a line?

2. To what extent do Galvin's line breaks capitalize on or spring similarities in sound ("fog"/"hollows," "Cathedral"/"are," "Brooks"/"back," and so forth)?

3. What is the effect of the pauses marked by punctuation *within* lines?

4. Continue to explore the differences among the three revisions of Galvin's lines.

5. What is the fewest number of syllables per line? The most? The norm (most frequently found or average)?

Here is the rest of "Fog Township":

> the spring genius of this
> foggy township knitting up
> cable and chain to bind
> the acres, among moss stitches
> laying down her simple
> seed and fern stitch,

> complicating the landscape
> a pattern a day: daisy
> stitches and wild oats,
> berry knots interspersed
> with traveling vine
> and dogwood. Her needles
> cut from oak tips,
> click like sparks fired
> across a gap, and I
> imagine her crouched on
> a stump, hair wet, pulling
> April back together.
> But for the lethargy that's
> floating in this fog
> in nets so fine they can't
> be seen, I might walk around
> out there until I meet her,
> or scare off the jay
> who's chipping for sustenance
> along a pine's gray limb.

from *Seals in the Inner Harbor*

EXERCISE

1. Recast this poem in lines ranging from eight to ten syllables. How do the effects of the two versions differ?

2. Recast the poem in widely varying line lengths. What has happened to the experience?

3. Recast the poem as prose. How does the prose version differ from the original? Now, without looking at the original, can you reconstruct the line breaks?

4. Write your own poem about fog and how it makes you feel. Pay special attention to how fog alters things. Employ as many different senses as you can. Experiment extensively with line lengths and line break.

5. Experiment with line length and line break to communicate the different effects of fog, rain, snow, and bright sunshine.

◆ *Question:* Is line length a function of seeing or of hearing?

By now, we hope one thing is clear: your lines and line breaks should not be the result of accident or whimsy. The line is a unit of composition and revision, not an afterthought practiced upon a stretch of prose. As a fundamental principle of composition, the line must become *a way of thinking*.

THE LINE AND METER

Poets don't invent the sounds and accents of the language while in the process of writing poems. These features are inherent in the language itself as it is spoken and heard by everyone. **Rhythm**, loosely defined as the recurrence of stressed (accented) syllables, is not a device but a given. Poets pay special attention to this natural dimension of language: heightening it, systematizing it, and using it expressively.

One convention of the poetic line is to identify it with the repetition that is rhythm. Knowledge of how this convention operates is a means to expressive power. Though this knowledge is not essential—you can certainly begin writing a poem without any consideration of these matters—it is most useful for you to examine the means by which you can create desired effects.

The special terms we use to discuss these physical features of language sound curious and remote, but they are our only available means of sharing observations about how poems work.

Traditionally, line length in English poetry is defined by a system of measurement called **meter**. There are three basic conventions of measurement in English poetry: the counting of stressed syllables, the counting of total syllables, and the counting of units comprised of some combination of stressed and unstressed syllables. *Note*: when we say a syllable has *stress,* we mean this relatively; it has more stress (takes more emphasis in natural pronunciation) than those that surround it.

The earliest English poetry—called Old English or Anglo-Saxon verse—was based on a line in which only stressed (or accented) syllables were counted without regard to the total number of syllables. It was as if the poets and their audiences heard verbal music only in terms of the stresses and somehow filtered out the unstressed syllables. This poetry was dominated by the convention of a four-stress line, the accented syllables emphasized by repeated initial sounds (**alliteration**). The lines typically had a strong internal pause (**caesura**) between the second and third stressed syllable:

> They *came* to the *court*yard | | *fac*es a-*flame*

This is a tradition that has never vanished, and a good deal of contemporary verse that seems unmeasured is really a version of the long-lived accentual line. Poetry whose lines are defined in this way is called **accentual verse**.

Read aloud the following lines from Dave Smith's "Night Fishing for Blues" and you will hear the strong-stress accentual rhythms.

At Fortress Monroe, Virginia,
the big-jawed Bluefish, ravenous, sleek muscle slamming
at *rock*, at *pier* legs, *drives* into *Che*sapeake
*sha*llows, *con*voys *rank* after *rank*,
          *wheel*ing through *flume* and *flute* of *blood*,   5
          *some*thing like *hun*ger's *throb hook*ing
un*til* you *hear* it and *know* them *there*,
                                        the family.
          Tonight, not far from where Jefferson Davis

hunched in a harrowing cell, gray eyes quick   10
as crabs' nubs, I come back over plants
deep drummed under boots years ago, tufts of hair

*floa*ting at my *eyes*, *think*ing it *right* now
          to *pitch* through *tide*turn and *mud*slur
          for *fish* with *teeth* like *snapped sa*bers.   15

                                        from *Cumberland Station*

There is no fixed line length here; rather, an insistent beat emerges from the piling up of stressed syllables in lines that roughly approximate the traditional four-stress measure. Many lines (3–7, 13–15) reinforce the four-stress pattern—the norm—though the variation from it is pronounced. Lines 5 and 6 illustrate the interplay of sound and stress, not only by alliteration, but through repetition of internal vowel sounds (**assonance**) as well. Note the long "u" sound in "flume" and "flute" and the more subtle short "u" linking "blood," "something," and "hunger."

EXERCISES

1. Write a short poem using a four-stress line. In writing accentual verse, pay no attention to the *total* number of syllables in a line—only the stressed syllables.

2. Develop an accentual stanza using a preset variation. For example, let lines 1 and 4 have three stresses per line, let line 2 have four stresses, and let line 3 have five stresses:

(1)   /   /   /
(2)   /   /   /   /
(3)   /   /   /   /   /
(4)   /   /   /

Repeat your pattern for three stanzas.

In contrast to accentual verse, lines in **syllabic verse** are defined by the total number of syllables without regard to accent. This is not a highly expressive system in English poetry or in the poetry of other languages in which the contrast between stressed and unstressed syllables is pronounced. Syllabic measures do dominate the poetry of some languages, such as Japanese and French. Syllabic verse *has* had its English language partisans. Many feel that the arbitrary discipline forces decisions that bring surprising results. Marianne Moore's work represents syllabic poetry at its most inventive. Her elaborate stanzaic poems may be analyzed as intricate syllabic patterns. Here are the last three stanzas of "The Fish":

> All
> external
>   marks of abuse are present on this
>   defiant edifice—
>   all the physical features of
>
> ac-
> cident—lack
>   of cornice, dynamite grooves, burns, and
>   hatchet strokes, these things stand
>   out on it; the chasm is
>
> dead.
> Repeated
>   evidence has proved that it can live
>   on what can not revive
>   its youth. The sea grows old in it.
>
>   from *Collected Poems*

EXERCISE

1. Reline Moore's stanzas. Can you discover any changes in expressiveness?

2. Experiment with a set syllabic line of seven or more syllables. Then try a shorter line. Finally, try a stanza of alternate syllabic line lengths (like Moore's).

When most people think of meter, they think of the system that measures units of stressed and unstressed syllables called **feet**. This system came into English poetry after the Norman Conquest (1066), perhaps from the mixing of the accentual Anglo-Saxon tradition with the syllabic tradition of the Norman

French. We call the poetic system that counts these packages of stressed and unstressed syllables **accentual-syllabic verse**.

Four distinctive units (or **feet**) are the building blocks for poetry in the accentual-syllabic tradition. Each is named by a term borrowed from ancient Greek **prosody**. The dominant unit is the **iamb**, a package that consists of an unstressed syllable followed by a stressed one (˘/), as in the word "up*on*." The great majority of poems in accentual-syllabic verse have their lines defined by the iamb. The inverse of the iamb is the **trochee**, in which a stressed syllable is followed by an unstressed syllable (/˘), as in the word "*but*ton." The **anapest** is a sort of stretched iamb; it contains two unstressed syllables followed by a stressed syllable (˘˘/), as in the phrase "in the *phrase.*" Its inverse (/˘˘) is the **dactyl**, an elongated trochee, as in the word "*bat*tery."

Lines dominated by one or another of these feet are named by adjective-noun combinations in which the first term announces the type of foot and the second the number of feet in the line. Thus, we may have iambic, trochaic, anapestic, or dactylic *monometer, dimeter, trimeter, tetrameter, pentameter, hexameter, heptameter,* and so forth. For example, an "anapestic trimeter" is a line of three anapests. Though these terms are sometimes annoying, they are analogous to more familiar constructions from other systems: "dual exhausts," "triple play," "quadraphonic sound," and "quintuple bypass," for example. The point is that they form the available language for talking about what we observe.

To discover and indicate the metrical nature of a poem, we employ the process called **scansion**, in which we mark the stressed and unstressed syllables and divide the line, when appropriate, into feet. This technique makes visible what our ears tell us. By carefully scanning—reading, listening, and marking—we can discover that Andrew Marvell's "Thoughts in a Garden" is cast in iambic tetrameter:

> ˘ /| ˘ /| ˘ /| ˘ /
> How vainly men themselves amaze
> ˘ /| ˘ / | ˘ /| ˘ /
> To win the palm, the oak, or bays,
> ˘ / |˘ / | ˘ /| ˘ /
> And their incessant labours see
> / ˘ | ˘ /| ˘ /| ˘ /
> Crown'd from some single herb or tree,   4
> ˘ /| ˘ /| ˘ /| ˘ /
> Whose short and narrow-verged shade
> ˘ /| ˘ ⌐ ˘ /| ˘ /
> Does prudently their toils upbraid;
> ˘ /| ˘ / |˘ /| ˘ /
> While all the flowers and trees do close
> ˘ / |˘ /| ˘ ˘ |˘ /
> To weave the garlands of repose!   8

Though Marvell's use of his measure seems quite regular by the standards of modern practice, we can see that he was not a slavish metermonger. The life of metrical poetry is not in the endless reproduction of a pattern, but in the lively interplay of a background beat—the norm—with expressive variation. Marvell's first three lines march briskly along, establishing the pattern. However, the fourth line begins with a variation (or substitution) before settling down once again into the iambic groove. The fifth and seventh lines are again regular, while the sixth and eighth stray playfully from the norm.

You can create variations for emphasis: notice how the word "crown'd" gains extra force as a consequence of the unexpected change in meter: a trochaic for an iambic foot at the beginning of the line. Another effect of substitution is to change pace. In line 6, the valley (made visible by scansion) of unstressed syllables after the initial iamb quickens that line in relation to those around it.

The unit of two unstressed syllables that we discover in lines 6 and 8 is called the **pyrrhic foot**. This unit is often found in poetry dominated by iambs or another of the four major poetic feet, but it can never in itself be the basis for a line. If you try to write a pyrrhic line, you'll soon discover how the nature of the English language defies you. Another foot used only for variation is the **spondee**, a unit of two stressed syllables. The effect of the spondee, or of any piling up of stressed syllables, is to create illusions of deliberateness, weight, slowness, or power—quite the opposite of the effects made possible by pyrrhic substitution. The pyrrhic-spondee combination in the second line of the following passage (also from Marvell's "Garden") illustrates the sharp contrast, pushing against the iambic norm, that lifts the poet's adjective-noun combinations off the page:

> Annihilating all that's made
> to a green thought in a green shade.

Here is the opening stanza of Wyatt Prunty's "What Doesn't Go Away." After scanning it for yourself, compare Prunty's contemporary handling of iambic tetrameter to Marvell's:

> His heart was like a butterfly
> dropped through a vacuum tube,
> no air to lift it up again;
> each time the fluttering began,
> he opened his eyes, first seeing
> his family staggered around the bed,
> then seeing that he didn't see.
> While he died, the nurses wouldn't budge,
> blood pressure gone too low, they said.

from *What Women Know, What Men Believe*

Notice how Prunty fashions a compromise between the artifice of iambic tetrameter and the colloquial flow of contemporary speech patterns. Observe also, in the stanzas by both Marvell and Prunty, the role that internal pauses play in breaking up what might otherwise become too mechanical and repetitious. You can vary meter and caesura placement to create energy and pace.

EXERCISE

Here are some workshop exercises done by Lisa Schenkel, a student in one of our classes. She was asked to write a short passage in strict iambic lines, then to introduce a preponderance of stressed syllables, and then to work it through once again with the metrical balance leaning toward unstressed syllables. Study the results and give yourself the same assignment.

Sunday Evening Matisse

1. Strict iambic

> Unlike the other nudes, she stands at ease
> and watches. Paint in hand, he strokes a breast
> with quickness. Black, the lines relax the splash
> of pink—her feathered hat. Undaunted
> and ready, Barbra breaks her silent stance
> and laughs until he puts his paints away.

2. With piled stresses

> Unlike other nudes, she stands, slouches, smiles
> from the door, winks and watches. Black strokes
> curve to breasts, pink splashes feather a hat.
> Playful, he paints her unposed. Teasing, she flings
> pink her hat, spills blue paint slick on tile floors,
> slips into the room laughing, and leaves footprints.

3. With unstressed

> So at ease, she's a bit unlike the other nudes.
> She stands with her hands on her hips, as if
> impatient for him to finish. Her lips tilt in a
> smile as he hurries to capture her. With a dab
> of paint he attacks the canvas with a clutter of pink
> hat, and black brushstrokes below match her stance.

LINES AND RHYMES

You will want to control how sharply lines are defined and how regularly that definition is reinforced. It is easy for readers to respond to a line that ends with a pause marked by punctuation. Such a line is called an **end-stopped** line. One that concludes with no such syntactical pause is called **run-on** or **enjambed**. You can sense the difference by comparing the following passages from Alexander Pope's "Eloisa to Abelard" and Robert Browning's "My Last Duchess." Read each passage aloud and jot down your reactions to how each poet handles the line.

> Those smiling eyes, attempering every ray,
> Shone sweetly lambent with celestial day.
> Guiltless I gazed; heaven listened while you sung;
> And truths divine came mended from that tongue.
> From lips like those what precept failed to move?
> Too soon they taught me was no sin to love:
> Back thro' the paths of pleasing sense I ran,
> Nor wished an angel whom I loved a man.
>
> Pope, 63–70

> Sir, 'twas not
> Her husband's presence only, called that spot
> Of joy into the Duchess' cheek; perhaps
> Fra Pandolf chanced to say, "Her mantle laps
> Over my lady's wrist too much," or, "Paint
> Must never hope to reproduce the faint
> Half-flush that dies along her throat." Such stuff
> Was courtesy, she thought, and cause enough
> For calling up that spot of joy. . . .
>
> Browning, 13–21

Even though both poets are writing in the same verse form, rhymed iambic pentameter couplets, each uses the line in a rather extreme and distinctive way. Pope, by ending each line with a pause, reinforces his rhyme words and creates the feeling of sharply isolated lines and couplets being added one to another. Browning, on the other hand, weakens the impact of the rhyme words and so we feel that the lines and couplets flow into one another. Each writer's technique is appropriate for his ends.

The preceding examples reveal one more fact about the poetic line. **End rhyme** is its most powerful signal. Indeed, end rhyme communicates line length to the ear, and this device can have as much force as the visual signal of the wide white space that follows a line break in print. However, because end rhyme is such a powerful attention getter and one so strongly identified with poetry, beginning writers often overuse it. The result can be noise that obscures meaning.

Contemporary poetry is characterized by less emphatic rhyming as well as less predictable line lengths. In Maxine Kumin's poem, there are instances of true rhyme on stressed syllables as well as the more subdued echoes of **off-rhyme**:

Stopped Time in Blue and Yellow

Today the violets turn up blue
in the long grass as ever
a heaven can, the sea-calm color
of promises ballooning into view.
Stems long enough to lace
around your oval wrist,
small petal face
the wash of Waterman's ink,
vigilant cat's eye at the center
yellow as the sluice box where cows drink.

Today under the blue line
that covers your pulse I feel
the small purling sounds
your body makes, going on.
Time squats in the blue-spurred grass
like a yellow blister
and love in the long foreplay of spring
follows skyblue after.

from *Our Ground Time Here Will Be Brief*

QUESTIONS

1. Why do you think Kumin uses less prominent repetitions of sounds in the second stanza than in the first?

2. What principle governs Kumin's line breaks?

3. How do the shortest and longest lines in this poem work expressively?

EXERCISE

Write a poem in which you experiment with various line lengths. Make your shortest line a single word.

THE LINE AND FREE VERSE

Most poets today write in **free verse**, a term describing a wide variety of practices in which the traditional, quantitatively defined line is replaced by lines defined far more loosely and subjectively. The poems by Galvin and Kumin that we have already examined are, relatively speaking, "free"—especially if we set them alongside the excerpts from Pope or Browning or even Prunty. If you read Kumin's poem aloud, you will hear a slight pause at many of the line breaks, even when no punctuation occurs. Kumin separates sentence parts in a fairly predictable manner, trusting her ear for colloquial speech patterns. *One convention of free verse is to break lines at natural, syntactical pauses, whether they are punctuated or not.*

    In the following excerpt from Margaret Gibson's "Affirmations," line break works similarly. However, Gibson sometimes departs from line breaks governed by syntax. Such variations depend more for their effects on what the eye sees than what the ear hears. *This visual focusing is one major device for emphasis in free verse.*

> An Eskimo shaman
> will take stone, and with a pebble sit quietly
> for days tracing on stone a circle,
> until snow and mind are one.
>
> Gazing into the whirl of a knothole   5
> I sit out winter. Someone mutters inside.
> Just one tremor before the walls give me
> another white word for snow
> this wood desk shimmers, as if wind
> had reached wood's spellbound   10
> galaxies and seen
> the pole star
> turning.

from *Long Walks in the Afternoon*

Gibson allows line break to replace punctuation on occasion, as in lines 5 and 8. Her practice suggests that for the free verse poet, *line break serves as a kind of punctuation.* As such, it is a way of visually scoring a feature of the *spoken* poem.

    Another device illustrated by this passage, a device explored in our examination of Galvin's poem, is the power of position. The placing of "spellbound" at the end of one line and "galaxies" at the beginning of the next gives the word "spellbound" more emphasis. Moreover, the hesitation at the line break creates a moment of suspense: we know that the line has ended with an adjective that demands a noun, and when the fulfillment of our expectation comes at the beginning of the next line, it comes with extra force. *Many free verse poets use line break as a strategy for surprise and suspense—or even for multiple meanings.*

Consider the various ways of reading the following lines:

> When she cried
> Wolf
> Tears down her face
> Ran

Is "Wolf" the object of the verb, as in the half-dead metaphor of "crying wolf," or is it the subject of the main clause that follows an introductory "when . . ." clause? Is the first word on the third line a reference to crying or a synonym for "rips"? This kind of controlled ambiguity is a device used by many contemporary poets.

When all is going well, every decision a poet makes about the length of lines and the placement of end words and opening words helps the poem communicate. In "Figure Eights" by Siv Cedering, even the white spaces between stanzas are functional. One could almost say that these spaces "mean" something in this brilliant reproduction of the experience of skating:

> My back toward the circle, I skate,
> shift my weight, turn toward the center.
>
> The skill is in the balance, the ability
> to choose an edge, and let it cut
>
> its smooth line. The moon is trapped
> in the ice. My body flows
>
> across it. The evening's cold. The space
> limited. There is not much room
>
> for hesitation. But I have learned a lot
> about grace, in my thirty-third year.
>
> I lean into the cutting edge: two circles
> interlock, number eight drawn
>
> by a child, a mathematician's
> infinity.

from *Letters from the Floating
World: Selected and New Poems*

The stanza breaks at "cut / its smooth line," "flows / across it," and "room/ for hesitation" seem to enact what the words describe.

Cedering's decision to shape this poem in unrhymed couplets has other consequences. The most obvious of these is that the appearance of the poem becomes a visual imaging of its content: the paired lines help us "see" the idea of pairing represented in the poem by the skates. Such visual communication is another element in much free verse poetry—and even in traditional poetry. *Poems on the printed page have a visual (typographical) level of communication; they have shapes that may or may not correspond to the poem as an experience for the ear.*

LINES IN COMBINATION

Broadly speaking, you can choose one of two major traditions for combining lines into poems: the **stichic** and the **stanzaic** (or **strophic**). The stichic tradition is to write a continuous poem whose overriding unity and cohesiveness are promised by the unbroken column of type. An example of this tradition is Galvin's "Fog Township." The stanzaic tradition is to write a segmented poem in which white spaces (blank lines) divide the total work into smaller, quasi-independent units, as in the Wordsworth poem below.

The contrasting visual experiences send the reader different signals, creating different kinds of expectations. While we recognize the general look of poetry—the fairly uniform left-hand margin, the ragged (unjustified) right margin, the narrower-than-prose column shape—we further recognize and are "preset" to respond to a range of more particular typographical designs. The following two-stanza poem by William Wordsworth promises something even before we begin reading it:

> A slumber did my spirit seal;
>   I had no human fears:
> She seemed a thing that could not feel
>   The touch of earthly years.
>
> No motion has she now, no force;
>   She neither hears nor sees;
> Rolls round in earth's diurnal course,
>   With rocks, and stones, and trees.

The visual message of this poem immediately suggests two foldedness and symmetry: we expect that the shape of thought or emotion will somehow correspond to the halved whole—and it does. The shift from past tense to present tense is the key to the "before and after" structure. In turn, that structure justifies the decision to cast the material in two *equal* stanzas. The line indentations suggest a further division of each stanza, a division echoed by the end rhyme (*ab/ab*).

Stanzaic poems and poems in **fixed forms** are most effective when some kind of correspondence exists between outer and inner divisions or form. Each of the following Italian sonnets by Jay Rogoff pivots between the eighth and ninth line; when the rhyme scheme changes, the poet takes us from the scene of the crime to the interrogation room:

Murder Mystery 1

Inkstains upon the oriental rug.
Blood mingles with them. Blood today is king.
The lyre lies on the bed strung with one string.
Protruding from her wounds are points stuck snug
as bees' abandoned stingers, which cops unplug.
Only the radio is left to sing.
The floor littered with crow quill pens. "Bring
'em here," says the sergeant with a shrug.

The poet, crammed into his seat with bright
lights blinding, when interrogated, said,
"I don't know what you mean." A lie. The light
was brightened, handcuffs clamped. He stood and read
a poem. Finished, he sobbed, "We used to fight.
I'd never *kill* her. But I'm glad she's dead."

Murder Mystery 2

Inkstains upon the oriental rug.
The poet at a queer angle. Like a spring
wound round his neck, a strangling catgut string
has popped his eyes. His hands clutch poems and hug
them to his heart. The cops' most violent tug
won't pry them. A pen lies like a torn wing.
From the hall a woman's voice begins to sing.
"Book'er," the sergeant says. "Prints and a mug."

She sat handcuffed. Her robe trailed on the floor.
"What do you know?" "Nothing." "A man is dead."
"A poet," she corrected. "I know no more."
The light was thrown upon her laureled head.
"He did it to himself," she added. "You're
a liar." "No, this is my lyre," she said.

Some poets might emphasize the overall unity of the sonnet; others, like Rogoff, develop material that coincides with the divisions signaled by the rhyme scheme. To put it simply, a mitten tells us one thing about a hand, a glove tells us something else.

If you think about it, the business of defining lines and line combinations leads to a prior consideration of whether your poem exists primarily in *time*, as a sequence of words, sounds, and rhythms to be heard, or in *space*, as a sequence of signs printed on the page. The work of most contemporary poets hovers somewhere in between, so that reading—finding the essential poem—becomes an act of mediation between what we hear, however silently, and what we see. In addition, you must consider how much the full communicative strength of your work depends on your reader's knowledge of traditions either employed, alluded to, or intentionally defied. You must be aware of your assumptions and the demands they place on your readers: you need to gauge the risks you are taking by depending on or ignoring conventions—even the conventions of free verse.

The two poems that follow illustrate contrasting assumptions about the essential nature of poetry and about the audience. Harold Witt's "Friends" is in a fixed form, the **villanelle**, and it gets much of its strength from manipulating the conventions of that form. Consequently, while the poem can reach any reader, it has greater resonance for the reader who is aware of the dynamics of the form and who is familiar with other villanelles. "The Waves," by Mary Oliver, follows only the rules that the poet has discovered for this individual poem. Moreover, Oliver has given special emphasis to the typographical level of the poem, allowing that experience to sit in sharp contrast to sounds, rhythms, and even syntax. Witt's poem also has a strong typographical impact; the visual shape underscores—or outlines—a musical shape that communicates to the ear. These patterned repetitions of sounds delineate the poem in time.

Friends

The Quakers, speaking plainly, knew
that Friends are what we're meant to be,
that they were right, though they were few,

in keeping to a loving view.
A brotherly society,
the Quakers, speaking plainly, knew

they had to act as Christians do
no matter who might not agree
that they were right. Though they were few—

bonnets and hats of somber hue,
quaintly saying "thou" and "thee"—
the Quakers, speaking plainly, knew

war's not peace and lies aren't true
and man's his own worst enemy.
That they were right (though they were few)

in light of what we're going through
today—it's easier to see.

The Quakers, speaking plainly, *knew*
that they were right. Though they were few.

from *The Snow Prince*

The Waves

The sea
  isn't a place
    but a fact, and
    a mystery

under its green and black
  cobbled coat that never
    stops moving.
      When death

happens on land, on some
  hairpin piece of road,
    we crawl past,
      imagining

over and over that moment
  of disaster. After the storm
    the other boats didn't
      hesitate—they spun out

from the rickety pier, the men
  bent to the nets or turning
    the weedy winches.
    Surely the sea

is the most beautiful fact
  in our universe, but
    you won't find a fisherman
    who will say so;

what they say is,
  See you later.
    Gulls white as angels scream
    as they float in the sun

just off the sterns;
  everything is here
    that you could ever imagine.
    and the bones

of the drowned fisherman
  are returned, half a year later,

in the glittering,
laden nets.

from *Dream Work*

QUESTIONS AND EXERCISES

1. From Witt's example, describe the villanelle form. What is repeated? How many times?

2. What is the effect of the difference between the first five sections and the longer final section with its concluding couplet?

3. Can you determine if Witt is taking any liberties with an even more restrictive tradition?

4. Witt begins his lines with lowercase letters (unless uppercase is otherwise demanded). Why this contemporary practice in a long-lived fixed form?

5. Find and study five or six other English villanelles, including Dylan Thomas's "Do Not Go Gentle Into That Good Night." After exploring the possibilities, try a villanelle of your own.

6. Compare and contrast the conventions and effects of the villanelle with those of the English (Shakespearean) sonnet (see p. 141) and the Italian sonnet (see Rogoff's "Murder Mystery" sequence, p. 126).

7. Invent a form that borrows some of its features from the villanelle and some from the sonnet.

8. What is the relationship between (visual) form and content in "The Waves"?

9. Does the fact that the stanzas are not self-contained seem accidental or purposeful?

10. Is there any inner logic that insists on or justifies the stanzaic appearance of this poem?

11. Can this poem be read aloud so its stanzaic nature is communicated?

12. Does a free verse poem cast in visual stanzas work with or against our expectations in order to gain its effects?

IMAGERY

For many poets, a poem begins with an **image**—a piece of language that relates sensory experience. While all writers employ **imagery** and the many figures of speech that are built from images, poets *depend* on this type of language. (See the discussions of **concreteness** and **figurative language** in Chapter 4, "Language Is Your Medium.") Because poetry aims at intensity and economy of expression, imagery and figures of speech have special value to the poet. Sensory experience is primary experience: we see, feel, taste, smell, and hear before we think, analyze, choose, and argue. By staying close to imagery, the language of the senses, you can bring your readers close to a fundamental animal awareness of the world we inhabit. At the same time, by choosing carefully and by letting associated images coalesce, you can evoke complex states of awareness.

The image in the title of this Roland Flint poem controls the poem by giving it a center and a circumference. If we let ourselves respond fully to what the earthworm image generates, we find a poem that is about processes, transformations—perhaps about poetry itself.

Earthworm

> I think of a girl who hated to walk in the rain,
> Loathing to step on them. I hope she got over that.
> We liked to keep one on the sidewalk
> And line it up with another
> For an excruciating race,
> Or put it back in the grass
> And watch its progress. Burrowing.
>
> We said, when he's underground,
> And worming, the earth goes right through him.
>
> I still think of him that way, lank, blind,
> Both ends open, refining whatever comes,
> Dirt among rose roots, yeasty bodies.
>
> He doesn't look for trouble. He just follows warmth,
> At the earth's curve, coming up only for rain
> And the feet of girls.

from *Resuming Green*

Flint's poem works through a series of sensory triggers to reach out for emotions and ideas. By building upon his central, generative image, the poet keeps his writing concrete, cohesive, and immediate. The earthworm changes what passes through it. The language of the poem invites us to ask *what else works in this way* without ever leaving the heat-seeking earthworm behind. The poem also asks *what, like the earthworm, is undervalued because it seems unattractive or doesn't call much attention to itself.*

Observations that discover likenesses are the geneses of many successful poems. Even such rarefied emotional experiences as the sudden sense of absence can be captured by the patient poet who asks "What is it like?" over and over again. "Gloves," by Jean Nordhaus, is alive with focused images that finally take us to a place beyond and within.

> When all the birds roost
> suddenly
> the bare tree
> bursts into leaf.
>
> plumb, tapered, brown, true
> a flock of
> weathervanes
> nosing into
>
> the wind, they hang
> to the branches
> like gloves, then
> leave suddenly
>
> leaving the branches,
> the branches
> full of in-
> visible hands.

from *A Language of Hands*

EXERCISE

1. Trace the connections between the images and figures of speech in these two poems.

2. How does each poet use the line to isolate or connect images?

3. Examine each poem in this chapter to see if line, imagery, or something else functions as the primary structural element.

4. Write your own poem by enlarging upon a central image or building a series of associated images.

The interplay between lines and images creates much of the dramatic tension in contemporary poetry. Investigating the possibilities of various line–image units will lead you to an understanding of one more expressive convention.

EXERCISE

Analyze the following poem by William Heyen in terms of line construction, line break, lines in combination, stanza breaks, and imagery. Pay special attention to the images of light. What are the key organizational devices of this poem? How can you use what you have learned from reading like a writer?

The Return

I will touch things and things and no more thoughts.
—Robinson Jeffers

My boat slowed on the still water,
stopped in a thatch of lilies.
The moon leaned over the white lilies.

I waited for a sign, and stared
at the hooded water. On the far shore
brush broke, a deer broke cover.

I waited for a sign, and waited.
The moon lit the lilies to candles.
Their light reached down the water

to a dark flame, a fish. It hovered
under the pads, the pond held it
in its dim depths as in amber.

Green, still, balanced in its own life,
breathing small breaths of light, this
was the world's oldest wonder, the arrow

of thought, the branch that all words
break against, the deep fire, the pure poise
of an object, the pond's presence, the pike.

from *Long Island Light: Poems and a Memoir*

1. What happens between stanzas 3 and 4, 5 and 6?

2. What sound dominates the close of the poem? What is its effect? (You might want to review this question after reading the next section.)

3. What figure of speech is "small breaths of light"? How does it work?

4. What does the poem have to say about the concrete versus the abstract?

5. Write your own poem in which you use one or two enjambed stanzas that force the reader to move over the white space in a way that underscores meaning.

SOUND PATTERNS

In our discussion of the line, we referred to the basic sonic devices: rhyme, alliteration, and assonance. Now it is time to look more closely into the expressiveness of sounds and sound patterns. In speech and in most prose, the various sounds in our language system occur at random. However, the poet can pattern the occurrence of sounds by repeating them in close proximity or at regular intervals. As with meter, some feature of language that occurs in a haphazard way when we speak or when we write prose is now given a conscious patterning for purposes of emphasis, cohesiveness, or organization.

When Poe, in "The Raven," writes of "this *g*rim, un*g*ainly, *g*hastly, *g*aunt, and ominous bird of yore," he is employing alliteration (repetition of initial consonant) on four stressed syllables in order to underscore his adjectives by linking them sonically. When Shelley, in "Mont Blanc," writes of pines that "in the m*a*ngled soil/ Br*a*nchless and sh*a*ttered st*a*nd," a similar—though somewhat quieter—effect is achieved through assonance (repetition of vowel sound). In both cases, the reader's attention is drawn to words linked by sounds, and the words themselves are linked together. *Note:* we are not referring to the *spelling* of words, since identical sounds are often spelled differently: "stuff"/ "enough."

Rhyme is simply a more complex echoing: usually a repeated vowel–consonant combination, as in the pair "streams"/ "dreams." Often, as in the pair "free"/"see," the matching of the final vowel constitutes the rhyme. Because rhyme (or "true rhyme") is more emphatic than the other devices, it is customarily used, as we have seen, to signal the ends of lines and to define stanzas. Rhyme sharpens meanings by asking readers to consider the semantic relationships between the words whose sounds mirror one another.

The following lines resulted from an assignment to develop a six-line stanza using true rhyme:

> Early one morning, an Amtrak train
> Rumbles north through the ivory expanse
> Of Maryland landscape. The muffled terrain
> Is sliced by the tracks. Slung like a lance,
> The careless freight, by folly and chance,
> Splatters the snowbank with that human stain.

This first draft exploits the power of rhyme effectively by emphasizing words important enough to carry the extra attention they receive. After leading us to anticipate alternating rhyme (*abab* through line 4), the poet makes a couplet (lines 4 and 5) that interrupts the pattern. This interruption unsettles the reader, who waits for some new resolution of pattern. The waiting produces suspense, and then surprise, as the culminating image is delivered with the return of the *a* rhyme.

While repetition of any sound has the broad effect of calling attention, more specialized effects can be achieved through a sensitivity—in both writer and reader—to the nuances of the various sounds. When Poe repeats the harsh gutteral *g,* the effect is quite different from that of Keats's lines from "To August": "Thy hair soft-lifted by the winnowing wing;/ Or on a half-reaped furrow sound asleep." In Keats's lines, harsh sounds are almost altogether absent and never prominent.

While we hesitate to say that sounds *mean* anything, we do feel that they *suggest.* Let's consider consonants first. The following chart shows the range of consonant sounds. The family groupings have to do with how the sounds are pronounced as well as how they strike the ear.

CONSONANT SOUNDS

liquids: *r, l*	"semivowels" along with *w* and *y,* considered the most musical consonants
nasals: *m, n, ng*	firmer, but still "soft"
fricatives: *h, f, v, th, dh, s, z, sh, zh*	produced by vibration or friction, abrasive
plosives: *p, b, k, g, t, d*	produced by blasting open a closed space . . . can't be prolonged . . . called "hard" consonants

Here is a student experiment in using sounds. The assignment was to write two short passages of poetry, the first with language that is dominated by softer consonants, and the second emphasizing the plosives.

1. Summer came on slow as a lizard's blink,
   on a flotilla of white wicker chairs and lawn games,
   and all we knew of time was a lurid glow
   in the West-Northwest that we watched from the headland,
   watched it sink seamless into Thursday.

2. Kirk burned for a while on alternate doses
   of hard bop and crack. He smoked Kents tit for tat
   with the most brutal of the night beasts and
       once hocked his axe
   for a Palo Alto whore. Even now, dead by the hand
   of an outraged husband, he looms over my shoulder
   slipping me jacks to cinch a high straight.

EXERCISE

1. In the preceding experiment, which lines or passages seem most successful at linking sound and sense? Where would you make improvements? Revise these passages; then go on to do your own experiments with the consonant

groups. Recite your work out loud. Listen for the similarities among sounds from the same family. Notice how they can almost be mistaken for one another. For example, the word "fish" and the first syllable of "visual" create a near rhyme—in fact, a near identity.

2. Listen and respond to the sounds in the following word pairs. How do the contrasting sounds make you feel?

a. pillow / cushion
b. coast / shore
c. beast / animal
d. referee / umpire
e. whiskey / booze

Now pronounce each word in the following vowel chart slowly and deliberately. Feel the work your mouth has to do to make the sounds.

VOWEL SOUNDS

bee	high-frequency	vitality, speed,
bay	(alto) vowels	excitement, stridency,
buy		exhilaration, light
bit	middle-frequency	
bet	(tenor) vowels	
bat		
bird		
bud		
bar	low-frequency	sobriety, awe, gloom,
bough	(bass) vowels	doom, largeness,
boy		darkness
bought		
book		
bone		
boot		

This vowel scale groups families by frequency characteristics that can be graphed on an oscilloscope. An interval of high-frequency sounds shows a busy, jagged pattern with many peaks and valleys. Low-frequency vowels, on the other hand, show fewer oscillations over the same interval. Like the consonant families, the vowel families are related by how they are produced. The high-frequency vowels are made toward the front of the mouth in a relatively closed space. You can feel a tension in the facial muscles as you pronounce them. The low-frequency vowels begin far back in the mouth, which is open and rounded as these sounds are manufactured.

As with the consonants, repetition of vowels from one or another category can help give emotional coloring to the passages bonded together by these related sounds. For example, the last stanza of Dylan Thomas's "The Hand That Signed the Paper" gains much of its solemnity from the way in which low-frequency vowel sounds dominate the passage, especially toward the end of lines.

> The five kings count the dead but do not soften
> The crusted wound nor stroke the brow;
> A hand rules pity as a hand rules heaven;
> Hands have no tears to flow.

Conversely, in his elegiac "Do Not Go Gentle Into That Good Night," Thomas urges not self-pity or gloom, but active resistance to death; here the strident high-frequency vowels take over:

> Grave men, near death, who see with blinding sight
> Blind eyes could blaze like meteors and be gay,
> Rage, rage against the dying of the light.

Turn back to the six-line stanza on page 133. Notice how the strident *a* sound promotes the feeling that the speaker's otherwise flat voice can veil but not hide his recognition of anguish.

EXERCISE

As you have already done with the consonant sounds, explore the effects of piling up vowel sounds from one and then the other side of the spectrum.

1. Write an "aw" poem in which the vowel in words like "call" and "appall" and "thought" is dominant. Notice, again, that spelling is not the key to pronunciation.

2. Write an "ee" poem.

3. Experiment with the ways in which various classes of consonants and vowels work in combination. For example, mix high-frequency vowels and fricative consonants.

OFF-RHYME

Contemporary practice tends to favor subdued sound patterns. **Off-rhyme** (also called **slant rhyme**, *near rhyme,* and *half rhyme)* is used more frequently than true rhyme, and the aspiring poet should experiment with the varying intensities of rhyme in order to discover what kinds of effects are possible. One form of off-rhyme is **consonance**. This is a matching of consonant clusters around changing vowel sounds: "blood/ blade," "cut/ cat/ cot/ caught," "dance/ dunce." The following lines from John Ciardi's "At My Father's Grave" indicate the power of this slight discord.

> A leaf is not too little. A world may rest
> in no more shade than spiders weave. Defend
> the nit on every underside. I roost
> on less than it, and I must yet be found
> by the same bird that found St. Francis dead.

Two lines later, "dead" is echoed by "deed." There is something slightly grating in this kind of rhyming, and it is appropriate to the emotion that Ciardi expresses.

EXERCISE

Experiment by alternating full rhymes with consonance.

1. Try these end words in your poem: "blend, blonde, blind, bland."

2. Now use these: "cuff, cough, calf; meat, mat, might, moat."

Consonance has an eerie richness about it; other types of echoing in use today are far more subdued. Often the repetition of final consonant sounds, or the pairing of related consonant sounds, serves for rhyme. Listen to the end sounds in the first stanza of Philip Levine's "For Fran."

> She packs the flower beds with leaves,
> Rags, dampened paper, ties with twine
> The lemon tree, but winter carves
> Its features on the uprooted stem.

The quiet alternate rhyming of the fricative "vs" pattern and the nasals sets just the degree of containment Levine needs for his gentle homage to his wife.

Another kind of off-rhyme uses assonance in the end words: "ice/ prize," "crisp/ din," "loud/ growl."

EXERCISE

1. Write six lines of alternating rhyme in which the odd-numbered lines end with dental consonants (*d,t*) and the even-numbered ones end with fricatives (see chart).

2. Write a five-line passage in which the end words' final consonants are nasals but the other sounds are in contrast.

There is no point in arguing, as some conservatives are apt to do, that this isn't rhyme or that poets just can't rhyme anymore. The subdued echoes illustrated by Levine's quatrain are the convention of our time for those who choose to rhyme at all. These modulated echoes can move a sensitive reader (listener). A skilled poet will have mastered their effects.

The sounds of the language are among your most important tools. While it is possible to write without regard to sound or meter, these physical phenomena do their work anyway. In a sense, they just *will not* be ignored. Any dimension of language that we choose to ignore is ignored at the risk of our sending unintended, ineffective messages to the reader, even the reader who has no conscious concern with these matters. The subterranean effects of sounds and rhythms are part of the "magic" of poetry. As with all magic, knowledge is power.

Our review of the fundamentals is now over. Of course, we have only skimmed the surface of these issues. Each poet chooses the devices and strategies that solve the problems of each developing poem—but there can be little in the way of informed choice without information. The conventions of poetry are, finally, the features by which poems are recognized and do their work.

7

Practicing Poetry

1. Unscrambling

We have scrambled the fifteen lines of Susan Astor's poem, "The Poem Queen." The original has five 3-line stanzas rhyming *aab*. Reconstruct Astor's poem. *Hint:* the first and last lines are in the right place.

> The Poem Queen writes a poem a day,
> To please her when she is alone
> She has more power than they know,
> It will be read.
>
> Some say hers is a magic throne
> Has found a way to burn the snow;
> Her pen is her divining rod;
> Turns gold to lead.
>
> She uses it to handle God,
> In her spare time pauses to pray
> She has a soldier and a drone
> And blossom bread.

> That she eats custard made of bone
> Or in her bed.
> And tame the dead.

Now exchange your reconstruction with those done by others in the class. Discuss the pros and cons of each version, as well as the original—which most people will be able to discover after a little trial and error. Astor's poem appears at the end of this chapter. Answer these questions about it:

a. By what logic are the stanzas ordered?
b. What is the effect of the repeated rhyme sound in the half-size third line of each stanza?
c. What about the short line in itself? What effect does it create?

2. IMITATION

Model a "character poem" of your own on Susan Astor's. Use her stanza form five times. Titles might be "The Prom Queen," "The Car King," "The Duke of Disco," "The Computer King," "The Punk Queen." Exchange and discuss the results with your classmates.

3. RECASTING

Recast the poem you have just written into the following forms.

Ballad Quatrain. This form rhymes *abxb* or *abab* and alternates iambic tetrameter with iambic trimeter, as in the following example.

> About the dead hour o' the night
> She heard the bridles ring;
> And Janet was as glad at that
> As any earthly thing.

Write four stanzas (you'll need sixteen lines instead of the fifteen in your original version).

Terza Rima. This is a three-line stanza that rhymes *aba bcb cdc* and so forth, the enclosed sound of each stanza becoming the enveloping sound of the next. Write five stanzas, and stretch the lines out to iambic pentameter. Compare these two variations with each other and with your original.

Shakespearean Sonnet. This is an English form rhyming *abab cdcd efef gg*. Take notes on the different effects the different forms create, as well as the problems each form creates for you.

Blank Verse. Write twelve lines of unrhymed iambic pentameter. This time the poem should be **stichic** (continuous) rather than divided into sections. How difficult is it to get rid of the rhymes?

4. MORE UNSCRAMBLING

Here is a scrambled free verse poem by Roland Flint. See if you can recover the original. To make things difficult, we have changed some of the punctuation and capitalization. When you have taken your best shot at this, compare your version with those of your classmates before looking at the original (found at the end of this chapter).

> Too young to be dying this way,
> he checks his meters, checks his flaps,
> and I am drifting back to North Dakota
> and airplanes.
>
> With the white silk scarf of his sleeve
> he pulls back the stick,
> steers a laborious, self-propelled combine,
> where butterflies are all gone brown with wheat dust.
> It is hot today, dry enough for cutting grain.
> and hurtles into the sun.
>
> Engines roaring,
> red-faced, sweating, chafed,
> he shines and shines his goggles,
> dreaming of cities, and blizzards—
> And where some boy
> screams contact at his dreamless father.

Hint: the original has four sections, the last consisting of a single line.

5. MEMORY POEM

Try a free verse "memory poem" of your own. Begin with some feeling, image, or event in the present that triggers a flashback to an earlier version of yourself. Perhaps you can fashion the poem around an action like swimming, running, dancing, or driving a car.

6. FORMULA POEMS

One kind of structure is the familiar formula, in which a cataloging or listing of directions and ingredients gives the material a focus, a limit, and—if some degree of parallel grammatical structure is used—a basic rhythm. Here is an old recipe for a cocktail called "Golf Links."

> 1/2 wineglass rye
> 1/2 wineglass sweet catawba
> 2 dashes lemon juice
> 1 teaspoon syrup
> 2 dashes orange bitters
> 1 dash angostura bitters
> 1 dash rum

> rinse cocktail glass with Abricotine, strain into same, dash with Appolinaris and dress with fruit.

Allowing our imaginations to take over, we can alter the proportions, ingredients, and procedures in order to provide, let's say, recipes for hate, ambition, or love. How are you feeling right now? Can you devise a recipe for a drink that will reproduce that feeling? It might include a jigger of stars, a dumpster full of dandelions, a twist of madness, a pinch of turpentine, a teaspoon of powdered California. Get the idea?

Here is a student "recipe poem" that relates two kinds of pleasure.

Jazz Sundae

> I love that sultry flavored trumpet
> topped with rich, creamy, soothing sax.
> Add a dash of drums, and a sprinkle of keyboard.
> Then cool to taste.

And here are some other formula ideas: menus (how about one for a restaurant called Nuclear Café?); 15,000-mile service (on your heart, perhaps); a weather report; a state of the union address; a promissory note; being read your rights (*Mirandized*); a pledge of allegiance; prayer; an ad in the personals column; the box score of a baseball game.

A major kind of formula, related to the recipe, gives directions (to go somewhere, to fix something, to assess something). Of course, one kind of process can always be imaginatively transformed into another, gaining strength from the contrast between the familiar formula and the new material it holds. Working with an imaginary map, give directions (in a poem) for getting to forgiveness, ecstasy, indifference, the fountain of youth, inner space, hysteria, or the end of a poem.

Examine a process that you know very well: how a bill becomes a law, how to knit a sweater, how to pitch a curve ball, how to parallel park, how to build a kite, how to drive on ice. Now give someone else directions—allowing, of course, an imaginative transformation to take place. For example, turn building a kite into a love poem.

Another kind of formula poem involves playing with plot patterns or similar literary conventions. "French Movie," by Pat Shelley, is a response to this assignment: *set the scene; put a person or persons in it; bring in another person or element and make something happen.* Here's the poem:

> Apricots are falling in the rain;
> The new young prunes are growing whiskers;
> Two old grandfathers, lost in ruminant thoughts,
> Sit among the pails of geraniums
> Eating the morning's squash blossoms.
>
> When the old nurse comes out
> And leans to pour them a cup of soup
> One old grandfather pinches her tit.
>
> from *Bogg* #56, 1986

Try a formula poem of your own based on the directions given in italics preceding the Shelley poem.

7. RITUAL POEMS

Ritual poems are closely related to formula poems but have more to do with behavior patterns outside those of language and literature. The job of a ritual poem is to discover or assess the feeling and meaning latent in such patterned behavior. Because ritual implies order, structure, and a sense of inevitability, poems that deal with ritual have a ready-made attraction for the formalist poet. Here is a poem by Baron Wormser that says something about the impact of soap opera patterns on the patterns of our lives, and vice versa.

Soap Opera

> If each witless age creates an image of itself,
> Ours is of a woman crying for help
> Amid a crowd of well-groomed friends.
> She is hysterical, tormented, saddened, upset.
> In a few minutes she will be better

And stay that way until she cries again.
It was nothing that made her cry.
Ralph had told Joan that Bill might die.
She looks at us through harsh light
That jumps off the linoleum and glass.

She is crying again and has locked the door.
She is not ugly or stupid or poor.
That's why she cries like this.
No one has told her what to do,
And she is forced to always look for clues,

To check the way adolescents dress and swear,
To listen to commentators
And remember the news.
She has opened the door.
Tom looks at her and smiles.

They kiss. It might be reconciliation
Or tenderness or thoughtless urge.
Adroit music surges over the throw rugs
And well-waxed tiles. We are convinced.
Happiness is the best of styles.

from *Good Trembling*

Write a ritual poem about a sporting event, a wedding, a holiday meal, a shopping trip. How do you get ready for work, for a test, for a date? What were Sunday mornings like when you were a child? Friday nights? Are there rituals at the restaurants or bars you go to? Employ some kind of formal repetition of sound, rhythm, phrase, or line that enhances the feeling of ritual, of routine, that you are describing.

Having trouble getting started? Here is a suggestion that we've adapted from Ross Talarico's book, *Creative Writing Exercises*. Divide a sheet of paper into two columns. Head one column "hunter" or "fisherman" or "soldier" and the other column "priest." Now, under each column make a list of five items connected with the person (occupation) named. Now add to the list three action verbs associated with each heading. These word lists are the raw materials for your poem. Try to interweave the words from each list ("stalking the Bible," "chalice of bait," "plaid flannel cassock") rather than allowing the poem to fall into two separate sections. The name of the poem? *Ritual*.

8. LIST POEMS

Inventories and lists are useful ways to brainstorm for a poem and good journal exercises. More than that, however, many successful poems are little more than well-selected lists ordered and phrased for maximum effect. Lists are forms of analysis and classification; as such, they can help us come to terms with large subjects or issues without resorting to abstract language or generality. In Shakespeare's *The Tempest,* Prospero threatens to punish Caliban with this list of traumas:

> For this, be sure, to-night thou shalt have cramps,
> Side-stitches that shall pen thy breath up; urchins
> Shall, for that vast of night that they may work,
> All exercise on thee; thou shalt be pinched
> As thick as honeycomb, each pinch more stinging
> Than bees that made'em.

Lists can be narrowly restricted: things in the pantry, in a bureau drawer, on a desk, in a supermarket, in a wallet or pocketbook. Many lists lead to poems that gain their strength not only from the selection, but from careful decisions about which arrangement of items is most telling. Often, successful poems are constructed out of lists that contain items at once literal and figurative, or that mix the two together. Examine Sue Standing's "A Woman Disappears Inside Her Own Life":

> There comes a time when she has to say goodbye
> to the cat, and stop watering the plants.
>
> She wants to be more than a curator
> of dissolving objects.
>
> The song her tongue keeps
> reaching for stays out of tune.
> The nautilus adds one chamber each moon,
> while she fills a room with rue.
> She leaves a clue
> inside the telephone book:
>
> underlines the names of friends
> who have already left town.
>
> She puts on all her necklaces—
> the clay beads from Peru,
>
> the feathers from New Mexico,
> the ostrich eggshells from Africa.
>
> She wears her lapis lazuli earrings
> and her aquamarine ring,
>
> the lightning bracelet
> and the tortoise shell combs.

She tries to fix one emotion
like a photograph of the room.

Someone has stolen her maps,
except one drawn in mauve

on thin parchment.
She will go there.

from *Deception Pass*

Walt Whitman, Allen Ginsberg, and Gerald Stern have created many fine poems using the list or inventory. Apply some of their techniques to a few list poems of your own. Don't always let logic rule in stringing items together; see where your imagination takes you. Put at least one of your poems in unrhymed, uneven couplets. Consider some of the following ideas: a basket full of gifts (wishes) for someone, an auction catalog for a hypochondriac's estate, items in a patrolman's memo pad, a time capsule for yourself to be opened twenty years from now, what Thomas Jefferson might bring back home if he visited a major city of today, a vegetable for each month of the year.

Anaphora is a device connected with formulas, rituals, and lists. It is the repetition of a word or words at the beginning of lines. Cornelius Eady takes it a bit further than usual, repeating whole lines and phrases. The effect is incantatory.

The Dance

When the world ends,
I will be in a red dress.
When the world ends,
I will be in a smoky bar
    on Friday night.
When the world ends,
I will be a thought-cloud.
When the world ends,
I will be steam in a tea kettle.
When the world ends,
I will be a sunbeam through
    a lead window,
And I will shake like the
    semis on the interstate,
And I will shake like the tree
    kissed by lightning,
And I will move; the earth will move
    too,
And I will move; the cities will move
    too,

And I will move; with the remains of
   my last paycheck in my pocket.
It will be Friday night
And I will be in a red dress,
My feet relieved of duty,
My body in free-fall,
Loose as a ballerina
   in zero gravity,
Equal at last with feathers
   and dust,
As the world faints and tumbles
   down the stairs,
The jukebox is overtaken at last,
And the cicadas, under the eaves,
   warm up their legs.

from *Victims of the Latest Dance Craze*

9. DRAMATIC POEMS/CHARACTER POEMS

In "The Dance," Eady is not the woman in the red dress. He has invented a character and spoken in her voice. This kind of poem, called a dramatic poem, comes in two major types. One is the **soliloquy**, in which a character speaks (or thinks out loud) to no one in particular. The other type, the **dramatic monologue,** imagines a full dramatic scene in which the occasion for the utterance is clear. In such poems, we can usually sense that a particular listener is intended, as in a play.

You are probably already familiar with works like Tennyson's "Ulysses" and Browning's "My Last Duchess." Eliot's "The Love Song of J. Alfred Prufrock" is a variation of that mode, an interior monologue in which Prufrock's character is revealed while the dramatic situation is subdued. Pretending to be someone else and speaking through that other person requires imaginative leaps and new considerations of language: just how would that character see the world, meditate, speak. Paul Zimmer has peopled book-length collections with a variety of fascinating characters. Here Eli speaks of Wanda, the central character of Zimmer's most engaging volume:

Eli and the Coal Strippers

At last I could not bear
The heavy memories of Wanda
And the farm. I sold out
To the bulldozers, let them
Slaughter woods, knock down

The old barn, topple great
Stones of the ancient people
And rip the top soil back
Till they had taken what
They wanted. They covered
It again as a dog would
With its turds.

Now I taste
The blood of the farm in
My water. When wind blows
Hard I smell the agony
Of the land rising like
My memory of Wanda at
The windows of this house,
Looking at fields in early
August, foretelling the end
Of all we had begun.

from *With Wanda:*
Town and Country Poems

Through how he presents his vision of experience, Eli tells us about himself. That is, Zimmer invents Eli and knows him well enough to let Eli do the talking. Perhaps it is easiest to begin working in this mode by transporting yourself into the mind of someone you know or into that of an historical character. Can you imagine Marilyn Monroe's last phone call? Suppose Bill Clinton had a chance to talk to George Washington; what would he say?

Employ the figure of speech called **personification** to give life—personalities and voices—to nonhuman entities. There is an old cliché about the tales walls could tell if they had ears. Why not *become* that wall? Find speech for an overturned motorcycle, a perfume bottle, a hairpin. (Leave out the identifying label, and you will have a riddle.) In the following poem, Karl Shapiro gives voice to a cut flower.

A Cut Flower

I stand on slenderness all fresh and fair,
I feel root-firmness in the earth far down,
I catch in the wind and loose my scent for bees
That sack my throat for kisses and suck love.
What is the wind that brings thy body over?
Wind, I am beautiful and sick. I long
For rain that strikes and bites like cold and hurts.
Be angry, rain, for dew is kind to me
When I am cool from sleep and take my bath.

Who softens the sweet earth about my feet,
Touches my face so often and brings water?
Where does she go, taller than any sunflower
Over the grass like birds? Has she a root?
These are great animals that kneel to us,
Sent by the sun perhaps to help us grow.
I have seen death. The colors went away,
The petals grasped at nothing and curled tight.
Then the whole head fell off and left the sky.

She tended me and held me by my stalk.
Yesterday I was well, and then the gleam,
The thing sharper than frost cut me in half.
I fainted and was lifted high. I feel
Waist-deep in rain. My face is dry and drawn.
My beauty leaks into the glass like rain.
When first I opened to the sun I thought
My colors would be parched. Where are my bees?
Must I die now? Is this a part of life?

From *Collected Poems*

Effective dramatic monologues are dramatic because they are little scenes, usually with a specific listener. Set your persona in a situation that will force revelations. What will the pot have to say to the kettle? What will a woman who has changed her mind say to the man she was about to marry? What will an election loser have to say to his or her loyal supporters?

10. EPISTOLARY POEMS

Epistolary poems, that is, poems written in the form of letters, can be voiced through invented characters or, as in the opening passage from the following poem by Richard Hugo, they can be modes of expression for very personal material.

Letter to Kathy from Wisdom

My dearest Kathy: When I heard your tears and those of your
mother over the phone from Moore, from the farm
I've never seen and see again and again under the most
uncaring of skies, I thought of this town I'm writing from,
where we came lovers years ago to fish. How odd
we seemed to them here, a lovely young girl and a fat
middle 40's man they mistook for father and daughter
before the sucker lights in their eyes flashed on. That was
when we kissed their petty scorn to dust. Now, I eat alone

> in the cafe we ate in then, thinking of your demons, the sad
> days you've seen, the hospitals, doctors, the agonizing
> breakdowns that left you ashamed. . . .
>
> from *Selected Poems*

Now, how about trying an epistolary poem that

- reviews your qualifications for an imaginary job.
- describes the highlights of a trip you are taking.
- asks forgiveness from someone you've betrayed, insulted, or somehow brought suffering to.
- admits that you might have been wrong about something.
- admits your fondness for chocolate, Mickey Mouse, old clothes, sentimental greeting cards, liver, gossip columns.

11. WORDPLAY POEMS

Wordplay poems are generated by the inspiration of words in themselves or through language experiments. The idea is to surprise yourself, expand your vocabulary, and discover the full denotative and connotative power of individual words and words in combination. (See Rod Jellema's poem on p. 68.)

a. Build a short list of consecutive entries in the dictionary. Study the meanings, including the etymologies, of each. Use all of the words in a poem, paying attention to both sound, sense, and intriguing nonsense. Here is a promising list if you need one: delight, delineate, deliquesce, delirium, deliver, dell, Delphic, delphinium, delta, delude, deluge, delve, demagogue, demand.

b. Make separate lists of nouns, adjectives, and verbs. For example, list nouns that have to do with furniture, verbs that have to do with sports, adjectives that have to do with taste. Now, shake well and see what happens when you crash them together.

12. SYNESTHETIC POEMS

Synesthesia is the mixing of senses, or the describing of one sense in terms of another. It is a natural phenomenon of thought and language to experience one sense in terms of another. For example, a friend's tie can be called *loud,* a musical performance can be *hot,* a smile can be *sweet.* May Swenson uses this technique in "The Blindman."

The blindman placed
a tulip on his tongue for purple's taste.
Cheek to grass, his green

was rough excitement's sheen
of little whips.
In water to his lips

he named the sea blue and white,
the basin of his tears and fallen beads of sight.
He said: This scarf is red;

I feel the vectors to its thread
that dance down from the sun. I know
the seven fragrances of the rainbow.

I have caressed
the orange hair of flames. Pressed
to my ear,

a pomegranate lets me hear
crimson's flute.
Trumpets tell me yellow. Only ebony is mute.

from *New & Selected.: Things Taking Place*

Swenson uses synesthesia to paint with hearing, taste, touch, smell. Write a poem in which you describe the tastes of music, the feel of colors, the sound of fragrances, or the smell of touch (or some combination of these blendings). Refer to "Jazz Sundae" on page 142. Which senses are being mixed there?

13. PICTURE POEMS

Use a painting, sculpture, or photograph that you admire as the inspiration for a poem. Try to capture in language the energy, technique, and vision of life that the artwork has to offer. Here is a famous poem of this type by William Carlos Williams. What relationships can you discover between the way poetry works and the way the visual arts work? How about poetry and music?

The Dance

In Breughel's great picture, The Kermess,
the dancers go round, they go round and
around, the squeal and the blare and the
tweedle of bagpipes, a bugle and fiddles
tipping their bellies (round as the thick-
sided glasses whose wash they impound)

their hips and their bellies off balance
to turn them. Kicking and rolling about
the Fair Grounds, swinging their butts, those
shanks must be sound to bear up under such
rollicking measures, prance as they dance
in Breughel's great picture, The Kermess.

from *Collected Later Poems*

14. MUSIC POEMS

Choose a piece of instrumental music that has affected you deeply. Play it over a number of times, paying special attention to its rhythms and emotional colorings. Now try to render those same rhythms and emotions in a poem. Don't write *about* the piece of music, "translate" it into poetry.

15. FOUND POEMS

When nothing else works, pushing someone else's language around can be fun. It can be revealing too. Here are some things to do:

a. Look for ready-made poetry in your everyday reading (such as the *Beaufort Scale* reproduced in Chapter 5). Bulletin boards are good places to look. After you have selected a few of these found poems and copied them into your journal, take some notes on what qualities of expression make them seem poetic. Some possibilities: advertising copy, operating manuals for various products, weekly school lunch menus in local newspapers, announcements for auctions, correction notices (apologies) for errors in the daily paper. Pay special attention to material that is highly patterned. The language of bridge and astrology columns is, in some ways, remarkably poetic. Share your discoveries in class.

b. Cut and paste! Take a column from a newspaper or magazine and cut it in half or in thirds lengthwise. Now rearrange the strips of type and look for vivid passages. Slide the strips up and down until effective word combinations appear. Now use them. Line up half-columns from different articles or news stories and see what happens.

c. Sculpt! photocopy a solid page of print from a book, newspaper, or magazine. Now, working with masking tape or correction fluid (white-out), cover over (discard) the least interesting stretches of language, letting the more evocative words and phrases reveal themselves. Can you get a poem to emerge by chiseling away the unnecessary words?

d. X-ray! If sculpting is too messy for you, use a yellow highlighting marker to display the words and phrases you find most striking. Now try linking together what you have found into a poem.

These exercises, along with the ones presented in Chapter 6, should give you some feeling for the wide range of techniques, tools, and approaches to writing poetry. However, unless you have been especially fortunate, you are not yet likely to have produced anything of major consequence. Beginners have to begin. It is now time to write from your own need, your own imagination, and your own sense of what will be significant for yourself and for your readers.

Warning: don't let the shape of the illustrative poems we have provided or the expected shape of finished drafts inhibit the process by which you explore. Poems can grow in many ways, not necessarily from beginning to end. If you work with a word processor, try the following.

EXERCISE

1. Enter a tentative concluding line for a poem so that it appears at the top of the screen. Now compose a line that will precede the line already written, entering it above the line written first so that that line is pushed down. Add lines in this fashion until the first line you wrote has reached the bottom of the screen.

2. Write a line to get started and then compose by alternating additions both above and below the original line.

In the next chapter we will review some of the problems you are likely to encounter on your way to mastering this demanding genre.

The Poem Queen
SUSAN ASTOR

The Poem Queen writes a poem a day,
In her spare time pauses to pray
It will be read.

She has a soldier and a drone
To please her when she is alone
Or in her bed.

Some say hers is a magic throne
That she eats custard made of bone
And blossom bread.

She has more power than they know,
Has found a way to burn the snow;
Turns gold to lead.

Her pen is her divining rod;
She uses it to handle God,
And tame the dead.

from *Dame*

August from My Desk

ROLAND FLINT

It is hot today, dry enough for cutting grain,
And I am drifting back to North Dakota
Where butterflies are all gone brown with wheat dust.

And where some boy,
Red-faced, sweating, chafed,
Too young to be dying this way,
Steers a laborious, self-propelled combine,
Dreaming of cities, and blizzards—
And airplanes.

With the white silk scarf of his sleeve
He shines and shines his goggles,
He checks his meters, checks his flaps,
Screams contact at his dreamless father,
He pulls back the stick,
Engines roaring,

And hurtles into the sun.

from *Resuming Green*

8

Poetry Problems

As we have said before and will say again, all good writing is finally the result of editing and revising. Rarely do we put down in first draft what will be a finished work. This is certainly true in poetry. Even poems that we want to believe are ready to go soon after we have drafted them usually benefit from second thoughts. We need to look at the poem again, honestly, and with a rigorous editorial eye. Often, having solved the technical problems in a poem, we are ready to congratulate ourselves prematurely. Here are some common problems in the poems of beginning writers (and some experienced ones, too).

ARCHAIC DICTION

Some of the more obvious archaic words and phrases in the following poem have been set in italics. The problem with language that is so remote from common usage is that it sounds insincere. Paradoxically, the writer probably chose it because it sounded "poetic"; nonetheless, it is hard to take these formulations seriously. Though this student's technical skill is apparent, that skill is being undermined by bad habits of diction.

The Thief

The warm, the fevered pillows pushed aside,
I lay *amidst* the ever-present Night
While his sweet handmaid, his euphoric bride
Beamed through glazed panels with a *pallid* light.
Mid hoary trees her shadows could be seen
In contrast to that phosphorescent sheen.
I sighed, unshackled from my *torpid shrouds,*
And sleep's last fetters from the covers fell
Away. As I peered out, a sable cloud
Swirled *round* the *orb*—as if its soul to quell.
Who else but Luna would steal *o'er* my sill
While I, bedazzled, could no more lay still?

Diction like this is often accompanied by the old-fashioned poetic contractions—"o'er," in this case—and by a tendency to disguise experience rather than reveal it. "Glazed panels" are only windows: why not say so? Writing like this tends to become formulaic; it expresses kinds of actions or emotions rather than particular ones.

Can you find other diction problems in this poem? What revisions (substitutions) do you suggest? Can any of the poem be salvaged, or should the poet begin again? Do you spot any problems in word order? Can you solve them?

THE ANONYMOUS VOICE

Characteristic of much greeting card verse—and of much unsuccessful poetry—is the anonymous voice. The following poem by James J. Dorbin is an example of the kind of writing that sounds like it could be by almost anyone and is therefore unconvincing. Along with problems in mastering the stanza form, this poem suffers from the hackneyed figures of speech, the absence of particulars, the yearning after vastness, and the overt **sentimentality** that add up to a typical beginner's effort.

Dreams

In a world of fantasy
dreams, like nets, were thrown
from a vessel hopelessly
adrift and all alone.

To cast a net and catch a dream
is no simple task.

JARRING DICTION

The result of not paying enough attention to connotation and to words in context can be diction that is jarring. The next poem, cast in free verse, mixes diction in unattractive ways.

Land Lord Dharma

I kneel
head erect
shoulders straight
hands on thighs
the warrior's posture

he enters
in long white silk robes
he looks so elegant—
from the warrior's shrine
he hands me implements
for my new quarters

first a flashing sword
with a slightly curved tip
to cut neurosis
and allow gentleness

then comes the black pen
with a rolled white scroll
tied with a ribbon . . .

The words "implements" and "neurosis" are in conflict with the poem's general diction. Additionally, "quarters" may be a questionable choice. The gains are obvious when we substitute "blessings" for "implements" and "masks" for "neurosis." Now "cut" seems off, if it wasn't clearly so before. What would be a better verb here? What substitute can you find for "quarters"?

FOR THE SAKE OF RHYME

Solving the puzzle of an intricate rhyme scheme is so exhilarating that you can become lost in a single dimension of a poem. The poet who wrote "Departure" conjured up the "braided ballad" form that rhymes *abcb/cede/dfgf* and so forth.

Departure

The smell of guava blossoms
appears to fill the air

> and in the wind are waving
> the palm leaves . . . and your hair.
>
> I sit on the porch, craving   5
> those kisses that you give
> and think that these are times
> in which it's good to live.
>
> But in the end our crimes
> seem to catch up with us,   10
> and I must take a trip
> with a distant terminus.
>
> I board the hated ship
> as you wave from the sand
> and dream I cup your bosom   15
> and feel it on my hand.

Among the problems lurking in this draft are the following:

1. Line 2 lacks poetic density; that is, the only function of most of the language is to get in enough syllables ahead of the rhyme word.
2. Unnatural (unidiomatic) word order undermines lines 7 and 8. More natural alternatives would be "and think that these are good times to live in" or "and think that it's good to live in these times." The poet has solved the problem of rhyme, but created a new one.
3. Inappropriate diction. The use of "terminus" in line 12 creates a clever rhyme but ruptures the poem's simple diction and earnest tone. It seems far-fetched, and it is.

There are a few other instances of these and related problems in the poem. Can you find them? What kinds of revision would you suggest? Should the poet stay with this demanding form, or should he abandon it?

Rose MacMurray's poem that follows is a more successful handling of the same form. Compare the two efforts (trimeter quatrains) before attempting your own.

Teen Mall-Rats Die
in Suicide Pact

> After the Mall closed down
> they came and built a nest.
> Monoxide was a high
> and they could charge the rest.
>
> No sweat to say goodbye,
> monoxide was a gas.

The mall rats, curled in death,
have solved their maze at last.

We lay a discount wreath.
May their eternity
be one long shopping mall,
one Gold Card spending spree

and may their parents all
sign up for every course
in "Interfacing Grief"
and "Creative Remorse."

THE CLASH OF POETIC ELEMENTS

This is a broad category, covering scores of discordant permutations of image, mood, sense, rhythm, sound, and other poetic ingredients. In the following example, the picture being painted and the meter used to reveal it are at odds with one another:

They glide like spirits by the water
Open to the tepid twilight
Bearing alabaster candles:
Rush-like figures clad in white.
Thin and spectral, like the Shee-folk
With their dripping, glowing wands . . .

This poet, who has such marvelous control over sound, meter, and language, does not coordinate the elements especially well. Whatever can "glide like spirits" will not move in this insistent, choppy rhythm. The pushy trochaic beat conflicts with anyone's notion of ethereality. A simple lengthening of the lines would help, but getting rid of those initial stressed syllables is mandatory. Things can't glide and march at the same time.

WRITING PAST THE POEM

Sometimes poets are unable to throw away what they have put down on paper. They are more willing to revise than to delete. In Karen Malloy's "Bagged Air," the poet's inventiveness goes beyond the poem's need:

The signs say no balloons.

You are just another visitor,
Hunted, fearful of the telltale coughs,
the dripping of mysterious liquids suspended

in bags,
and harried eyes
of people in white.
Frailty, mortality, futility,
the cheap pictures on the wall say it,
so do the eyes from the beds,
watching you pass.
You walk on, holding roses for a shield
against these exposed truths.
Brown has begun to claim the healthy pink domain
of a petal.

Among carefree balloons, even the best
leak gaseous blood,
and submit
to the most basic laws of nature,
pulling them earthward.
That admonishing sign is humane—
stopping those who would give a doomed
bag of air
as a gift of cheer
here.

How can the last stanza be pruned? What is essential to conclude the poem?
Most of the poem *shows,* whereas the last stanza is dominated by *telling.* Can
the "message" of the conclusion be derived from a minor revision of the main
part of the poem, eliminating the need for the last stanza?

TREASURE BURYING

Burying treasure in an otherwise unsuccessful poem is the unfortunate practice
of overwriters. In the following piece, Alice S. James employs predictable
rhymes and overuses repetition. Moreover, she breaks the logic of her own figurative expressions. Still, one extremely vivid and evocative stanza sings out.
We have set it in italics.

Desert Rain Poem

I am the desert
Dry and desolate
Shimmering in the sun
You were rain
And I watched the rain
Coming down
Against my sun-drenched pain

I am the African steppe
Dying into desert
The wind tosses over me
A blanket of sand

Shrouding once verdant trees,
Big dry holes—once lakes
Maybe small seas
Into oblivion

Some fountain of sorrow
Fountain of life
An ancient aching love
Brings on the spring rain
Just to pass my way again

Only searing sun-drenched
Pain, reigns
Raining down on me

I am the desert at night
Cold dark sand
Blows against my stark
Countenance
When I love, I rain
My rains to come
As long as the love
Keeps coming
So will the rains

Our suggestion to this writer is to start over again, rebuilding the poem from the third stanza, which could be an effective beginning. Three additional four-line stanzas, if they are equally compact and focused, should do to complete the idea of the earlier draft.

SAYING TOO MUCH

Even sophisticated writers can overwrite by saying too much. The following draft is slightly heavy-handed, though it is clearly the work of a careful and skillful writer.

January Thunder

As the heavy presence nears
bare branches falter and twist.
At the first crash of the axe

pines flail and lash,
stoop to the snow.

At the iron boom of the hammer
gusts of summer flare at the window,
ice pellets surge up.
Snow flooded by lightning,
blazes white beyond white.

In a workshop session the author agreed that the poem would be strengthened by the elimination of "heavy" and "blazes." Why do you think the poet agreed? Do you see other possibilities for paring back so that less does more?

THE FALSE START

It should be obvious to a practiced writer that we often find our subject and warm up our language engines only after we have been writing for a while. In composition classes, students are warned about introductions that no longer work when the act of writing has taken the writer in unexpected directions. This happens in poems too.

Here is an early draft of a poem by Elizabeth Bennett.

A Small Explosion

Is it a coincidence
This forty years later
soft knock at the door?
the young girl, Makiko
with her father, Yasuo
their car broken down.
I pronounce her name wrong.
Her father explains
it means little jewel.

She looks at me
little jewel, eyes clear
as a freshwater pool
where fish still swim, hair
paint brush straight.
In the kitchen
she takes off her coat
Her T shirt says
Washington A Capitol City.

While her father phones
she plays with my infant son's
Steiff bear, fondles

its stiff fur.
When the baby cries
she makes a face
She pulls her long arms
inside her shirt.
See, I have no arms
she says to make him laugh.

This was not a first draft, nor is it the final one. In the published version, a number of changes have been made. Notice how the poem gets off to a quicker start by beginning with what had been the third line. Locate and discuss the other changes.

Small Explosion
August 6th, 1985

A knock at the door,
the young girl, Makiko
with her father, Yasuo
their car broken down.
I pronounce her name wrong.
Her father explains
it means little jewel.

She looks at me,
　　　　　　little jewel,
eyes clear as a freshwater pool
where fish still swim,
hair paint brush straight.
Her T shirt says,
　　　　　　Washington A Capitol City

While her father phones
she plays with my infant son's Steiff bear,
fondles its stiff fur.
When he cries she makes a face,
pulls her arms inside her shirt,
See I have no arms, she says
to make him laugh.

It is forty years later.

from *Poet Lore*, Fall 1986

PUNCH-LINE ENDINGS

Although they can be successful, too often punch-line endings reach for too much or too little. Poets can be tempted to rescue weak or trivial poems by clever resolutions. The next poem leans too heavily on its pressured close, a close that isn't strong enough to take the weight.

Lifeguards

Gopher holes blemished our back-
yard like acne
when the swimming hole
was dry
and it was too hot for kickball
Henry and I
took the hose
and filled them up
to the brim
We waited for gophers
to surface gasping
Patient hours
we sat on our shadows
but never saw
one

Back then
we didn't know
of escape tunnels.

The idea of bringing in a new perspective that answers a question is a good one, but the execution falls flat. The shift seems too self-conscious, and, once again, the decision to "tell" rather than "show" is part of the problem.

INEFFECTIVE LINE BREAK

It is often hard to detect an unsatisfactory line break without the frequent testing of alternatives. It is easy to cure such diseases as ending on function words (articles, prepositions, conjunctions) for no good reason, calling too much attention to words whose only job is to link more important words together. Most often, line-break problems result in obscuring key images and relationships between images and ideas. Examine the following passage:

I hold a desperate starfish before I toss him back
matched with my hand, our common five-shape
a reminder of where we begin.

Here the writer wants us to observe the relationship between the human hand and the starfish, but both words are lost in the middle of lines. One solution would be to reconstruct these lines:

> Before I toss him back, I hold a desperate starfish,
> our common five-shape, matched with my hand—
> a reminder of where we begin.

There is some strategic improvement in placing the "before" clause in front of the rest. However, "our common five-shape" now has less emphasis, and its proper place in the movement from specific to general has been lost. Stronger yet is this shaping:

> Before I toss him back,
> I hold a desperate starfish,
> matched with my hand—
> this, our common five-shape,
> reminder of where we begin.

The language still needs some smoothing, but at least the key words/images—"starfish," "hand," and "five-shape"—are properly emphasized and clearly related to one another. Line break has controlled the emerging picture and idea.

OUT OF ORDER

Lines or sections that are not in the proper order can cause a poem to lack cohesiveness and focus. Linda Replogle's untitled poem is fairly effective as it stands, but it could be argued that the transposition of stanzas 2 and 3 would make an even stronger poem.

> The old man sits
> at the white kitchen table,
> his eyes big
> behind thick glasses.
>
> Behind him, his wife
> in a large apron
> fries fish
> at the kitchen stove.
>
> He looks out, away,
> into the garden.
> Rain separates him
> from the green hydrangea.
>
> He puts the magnifying glass
> down on the newspaper
> and lifts the cup

> hot from tea
> with his fragile hands.

What are the losses and gains in the suggested rearrangement? What other arrangements are possible?

DERIVATIVE DRIVEL

Many beginning poets get lost in the worst habits of a poet whom they consciously or unconsciously imitate. Usually they capture only the most obvious surface features of a style or technique. The resulting poems are simply clumsy posturings: piles of mannerisms. Of course, the worse the model, the worse the imitation is likely to be. Here is an example of a poet striving for poetic density. The cop-out is at the end.

> Red rock in the brain
> and the proud darkness settles like a sifted house
> deep in the synapse of ultimate mind.
> Do you know what I mean?

And here is imitation beat generation sprawl:

> I wandered in the big, empty, people-filled city
> an ant in Miami Beach where I saw
> dopers, fat landladies, displaced californians, cops
> in Porsches right out of tv . . . and scrawled walls of
> sneering, scarred, fearing, raging . . .
> pimps and smarmy politicians, supermarket grandmas,
> and I wanted to kick and smash and trash them all!

These are only a sampling of the many problems both beginners and experienced poets encounter. We could fill a book with additional instances such as predictable rhyme, lack of unity caused by two poems being pressed into one, and stumbling rhythms. While writing poetry requires more than technical skill, without that skill no amount of vision or largeness of soul will be turned into a living poem.

We began this unit on poetry by talking about the line—the most obvious signal that we may be in the presence of a poem. It should be clear by now, however, that the mere ragged right-hand margin does not a poem make. To borrow the prestige of poetry by presenting pedantry, political argument, exhortation, or preaching in "poetic" lines—without *attending to craft* in the ways we have explored—is more likely to fool you than your reader.

> We have to shed ourselves of these snake
> politicians who crawl around each year
> and cover up all graft they take . . .
> Impeach those who dip into and make
> our pockets empty and dishonor this greatest land of all
> where men and women should stand tall!

The less said about this stuff the better.

REVISION: A BRIEF CASE STUDY

By examining the material presented here, you will be able to follow the development of a short poem from its initial draft to its final form. Because this poem was short, and because the poet had worked with related material for a long time, the journey from inception to completion was relatively brief. Here is the first draft, actually eight lines of notes toward a poem that had the good luck of getting off on the right foot.

> (1) His hands are fish that dart
> toward the center of ripples
> at the surface of his name,
> his neck a knotted trunk
> that shoots from a mulch of collar.
> Pull on the tie
> and his eyes will dance
> like paired skaters

To the right of the typescript, the poet later wrote some additional material:

> His heart is pumping coffee,
> he is counting out bus fare
> in ~~the dark~~ his pocket's dark.
> He hears the garbage truck's approach
> He is late with everything
> He is going to work

The next draft works at consolidating this material:

> (2) His hands are fish that dart
> to the center of ripples
> at the surface of his name,
> his heart is pumping coffee,   /arteries surge with
> his neck/a knotted trunk   /is
> that shoots from a mulch of collar.

> He hears the garbage truck's approach,
> he counts out busfare in his pocket's dark,
> he pulls on his tie
> and his eyes dance like paired skaters
> gliding through red creases of ~~light~~ dawn.
> Today, he is going to be on time.

While the consolidation was in process, additional changes were introduced, the most important being the alternative phrasing for line 4. This, and the earlier revision of "in the dark" to "in his pocket's dark," are the most significant so far. The next run through the typewriter produced this:

> (3)   His hands are fish that dart
> to the center of ripples
> at the surface of his name;
> his neck is a knotted trunk
> that shoots from a mulch of collar;
> his arteries surge with coffee.
> He hears the garbage truck's ~~approach~~ moan.
> and counts out busfare in his pocket's dark.
> He pulls on his tie
> and his eyes dance like paired skaters
> gliding through red creases of dawn.
> Today, he is going to be on time.

Notice that the revised fourth line of draft 2 has been moved down, anchoring a series of clauses that now move more logically through this segment of the morning. Moreover, by making each clause a line shorter than the one before it, the writer has echoed the focusing of awareness that is conveyed in the series of images: the disoriented initial coming awake, the body stiffness as he finished getting dressed, the boost of the caffeine. All along the way, the poem's rhythms have been improved.

In the next draft, the poem receives its title:

Meeting the Day

> (4)   His hands are fish that dart
> to the center of ripples
> at the surface of his name;
> his neck is a knotted trunk
> that shoots from a mulch of collar;
> his arteries surge with coffee.
> He moves to the garbage truck's moan
> and counts out busfare in his pocket's dark.
> Today, he is going to be on time.

> He pulls on his tie
> and his eyes veer like paired skaters
> ~~gliding through~~ that dance through
> the red creases of dawn.

Notable here is the decision to shift what had been the concluding line in previous versions, letting that intention—to be on time—serve as a bridge between the man's preliminary struggles and his final action of adjusting his tie—a sign of determination—and the visionary resolving image.

Looking back to the poet's initial jottings, we can see that his first idea was to present the man as a kind of marionette whose eyes would move if someone pulled on his tie. This possibility has not entirely disappeared from the succeeding versions, though it is no longer the main thrust of the image. The poet is still struggling with the complex "eyes . . . skaters . . . creases" business. In the final (published) version, the conclusion is less cluttered: the simile formula is dropped and one action verb controls the passage. Additionally, the close is visually reinforced by the lengthening lines.

Meeting the Day

> His hands are fish that dart
> to the center of ripples
> at the surface of his name;
> his neck is a knotted trunk
> that shoots from a mulch of collar;
> his arteries surge with coffee.
> He moves to the garbage truck's moan
> and counts out busfare in his pocket's dark.
> Today, he is going to be on time.
> He pulls on his tie
> and his eyes become paired skaters
> that veer through the red creases of dawn.

from Philip K. Jason's Near the Fire

9

The Elements of Fiction

THE NATURE OF FICTION

Like all narrative, prose fiction contains the *history* of one or more characters or something that acts like a character (a talking dog, yellow Rolls-Royce, or computer). The writer shapes that *history* with the same tools one would use in literal **history**—except that "people" become *characters*, "talk" becomes dialogue, "reporting" becomes *narration*, and "places" become *settings*. The stories contain descriptions of where and how the characters live, what they do, and what they say, believe, or think:

> There was once upon a time a Fisherman who lived with his wife in a miserable hovel close by the sea, and every day he went out fishing. And once as he was sitting with his rod, looking at the clear water, his line suddenly went down, far down below and when he drew it up again, he brought out a large Flounder. Then the Flounder said to him, "Hark, you Fisherman, I pray you, let me live, I am no Flounder really, but an enchanted prince. What good will it do you to kill me? I should not be good to eat, put me in the water again, and let me go."
>
> "Come," said the Fisherman, "there is no need for so many words about it—a fish that can talk I should certainly let go, anyhow." With

that he put him back again into the clear water. . . . Then the Fisherman got up and went to his wife in the hovel.

"Husband," said the woman, "have you caught nothing today?"

"No," said the man, "I did catch a Flounder, who said he was an enchanted prince, so I let him go again."

"Did you not wish for anything first?" said the woman.

"No," said the man, "what should I wish for?"

"Ah," said the woman, "it is surely hard to have to live always in this dirty hovel; you might have wished for a small cottage for us. Go back and call him. Tell him we want to have a small cottage, he will certainly give us that."

Jakob and Wilhelm Grimm, "The Fisherman and His Wife"

Notice that the Grimms's story has the following elements:

+ *time*—a "once upon a time" that is vague but efficient
+ *setting*—hovel by the sea (a place related to the action) in a fairyland with real poverty
+ *characters*—fisherman, wife, and Flounder-prince
+ *reported actions*—catching Flounder and throwing prince back
+ *dialogue*—which reveals the Fisherman's easily satisfied nature and the wife's materialism

Even Charles Dickens's *Great Expectations,* Virginia Woolf's *To the Lighthouse,* and J. D. Salinger's *Catcher in the Rye* are made up of these elements. Whether you wish to write traditionally or experimentally, there is no way around gaining a mastery of them.

Of course, the story of your character in fiction will be different from a literal biography. One of the major differences is that in fiction it is legitimate to choose the events and make them come out as you like. In your story, fish can be turned into princes who make wishes come true. To put the matter another way, in fiction you can travel anywhere you want so long as you can convince your reader to take the trip with you.

Your story may grow from actual or imagined experience(s), character(s), image(s), or concept(s). No matter what generates your story line, you will have to create a **plot line** to carry it. As you can guess, we are not using "story" and "plot" interchangeably as we do in everyday speech. Here "story" is the name we give to imagined lives presented chronologically—an imitation of how we present events in a chronicle biography or history. Story, in that sense, is A to Z. "Plot," on the other hand, is the name for the shape we give to the story materials by selection, arrangement, and emphasis. **Plot** involves (1) *what* of the story is told and shown, and (2) *when* each unit of showing and telling is presented to the reader.

In this chapter we present an overview of the elements of fiction, stopping for short examples and a number of exercises along the way. Some of the discussion refers to the six stories in Chapter 11. You might want to read them before going on and then again as they are brought into discussion. Between the overview and the stories is a chapter on student problems in fiction.

PLOT AND WHAT IT DOES

Though the writing process itself can begin anywhere, we are beginning the discussion of fiction with plot because plot is the vehicle that carries all the other elements. Like a sentence and love, you should know a plot when you see one—though you may be deceived.

Here are several dictionary definitions for "plot":

1. a secret plan or scheme
2. the plan, scheme, or main story of a play, novel, poem, or short story
3. in *artillery,* a point or points located on a map or chart
4. in *navigation,* to mark on a plan, map, or chart, as the course of a ship or aircraft

Beginning writers often take the first definition as the significant one and so think their task as writers is to hide what is going on from the reader until they spring their surprise. The second definition, while accurate, is about as useful as saying that your plot should have a beginning, middle, and end. A rope needs the same thing. (The real problem for a writer is *how* to make particular beginnings, middles, and ends.)

Strangely enough the third definition is a bit more to the point; in a way, the plot is the direction in which you have aimed the reader. The fourth definition is the most appropriate of all for writers. Sailors plot a course to get from here to there as safely and efficiently as possible considering their purposes and what is in the way. What the plot does is to organize the voyage.

For your reader, the plot may appear to be the equivalent of the story, the sum of all the events that "happen." Even a writer might try to report the chronological story line if asked "what is it all about?"

> "It's the story of this man and woman who are caught in a cave-in. She doesn't like him and, at first, they fight all the time. Then, when they think they are going to die, they fall in love. Then they feel this breeze and then start to—"

The potential reader breaks in:

"Wait a minute. How did they get into the cave in the first place? Why doesn't she like him? How come they didn't feel the breeze right off?"

And when the answers to these questions cause more questions, the writer most likely will say, "Look. You'd better read it." The reason the writer can't satisfactorily tell you the plot by giving the chronological events is the same reason a chocolate chip cookie can't be experienced by having you taste butter, chips, flour, sugar, and vanilla. Because the story is mixed and baked in the plot, it is an error to think that a mere sequence of events is what the work is about.

This common error is understandable, however, because the actions the characters perform are usually the most visible element in the plot. Indeed, through these actions the reader sees what the writer has prepared: (1) a conflict or conflicts with complications, (2) a crisis or crises, and (3) a resolution—all contained within a series of actions the characters perform. For some readers, the plot is the writer's plan for keeping the characters in danger in order to keep the reader interested. And, for some readers, the only worthwhile plot is the type that keeps them at the edge of their seats or up past midnight waiting *for what comes next.*

These types of plots are not easy to make, and those who, like Stephen King or Ross Thomas, can hold our attention with their plots and satisfy our need to be on tenterhooks deserve our gratitude. They haven't written *Sons and Lovers* or *The Color Purple,* but they have entertained us. On the other end of the spectrum, some plots may be made up of subtler actions, not so "dramatic" in nature. Such plots satisfy us less by presenting a series of slambang actions that bring the characters to success or failure and more by expanding our understanding of human circumstances (see Joyce's "The Boarding House").

Both types of plots share with all plots the same purpose: to put the characters in motion so the reader can follow them to a satisfactory—that is, convincing—end. They provide a line to follow, they explain how and why what is happening is happening, and they involve us with the fate of the characters because the elements that make up the plot connect the character to our world (or wished for world) in a logical way. By "a logical way" we mean "*a process* to which our minds may give assent without believing." *This process need not be revealed chronologically.*

Experienced as well as inexperienced writers may confuse a situation (a premise, image, idea) with a plot, though the experienced writer will soon realize that something is wrong. The following list, for example, contains the root situations for six specific American works. These obviously could be the root situations for a million other works.

1. A young boy runs away from his cruel father.
2. A woman commits adultery in a rigidly puritanical society.
3. A family driven from its land seeks work and dignity in a foreign place.
4. In order to help his family, an old man commits suicide.
5. A young man loses the woman he loves.
6. A young black man comes North.

At this point, the preceding situations share one feature—each is a frozen statement of the character's circumstances. In a plot, however, the situation is in motion.

The situations just listed may be thought of as images or pictures about which the story has yet to be told. Indeed, writers often begin with even less in mind:

1. The seventeen-year locusts come out.
2. Going to Wicoma Lake.
3. What if a man always told the truth?
4. An intelligent computer that wants to be fed graphics of food.
5. The last living veteran from World War I.
6. The last living veteran from World War IV.
7. The bag lady who has a Ph.D. in nutrition.
8. Aunt Susan who disappeared and no one talks about her.

These notebook jottings, the kind of pictures or ideas always popping into our minds, are the stuff from which we might build anything—poems, fiction, essays, or plays.

Here we should point out that writers work out plots in many ways. Some find out what will happen by writing along until the direction reveals itself, almost magically. Then they go back and make it all match up. Some construct elaborate outlines of each scene and transition and will not begin writing until they know every part of their story. Some start with characters and invent situations and plots for them to act in. Some start with plots and invent characters. Some start with abstract ideas and invent everything else to express those ideas. The starting places, if not infinite, are various, and you will find a way to work that is most congenial and productive for you. It is a sign of inexperience to ask a writer or a workshop leader: What is *the* way to go about developing a plot?

Wherever you start, you have to construct incidents—opportunities for your characters to be in psychological and physical conflict or motion. Keep in mind, however, that though a plot is made up of incidents, a mere series of incidents do not a plot make. Here is an example of a plot a student outlined:

A. Kane never liked school much and one day had a major fight with Mr. Sonwil, his English teacher.

B. Another time, Kane and Leon, his brother, are wrestling, when Kane kills Leon.

C. Kane moves to NYC where he gets a job washing windows on the Empire State Building.

D. He meets a young woman who is free with her favors.

E. Kane decides to go to night school.

F. The woman goes to Africa with a wealthy man and there she kills a tiger.

G. Kane goes back to the family farm.

H. One day, while plowing, he unearths a treasure.

I. The next day a bee stings him and he dies.

Each of these is certainly an incident. One can even imagine building from this outline a series of scenes in which actions occur (think of the opportunities for action in event C). However, we would be hard put to find any *connections* that make event A flow into event B and B into C with event C also connecting to event A . . . and so on until they are all woven together. You might argue, of course, that if one eliminates item F, the events are connected because they happen to one character. Or, they are connected because they happen after each other to the same character. Or, that if all the events happen in New York to one character, and one event follows the other, everything will be connected. Such connections in time, place, and character can be virtues, but they do not create a sense that the events have a necessary and logical relationship, a syntax, that allows us to understand the events individually and as a whole.

EXERCISE

1. Take the incidents previously listed and try to find a syntactical relationship between them—some reason that Kane goes to New York and takes such a dangerous job, a reason to go home, a reason to find a treasure, a reason to die. Feel free to drop items out, change them around, and bring items in. Don't expect to end up with anything useful. It is the process of finding the connections and adjusting the events that is important for developing a plot from Kane's biography. Is there anything you can do with the name Kane? Is it necessary to begin telling the story with Kane's school days?

2. Once you have selected the key events, determined their relative importance (show or tell), and their connections, rethink the strategy of your plot line. Will simple chronology suffice? *When does the reader need to know* that Kane killed his brother? This is a different question than "when did it happen?" Reconstruct your plot as a sequence of revelations to the reader.

3. Create a list of incidents that might surround the following poem:

> *Written in Pencil*
> *in the Sealed*
> *Railway Car*
>
> Here in this carload
> I am eve
> with abel my son
> if you see my other son
> cane son of man
> tell him i
>
> Dan Pagis, *Variable*
> *Directions*

In a sense, writers have to construct plots as they might sentences. All the nouns, verbs, adjectives, adverbs, articles, and conjunctions must be in their proper grammatical form and place to produce the effect of a sentence. You don't have a plot until all the parts produce an understanding of what each part is doing in the work. Just as a vase is not the space it contains, so a plot is not the simple addition of events; the plot *contains* events.

SETTING

We generally use the word "setting" in two senses. One sense has to do with the particular "somewhere" in which the characters function for a single scene—the kitchen, the palace, the street. That kind of "where" has to do with **scene**, and we discuss it later. In its second sense, **setting** refers to more than a specific space. It refers to the total environment for your story, with all of its cultural shadings as well as its physical landmarks and characteristics—medieval Burgundy, turn-of-the-century Sacramento, a boarding house inhabited by men at the edge of society in Dublin, contemporary cubistic Houston. These settings are not and should not be flat backdrops in front of which the action happens.

An effective setting is intimately related to the plot because what happens to the characters could happen *in the way it happens* only in that particular setting. Goyen's "Rhody's Path" cannot be divorced from its setting in rural Texas—the food, the way people talk, the pasture and porch, the values—and still have the same kind of impact and make the same kind of sense. The very existence of the family's New England summer place in Leavitt's "The Lost Cottage" is significant because it brings the family together for one last time and, through its peculiarities (its decrepitude), we see the characters interact.

The characters in both stories know that they are somewhere; therefore, the reader is more inclined to believe in and respond to their lives.

The physical place the writer directly invokes in a particular scene is surrounded by a larger environment that the writer may directly or indirectly suggest. In stories such as Joyce's "The Boarding House" and Rushdie's "Good Advice Is Rarer Than Rubies," the particular settings include more than material culture. Early twentieth-century Dublin and late twentieth-century New Delhi are not only churches and embassies, they are societies and all that societies mean. Such environments are as instrumental to what happens as any individual character.

Chapter 5, "Invention and Research," provides many suggestions for working toward a control over setting. The following excerpts show how various writers communicate a sense of place.

> It was a tiny town, worse than a village, inhabited chiefly by old people who so seldom died that it was really vexatious. Very few coffins were needed for the hospital and the jail; in a word, business was bad. If Yakov Ivanov had been a maker of coffins in the county town, he would probably have owned a house of his own by now, and would have been called Mr. Ivanov, but here in this little place he was simply called Yakov, and for some reason his nickname was Bronze. He lived as poorly as any common peasant in a little old hut of one room, in which he and Martha, and the stove, and a double bed, and the coffins and his joiner's bench, and all the necessities of housekeeping were stowed away.
>
> from Anton Chekhov, "Rothschild's Fiddle"

> It was a bad time. Billy Boy Watkins was dead, and so was Frenchie Tucker. Billy Boy had died of fright, scared to death on the field of battle, and Frenchie Tucker had been shot through the nose. Bernie Lynn and Lieutenant Sidney Martin had died in tunnels. Pederson was dead and Rudy Chassler was dead. Buff was dead. Ready Mix was dead. They were all among the dead. The rain fed fungus that grew in the men's boots and socks, and their socks rotted, and their feet turned white and soft so that the skin could be scraped off with a fingernail, and Stink Harris woke up screaming one night with a leech on his tongue. When it was not raining, a low mist moved across the paddies, blending the elements into a single gray element, and the war was cold and pasty and rotten . . . The ammunition corroded and the foxholes filled with mud and water during the nights, and in the mornings there was always the next village and the war was always the same.
>
> from Tim O'Brien, *Going After Cacciato*

> The school was on a large lake in the breast-pocket of the continent, pouched and crouched in inwardness. It was as though it had a horror

of coasts and margins; of edges and extremes of any sort. The school was of the middle and in the middle. Its three buildings were middling-high, flat-roofed, moderately modern. Behind them, the lake cast out glimmers of things primeval, cryptic, obscure. These waters had a history of turbulence: they had knocked freighters to pieces in tidal storms. Now and then the lake took a human life.

from Cynthia Ozick, *The Cannibal Galaxy*

We don't mean to suggest, with these examples, that the first thing you do in your story is to lay out the setting in full detail. More often, the impact of setting on the reader is cumulative, as it is in James Dickey's novel *Deliverance* or in any of the fictions that Saul Bellow has placed in Chicago. When the writer has fully imagined the place (even if the place is only imaginary), that necessary sense of "being somewhere" will permeate the writing in hundreds of seemingly incidental details. The two worlds in Ursula Le Guin's *The Dispossessed* are her own inventions, but the characters who live there know them with the same sense of their own belonging or alienation as we know the settings of our own lives—or so it seems while we're reading. To put it another way, the reader believes in a setting—natural or imaginary—precisely because the writer has made one in which the characters believe.

If you look back over the examples, you will see that each passage not only conveys a material reality, but also projects attitudes and emotion. Places are associated with feelings, often because of the events that happen there. The setting in "Rothschild's Fiddle," for example, is not simply a tiny town. Chekhov establishes that it is boring—a funeral would be more exciting. Economic conditions are poor. Existence is dingy. People have a sense of somehow being better than their circumstances—he's Yakov here and would be Mr. Ivanov in a bigger town. By implication, status is important to them. When handled effectively, then, setting—like everything else—is not only literal, but suggestive. How the character feels about and relates to the setting is often the "background music" of the work.

EXERCISE

Review the three preceding examples and answer the following questions:

1. Describe as fully as possible the worlds that the characters live in: material, social, spiritual.

2. What devices of language—diction and imagery—are used suggestively?

3. Do any of the passages contain **foreshadowing**, that is, suggestions of events to come?

4. Invent two or three additional sentences for each passage that maintain consistency of setting in both tangible and intangible terms.

5. Draft four descriptions of the same place, such as a shopping mall, a mountain vacation spot, a college or university, or an urban business office. Let each description register a different emotion or tone: nostalgia, torment, mystery, or farcical humor.

POINT OF ATTACK

Think of your narrative as being composed of two movements. One movement is *forward,* an unfolding of events in scenes that the characters have yet to experience. From their point of view, the future is as unknown as it is to the reader. Indeed, in some cases the audience knows what will happen even when the characters don't. As the characters move forward in time, the writer communicates to the reader (or viewer or listener) *past* events that are necessary for understanding the characters' present situation. This other movement, sometimes called backgrounding or **exposition**, evolves in the process of shaping a plot from a story line. Sooner or later your shaping of plot requires a place at which you are going to have your reader begin reading.

The *first* forward-moving scene that you choose to show the reader is your **point of attack**.

Wherever you begin drafting (and it can be anywhere), locating the point in the time line of the story at which the plot—*not the story*—begins is one of your major decisions. Many other decisions follow from it. This is the rule of thumb: *have the reader start reading as far along the time line as is consistent with the effects you are trying to achieve.* The principle of beginning somewhere along the way—*in medias res*—has been distilled from the practice that worked even before Aristotle and still works for us. Start as late as you can.

The following Aesop fable, "Belling the Cat," gets to its one scene quickly, and that scene is within moments of the story's end.

> One day the mice held a general council to consider what they might do to protect themselves against their common enemy, the Cat. Some said one thing and some said another, but at last a Young Mouse stood up and announced that he had a plan which he thought would solve the problem.
>
> "You will all agree," said he, "that our chief danger lies in the unexpected and sly manner in which our enemy comes upon us. Now if we could receive some warning of her approach, we could easily hide from her. I propose, therefore, that a small bell be obtained and attached by a ribbon to the neck of the Cat. In this way we could always know when she was coming and be able to make our escape."

This proposal was met with great applause, until an Old Mouse arose and said, "This is all very fine, but who among us is so brave? Who will bell the Cat?" The mice looked at one another in silence and nobody volunteered.

from Aesop's *Fables*

The story dramatizes that it is easier to suggest a plan than to carry it out. Aesop relies on conventional characters (a foolish youth and a wise old mouse) and a conventional situation—we expect that mice will want protection from cats. The exposition is rapid: time = one day, place = a meeting, situation = an enemy to be frustrated. For the point Aesop wishes to make, we don't have to experience in detail the Cat's deprecations among the legions of mice, the process by which the meeting was called, or even the description of where it is being held (between walls, one is sure). Not only is the point of attack at the first and, one presumes, last meeting, but that meeting is the only scene. Notice where we really enter the action: close to the end of the meeting when the Young Mouse stands to deliver his plan.

This basic principle cannot be repeated too often: *have your reader enter the story at a point which allows all irrelevant effects to be excluded.* We return to this point shortly.

EXERCISE

List all the information that happened before the point of attack in the following story excerpts.

1. A Fox was eagerly watching a Crow as she settled in the branch of a tree because in her beak he spied a large piece of cheese. "That's for me, as sure as I'm a Fox," he said to himself as he walked up to the tree.

    "Good morning, Mistress Crow," he began, "how lovely you look today. How black and glossy are your feathers, how bright your eyes. I am sure that your voice, like your beauty, surpasses all the other birds. Just let me hear you sing a little song, so that I may know that you are really the Queen of Birds."

    The Crow was so pleased with all these compliments that she lifted up her head and began to caw. Naturally the moment she opened her mouth the piece of cheese dropped to the ground and was snapped up by the Fox. "That will do," said he. "This is all I wanted."

    from Aesop's *Fables*

2. Alice was beginning to get very tired of sitting by her sister on the bank and of having nothing to do: once or twice she had peeped into the book her sister was reading, but it had no pictures or conversations in

it, "and what is the use of a book," thought Alice, "without pictures or conversations?"

So she was considering, in her own mind (as well as she could, for the hot day made her feel very sleepy and stupid), whether the pleasure of making a daisy-chain would be worth the trouble of getting up and picking the daisies, when suddenly a White Rabbit with pink eyes ran close by her.

Lewis Carroll, *Alice's Adventures in Wonderland*

3.   Do the same thing for the first two paragraphs of Salman Rushdie's *Good Advice Is Rarer Than Rubies* (p. 258).

Essentially, there are three reasons for choosing as late a point of attack as possible:

1. You have less to account for.
2. You get the reader into the story faster.
3. You increase the tension because the reader waits for the unfolding of both the past and the present.

Had we met Crow in Aesop's story before she got the cheese, we probably would want to know how she got it. The classic though deliberately amusing case of beginning too early and getting caught in too many explanations is Laurence Sterne's *Tristram Shandy*. Tristram decides to tell his life story from the beginning, his birth. Since he is an inexperienced storyteller, he feels he has to explain how he was conceived and that decision leads him back and back into the past. As a result, he never gets born in the novel. Remember, the later the entrance, the fewer the explanations.

Getting the reader into the story quickly is not simply a matter of exploding into action as in the following opener:

John grabbed the gun from the wall and shot the two men Swenson had sent to kill him. Then he flung himself out the window, crashing through the convertible top of the Maserati waiting below. Sheila gunned the 460cc engine and squealed away from the curb. The Bolix XG-5 on the other side of the street took off after them.

How did John and Sheila get themselves into this bind? Well, six months before, Karl Ambler had called them and . . .

Sure, this story begins quickly, but then it comes to a dead halt to orient us. And it starts on such a high level of action that the writer will have a hard time building up to it again. In fact, this point of attack feels like the final moment of the final scene.

A late point of attack works on your readers' natural curiosity about the purpose of or reason for something they are experiencing. The reader will trust you to fill in the background if there is something happening in the foreground. Only in rare circumstances will the reader tolerate investing hours of energy in a story before it really gets started. Of course, decisions about point of attack are connected to the nature of the fiction: a novel may begin earlier than a short story. In short stories or plays or poems, the point of attack is usually near the concluding event.

EXERCISE

List all the information (and scenes) you might have to prepare if you started *Alice in Wonderland* with Alice getting up in the morning.

Though you never begin at the beginning—can one ever?—you still need to find an effective point of attack. The most practical point of attack is a natural one, one that is natural to life itself. Start with actual beginnings (weddings, new jobs, births, graduations, vacations); waitings (for friends, dinner, trains, mail, the long lost cousins, news); movings or relocations (into the forest, into a vehicle, out of town). Moments like these involve the kinds of tensions we are all familiar with, allowing readers to enter willingly the "let's pretend" of fiction.

Also these are moments connected to change in the lives of our characters. Readers are inclined to suspect that something is up with a character who is excitedly passing through an airport (Kornblatt's "Balancing Act") or getting off a bus in a cloud of dust (Rushdie's "Good Advice Is Rarer Than Rubies") or coming home after a long absence (Goyen's "Rhody's Path"). Such natural beginnings focus your readers' attention. They raise questions about the future *and* the past that will pull the reader into your material.

EXERCISE

What is the effect of each of the following opening scenes?

1. She was a large woman with a large purse that had everything in it but a hammer and nails. It had a long strap, and she carried it slung across her shoulder. It was about eleven o'clock at night, dark, and she was walking alone, when a boy ran up behind her and tried to snatch her purse. The strap broke with the sudden single tug the boy gave it from behind. But the boy's weight and the weight of the purse combined

caused him to lose his balance. Instead of taking off full blast as he had hoped, the boy fell on his back on the sidewalk and his legs flew up. The large woman simply turned around and kicked him right square in his bluejeaned sitter. Then she reached down, picked the boy up by his shirt front and shook him until his teeth rattled.

Langston Hughes, "Thank You, M'am"

2.
> The king sits in Dumferling town
>   Drinking the blood-red wine:
> "O where will I get a good sailor,
>   To sail this ship of mine?"
>
> Up and spake an elder knight
>   Sat on the king's right knee:
> "Sir Patrick Spence is the best sailor,
>   That sails upon the sea."

3. All of Olga Ivanovna's friends and acquaintances went to her wedding.
"Look at him—there *is* something about him, isn't there?" she said to her friends, nodding towards her husband—apparently anxious to explain how it was that she had agreed to marry a commonplace, in no way remarkable man.

Anton Chekhov, "The Grasshopper"

4. It is five o'clock in the morning, Daylight Saving Time. I have been sitting on the balcony of the down-river room on the second floor of the Howard Johnson's motel on Canona Boulevard almost all night. In other cities motels may be escape routes to anonymity, but not for me, not in Canona, and not this morning.

Mary Lee Settle, *The Killing Ground*

CHARACTER AND CHARACTERIZATION

The story from which your plot grows through exposition (largely *telling*) and scenes *(showing)* is about the life or a portion of the life of characters. Remember, you are writing fictional biography or autobiography or history that the reader will take as "real" during the time of reading. Even in pure allegories or the most action-oriented plot, we expect that what happens to the characters and what they do will grow from their natures, *or will appear to*. So, whether you create characters to fulfill a situation or a situation to fulfill characters, the reader expects situation and characters to match. By "match" we mean:

1. What the characters do always reflects who they are or what happens to them as the story unfolds.

2. Their natures are understandable both in terms of the conventions of fiction or what *has* happened to them. (Remember, the environment or **setting** is always happening to them.)

For the characters, there is no plot (usually). They do not think of themselves as characters (usually). From their point of view, they have lived and are living through events. They may plan or try to "plot" their lives in order to reach goals. They may "plot" against some other characters or vice versa. Like people, within the flow of events that *you* are charting for them, your characters wish to achieve their desires.

There are three possible types of characters in your stories or novels: primary characters, whose story you are telling; secondary characters, who are necessary for understanding the primary characters or carrying out the plot; and "uniformed" characters—doormen, waitresses, crowds—who are in the story to open doors, serve meals, and jostle the other characters; that is, to provide a credibly populated fictional world. (In a way, this last type of character is a component of setting.) No character should be given more weight of characterization than his or her place in the story requires. (See the later section, "Functionaries and Stock Characters.")

The word "character" comes from the Greek word meaning "an instrument for marking or engraving." By the fourteenth century the word in English had come to mean *distinctive mark,* and by the fifteenth, *graphic symbol.* Not until the seventeenth century was it used in anything like our modern sense—the sum of mental and moral qualities—and not until the eighteenth do we find it used in place of "personage" and "personality." The history of the word suggests that character is something imprinted, impressed upon, or scratched into universal human material to distinguish it from other material. It is the individual in the universal. A character in a literary or dramatic work is a *fictional personage* who the reader recognizes by the distinctive traits the author has stamped upon or etched into the raw material. That character is "branded" so as not to be mistaken for anyone else.

A major error of beginning writers is to equate "character" with "actor"—to think that simply because one has given different names to the personages carrying out the plot, the task of characterizing has been done. What the writer should strive for is to convince the reader that (1) what happens, (2) where it happens, and (3) to whom it happens are intimately related. In fact, when you inspire in your reader a belief in the character, you usually can get your reader to believe any other aspect of the story. This "belief" we are speaking of refers to recognizing the character's reality *in the story* rather than its reality as part of the natural world. When we identify and individualize the characters, the reader can believe even in talking flounders.

The writer gives the reader four basic ways of identifying each character. For every Roderick Usher, Ahab, Elizabeth Bennett, or Holden Caulfield, the writer constructs

- an identifiable way of behaving
- an identifiable way of speaking
- an identifiable appearance
- an identifiable way of thinking

The writer sets up and develops the identification either (1) by *telling* us information through straight exposition or (2) by *showing* us how the character acts. This showing includes, of course, how the character looks, speaks, and thinks and how other characters respond.

In practice, the writer shapes our sense of the character's identity by mixing the basic techniques, as in the following passage:

> Grant was surprisingly relaxed, yet serious.
> "We may as well admit it's over, really over this time," he said.
> Alice wasn't convinced that this time was any different from the others. Her hand smoothed her straight hair in a gesture that was part of her little arsenal of weapons in such situations. The gesture was always the first step in a delicate series of maneuvers that had kept them together. But Grant had prepared himself. "That's not going to work, you know." He had had enough. He was through.

Even in this brief passage, the writer uses all the tools of characterization. The first sentence presents the narrator's assessment of the situation. He (or she) tells us something about Grant. Then Grant, in his own words, reveals where he stands—and thus something about himself. Alice's actions characterize her and, in passing, give us some sense of how she looks while helping us understand the history of their relationship. But it also says something about Grant. We know that up to this point he has been indecisive about ending the relationship and that he had a weakness for Alice's physical charms which she could exploit. Grant's own words finish the job of establishing a changed situation, and the very way he speaks tells us something about his quiet but firm approach to this difficult moment. The closing sentences appear to be the narrator's report of what Grant is thinking, almost as if Grant had said it aloud. The reader understands by this point not only that the situation has changed but also a little bit about the nature of both characters. Such moments, repeated dozens of times in any particular narrative, give the reader a sense that a character has a specific psychological and moral organization, an identifiable way of looking at and responding to situations.

One thing to notice about the preceding sample is that it doesn't sit there screaming *characterization*. The ongoing business of characterization gets done while everything else is getting done. Only when a character is first introduced or at special moments in an extended narrative is a long, static section of characterization ever appropriate. Characters are more effectively presented to readers by actions, words, and deeds than by analytical descriptions.

The problem with long, analytical descriptions is that the audience is given the end product—the summary case history—rather than being allowed to experience the character in action. The writer creates a greater sense of intimacy and engagement when a reader deduces the nature of characters from what they do, think, or say. This is the way we get to know an individual's nature in life itself. Indeed, one of the reasons a reader comes to believe in a character is that the writer provides the same kinds of information by which we come to know real people; we don't come to know *them* through lengthy analyses. Remember, the characters created in a work of fiction are not "real" because they pass the test of measurement against real models. They are fictional personages whom we agree to believe in because of accepted, conventional means the writer has employed.

To create these believable characters, you must know more about them than can ever be told or shown to the reader. This is particularly true of major characters. The writer sets the game in motion by knowing the fictional personages so well that every move they make, every word they speak, every thought they have grows from a kind of intimate biography that would allow the writer to answer the following questions:

1. When and where was the character born? Why does the character have that name? What is the character's background—economically, spiritually, educationally? Does the character have brothers and sisters? What are the family dynamics?

2. What does the character look like? How does the character speak? Move? Relate to others? What are the behavioral tics (like rubbing the side of his nose or hiccuping when nervous)?

3. What does the character do for a living? For fun? For a hobby? To kill time?

4. What is the character's psychological makeup? What are the character's memories—conscious and unconscious (as revealed in dreams and actions)? How self-aware is the character?

5. What significant events shaped the character's views and reactions?

6. *What does the character want and why?*

While all of these questions are important, the last is crucial.

Knowing what your characters want can help you find situations that will put them in conflict with other characters or with the environment. It is the question that can connect character and plot, not in the sense that the pursuit of a goal is all that makes for a story line, but in the sense that knowing what the character wants (even if the character doesn't) is the key to knowing how that figure will react to various circumstances. As in life, the clash between the wants of a character and the blocking forces of nature, social conditions, or the wishes of other characters is what creates tension. Without tension, stories and life are ho-hum—which is acceptable in life but not in stories.

Once you know your character, you will be able to present that character as a unique identity rather than just as a type (see "Functionaries and Stock Characters"). And once you know your character that well, you cannot avoid keeping to what may be the only unbreakable rule in fiction: *the character must behave according to his or her nature as the writer has established that nature for us.* Tom Sawyer may leave off being a romantic and become a cynic, but we'll have to see how that happened. Merely for the convenience of the writer in a particular scene, a character who studied atomic physics cannot ask who Einstein was.

Writers often develop elaborate journal sketches of their characters' lives so that they can give those characters the degree of complexity, the multiple edges required for the type of fiction they are writing. In sum: individuality, consistency, and complexity are the goals of successful characterization. They give the reader the opportunity to believe in the character.

You should, however, avoid the temptation to push everything you used in a character sketch into your story. The sketch is there only as a reference, a resource. The materials in the sketch must be used selectively and suggestively. You will need to choose or invent *representative* items that economically stand for many omitted possibilities. Essentially, doing the sketch will give you the knowledge and the insight necessary to set the character in motion. You can draw on that insight as you follow the character through a series of actions and reactions.

EXERCISES

1. Write three elaborate character sketches. Make one of the characters approximately your own age, one five years younger, and one five years older. Two of them should be the same sex as yourself, the other of the opposite sex. Answer all of the questions listed earlier as well as others that you think of. Write the sketches out in full sentences and paragraphs. (If you are assigned to do this in a short period of time, do the best you can and go back to amplify your sketches later.)

2. Test out your character sketches with someone else. Find out what the sketch has not covered or made clear about your characters.

3. Make a list of situations for each character. In making the list, consider the kind of problem or set of circumstances that will best reveal what the character is made of. Take situation suggestions from others who have read your character sketches.

4. Imagine one of your characters ten years older. Take some additional notes on the character at that age.

5. Have one of your characters look in the mirror and record what he or she sees (some first-person introspection). *Note:* this ploy has become a cliché—useful in practice, dangerous in serious work.

6. Write about one character through the eyes of another.

7. Obtain some tests that are used for psychological profiles, such as aptitude/interest tests. Have one or more of your characters fill them out.

8. Have one of your characters fill out a job application and write a covering letter to go along with it.

Action

What characters do defines them, and these same actions are part of the materials that constitute plot. In a story or novel, every action must be convincing in this double way: (1) it must be consistent with what we know or will come to know about the character's inner state; (2) it must be necessary to the advancement of the plot and the revelation of theme.

Actions are directly related to motivations. In "The Lost Cottage," for example, Alex arranges to have his lover, Marian, nearby while he goes through the motions of the traditional family vacation. This action reveals his character, while the exposure of the action to others brings the plot to its crisis. When, in "Good Advice Is Rarer Than Rubies," Muhammad Ali leads Miss Rehana to his corner of the shantytown, he is asserting his authority by taking her from neutral territory to his personal terrain. When he offers her advice from his desk, he does so with great confidence that he knows her needs. Through what he does, the old man is defined: we discover his true nature. Conversely, his very personality gives rise to what happens. In this case, there is a conflict within Muhammad Ali. He wants to earn his living, and yet he is moved to impress Miss Rehana because of her beauty. The characterization becomes complicated by a tension between what the old man does and what he intends.

EXERCISE

1. Analyze, as we have done, how the other characters in "The Lost Cottage" are revealed through their actions.

2. From one of the character sketches you have drawn up, develop a scene in which a character trait—impatience, for example—is revealed in action or actions. See if, at the same time, you can show how that trait developed.

Appearance

In life, appearances are significant, even if they are deceiving. When we meet people, they strike us first as images, and it is this first impression that we remember. How people respond to *our* images and how we believe we look are important to us (consciously or unconsciously), as is made quite clear when we consider the time we devote to our weight, our hairstyles, our clothing, and even our gestures. In fiction, even a single detail (Huck Finn's ragged pants) gives the reader some tangible image to hang on to. Such details usually hint at other aspects of the character. In the collection of physical features that meets the eye is something of the buried individual.

The amount and kind of detail about your character that you give needs to be carefully measured and selected. Beginning writers tend to go to extremes, either (1) giving their characters too much of a physical embodiment or (2) neglecting to visualize their characters altogether, often insisting that they want to leave it to the reader's imagination. The writers who go overboard elaborate the appearance of the character far beyond what the reader needs or wants. In fact, when a writer spends pages of excruciating detail on the character's appearance, the reader is likely to lose the *essential* picture. There is simply too much for the reader's imagination to carry. On the other hand, a character who is totally faceless (except for age and sex) has so many possibilities that the reader is left without anything to hold on to. Readers are also confused when too many different characters are described one right after another.

EXERCISE

The following physical descriptions suggest the nature of the character. Examine the extent of such description in each passage and the techniques for presenting the description. See our comments following the first example.

1. Zadok Hoyle presented a fine figure on the box of carriage or hearse, for he was a large, muscular man of upright bearing, black-haired and dark-skinned, possessed of a moustache that swept from under his nose in two fine ebony curls. On closer inspection it could be seen that he was cock-eyed, that his nose was of a rich red, and that his snowy collar and stock were washed less often than they were touched up with chalk. The seams of the frock coat he wore when driving the hearse would have been white if he had not painted them with ink. His top hat was glossy, but its nap was kept smooth with vaseline. His voice was deep and caressing. The story was that he was an old soldier, a veteran of the Boer War, and that he had learned about horses in the army.

    Robertson Davies, *What's Bred in the Bone*

Nothing is directly said about Hoyle's personality here, though the narrator has begun to show the character in a way that allows us to draw inferences we will test later in the novel. What Hoyle does to maintain his clothes suggests his pride in his appearance, as does his posture. The "fine figure" is a manipulated image. Nonetheless, we receive the impression of a man who is competent within a limited sphere and who can be endearing (note the qualities of his voice).

Make a list of expectations about Zadok Hoyle from the materials presented in the paragraph. After each, answer the question, "What makes you think so?" Notice that Davies comes right out and *tells* us what Hoyle's appearance is rather than trying to find more "subtle" ways (i.e., having Hoyle look in a mirror or seeing Hoyle's appearance through another character's eyes).

Ask the same questions about the following passages. Note, for each, how much is *told*, how much *shown*. What role does *appearance* play in each passage?

2. My grandfather, when I first remember him, lived over in the next county from us, forty miles west of Nashville. But he was always and forever driving over for those visits of his—visits of three or four days, or longer—transporting himself back and forth from Hunt County to Nashville in his big tan touring car, with the canvas top put back in almost all weather, and usually wearing a broad-brimmed hat—a straw in summer, a felt in winter—and an ankle-length gabardine topcoat no matter what the season was.

    He was my maternal grandfather and was known to everyone as Major Basil Manley. Seeing Major Manley like that at the wheel of his tan touring car, swinging into our driveway, it wasn't hard to imagine how he had once looked riding horseback or muleback through the wilds of West Tennessee when he was a young boy in Forrest's cavalry, or how he had looked, for that matter, in 1912, nearly half a century after he had ridden with General Forrest, at the time when he escaped from a band of hooded nightriders who had kidnapped him then—him and his law partner (and who had murdered his law partner before his eyes, on the banks of Bayou du Chien, near Reelfoot Lake). He would plant one of the canvas yard chairs on the very spot where I had been building a little airfield or a horse farm in the grass. Then he would undo his collar button and remove his starched collar—he seldom wore a tie in those days—and next he would pull his straw hat down over his face and begin his inevitable dialogue with me without our having exchanged so much as a glance or how-do-you-do.

    Peter Taylor, "In the Miro District"

3. On this particular evening, a Tuesday, most of the regular people . . . were down at the Rachel River V.F.W. Lounge. Drinks, for once, were at half price, in honor of Mr. and Mrs. Kevin Ohlaugs's son, Curt [who was back from the service]. . . . The local radio-news lady, a thirty-three-year-old divorcee named Mary Graving, sat in the best corner booth of the V.F.W. Lounge. She was celebrating something secretly.

From the beginning, she had intended to spend the whole evening there, so she had had the foresight to prop herself up in the right angle between the back of the booth and the wall. By her elbow, someone had scratched on the wall a suggestion to the I.R.S. about what it could do with itself. Mary had arranged a smile on her face quite a while ago; now it was safely fixed there, and she herself was safely fixed, and although she was immensely drunk, she was not so drunk as the others, which meant she counted as dead sober.

When Mary Graving was sober, her face was too decided and twitchy to look good with the large plain earrings she always wore. She thought she was generally too grim-looking, and her earrings looked too cheerful at the edges of her face. Now that she was drunk, though, and wearing a red dress, her face felt hot and rosy. Her smile stayed stuck on, and she knew that the earrings—a new pair, especially cheap, not from Bagley's in Duluth but a product of the Ben Franklin Store in Rachel River—looked fine. She was not beautiful but she was all right.

Carol Bly, "The Last of the Gold Star Mothers"

Thought

There are two basic ways of letting a reader know the action of a character's mind: (1) The narrator *reports* what a character thought, dreamed, or felt. (2) The narrator directly *presents* the flow of the character's thoughts. Sometimes the narrator may present the flow as an **interior monologue**—an apparently realistic, because apparently uncut, recording of the complex flow of diverse thoughts, feelings, and images welling up within the character. **Stream of consciousness** is the extended form of interior monologue often going on for whole chapters, as in the works of Virginia Woolf and William Faulkner.

An omniscient narrator can enter the mind of any character, but in most fiction the narrator chooses one character as a point of psychological reference, limiting our access to the thoughts (feelings, dreams) of that individual. Jumping back and forth among the minds of many characters is unconventional because it is difficult for the reader to follow. It *seems* unrealistic. Given the brevity of "The Boarding House," Joyce's decision to take us into the minds of three characters is especially unusual. He chooses to do this because his story is largely *about* their different perspectives and their understandings of one another. In recording his characters' thoughts, Joyce rarely tags the passages with phrases like "he thought" or "she pondered." The narrator slips into the character's mind and tells us what's going on with a minimum of fuss. Here are Mrs. Mooney's thoughts as she prepares to maneuver Mr. Doran into a proposal to Polly Mooney:

There must be reparation made in such a case. It is all very well for the man: he can go his ways as if nothing happened, having had his moment of pleasure, but the girl has to bear the brunt. Some mothers would be content to patch up such an affair for a sum of money; she had known cases of it. But she would not do so. For her only one reparation could make up for the loss of her daughter's honour: marriage.

Here, Joyce's report of her thought comes very close to authorial comment, another means of characterization that we will discuss later. Joyce's intention, however, is to bring us close to Mrs. Mooney's thoughts, not to access them directly.

A more typical handling of a character's thoughts is this passage from Kornblatt's "Balancing Act."

> The hotel was old and sumptuous, and she was pleased that they would not be confined for five days to a stripped-down, thin-walled Holiday Inn. She often wished that environment did not mean so much to her mood, did not contribute so heavily to her frame of mind. She would have liked to have been as happy with him in a sterile motel as in this gracious building, but it was not the case and she allowed the atmosphere to work on her like a martini.

Even more direct is this treatment:

> *Breathe in the elegance,* she wanted to tell him. *Absorb and retain it.*

The more the character concentrates on his or her own thoughts, the closer the author makes the language of thought approximate the language of speech, and the more the reader feels like a direct observer of a portion of the character's life.

EXERCISE

1. Report the thoughts of two characters you have sketched. Work them into the flow of a scene.

2. Write interior monologues for two of the characters you have sketched, one of each sex.

Dialogue

What characters say to one another plays a vital role in fictional representations. While action, appearance, and thought reveal the character in ways that heighten his or her individuality, dialogue also insists that we see the character in immediate relationship to others. We might say that speech somehow contains the other methods: it is the way in which *thought* becomes *appearance*. It is also a special kind of *action*. Dialogue used merely as a way of presenting exposition (facts necessary for the reader to understand the plot) will be stilted and boring.

The writer who uses dialogue well understands that it is in a story not only to relate its ostensible subject, but to do other work as well. Let us say two characters are talking about whether or not to go to Boston. Ideally, the way they talk about going to Boston should carry the plot forward, reveal character, focus relationships, carry thematic implications, and—if convenient—provide some exposition. If a stretch of dialogue isn't working on many levels, then dialogue is not likely to be the best tool to use at that point.

Here is a passage from David Leavitt's "The Lost Cottage" developed primarily through a conversation between father and son. The scene is a flashback in which Mark, the son, remembers a dinner with his father in which the future family get-together that constitutes the unfolding present of the story was discussed. Marian is the father's lover.

> "Well," Alex said, halfway through the meal, "I'll be on Cape Cod this June, as usual. Will you?"
> "Dad," Mark said. "Of course."
> "Of course. But Marian won't be coming, I'm afraid."
> "Oh?"
> "I wish she could, but your mother won't allow it."
> "Really," Mark said, looking sideways at Marian for some hint of how he should go on. She looked resolute, so he decided to be honest. "Are you really surprised?" he said.
> "Nothing surprises me where your mother is concerned," Alex said. Mark supposed Alex had tried to test how far he could trespass the carefully guarded borders of Lydia's tolerance, how much he could get away with, and found he could not get away with that much. Apparently, Lydia had panicked, overcome by thoughts of bedroom arrangements, and insisted the children wouldn't be able to bear Marian's presence. "And is that true?" he asked Mark, leaning toward him. "Would the children not be able to bear it?"

In this scene Alex is testing the waters, seeing if he can find some way of bringing Marian to what is likely to be the final family gathering on Cape Cod. The relationship between father and son is simultaneously warm and guarded. Leavitt mixes thought and action with the speeches, reproducing the necessary psychological and physical context. The strain put on Mark by having to deal with his father in such a way—talking about his mother, Lydia, in front of the "other woman"—comes through, as does Mark's genuine fondness for his father.

The passage can serve to illustrate some of the conventions of dialogue. Notice how *a paragraph indentation signals a shift in speaker*. Rarely do we find the speeches of two characters in the same paragraph (though, if you turn to the story, you'll see that Leavitt breaks this convention in the paragraph that follows). This convention is a way of helping the reader keep the characters straight. We are so used to it that it has become an unconscious expectation when we read. As writers, we need to be helpful in these most ordinary ways.

Notice how Leavitt keeps the **designators**—the words that tell us who is speaking—simple. Beginning writers tend to become heavy-handed with these tags, no doubt out of a false worry about repetition. They try to juice up their prose by being inventive when they should be almost silent. "He snarled" and the like should be used sparingly, if ever. Not only are elaborate designators more comic than helpful, but they also signal the writer's insecurity about whether the reader will respond properly to what the characters have said. When the writer has shown the state of mind or the tone of voice in the dialogue, it is not necessary to do so in the designator. If the writer hasn't shown it in the dialogue, then the dialogue needs revision.

The designator in the following speech is both redundant and silly:

> "For God's sake, please don't go, Lettie," he implored in a piteous voice.

"He said" is sufficient. When the designator remains almost invisible, the reader is in closer contact with the dialogue and therefore with the characters. In fact, the writer can increase direct contact by judiciously dropping the designator altogether, as Leavitt has sometimes done in the passage above.

You will want to read the extended discussion of how to create expressive dialogue in Chapter 13.

QUESTIONS

1. Why does Leavitt change to "he asked" for Alex's last speeches?

2. Those final questions do not grow logically or naturally out of what has been already spoken. It's almost as if the characters are reading each other's minds. Is this disjunction a slip-up on Leavitt's part, or is there some other way to explain it?

3. Here is a brief subscene from Joyce Kornblatt's "Balancing Act." What are the surface and subsurface meanings (**text** and **subtext**) of the dialogue?

> "I think I'll buy a magazine," she said as they approached a newsstand.

"They've got plenty on the plane," he said.

"They might not have what I really want."

He shrugged. "That's entirely possible."

She caught his ironic smirk, the momentary despair of his retort, and turned away from it nervously. She studied the racks while he scanned headlines from all over the world.

Along with her magazine, he bought a pack of gum. He handed her a stick as they walked through the gate. "Here," he said, "for your ears."

"Thanks," she deadpanned. "Could I have a piece for my mouth, too?"

He gave her a small smile, but he had no comeback and her appetite for banter reluctantly receded.

"Really, thanks," she said. "You're nice."

"Cub scout training. I've been nice since I was seven."

EXERCISE

Write two pages of dialogue for any two characters. Create a simple conflict (should they go someplace or not; should they buy something or not). Do not use designators for any of the characters' speeches. Remember: the characters know what they are doing and what their situation is, so they are not likely to talk about it directly. Show your dialogue to someone else to see if they can understand the situation and keep track of each character.

Indirect Discourse

At times you will want to report dialogue in the narrator's voice rather than render it as speech. This reporting, often really summarizing, is called **indirect discourse**. Let us suppose that you have developed a scene in which one character has to tell another character about something the reader has either already experienced or doesn't need to have tediously elaborated:

Addie entered the room where Franklyn was setting the table.

"Hi, Frank."

"Hi, Addie."

"How you feeling?"

"O.K., I guess. And you?"

"O.K."

"How did it go with Scotty?"

"I went over there and we started to talk."

"What did she tell you?"

"It's not what she told me. It's what happened."

"What happened?"

[Now Addie launches in a long retelling of a squabble that turned into a shoving match.]

With indirect discourse you can quickly get over such repetitious or dramatically weak material:

Addie entered the room where Franklyn was setting the table, and after they exchanged greetings told him what had happened with Scotty—including the business about the fight.

Indirect discourse can also be used within stretches of dialogue to quickly summarize exchanges in which characters give one another information. A subtle example of this device occurs in "The Lost Cottage" when the narrator indicates that Alex has told Mark about the conversation with Lydia that leads to Alex's question: "And is that true?"

Indirect discourse is also a way of avoiding the presentation of *any* dialogue that would be downright tedious or purely informational (not characterizing). In some instances, this technique serves when characterization is called for but the use of dialogue would force you to invent speeches for *other* characters. Notice, in the following example, how dialogue and indirect discourse are combined for maximum flavor and efficiency. A son has come home late:

"I'm only an hour after I promised, Ma. What do you want from—"
"It wasn't you who was doing the waiting."
"But, Ma, I'm eighteen."
He might be eighteen, she told him, but he wasn't a very grown-up eighteen. Because if he was he would understand exactly how she felt. What with no husband and Marcy and Joe gone heaven knows where, he should plan his time a little better. In any case, he was home now and she wanted him to get down to his homework right away. At least one of them would amount to something. . . .

The narrator can go on for quite a while like this, giving information as well as a sense of character without having to worry about the mother's exact words or the son's responses.

The consideration of indirect discourse is a reminder that it is easy to overuse or misuse dialogue. As a general rule, save dialogue for what only dialogue can accomplish. Indirect discourse is often the more effective choice.

EXERCISE

Finish what the mother in the example tells the son. Then break into a brief dialogue in which she demands an explanation as to why he was late. Then use indirect discourse to report his story.

Other Means

So far we have reviewed the direct means of characterization: what a character looks like and what that character does, thinks, and says. Often the delineation of a character is aided by what other characters say and think about him or her. In "The Boarding House" Joyce presents Mr. Doran's character, in part, by providing Mrs. Mooney's estimate of it. In "The Lost Cottage" our understanding of Marian is through David's perspective. In "Rhody's Path" the narrator quotes Aunt Idalou to help the reader evaluate Rhody.

A more important, and more dangerous, technique is that of *authorial comment*. It has the advantage of great economy, but the disadvantage of seeming coercive—as if the author doesn't trust our understanding. James Joyce allows himself this method in a well-known line from "The Boarding House": "She [Mrs. Mooney] dealt with moral problems as a cleaver deals with meat."

Functionaries and Stock Characters

In selecting characters and building them, you can exploit what the reader already is likely to know. Indeed, to have your narrator demonstrate that an aging mercenary soldier is cynical about the glory of war is to ignore that we know this by convention, just as we know that dissolute younger brothers of murdered noblemen might be logical suspects in the case. Because your work is not the first your readers have read, you can rely on such types for less important characters, giving the readers' imagination and experience some room. Foxes are clever and hungry: *always.*

Most of the figures who populate your work are merely functionaries: the drunk show girls at Gatsby's parties, for example. At one level functionaries may be part of the scenery; on another level they may have a line or two. The writer is best off relying on the reader's knowledge of the function or the type so that the figure can be sketched in quickly:

> The *waitress* brought our drinks and we got down to business. It was difficult to talk in whispers because a *well-dressed and well-lubricated stockbroker was telling all the world why the market had crashed.* Leroy wanted to go to another bar but I thought it would be a waste of time. He was annoyed and at every other word he'd ask me to repeat what I just said. He didn't touch his martini so I took it.

Had the writer said anything more than this about the waitress and stockbroker, we would feel our attention diverted from the central issue of the scene. Unless the functionaries have a significant role in the plot, they need not be characterized.

Using **stock characters**, on the other hand, requires more complex decisions. Stock characters are derived either from commonly held generalizations about racial or social types or from conventions of literature. Sometimes it is difficult to separate the generalization from the convention, as in the following list: the disrespectful, clever servant; the braggart, cowardly soldier; the tough prostitute with a heart of gold; the silent cowboy; the snobby Harvard grad; the farmer's daughter; the cynic; the incorruptible but sarcastic private eye; the shylock; the step'n fetch-it; the redneck; the hippie; the gay; and so on. On the one hand, stock characters can easily become mere reflections of popular prejudices. On the other hand, stock figures can behave so much according to type that they never become characters with their own wants.

A social type (the dull professor or the airhead yuppie), of course, will not offend the reader as may the racial, religious, or sexual stock character. Offensive or not, such stock figures can play major roles in satire or comedy. The dirty old man lusting after a young bride has supplied the central focus for many plots. When you want only a "stock response," use a stock character, but be careful to weigh the risks involved.

The stock character can also provide the seed from which the writer builds a more complex character. Just as our understanding of real people may begin with placing them in general categories by which we first know them (gender, age, occupation, class), so may we begin developing our fictional people by first seeing them as types and then learning about them as individuals. For an extended discussion of this process, see the section on stock characters in Chapter 12.

EXERCISES

1. List the functionaries and stock characters in "The Boarding House." How does Joyce signal their identity?

2. Examine the major characters from "Balancing Act" and "Rhody's Path." In what ways can you see them as stock characters? What characterizing techniques did the authors use to develop them into complex characters?

3. There is a fine line distinguishing **stock characters**, an artistic convenience, and **stereotypes**, a potentially hazardous playing on prejudices. How would you categorize each of the following?

a. a redheaded, gum-chewing waitress

b. a jock

c. a "yes, dear" husband

d. an "old salt"

e. a Jewish-American princess

f. a wicked stepmother

g. a Puerto Rican thief

h. a couple in polyester leisure wear

i. a nerd or geek

j. a television evangelist

k. an aging spinster

l. an unmarried career woman

m. a punk rocker

n. a male nurse

Naming Characters

Finding appropriate names for characters is not a trivial task, since your reader is often attracted or distracted by the name itself and by its seeming "rightness" for that particular fictional personage. A name must have credibility without being a cliché, and sometimes the name may have significance or suggestiveness. In choosing names, the writer must consider:

1. cultural stereotypes (if only to avoid them)
2. historical authenticity (is the name right for the times?)
3. regional probability (is a small-town Texan named Melvin?)
4. socioeconomic signals (is Poindexter the trucker?)
5. symbolic overtones (is Joshua leader or wimp?)
6. auditory features (what's an Ebenezer Scrooge?)

The following list includes names of characters from drama, fiction, and poetry. For the characters you know, check the "ring" of each name against the traits of the character. For the others, make a list of traits you would expect and then find out how close your portrait comes to the original.

1. George F. Babbitt
2. J. Alfred Prufrock
3. Becky Thatcher
4. Willy Loman
5. Franny Glass
6. Quentin Compson
7. Stephen Dedalus
8. Emma Bovary
9. Nick Adams
10. Joseph Andrews
11. Lemuel Gulliver
12. Moll Flanders
13. Isabel Archer
14. Oliver Twist
15. Holden Caulfield
16. Daisy Buchanan

Beware of names that are overly allegorical—Lancelot Hero—as well as names that do nothing to distinguish your character—Bill Smith, Joan Jones.

An excellent way to get names for your characters is by "researching" in telephone directories, local newspapers, and—of course—high school and college yearbooks. Mix first names and last names. Try your characters' names out on your friends or an instructor.

The Relationship of Character, Plot, and Setting

Since fictional characters are "represented" persons, their lives are limited to the fictional work or works that shape them. A character has verisimilitude in terms of the *imagined* environment, not necessarily in terms of the world we know intimately or the larger world that we know something about. The reality of Rhody in "Rhody's Path" is bound up with the environment in which

Goyen places her: the impact she has on *that* world and that it has on her. This is true also of the characters in "Good Advice Is Rarer Than Rubies." It is easy to grasp this point when we consider fairly exotic settings (like East Texas or India) and characters. However, the same truth holds in the more familiar worlds created by Joyce Kornblatt, David Leavitt, and Bel Kaufman. The reality of the character is *inside* of the story, not *outside* of it. This means, in part, that the things the reader needs to know about a character are limited to the larger unity of the story. Not every character is given the same attention, the same degree of rounding.

The situation (or conflict) that springs the plot also limits or controls what the reader needs to know about the character. We, as readers, need to know those things that bear on the circumstances at hand. For example, in "The Boarding House," Mr. Doran's inexperience with women is important, and, by suggestion, so is Mrs. Mooney's upbringing as a butcher's daughter. In another set of circumstances, we might need to discover other things about these same characters. As writers, we will know much more about these characters than the story allows us to share with the reader. Our concern for overall unity and focus will help us select just what must be known about each character. When the seemingly sophisticated and independent Miss Rehana speaks of "Bradford, London"—instead of Bradford, England—(in "Good Advice Is Rarer Than Rubies"), Rushdie has given us all we need to know about the limits of her worldliness. This part of the character is important to the story, but it takes only two words plus Muhammad Ali's gentle correction to get the point across. We don't need to know, as readers, about her education or her reading habits. Salman Rushdie knows all this but gives us only what we must have. Miraculously, he has made her as memorable as if we had actually met her.

The art of characterization is at the heart of all successful fiction. For many writers, imagining their characters is where the process of storytelling begins. A sense of relationship to the characters is what keeps readers reading.

EXERCISE

1. Study the characters in David Leavitt's "The Lost Cottage." Now take the flashback scene in which the parents announce that they are getting a divorce and develop it into the central scene of a story. Be true to the characters as Leavitt has imagined them.

2. From two or three of the character sketches you have done, draft an introductory section like the ones by Davies, Taylor, and Bly in the section on "Appearance."

3. Choose two or three of the "situations" collected for exercise 3, page 189. Group whatever materials from your character sketch you will be most likely to use in developing each situation.

4. Reread "Eli and the Coal Strippers" (pp. 147–48) and develop a scene from Zimmer's hints about the relationship between Eli and Wanda. You might want to write about Wanda leaving the farm.

A NOTE ON THE NOVEL

Writing a novel involves all the basic techniques of writing shorter fiction— character and scene development, narration, dialogue—plus the demands brought on by the sheer magnitude of your promise to tell a long story. From a purely commercial point of view, when you undertake a novel, you commit yourself to writing a minimum of 40,000 to 60,000 words or 150 to 200 double-spaced typescript pages. And for some of the subgenres of the novel, like the historical romance, you will need to write 100,000 or more words. Even with word processing, the task is daunting—both the original drafting and the revising.

However, the more serious difficulties are not those of filling up pages or preparing a manuscript. While a short story generally focuses on a single event involving only one or two major characters, a novel enters far more fully into the imitation of an unfolding life (or series of lives) while it places that unfolding in an elaborated setting that traditionally includes social background. The novelist must exercise intense concentration over a long period of time to manage the intricacies of characters' lives in an expansive plot. Authors of long fictions, even more than writers of short stories, must truly live with their characters.

Generally speaking you will need to do much more prewriting than might be necessary for a short story. Since novels tend to imitate either biographies, autobiographies, or histories, you will need to determine how your imagination will substitute for the nonfiction writer's research. Of course, you will need to do much of the same kind of research (see Chapter 5) to create a sense of authenticity. And you will have to be flexible: because you will be working on the manuscript for months, even years, your reading will expand your writing tools, and your experience of the natural world and the world of your novel will deepen. You will have many opportunities, *while you are writing*, to make discoveries about your characters and the moral, physical, and intellectual world(s) they inhabit. Rigid adherence to a plan over the months and years of the writing process that novels require is likely to be a foolish faithfulness.

Though you will want to jot down notes as ideas come to you for all writing projects, writing a novel calls for even more note taking. Much more is happening, more characters are moving across your stage, more time has passed since you set up the action. Think of yourself as the person who takes care of the props in a play or the continuity in a film. Like such managers, you need to know what your character was wearing and had in her purse in the last scene. Or, since four years have gone by since Jay Gatsby left for the war, how does he find out where Daisy is living? The sheer volume of events, props, and characters, and the time that elapses between writing Chapter 1 and Chapter 10 qualitatively change the task before you. Some authors dedicate a journal to keeping track of their ideas and plans for a novel, and then for keeping track of their progress (see Steinbeck excerpt, pp. 14–15).

If you have read this far, you already know that you have to study the genre and subgenre in which you plan to write. Particular subgenres—mystery, adventure, science fiction, romance, historical—are subdivided into even more types, and you should master the conventions and expectations of the audience (even if you intend to upset those expectations). You should have read in the genre for a long time before you try, let us say, an adventure story. If you try to write in a subgenre just because it is popular, you will probably fail.

A good part of your preplanning should involve especially careful thinking about who is going to tell the story (see Chapter 3). For example, if you are going to have to do a great deal of exposition (as, for example, in an historical novel), a first-person point of view may cause difficulties. How are you going to get a piece of information to your narrator? On the other hand, a story about growing up or a hard-boiled detective story may flow easily in the first person. If your point of view in a short story is not working, you have relatively little revising to do. Going back after writing a hundred pages of a novel can be a burden so daunting that you throw the manuscript in a drawer.

Always tell your novel in the past tense. Though you might have a prologue in the present tense to set the atmosphere, telling a whole novel in the present tense usually puts off a reader and poses exposition problems for the writer. It's been done, of course, but seldom successfully. Page after page of "she meets John and they go to the zoo where they look at the monkeys" creates unnecessary demands on the reader's attention. The novel has no emotional resting place. Everything appears to be so important and significant. Everything is happening now. The present tense may work in some short stories but, ultimately, it tends to create an evenness in the prose, an immediacy that allows for no hills and valleys.

All the decisions regarding plot, point of attack, character and characterization, and setting that we have already discussed become increasingly complicated when you tackle a novel. Perhaps the most important is to determine what to show and what to tell—and to be sure you know why. Because the novelist has to create a more sustained illusion of time passing, decisions about scene and summary are far more complex than they are for short stories. And, of course, such decisions must be made over and over again.

As a practical matter, what you show will be in scenes that combine description, narration, and dialogue (or interior monologue). Each scene will exist to reveal character and present action. If information is conveyed, it will be conveyed as a side effect of the scene. The scene must never appear to exist for the purpose of giving the information. When Hawthorne, in *The Scarlet Letter*, creates the scene in which Chillingworth doctors Hester and attempts to pull from her the identity of Pearl's father, we also learn about Chillingworth and Hester's marriage.

Most novels have twenty to forty major scenes of two to ten or more pages. Often one scene, with attendant description and exposition, makes up a chapter. If you find your scenes are a page or less and/or you have dozens in a chapter, you probably are writing scenes that exist only to give information (either to the reader or the other characters) or to provide a transition to another scene. In either case, the scenes are probably only for exposition and should be eliminated in favor of having your narrator simply tell the reader the key information.

Some novelists develop a complete life for each character: birthdate, parents, schooling, allergies, and so on. Many of your characters will exist only to help your major characters in their conflicts or to serve the plot. Ask yourself if it is really necessary to give a complete physical description of the doorman who only appears in a single scene. If you do need supporting characters, try to make those characters serve several functions. For example, Jordan Baker in *The Great Gatsby* not only serves as a foil to Daisy Buchanan, not only delivers necessary expository material, and not only becomes Nick Carraway's date for the summer (a parallel "love" story), she also is one of the characters who illustrates the decadence of contemporary society (she cheats at golf). A less sophisticated novelist might have employed several characters to fulfill these various roles.

Warnings: do not revise while the novel is developing. When you discover in Chapter 4 that you need to revise one or more earlier chapters—anything from the name of a character to adding a scene—just put down a note to yourself to make the revision. Continue writing as if you had already made the change. Why? Because when you get to Chapter 5 and 6 and so on, you will find other revisions necessary for the earlier chapters. If you keep revising you will never finish the novel. (Word processing has the advantage of letting you return to the earlier chapters and drop in notes to yourself about the changes that will be needed and then jumping back to where you were.)

The challenge of the novel, then, brings a mixture of pleasure and pain. Most fiction writer's (but certainly not all) learn to control the essential elements of their craft by working first in the short story, then going on to the longer form. The rewards of creating a peopled edifice in words are enormous, but the writer who accepts the challenge must camp out for a long season in those construction sites of the imagination, through bad weather and occasional strikes, while the structure takes shape.

EXERCISE

1. Prepare a chapter outline for a novel based on Hemingway's "A Very Short Story." Include comments on new characters, new scenes, and point of view.

2. Prepare dust jacket copy for your novel. This task should force you to focus on the essentials.

3. Review the World's Fair Paroposal (pp. 108–9) and prepare a proposal for a novel-length project of your own.

10

Narration and Its Problems

Your story, the interaction of situation (focused in the point of attack), setting, and characters, is **plotted** through alternating units of telling and showing: exposition, flashback, scene, and summary.

EXPOSITION

A writer needs ways to communicate information that will round out the readers' understanding of the unfolding story, which is **narrated** primarily through scenes and linking summaries. Most often this information has to do with events that precede the point of attack. The writing that supplies this information is called **exposition.** In Joyce's "The Boarding House," five introductory paragraphs supply family background necessary to our full comprehension of the dramatized events. We are told about Mrs. Mooney's unfortunate marriage, the reputation of the boarding house, and Polly's character and situation. The events that follow make sense—a particular kind of sense—because of what has been exposed.

The bridges between scenes also function as exposition when they prepare us for the point of attack of the coming scene. The term, however, usually applies to everything that we do not see happen in the forward movement of the story. In any case, exposition is almost always handled by *telling*, whereas scenes are conveyed by *showing*. Some of your most difficult decisions will involve discovering (1) how much of what happened before the point of attack is necessary to tell, (2) when to tell it, and (3) how to tell it most effectively and least obtrusively.

There are two kinds of information that the reader needs. First is information *about the world we all live in* that bears upon the characters in the story. If you are writing a story about, let's say, mountain climbing, how much does the reader need to know about Nepal, crampons, rappeling, hypothermia, atmospheric conditions? How much can you expect the reader to know already? How much can be gleaned from context? You need to gauge the reader's knowledge about the most relevant information and proceed accordingly, avoiding set explanatory passages that stop the action. When in doubt, the best principle is to expect the best of the reader. If you assume that you have to explain where New York City is, you will never make your way through the writing of a story.

Some fiction depends on introducing the reader to relatively unknown settings, the unfamiliar details of which engage the reader's imagination. For example, novelist Dick Francis has made a career of letting his readers experience the world of horse racing. In works like these, the absorbing of new information is a central pleasure. A classic case is Defoe's *Robinson Crusoe,* which gains much of its power from having us learn the same things that Crusoe must learn to survive.

Most short fiction, however, needs to tell us only that, for example, the main characters are two sisters who live in a six-bedroom house in a Chicago suburb and intend to become lawyers. Your reader can intuit a lot from this little bit.

The second type of information the reader needs is information about the lives and circumstances of the characters *in the story:*

> Once upon a time, in a distant kingdom, there lived a princess who was an only child. Her name was Esmeralda and in every way save one she was the most fortunate of young persons.
>
> Phyllis McGinley, *The Plain Princess*

Who, where, and *when* need to be established in almost every piece of fiction, and little is ever gained by hiding this material from the reader. Making puzzles out of basic information, a novice's idea of creating mystery, more often loses the reader altogether. Look at the first paragraph of Bel Kaufman's "Sunday in the Park" (pp. 231–32) to see how sure-handedly the basic expository work can be done and smoothed into the point of attack.

However much you tell the reader about the background, you will know ten times more than you can expose. Your job is to anticipate the reader's needs as the story unfolds and to offer the right information—and no more—in the right place.

Again, most expository information is *told* by summary overviews of conditions, backgrounds, and settings. Directness is a virtue; don't worry over cute ways to make a simple point:

> NO: He walked up to the door. When the tall woman answered it, he handed her his card. She read on it: "Will E. Seridy, 7803 Wilson Lane, Exterminator."
> NO: Will looked into the handsome reflection that showed him a six-foot man of thirty-two with an intriguing cowlick of reddish hair.

These passages call more attention to the means of communicating the facts than to the facts themselves. The next attempt is simple, yet far more effective:

> Will Seridy walked up to the front door. A handsome man of thirty-two, the lanky exterminator had reddish hair that fell in a cowlick.

Providing exposition is like giving your readers a map orientation before you show them where they are going: "You are right here. Now from this point . . ." In the following example, notice how Saxe establishes his authority by just laying down the facts.

> It was six men of Indostan
>   To learning much inclined
> Who went to see the Elephant
>   (though all of them were blind),
> That each by observation
>   Might satisfy his mind.
>
> John W. Saxe, "The Blind Man
and the Elephant"

In this poem for children, Saxe orients us quickly to the situation so he can get to the material he wishes to show: what, after touching a different part, each of the six blind men will say an elephant is.

Exposition is frequently not placed at the beginning of a work, as our examples so far might indicate. While chronologically it can convey information that precedes the point of attack, structurally exposition comes at the point the author feels is strategically effective. The following passage from Kornblatt's "Balancing Act" is the second of three paragraphs of exposition that come *after* the opening scene:

> She knew he was disheartened by her growing lack-luster. It was as if, over the years, she were a photograph in the process of fading. He could not articulate it, but she could see his discouragement, even terror, when she moved like a shadow through the rooms of their house. She behaved more and more like a person unable to remember

the most important fact of her life. He would ask her repeatedly, "What's wrong?" and she would reply, "Nothing. Just thinking," with a smile as tight as a fist and her brain shouting: *I am waiting for you to be able to read my mind.*

This information about the direction of the couple's relationship helps the reader grasp the importance of the unfolding events. Even though it contains dialogue, the passage does not become a scene, because the dialogue is representative rather than part of a particular event. Again, something is being exposed rather than demonstrated. In this case, the exposition strengthens our understanding of events that have *already* been shown as well as those yet to come.

FLASHBACKS

Except for relatively rare cases in which a character flashes back to an event that the reader has directly witnessed, **flashbacks** dramatize events that happened before the point of attack. While exposition may or may not be presumed to occur in the mind of the character, a flashback is always presumed to be a remembrance. A memory moment like "As she reached for the peanut butter, Josie saw again the knife-scarred kitchen counter on which rested the fixings of all those homemade snacks her mother used to give her" is not yet a flashback but rather a piece of generalized exposition. It contains no events. Flashbacks are remembered **scenes** that interrupt the ongoing action. They serve expository purposes, but they dramatize rather than tell about something in the past.

> It was on her thirteenth birthday that the ceremony had come to an abrupt halt, her mother handing over the tools of the trade and the responsibility.
> "No more waiting on you hand and foot," she said.
> Josie was stunned. The words and the kindly, loving look in her mother's eyes seemed in conflict. She walked over to the counter and picked up an apron. "Which do you put on first, the peanut butter or the jelly?"
> Today, she still imitated her mother's kitchen habits, though in everything else she had gone her own way.

Because flashbacks occur in the character's mind under the pressure of present circumstances, the reader assumes that whatever is revealed in the interrupting scene has some importance to the emotional development of the character. That is, a flashback should contain emotional facts, not simply material information. The placement of the flashback—or other exposition of past events—should be justified as a step in the experience you are creating for the reader.

The techniques of moving in and out of flashback scenes deserve special attention. You should get in and out of a flashback as quickly and directly as possible. Many times you can simply cut to the flashback, particularly if you use a typographical means (such as italics) to hold the flashback material. Here is an example of this technique. Miriam, at Phyllis's wedding, remembers a past event. Note the decision to put this flashback in the present tense for additional emphasis.

> Miriam heard the minister say, "Do you, Phyllis"—*She is standing at the punch bowl wondering why she came. She wants to be at the lab or back in her room listening to Bach. She sees the frenetic dancing and Robin talking animatedly at the other end of the room. Someone touches her on the shoulder and she turns to see Frank and he is saying, "Do you . . ."*
> And then she heard Phyllis saying "yes" and wondered how things would be now if she had said "yes" to Frank.

Normally you will cast flashbacks (and everything else) in the past tense. This is what readers are used to and what is easiest for them to follow. The present tense creates a greater degree of intensity than you usually want.

Readers are also used to the simple conventions of phrasing that introduce interrupting scenes: "He remembered the time when . . . ," "She wished she could get back to when she was everybody's favorite, like on the day . . . ," "The smell was just like . . . ," and so forth. Here is a movement backward from Joyce's "The Boarding House."

> It was not altogether his fault that it had happened. He remembered well, with the curious patient memory of the celibate, the first casual caresses her dress, her breath, her fingers had given him. Then late one night as he was undressing for bed she had tapped at his door, timidly. She wanted to relight her candle at his for hers had been blown out by a gust. It was her bath night. She wore a loose open combing-jacket of printed flannel. Her white instep shone in the opening of her furry slippers and the blood glowed warmly behind her perfumed skin. From her hands and wrists too as he lit and steadied the candle a faint perfume arose.

EXERCISE

1. Mark the interweaving of exposition and flashback with the unfolding present action in Leavitt's "The Lost Cottage."

2. Invent one or two flashback scenes for Bel Kaufman's "Sunday in the Park."

3. Outline a restructuring of "Rhody's Path" that uses the snakebite as the point of attack and presents most of the other material through exposition and flashback.

4. The constant task of the fiction writer is to move characters through time and space while getting a number of other tasks done simultaneously. Imagine a character you have developed in a character sketch getting ready to meet his new girlfriend's, or her boyfriend's, parents for the first time (or some similarly critical situation, such as getting ready for a job interview, a promotion review, or a trip to the doctor). Move your character through a believable landscape (or cityscape) and into the building and room where he or she will wait to meet the others. The character is apprehensive. Since this episode is your reader's introduction to the character (and the whole story), your writing must serve many functions at once without being too obvious. The character might be reminded of something in the past (which you could develop in a flashback), might notice certain details in the office building or home, might wish to escape the situation or else be eagerly looking forward to it. Keep the action moving. All aspects of fiction writing except dialogue can play a part here. If you use dialogue, keep it to a minimum. See Exercise 5 for some planning ideas.

5. Inspector A arrives at the home of Mr. and Mrs. X. He has come to interview them about their reported theft of a painting. Describe Inspector A's arrival at the X estate, his impressions of the owners from what his trained eye notices as he approaches the front of the house, enters, walks through the

SKETCH OF GROUND FLOOR LAYOUT; SITTING ROOM SCENE OF THEFT

A = STAIRCASE
B = FORMAL ROOM
C = SITTING ROOM
D = DINING ROOM
E = ENTRANCE
G = GARAGE
H = HALL
K = KITCHEN

entrance hall or lobby, and is shown into the sitting room, where he waits for Mr. and Mrs. X to join him. Through physical details, the inspector is building an understanding of the people he is about to meet. You might as well have a butler answer the door. You might want to prepare a sketch such as the one on p. 212, to help you visualize the situation.

SCENE AND SUMMARY

In *Writing Fiction,* R. V. Cassill tells us that **scenes** "bring the action and sometimes the dialogue of the characters before the reader with a fullness comparable to what a witness might observe or overhear." **Narrative passages,** on the other hand, "condense action into its largest movements." They tend to summarize and telescope events rather then present them in dramatic detail as scenes do. Janet Burroway, in her book *Writing Fiction,* considers "*scene*" and "*summary*" as ways of treating time: "A summary covers a relatively long period of time in relatively short compass; a scene deals with a relatively short period of time at length." Burroway believes that while a summary is a useful device, scenes are absolutely necessary.

Scenes create the illusion of an unbroken stretch of time and action, usually in a single place. The business of narrative passages or summaries is to introduce or link scenes while performing expository work. In your scenes you make your work come alive.

A crucial task for the writer is to determine which material demands development in a scene and which requires only summary handling. The principle of economy operates here: scenes should be chosen to perform multiple tasks, and no plot should have more scenes than it needs.

On the pages that follow, we discuss the development of plot through scenes in three short stories: Joyce's "The Boarding House," Kornblatt's "Balancing Act," and Rushdie's "Good Advice Is Rarer Than Rubies." Though we mainly concentrate on the selection and juxtapositioning of scenes, we will pay attention as well to point of attack, exposition, flashback, summary, and characterization. The idea here is to help you look at these issues as a writer.

"The Boarding House" by James Joyce provides a clear example of economy in scene selection. In fact, Joyce has handled his story so economically and suggestively that, with no loss of impact, he has been able to leap over a scene that we would expect to be dramatized. He has also presented us with a summary telling of another potential scene.

"The Boarding House" is built out of four scenes in the ongoing present into which are embedded past scenes and some observations about past events. The story begins slowly, as Joyce takes a leisurely five paragraphs to give us a fairly detailed backgrounding of the situation in which Mrs. Mooney and her daughter Polly find themselves. However, if we study these expository paragraphs carefully, we see that Joyce has established a vivid personal situation inside of a larger cultural one. The moral environment of the story is one of Joyce's main concerns, as it is throughout *Dubliners,* from which this story is taken.

Only after readers receive the background situation and the initial portraits of Polly and her mother does Joyce focus the story through dramatized scenes. The first scene establishes the time—Sunday morning—in which all of the unfolding action occurs. We see the respectable-looking churchgoers out on the street, while the fallen establishment that Mrs. Mooney runs is being aired out. We are given a close-up description of the breakfast remains, and we hear about the frugal measures taken by Mary under Mrs. Mooney's instruction. The images of propriety ("gloved hands") clash with the images of egg streaks and bacon fat, intensifying thematic concern with the distance between outward appearances and inner truths. So, too, the expansive gesture of the open windows and ballooning lace curtains conflict with the pettiness of putting "the sugar and butter safe under lock and key." Joyce's scene contains precise images that not only render the place concretely—materially—but also suggest the moral issues of his story.

Embedded in this scene is Mrs. Mooney's reconstruction of the previous night's conversation with Polly. *That* scene, however, is not dramatized: we get none of the conversation and only the barest summary of what transpired. Nonetheless, we know exactly what happened.

Scene 1 continues with Mrs. Mooney planning her attack on Mr. Doran. She knows that she holds all the cards of moral pressure. She and Polly have been silent accomplices in the pursuit of a proper marriage for Polly. Their plan is based on a reading of Mr. Doran's character and an intimate knowledge of how important reputation is in Dublin. The morally repugnant scheme depends on the concern for appearances, and it reinforces the superficiality of those appearances. Ironically, Joyce has Mrs. Mooney consider that she has just enough time to blackmail Mr. Doran and still make it to church by noon. She sees no inconsistency between the two acts.

We get to know Mr. Doran a bit through Mrs. Mooney's ruminations. The second scene presents Mr. Doran in his room puzzling over his fate. We learn that Polly had come to see him after discussing things with her mother the night before, and that she had told him about the mother and daughter conversation. He is remembering his confession to a priest, examining the overall situation, and retracing the steps of his involvement with Polly. Within this second scene is a flashback—Doran's vivid recollection of the night he succumbed to Polly's seductive behavior. The second scene concludes with Mary arriving to summon him to see Mrs. Mooney.

The third scene, Mr. Doran's journey down the stairs, intensifies his anxiety, especially as he passes Polly's brother Jack, a man capable of violence who has threatened anyone who would jeopardize his sister's reputation. Jack, we gather, is the strong-arm version of his mother.

Between the third scene and the concluding scene, we know that Mrs. Mooney and Mr. Doran have had their little chat. However, Joyce chose not to present it, trusting the reader to feel the full weight of the inevitable through silence.

Instead of following Doran into the parlour for his confrontation with Mrs. Mooney, we visit Polly's room and enter Polly's thoughts. We see her preparing for the news that is bound to come. It is an emotional moment for her, but her complex imaginings of the future are left unspecified. Joyce leaves us to ponder the kind of relationship these two can have, given the questionable foundation on which it is built. Mrs. Mooney's voice breaks through Polly's reverie, announcing that Mr. Doran has something to speak to her about.

In conveying this story, Joyce has made a series of decisions about plot. These decisions have had to do, in part, with how to get the essential material to the reader. That is, Joyce lays out not only a series of events, but also—and more importantly—a series of experiences for the reader. The plot is not the story, but rather is the strategy by which the story is communicated: the selection of scenes for dramatization, the selection of perspectives from which to render those scenes, the selection of materials to summarize and "tell" about rather than present dramatically, and the decision to let the reader's imagination do some work—that is, the selection of those story ingredients only implied or briefly sketched.

QUESTIONS

1. Joyce uses dialogue sparingly in this story. What does he save it for?

2. Joyce allows access to the thoughts of each of his three main characters. How is this omniscient technique handled? Why is it necessary? (*Note:* the selected scenes do not show the characters interacting.)

3. How does Joyce make the initial five paragraphs of exposition count? In particular, what do readers gain from knowing about Polly's father?

EXERCISES

1. Rewrite "The Boarding House" beginning with the sixth paragraph, layering in the material Joyce has presented in the first five paragraphs.

2. Invent the two "missing" scenes: the conversation between Mrs. Mooney and Polly and the one between Mrs. Mooney and Mr. Doran.

3. Imagine Jack Mooney's perspective on what has been going on. Develop one or two scenes from his point of view.

In "Balancing Act," Joyce Reiser Kornblatt employs six scenes to develop her story of a woman's hope for a reawakened marriage. The point of attack for her story is late in the long history of the relationship; it is a point just in advance of the false hope on which the story ends. Kornblatt's story moves into its first scene much more quickly than does James Joyce's.

The couple go on a trip together. The woman is accompanying her husband, who will attend a convention. This story could have been picked up (point of attack) with his first mention of the convention, her decision to come, the two of them packing, leaving the house, or driving to the airport. Kornblatt's decision to place them in the airport avoids unnecessary exposition or scenes and brings the reader immediately into the excitement of the airport environment.

The great variety of couples at the airport allows Kornblatt to enter quickly into the woman's concern: her own marriage. This first scene, partly summarized, concludes with a dramatized subscene at the newsstand. The bland civility of her conversation with her husband, with its undercurrent of frustration, focuses the more generalized treatment of the woman's dissatisfaction rendered just before. The scene ends with them heading for the plane.

In place of the next "realistic" moments—boarding the plane, taking their seats, preparing for takeoff—Kornblatt has her narrator expound on the woman's predicament. The focusing image, balancing on one foot, elaborates on the title, and the expository passage substitutes for one action we know is taking place: climbing the boarding ladder to the plane. Kornblatt presents the staleness of the relationship, the woman's loss of identity, and her psychological suspension or paralysis in a summary fashion—but notice that the expository paragraphs are filled with concrete details.

The phrase "The plane lifted" begins the second scene. Those three words allow the reader's imagination to relocate. No one questions the narrator's authority to put us here. No one feels that significant details have been omitted. This short scene, a smooth mixture of showing and telling, takes us from somewhere—the reader can decide where—to Chicago. It's a fifty-minute flight in which about thirty seconds of precisely focused dialogue handles the illusion of time while deepening our understanding of the woman's despair.

"They were waiting for the desk clerk to attend them" sets the third scene. No details of descent, the second airport, or ground transportation. No struggling with luggage. No wandering through the lobby. No writing a transition scene just to fulfill a trivial notion of verisimilitude. Nothing that doesn't count. Waiting is what this woman does, is what each of the partners does with respect to the other. Not only does the whole story have a point of attack, but each scene as well. The building is pleasing. The different ways in which each responds to the architecture—the man's profession—deepens our understanding of their emotional dissonance.

Although Kornblatt does not mark it as a separate scene by the typographical convention of skipped lines, we might consider the bedroom scene as the fourth scene of this story. Again, the transition is swift: "Their room was spacious and well appointed." The brief summary of their tepid lovemaking underscores everything we have already learned. Although both want this trip to be something special, neither has a way of breaking out of their lifeless routines. The wife wants energy, intensity, passion—something beyond the husband's matter-of-factness. However, the only passion is in the eyes of the wallpaper figures. (*Note*: Because this material is not actually dramatized, we might consider it part of the larger "arrival" scene.)

In the next scene, the woman's morning of shopping ends with a light meal in a coffee shop. The woman overhears the cheerful banter between two young mothers and their children. This experience triggers thoughts about her relationship with her two children, focusing down to memories of how each was born. These memories give us a more complex understanding of her tendency toward depression as well as her failure to achieve an idealized intimacy with her husband.

Following this scene is a summary treatment of the next few days. With nothing worth the reader's attention, Kornblatt feels no obligation to give equal weight to equal intervals of time. We learn that the woman's shopping becomes satisfying, that she begins to relax, and that their lovemaking improves. This little change-of-pace trip is making a small difference in the lives of this couple, even as they go their separate ways through most of it. The scene raises expectations (a kind of suspense) that will not be fulfilled in the long run.

The final scene takes place on Friday morning in the hotel lobby. Unnoticed, the woman sees her husband in conversation with a colleague. She is surprised by his dominance of the other man. In his commanding behavior toward the Philadelphia urban planner, she sees her husband acting as she wants him to act toward her. We know that she has been energized by her accidental discovery, and that she allows herself "a fragile crystal of hope."

The story concludes by quickly sketching the brief renewal of their relationship that precedes its ultimate failure. So surely have we been manipulated by Kornblatt that we feel the truth of the temporary resurgence of vitality and the truth of its ephemerality. In one way, the story has been about the whole of this couple's marriage. Yet what we have learned about these people, about the woman in particular, we have learned through bits and pieces of a few days and bits and pieces of the remembered past. Selectivity and focus. These are features that life doesn't have, but that any piece of fiction you write should have.

EXERCISE

1. Why is there so much detail in the coffee shop scene? What justifies this close look at characters who play no direct role in the story?

2. Rewrite that material as a summary. Consider the consequences of this different treatment.

3. How close is the narrator's perspective to the woman's? Is the narrator's treatment of the husband sufficient? Reliable?

4. Develop the "voluptuous breakfast" into a full scene. Use it to reinforce or replace another scene in the story. Keep in touch with Kornblatt's characters and style.

Salman Rushdie's "Good Advice Is Rarer Than Rubies," like many stories, is framed by an arrival and departure (see also "Balancing Act," "The Lost Cottage," and "Rhody's Path"). Rushdie's story, which depends largely on dialogue, is one of those many short pieces of fiction in which character seems to generate the plot. Though we come to understand that the story is "about" (1) Miss Rehana's need to fulfill the terms of the arranged marriage and her simultaneous need to avoid it, and (2) Muhammad Ali's need to fulfill his role as advice giver, these concerns are never directly addressed. Instead, we deduce them from their source: the actions, words, and thoughts of the two characters. Rushdie turns his story on the fine irony of Miss Rehana "failing" to get her passport by not listening to Muhammad Ali's advice and thereby managing a greater victory. At the same time, though he "failed" to persuade her to accept the forged passport, the old man was victorious in having the "correct" advice and in winning an apology from this most attractive young woman.

In this story, the "plot" is the series of events that reveal the shifting positions the characters take toward one another. There is a competition for mastery, for having the upper hand, that constitutes the **conflict** in this story. Each has unique tools for waging the struggle. The story needs only two scenes: one before and one after Miss Rehana's confrontation with the British Embassy officials.

Rushdie has organized the first scene so that we take Ali's position toward Miss Rehana's needs. His is the only perspective we have, and since he is deceived, so are we. The **crisis** comes in the second scene, when the consequences of the offstage action are revealed to Muhammad Ali and to the reader. Subtly, Rushdie brings Ali and the reader to understand that the original perception of Miss Rehana was false. The **resolution** occurs when Miss Rehana tells the old man he need not feel sorry for her. In fact, this resolution contains the moment of enlightenment, the **epiphany:** her real mission was *to make an attempt* at fulfilling her obligation.

At the point of attack, Miss Rehana's arrival on the morning bus, Rushdie playfully introduces a fabulous quality. (The title, an aphorism, also suggests a fable.) The bus is extremely colorful, and the woman arrives almost magically in "a cloud of dust." We never leave the small area bounded by the bus stop, the embassy gates, and the adjacent shantytown that includes a snack stand and Muhammad Ali's "special corner." In fact, the story ends with Miss Rehana—once again on the bus—disappearing into the same cloud of dust. For the old man, she has been a magical figure, almost a dream, through which his need for beauty and appreciation have, for part of one day, come true.

In "Good Advice Is Rarer Than Rubies," Rushie has shown us how a few well-chosen, focused moments can reflect significant aspects of a culture and types of individuals within that culture.

EXERCISE

1. Outline the personality traits of each character and note the means by which each is revealed.

2. Describe the plot without reference to the nature of the characters. Can this task be done? Why or why not?

3. Discuss the omission of Miss Rehana's "scene" inside the embassy. Why is it handled through her report to Muhammad Ali? Compare and contrast this "missing" scene with the one in Joyce's "The Boarding House."

4. Sketch alternative developments of the story in which Miss Rehana decides to (a) accept the passport or (b) go home without applying for one.

ADDITIONAL EXERCISES

1. Break down "The Lost Cottage" by David Leavitt into its major scenes, summary passages, and flashbacks. Describe Leavitt's point of attack and his method of shuttling back and forth in time.

2. Analyze the alternation of scene and summary in Bel Kaufman's "Sunday in the Park."

3. Outline or make marginal notes on the methods of characterization in Kaufman's story.

4. How would you describe the conflict in Kaufman's story? Is the ending a fortuitous surprise, or has the author built toward it carefully?

5. Read Hemingway's "A Very Short Story" in Chapter 11. Each paragraph contains the seed idea for at least one fully realized scene. Select one such idea and develop the scene.

6. Return to the detective story set in motion in Exercise 5 on p. 212. Imagine that some time has passed. The inspector has interviewed Mr. and Mrs. X, who are now left alone to respond to what has happened. Pick up the story with their interaction.

7. Recast Susan Glaspell's *Trifles* (Chapter 14) as a short story.

VERISIMILITUDE

We could have dealt with this topic in any of the previous sections because the writer's successful handling of characterization, plot, setting, and scene creates in the reader a feeling of **verisimilitude**—a sense that both individual elements and the whole fiction is *like the truth*.

A historian or biographer has to report precisely literal reality, something that anyone else who found the same evidence would report. (Differing interpretations, of course, are another matter.) Fiction writers have only to give the *impression* that their fictive history or biography follows the rules of evidence. Therefore, while writers cannot be arbitrary, they need not prove that the facts can be tested in the chemistry lab or FBI files. Verisimilitude is like Nutrasweet: it needs to taste like sugar but not *be* sugar.

Inexperienced writers often waste energy trying to recreate literal reality rather than an impression of it. Experienced writers understand that, for the sake of a good story, readers are willing to suspend their disbelief in the "facts" of the fictive world. Thus half the job of producing a feeling of reality is already done by the readers.

Readers don't task writers with explaining which chemical laws allow a prince to be turned into a flounder, or how a spaceship can go faster than light, or what motivates a white whale to go around eating legs, or exactly how a sudden coup managed to establish a patriarchal society in New England despite the Constitution and U.S. Army. Readers never ask how first-person narrators can remember verbatim conversations that happened two or ten or thirty years ago. We don't need to know how the couple gets from the airport to the hotel unless the "how" is important. *If the characters believe in the fictive world*, we'll believe.

In fact, when the writer goes about nervously matching the fictive world to the phenomenal world, the reader begins to question the fiction. It is best not to explain how it happens that your character can fly. Just let your hero fly early and late, have Lois Lane believe it, and we'll believe it so long as we are convinced that the unbelievable fact works in the story. Interestingly enough, a story will lack verisimilitude only if our flying character doesn't fly when, for example, abandoned on a lonely desert island (unless, of course, the writer has created a reason the character cannot fly in that particular circumstance).

Verisimilitude is maintained as long as the writer is careful about the following matters:

1. *The characters must behave consistently from scene to scene* (not just in one scene), or the reader must be prepared for a deviation from an expected behavior or trait. A personage who has been a coward throughout cannot suddenly save a child from a runaway horse because the writer has discovered that the situation requires the child to be saved and grow up to invent the electric light bulb. Nor can the writer finesse the point by saying "something just came over him." If you haven't done it in the first place, you need to **foreshadow**—to find some way to suggest the possibility that the coward can be brave. In brief, a story begins to lack verisimilitude when the special identity of the character is ignored merely to satisfy the plot.

2. *Don't insult the reader by surprising plot elements invented merely to get out of a dead end.* The long-lost rich uncle can't be made to appear just when the newlyweds are about to go down for the third time. (See **deus ex machina** in the Glossary.)

3. *All the props must be planted before they are needed.* The gun doesn't just happen to be in the purse. Either we see it put into the purse or we are convinced by other means that it is likely to be there. (Incidentally, if we are shown a loaded gun in a purse, it had better go off sometime in the story.) This principle is a variation of number 2.

4. *The outside reality that the story calls on the reader to know must be rendered accurately.* When a writer depends on the reader's knowledge of outside facts for some of the internal effects of the story, then the facts must (a) have verisimilitude in the story and (b) accurately reflect outside reality. A chase scene in New York City that has the pursuer's car traveling east on Broadway (a north-south street) is likely to offend the experienced reader's sense of reality with no gain for the fiction. Readers will more easily accept Superwoman deflecting bullets with her bracelets than they will accept that she did it on the border between Alabama and Arizona. The need for accuracy cannot be overstressed. If your readers catch you in a factual mistake, you may lose them.

5. *Your characters must interact with the environment or "set" you have created for them in credible ways.* If a scene occurs in a howling gale on the deck of a schooner, don't have them whisper to one another. If your characters are two recluses in a house full of cats, the cats will be rubbing up against the characters' legs, scratching at the Victorian sofa, and sniffing around the hamburger. One of your recluses will be forever shooing the cats away. For more on how characters interact with their

world, see the drama section. The essential point is that we believe in characters who see, hear, taste, touch, and smell the world in which the writer has placed them.

Creating verisimilitude requires that you plot (or replot) so the "equipment" necessary to move the story—straw, caves, knowledge, experience, ray-guns—does not magically or awkwardly appear in the scene just at the moment needed. If you don't plan (or go back and fix up), the sudden appearance of the new element will unpleasantly surprise the reader: "How did that get there? Did I miss something? Why would George kill Andrea? I think the writer got stuck." When you have destroyed verisimilitude in this way, readers begin to ask the kinds of questions that destroy belief in your story.

As you can see, foreshadowing in both a limited sense (getting the gun in the purse) and a more profound sense (suggesting changes in relationships) is at the heart of creating a sense that the story is like reality.

Unsophisticated writers often try to justify an event—a coincidence, for example—that is not convincing *in the story* by saying, "But that's the way it happened." Strange though it seems, some things, like coincidence, happen more in "real" life than they can in fiction or, to put the issue another way, coincidence happens differently in life than it can in fiction.

For example, in real life you might be broke and alone in a big city, let's say Chicago. Night is coming on. Your family can't be reached because they've gone to Nepal on vacation. Besides, you don't even have enough money to make a call. You are getting frightened as you walk the Loop in the crowd of homeward-bound people. Suddenly a fifty-dollar bill swirls down in the stiff breeze off Lake Michigan and lands right at your feet. Saved! Once in a billion times you have won the lottery of life. In real life, the chance may be a billion to one, but there is room in reality for that statistical *one*.

In plotting, there are no statistics. Everything that happens, even a coincidence, is part of the writer's plan. It is the writer who is dealing out the fifty-dollar bills for the character. The reader of a story would feel that the happy coincidence just described occurs only because the writer could not think of another, more logical solution to the character's dilemma. The wind-blown inheritance, no matter how well disguised, is a cop-out, a way of rescuing the character that does not grow from the situation (except that Chicago is windy) or from the character's identity. Because the writer has not plotted well, the surprise that has been sprung on us is not satisfying: no amount of foresight could have predicted it *in this story*.

In contrast, the surprise that grows from an inevitable but unanticipated event at the climax of the story is one of the pleasures you provide your reader, who says, "I should have realized that." Some stories are aimed directly at this pleasure—for example, O'Henry-type short stories or James Bond novels. But the surprise that is not inevitable, the surprise that readers cannot kick themselves for having missed because it was foreshadowed, the surprise that seems to exist only to keep the action going or to get the characters offstage—that kind of surprise destroys verisimilitude.

EXERCISE

1. Can you think of ways to use such an unexpected event as the wind-blown money without injuring the reader's sense of verisimilitude? For example, what if you did not use the event at the end of a story but at the beginning? Work out the first paragraph of a story that has the event as its central incident. Can you think of any other ways to give the event verisimilitude?

2. List the ways in which the authors convince (or fail to convince) the reader that the following potentially unlikely circumstances are in fact like reality (obviously, don't worry about the ones you haven't read).

a. Mr. Doran's accepting the trap set for him rather than just moving out of the boarding house to avoid marrying Polly.
b. The snake escaping in "Rhody's Path" and Rhody being the one whom it bites.
c. The mother becoming the bully at the end of "Sunday in the Park."
d. Alex's stashing Marian at a nearby motel while the family gathering is going on in "The Lost Cottage." Lydia just happening to see Marian while shopping.
e. Jay Gatsby acquiring all his money so quickly.
f. Lilliputians.
g. The planet Dune.

3. What techniques does Kornblatt use to set us up in "Balancing Act" so that we accept her story's reversals? Can you find elements of foreshadowing?

4. As a fiction writer, you will need to find the answers to questions like these. Can you?

a. Can a hand grenade turn over a Toyota truck?
b. What are beer brands from Argentina?
c. Will a typical college library have many windows or few?

PROBLEMS

In this section we discuss some typical problems of beginning writers. Some of these are illustrated here. Some would take perhaps an entire story to illustrate so we have merely described the problem. In a sense, we are protecting the guilty and saving you from reading too much ineffective prose.

Needless Complication

A misguided sense of what makes for verisimilitude, or a desire to surprise the reader, can lead a writer to give a character an unconvincing action. In the following opening passage the student writer is so intent on piling up details and creating a suspenseful mood that he fails to build the character and situation in a truly plausible way.

> Brian brushed his long blond hair out of his eyes, then quietly opened the door to his bedroom. He was tall and rather thin. As he gently closed the door, he thought himself lucky that his parent's hadn't heard him come in two hours late from his date. The room was consumed by darkness except for the narrow streak of light along the bottom of the door. He turned and tip-toed over to his desk.
>
> He opened the drawer slowly and began to carefully sort through the disarray. It was hopeless, groping about in the darkness, so he reached over and drew the curtains open slightly. Moonlight shown in illuminating the scene. Bending over to look into the drawer, he spied them—a small bottle of pills in the back right hand corner. He pulled the pills out of the drawer and set them on his nightstand.

Of course, you can spot any number of problems in style, diction, and even grammar and spelling. But the conceptual failure would remain even after you smoothed out the rough spots. Here it is: Brian is searching for drugs. When the reader learns this, the elaboration of the search becomes unconvincing. Who would "hide" drugs so carelessly? Brian should know just how to get his hands on the bottle. All the business about a hopeless disarray and letting in the moonlight rings false once we discover what he is actually doing.

Misuse of Dialogue

Too often in premise or adventure fiction, characterization is given no attention. As a result, dialogue serves only obvious expository purposes. Because the writer of the following material is so concerned that the reader understand the situation, the characters seem to exist only for that purpose.

> "Colonel Yeshnick, I refuse to sign this visa for Donnis to defect to the United States," responded General Alexeev in a rejecting manner.
>
> Colonel Yeshnick replied placatingly, "Sir, he will be immigrating, not defecting to the United States, and you are the only one left from the Premier on down who has to approve it. Sir, with all due respect, you promised him that he would be allowed to leave if he would not retire from athletics until after the Olympic Games. Not only did he compete, but he won the silver medal, and also set a new . . . ."

The dialogue seems forced and artificial because it is. It is in the service of exposition that could be handled more smoothly in another way. In fact, the entire story is told primarily through conversations between these two officers, while Donnis, the character whose fate is at stake, hardly gets any attention. Even though we are always hearing voices, we are never getting in touch with characters. They are doing the narrator's work. Note also the awkward, heavy-handed use of designators.

Here is a shorter example of dialogue being used, obviously and clumsily, to do the work of exposition.

"You must be that Penny fellow from Bangor. I'm Mrs. Johnson. We're the caretakers. The Cables are expecting you. Come with me."

This passage can also serve to illustrate another ineffective use of dialogue: the attempt at verisimilitude that comes from trying to detail the most trivial kinds of "actual" speech. In this category we include those interchanges of "hello" and "goodbye" that have no emotion or characterizing energy. Just because it is easy to make these exchanges sound authentic is no reason to use them in a piece of fiction. Better a few instances of **indirect discourse**—the narrator's "after saying hello" or "after stating his business" or "the introductions having been made"—than a tedious reproduction of speech. Rarely would we need to belabor this part of a scene or transition, and even more rarely would we need to have it dramatized. (See Chapter 13, "Dialogue and Its Problems.")

Sudden Comfort

Beginning writers often call too much attention to the contrivances that their stories depend upon. We have read too many stories in which, within the course of seven or eight pages, morose lovers or spouses become suicidal, and when they need a weapon to blast them out of their misery, the author conveniently provides one—all this just as the story is about to end.

Case in point: Bill's wife has left him. He regrets that he has been a drunk and a bully, often forcing himself on her in brutal ways. But now, seeing that she has moved out, he convinces himself that all is lost. His tortured mind leads him to set up a romantic dinner for himself and an imaginary version of his wife. Just before he brings that special bottle of wine to the table, something draws him to a nightstand: "Bill reached under the drawer and pulled off an object that had been obviously concealed." Well, of course, this mysterious object is identified a few sentences later as the "small 38 caliber pistol" that he fires into his temple. How convenient for Bill and for the author.

The sudden appearance of a gun or any other fortuitous plot saver happens, in part, because the story is weak and skeletal to begin with. However, only in first drafts, when the flow of events is taking on a shape, are such conveniences forgivable. Then it's time to recognize the problem and do something about it.

1. To revamp the whole story because it is hackneyed.
2. To create a plausible reason, long before it is needed, for a gun to be available, and to build that reason into the story with some subtlety.
3. To avoid depending on the gun gimmick altogether.

Sudden Omniscience

Once you have established a perspective from which events and information are revealed, you must stick to it. One student writer made his main character, Connor, the central intelligence. We go where he goes, see what he sees, and have access to his thoughts and feelings. Connor, who runs a bar, has decided to walk Katherine, one of his waitresses, to her car. It's late at night:

> As he walked her to where she had parked her rental car, he could see from her face that she was still upset over the night's events.

But wait! Nothing that comes earlier in the story allows Connor to know that she is driving a rented car. The narrator has moved too far outside of the limited perspective chosen for this story. We wonder whether this information has special importance (it doesn't) or is simply an attempt at verisimilitude—a fortuitous fact that backfires.

Ping-Pong

Shifting the point of view too rapidly, especially without any clear reason for breaking the convention of maintaining a single point of view throughout a scene (if not an entire work), disorients the reader and strains credibility.

In one student work we are asked to follow the path of a mysterious killer, taking things in through his perspective: "The night sounds were a calming friend to him" and "he noticed a car light stop on the bridge above him" and "his adrenaline began to flow freely" establish the reader's means of access to the story. When the author writes "After the killer had ascended the sloping hill up to the bridge, his form became visible to the stranger . . . ," we are momentarily jolted by the shift in perspective, and to no good end.

In a story about Michael Locklear, whose thoughts about a coming confrontation with the Soviet Union are generously provided, we suddenly encounter the following after Michael's conversation with Admiral Pete Mitchell: "Mitchell returned to his chair and levelled his gaze at the President. Damn it, he thought, there was no alternative." And then, in the next paragraph, "Locklear shifted in his seat." Nothing justifies this convenient presentation of Mitchell's thoughts, which fractures our illusion of *being with*

Locklear throughout the story. Furthermore, "Mitchell" is too easily confused with "Michael"—the main character's first name.

The same mistake occurs in the following scene, in which a policeman, Bob Bryant, is questioning Miss Lee about the death of her boyfriend. Bryant is the story's central intelligence whose perspective the reader shares.

> Boy, you're losing your touch and your sensitivity, Bob told himself. "I'm sorry to bother you, but we need to ask you some more questions. Can you think of any reason why someone would have wanted Wayne dead?"
>
> Miss Lee seemed calmer now, but she never got over her agitation during the half hour she spent with Bryant.

Unless Miss Lee's agitation is shown outwardly (and it isn't) or is somehow perceived by Bryant, we shouldn't be told about it.

Wrong Technique

In the same story treated in "Sudden Omniscience" section, the author has attempted to reproduce Connor's thoughts rather than simply characterize them:

> "God it's hot," thought Connor, "maybe I should think about investing in an air conditioner for the joint. Yeah, and I oughtta set the temperature *way* low. The girls wouldn't be wild about it, but I bet business would triple. Hah—I'm a damn funny guy."

These thoughts read too much like self-conscious speech; even Connor's habits of pronunciation are reproduced. Better to simplify:

> Connor wondered if he should buy an air conditioner. If he had one, he would set it way low. The girls wouldn't be wild about it, but business would probably triple. Connor was amazed at his own cleverness.

Notice how the revised second and third sentences come across clearly as Connor's thoughts even though they aren't given designators, quotation marks, or verbal quirks. The narrator has slid quietly in and out of Connor's mind.

Pogo Stick

Beginning writers often feel the need to sketch many short scenes, presenting some bit of information in each but not developing any of them fully enough to further the plot or deepen the character. This quick jumping around from scene to scene without any clear direction being established only confuses the reader.

In the Bob Bryant story discussed earlier, an early scene in the station house contains a celebration of Bob's successful "sting" operation in which a major narcotics organization was put out of business and the leader shot. The scene does nothing for the story at hand; none of its details have any relevance later on. All it establishes is that Bryant is a policeman, something the first mention of his current case would make clear anyway.

Descriptive Clutter

Sometimes the search for verisimilitude ends in amassed details that only slow the story down while the reader is forced to pay attention to "realistic" trivia. Here is an example:

> He went back to the van. The door on the driver's side was slightly rusting near the bottom front corner. He opened the door, climbed in, and closed the door. The sound of vibrating steel resounded throughout the car.

For this story, we don't need to know the degree or exact placement of the rust, nor the three steps the character takes to get behind the wheel. Essentially, the writer's job is to get him moving again. So, "He got back in the van and winced as the rusty door slammed shut" would do it.

Another kind of clutter comes from trying to introduce too many characters at once. Here is the opening of a novel that causes more confusion than clarification, especially since some of the characters mentioned here are never heard of again.

> Dolly McKee's timing was less than perfect. Sam Parker was just getting to the part of his meeting with the president that Ken Meyers had been patiently waiting to hear about.
>
> "I'm sorry to break in," Dolly said, her hand on the doorknob, little more than her birdlike face visible as she leaned into the room. "Levi says he's got to talk to Ken. He's upset about something. It sounds important. Can you handle it, or should I call Simpson?"
>
> Sonofabitch, Meyers thought. What a time for a housekeeping problem. Just when Parker might say something about whether Babcock was planning to reappoint him. He told Dolly to show the black man into his office.

Even though one could argue that these characters are real to one another, such a barrage of names, labels, and pronouns will raise any reader's anxiety level—and for no good reason.

Other Problems

We have no space to illustrate the story in which one action follows another and yet nothing happens. That is, the events don't reveal character or shape an understanding of some issue. Nor will we ask you to consider the other extreme: the story that constantly screams out its meaning by glossing every action and every physical detail as if the writer felt obliged to present both the story and its interpretation. Nor the kind in which the author has gone back and disguised all the evidence we need to make any sense out of what's going on, believing that bewildering the reader is a worthy goal if one can later show how cleverly the obscuring had been done. These and other problems take whole stories to illustrate.

It is very easy to go wrong in telling stories because so many demands come to bear at the same moment—character development, plot, exposition, description, narration. You can't let down your guard and cruise for a while, because what is said on page 20 has to connect with page 6 and both with page 23. You need constantly to anticipate, recognize, and then solve the problem. The payoff is an effective story.

11

Six Stories

A Very Short Story

ERNEST HEMINGWAY

One hot evening in Padua they carried him up onto the roof and he could look out over the top of the town. There were chimney swifts in the sky. After a while it got dark and the searchlights came out. The others went down and took the bottles with them. He and Luz could hear them below on the balcony. Luz sat on the bed. She was cool and fresh in the hot night.

Luz stayed on night duty for three months. They were glad to let her. When they operated on him she prepared him for the operating table; and they had a joke about friend or enema. He went under the anesthetic holding tight on to himself so he would not blab about anything during the silly, talky time. After he got on crutches he used to take the temperatures so Luz would not have to get up from the bed. There were only a few patients, and they all knew about it. They all liked Luz. As he walked back along the halls he thought of Luz in his bed.

Before he went back to the front they went into the Duomo and prayed. It was dim and quiet, and there were other people praying. They wanted to get married, but there was not enough time for the banns, and neither of them had birth certificates. They felt as though they were married, but they wanted everyone to know about it, and to make it so they could not lose it.

Luz wrote him many letters that he never got until after the armistice. Fifteen came in a bunch to the front and he sorted them by the dates and read them all straight through. They were all about the hospital, and how much she loved him, and how it was impossible to get along without him, and how terrible it was missing him at night.

After the armistice they agreed he should go home to get a job so they might be married. Luz would not come home until he had a good job and could come to New York to meet her. It was understood he would not drink, and he did not want to see his friends or anyone in the States. Only to get a job and be married. On the train from Padua to Milan they quarreled about her not being willing to come home at once. When they had to say goodbye, in the station at Milan, they kissed goodbye, but were not finished with the quarrel. He felt sick about saying goodbye like that.

He went to America on a boat from Genoa. Luz went back to Pordenone to open a hospital. It was lonely and rainy there, and there was a battalion of arditi quartered in the town. Living in the muddy, rainy town in the winter, the major of the battalion made love to Luz, and she had never known Italians before, and finally wrote to the States that theirs had been only a boy and girl affair. She was sorry, and she knew he would probably not be able to understand, but might someday forgive her, and be grateful to her, and she expected, absolutely unexpectedly, to be married in the spring. She loved him as always, but she realized now it was only a boy and girl love. She hoped he would have a great career and believed in him absolutely. She knew it was for the best.

The major did not marry her in the spring, or any other time. Luz never got an answer to the letter to Chicago about it. A short time after he contracted gonorrhea from a salesgirl in a loop department store while riding in a taxicab through Lincoln Park.

Sunday in the Park

Bel Kaufman

It was still warm in the late-afternoon sun, and the city noises came muffled through the trees in the park. She put her book down on the bench, removed her sunglasses, and sighed contentedly. Morton was reading the *Times Magazine* section, one arm flung around her shoulder; their three-year-old son, Larry, was playing in the sandbox: a faint breeze fanned her hair softly against her cheek. It was five-thirty of a Sunday afternoon, and the small playground, tucked away in a corner of the park, was all but deserted. The swings and see-saws stood motionless and abandoned, the slides were empty, and only in the sandbox two little boys squatted diligently side by side. *How good this is,* she thought, and almost smiled at her sense of well-being. They must go out in the sun more often; Morton was so city-pale, cooped up all week inside the gray factorylike university. She squeezed his arm affectionately and glanced at Larry, delighting in the pointed little face frowning in concentration over the tunnel he was digging. The other boy suddenly stood up and with a quick, deliberate swing of his chubby arm threw a spadeful of sand at Larry. It just missed his head. Larry continued digging; the boy remained standing, shovel raised, stolid and impassive.

"No, no, little boy." She shook her finger at him, her eyes searching for the child's mother or nurse. "We mustn't throw sand. It may get in someone's eyes and hurt. We must play nicely in the nice sandbox." The boy looked at her in unblinking expectancy. He was about Larry's age but perhaps ten pounds heavier, a husky little boy with none of Larry's quickness and sensitivity in his face. Where was his mother? The only other people left in the playground were two women and a little girl on roller skates leaving now through the gate, and a man on a bench a few feet away. He was a big man, and he seemed to be taking up the whole bench as he held the Sunday comics close to his face. She supposed he was the child's father. He did not look up from his comics, but spat once deftly out of the corner of his mouth. She turned her eyes away.

At that moment, as swiftly as before, the fat little boy threw another spadeful of sand at Larry. This time some of it landed on his hair and forehead. Larry looked up at his mother, his mouth tentative; her expression would tell him whether to cry or not.

Her first instinct was to rush to her son, brush the sand out of his hair, and punish the other child, but she controlled it. She always said that she wanted Larry to learn to fight his own battles.

"Don't *do* that, little boy," she said sharply, leaning forward on the bench. "You mustn't throw sand!"

The man on the bench moved his mouth as if to spit again, but instead he spoke. He did not look at her, but at the boy only.

"You go right ahead, Joe," he said loudly. "Throw all you want. This here is a *public* sandbox."

She felt a sudden weakness in her knees as she glanced at Morton. He had become aware of what was happening. He put his *Times* down carefully on his lap and turned his fine, lean face toward the man, smiling the shy, apologetic smile he might have offered a student in pointing out an error in his thinking. When he spoke to the man, it was with his usual reasonableness.

"You're quite right," he said pleasantly, "but just because this is a public place. . . ."

The man lowered his funnies and looked at Morton. He looked at him from head to foot, slowly and deliberately. "Yeah?" His insolent voice was edged with menace. "My kid's got just as good right here as yours, and if he feels like throwing sand, he'll throw it, and if you don't like it, you can take your kid the hell out of here."

The children were listening, their eyes and mouths wide open, their spades forgotten in small fists. She noticed the muscle in Morton's jaw tighten. He was rarely angry; he seldom lost his temper. She was suffused with a tenderness for her husband and an impotent rage against the man for involving him in a situation so alien and so distasteful to him.

"Now, just a minute," Morton said courteously, "you must realize. . . ."

"Aw, shut up," said the man.

Her heart began to pound. Morton half rose; the *Times* slid to the ground. Slowly the other man stood up. He took a couple of steps toward Morton, then stopped. He flexed his great arms, waiting. She pressed her trembling knees together. Would there be violence, fighting? How dreadful, how incredible. . . . She must do something, stop them, call for help. She wanted to put her hand on her husband's sleeve, to pull him down, but for some reason she didn't.

Morton adjusted his glasses. He was very pale. "This is ridiculous," he said unevenly. "I must ask you. . . ."

"Oh, yeah?" said the man. He stood with his legs spread apart, rocking a little, looking at Morton with utter scorn. "You and who else?"

For a moment the two men looked at each other nakedly. Then Morton turned his back on the man and said quietly, "Come on, let's get out of here." He walked awkwardly, almost limping with self-consciousness, to the sandbox. He stooped and lifted Larry and his shovel out.

At once Larry came to life; his face lost its rapt expression and he began to kick and cry. "I don't *want* to go home, I want to play better, I don't *want* any supper, I don't *like* supper. . . ." It became a chant as they walked, pulling their child between them, his feet dragging on the ground. In order to get to the exit gate they had to pass the bench where the man sat sprawling again. She was careful not to look at him. With all the dignity she could summon, she pulled Larry's sandy, perspiring little hand, while Morton pulled the other. Slowly and with head high she walked with her husband and child out of the playground.

Her first feeling was one of relief that a fight had been avoided, that no one was hurt. Yet beneath it there was a layer of something else, something heavy and inescapable. She sensed that it was more than just an unpleasant incident, more than defeat of reason by force. She felt dimly it had something to do with her and Morton, something acutely personal, familiar, and important.

Suddenly Morton spoke. "It wouldn't have proved anything."

"What?" she asked.

"A fight. It wouldn't have proved anything beyond the fact that he's bigger than I am."

"Of course," she said.

"The only possible outcome," he continued reasonably, "would have been—what? My glasses broken, perhaps a tooth or two replaced, a couple of days' work missed—and for what? For justice? For truth?"

"Of course," she repeated. She quickened her step. She wanted only to get home and to busy herself with her familiar tasks; perhaps then the feeling, glued like heavy plaster on her heart, would be gone. *Of all the stupid, despicable bullies,* she thought, pulling harder on Larry's hand. The child was still crying. Always before she had felt a tender pity for his defenseless little body, the frail arms, the narrow shoulders with sharp, winglike shoulder blades, the thin and unsure legs, but now her mouth tightened in resentment.

"Stop crying," she said sharply. "I'm ashamed of you!" She felt as if all three of them were tracking mud along the street. The child cried louder.

If there had been an issue involved, she thought, *if there had been something to fight for. . . . But what else could he possibly have done? Allow himself to be beaten? Attempt to educate the man? Call a policeman? "Officer, there's a man in the park who won't stop his child from throwing sand on mine. . . ."* The whole thing was as silly as that, and not worth thinking about.

"Can't you keep him quiet, for Pete's sake?" Morton asked irritably.

"What do you suppose I've been trying to do?" she said.

Larry pulled back, dragging his feet.

"If you can't discipline this child, I will," Morton snapped, making a move toward the boy.

But her voice stopped him. She was shocked to hear it, thin and cold and penetrating with contempt. "Indeed?" she heard herself say. "You and who else?"

Balancing Act

JOYCE REISER KORNBLATT

They walked through the airport without intimacy or particular joy in each other's company, but also without hostility. In the huge concourse, it seemed they passed every imaginable permutation of the mating equation. Couples crazed by the imminence of separation clung like Siamese twins to one another. Other pairs of men and women strolled the terminal with easy affection, fingers brushing, strides matched. Still others tried to outpace their partners, one and then the other forced into an embarrassing trot, a whispered "Dammit, slow down." Some argued loudly, their words strafing each other on the zoneless battleground on which they fought out their lives. Trying to fit herself and her husband in somewhere between the lovers and haters, she speculated that they probably appeared much as they were: eleven years married, prospering, fond of each other, bonded by domestic ritual, speaking in familial civilities, enjoying well-regulated pleasures. She had a funny vision of the terminal as a laboratory for an earnest psychologist—days spent posing as a traveler, working in phone booths, gathering data, grinding out an article: "Coupling Variations in Transit." She smiled at her own joke, but did not share it with her husband, fearing it would take too much exposition to get him to adjust his sight to hers. They seldom stood at the same perceptual location.

"I think I'll buy a magazine," she said as they approached a newsstand.

"They've got plenty on the plane," he said.

"They might not have what I really want."

He shrugged. "That's entirely possible."

She caught his ironic smirk, the momentary despair of his retort, and turned away from it nervously. She studied the racks while he scanned head-lines from all over the world.

Along with her magazine, he bought a pack of gum. He handed her a stick as they walked through the gate. "Here," he said, "for your ears."

"Thanks," she deadpanned. "Could I have a piece for my mouth, too?"

He gave a small smile, but he had no comeback and her appetite for banter reluctantly receded.

"Really, thanks," she said. "You're nice."

"Cub scout training. I've been nice since I was seven." Now a uniformed man was taking down the chain that held them from the field; they headed for the plane.

She stood with one foot raised above, held aloof from, the field of their marriage, and she waited for the force of his personality to emerge, to pull her completely down into the circle of their relationship. She did what she could to invest him with the energy he would need to attract and hold her; she tired herself in the effort to create him, to make him believe in his own power. She closeted her own possibilities. Half asleep like a pelican on one foot, she waited for his transformation. She was very patient; but the patience seemed to infuse itself into her very veins, diluting her blood. She became too quiet; she did not laugh easily or deeply enough; she forgot to use body lotion; at parties she distanced herself from drinkers and flirts. She was waiting, in reserve.

She knew he was disheartened by her growing lackluster. It was as if, over the years, she were a photograph in the process of fading. He could not articulate it, but she could see his discouragement, even terror, when she moved like a shadow through the rooms of their house. She behaved more and more like a person unable to remember the most important fact of her life. He would ask her repeatedly, "What's wrong?" and she would reply, "Nothing. Just thinking," with a smile as tight as a fist and her brain shouting: *I am waiting for you to be able to read my mind.*

She knew by standing on one foot for so long that her other leg might atrophy, that she might never recover its use even if he were to manage to pull her from her strained position. She looked for exercises that she could do which would not jeopardize her crucial, painful balance. Half-hooked rugs she'd begun and abandoned were rolled up in the basement; oil paintings and acrylics sat unframed, unhung in the cluttered sunroom she had used for a time as a studio; overly large gardens choked all summer on weeds, and vegetables she forgot to harvest rotted in the untended furrows; a piano she snatched up eagerly at a house sale stood in the corner of the living room, newspapers stacking up on the bench.

Once he told her, "Your trouble is that you don't stay with anything long enough to know if you really like it."

While she felt like someone who'd been drinking the same glass of water for years.

The plane lifted and she clutched at the armrest during the moments of disconnection with the ground. She shut her eyes and worked on her chewing gum. She wondered how he could not feel brief uneasiness, some small pang of danger. He nudged her. "We've leveled out," he said, "relax."

She opened her eyes. It astounded her how her terror of takeoffs could dissipate once they were high enough and moving smoothly. She was always grateful for his apparent equanimity while she suffered through her short ordeal. But she felt guilty about using his strength while, at the same time, resenting it for its passivity. She looked out at the diminishing city.

"Sometimes I think we should fly on separate planes when we travel," she said. "Because of the kids. Reduce their chances of being orphaned by fifty percent."

He shook his head, as if at a child. "That's what I love about you."

"What?"

"My wife the optimist."

She wanted to tell him, *I need you to have a sense of doom; so we can laugh like mad hyenas every time we escape with our miraculous lives.*

Instead, she capitulated: "I have a morbid streak, don't I?"

For the rest of the fifty-minute flight, until the terrible descent, she lost herself in her magazine. He opened his briefcase on his lap and read the agenda for the impending week-long convention of the American Society of Architects.

They were waiting for the desk clerk to attend them. The hotel was old and sumptuous, and she was pleased that they would not be confined for five days to a stripped-down, thin-walled Holiday Inn. She often wished that environment did not mean so much to her mood, did not contribute so heavily to her frame of mind. She would have liked to have been as happy with him in a sterile motel as in this gracious building, but it was not the case and she allowed the atmosphere to work on her like a martini.

"One thing you can say about architects," she said, "they pick nice places to convene."

He smiled and nodded at her pleasure, accepting the compliment as if he, personally, had chosen their lodgings. "You really like old buildings, don't you?" he asked, as if just discovering something about her he had not known for years.

Breathe in the elegance, she wanted to tell him. *Absorb and retain it.*

He was not an architect of elegance; he designed schools, gas stations, supermarkets. "I'm really a technician," he would tell people when they asked about his work. "Some architects are artists, but I am more of a technician."

Afterward, she would tell him, with a kind of frantic confidence, "Don't demean yourself, don't underestimate your talent."

Their room was spacious and well appointed. They hung up their clothes and arranged their toiletries on a shelf above the marble sink in the gilded bathroom. When they were done with domestication, she took out the telephone book and began perusing the "Restaurants" section. "What are you in the mood for?"

"You," he said. He had taken off his shirt and shoes and was lying on the bed; he was propped up on one elbow and a gentle lust washed over his features. She undressed quietly, with no effort at seductiveness. He watched her with wistful tolerance. They made efficient, kindly love. On the wallpaper behind the bed, seventeenth-century ladies and gentlemen touched only fingertips, but their eyes seared the air.

After a voluptuous breakfast—melon, eggs, Canadian bacon, English muffins, coffee in a silver urn—they separated. He went to register for the convention which was to begin at ten. She walked out onto Michigan Avenue and inserted herself into the flow of people. It was like being on a moving sidewalk, she thought, the way the crowds of a huge city like Chicago could move you along, block after block, allowing you to nearly forget your feet. She browsed in bookstores and little specialty shops, where scarves and bracelets and tiny bottles of perfume offered themselves up like gifts to her senses. By eleven-fifteen she was tired and slightly hungry, and she entered a coffee shop tucked into the lobby of a large office building. The place was nearly empty. Still, she wished she had bought something, that she could be carrying a package or a book and not look so much like a friendless wanderer. However, it did not keep her from settling into a booth and accepting a menu from the bored waitress. "A grilled-cheese sandwich and coffee, please." She relaxed as well as she could, fingering the icy rim of her water glass.

The only other customers in the shop were two young women and three small children; the women sat on one side of their table and the children on the other, so she could not tell to whom each belonged. The children, a boy and two girls, looked to be around six or seven years old, well-behaved but restless, held in line by the serious glances of the two mothers. The children sat on their hands and slurped Cokes through bent straws. The glasses wobbled dangerously on the table. "Hold on to your drinks," one of the women rebuked with a fair amount of gentleness. Little fingers rose reluctantly, and the woman who had given the order nodded approval. "Isn't that better?" she said. The other woman said, "All we need is three Coke-soaked kids." They all laughed at the inadvertent rhyme, and the boy sang out loud with delight, "Soaked by Coke! Soaked by Coke! Soaked by—" "Enough, Jimmy, enough." The woman spoke with humor, but also with urgency. They all calmed down.

It made her think of her own children. Six and eight, their features beginning to be firmed and angled by their short lifetimes. She had chosen ether when her first was born, and it was hours later when she finally got to look at her daughter; it was as if someone had slashed her balloon of a belly and the child—a vital organ—had slid out. It took weeks to comprehend that the separate creature had grown inside of her. She read volumes on postpartum depression. Finally she accepted. It made her determined, however, to be awake for the next birth.

He agreed. He felt it would weld them all closer. He coached her in the necessary exercises of breathing and control, and she was touched by his enthusiasm. She began to hope that, just as the baby was growing inside of her, cells of awareness were multiplying within him—and soon he would give birth to his own new self which she had seeded. When the labor began, they rushed to the hospital. He attended her with nervous tenderness, and she accepted his help. But as the contractions intensified, she felt the pain suck her away from him; she did not honestly care if he was there or not. Although she held his hand tightly in the delivery room and turned her face to his kiss when their son burst from her body, the weight of distance from him bore down on her as surely as the doctor's hand urging the placenta from her abdomen. The baby looked just like his father.

She would call home tonight, she decided. She paid her bill and walked back to the hotel to take an afternoon nap.

The week moved on with his meetings, her trips to museums and galleries and the endless variety of stores. She bought a few things: a teak tray in a shop of Scandinavian imports, a silk blouse for her mother, a wooden puzzle and a book about clowns for the children. In the evenings they ate well, saw a play, went one night to the convention banquet. She began to relax, to feel acclimated. On Thursday night they made love again, this time at her initiation. Afterward, lying under the sheets, he told her, "When you want to, you can be so good." She knew that was true, and was happy for her courage to please him, to offer what she knew she owed.

He had a final meeting the next morning; she decided to pack after breakfast, in order to have the day and early evening free from the chore. They had an eight-o'clock flight home. When she finished, she decided to take a walk before meeting him for lunch—they were going to drive out to a little Greek restaurant in Evanston that a convention colleague had recommended for its wonderful salads. Leaving the elevator, she realized that the architects were having a midmorning break: they were fanned out in small, talkative groups all over the mirrored lobby.

She scanned faces and spotted him off in a corner, engaged in serious conversation with an urban planner from Philadelphia, an old schoolmate of his. She moved close enough to hear them, but out of his line of vision. He was deep into technical jargon, he was gesturing emphatically, he was—she realized it with a shock—in control of the discussion. The other man was listening to her husband with real concentration, the Philadelphian's brow wrinkled with respect. Her husband had *power* over the man, he had *dominance* over his friend. She listened to her husband make his points with assurance, with pride in his own intelligence. She had never encountered him before this moment as a separate entity from herself—or had she, and forgotten?—and his obvious poise startled her, confused her. He was with the Philadelphian the way she wanted him to be with her. She was unsteadied.

The architects were beginning to move back to their conference, and as he strode toward the ballroom, she called to him. He turned, and she looked at him with intense warmth, with something like desire; she could see that he'd received the curious, exciting signal. "See you at noon," he mouthed, and she nodded. He turned back toward the ballroom, she toward the street. She felt as if she had been entrusted with a fragile crystal of hope.

She studied herself in the glass caverns of Michigan Avenue. She tried to keep intact, like an engraving, the image of his animated force, so she could summon it when the deadly doubts moved in, when the distance re-emerged, when the isolation threatened to freeze her, render her immobile. She knew he would be thinking of the warmth he had seen in her eyes, the falling away of fear, the liveliness which he craved. Something had, at least for a moment, thawed her out, given her color again, energized her. How determined he would be to preserve it.

The drive to Evanston and the lunch in the tiny Greek restaurant were like a courtship, each of them striving to maintain faith in the other's possibilities. Each walked a tightrope of need. That single afternoon, she later decided, was what had kept them together for another three full years.

The Boarding House

JAMES JOYCE

Mrs. Mooney was a butcher's daughter. She was a woman who was quite able to keep things to herself: a determined woman. She had married her father's foreman and opened a butcher's shop near Spring Gardens. But as soon as his

father-in-law was dead Mr. Mooney began to go to the devil. He drank, plun-
dered the till, ran headlong into debt. It was no use making him take the
pledge: he was sure to break out again a few days after. By fighting his wife in
the presence of customers and by buying bad meat he ruined his business. One
night he went for his wife with the cleaver and she had to sleep in a neighbour's
house.

After that they lived apart. She went to the priest and got a separation
from him with care of the children. She would give him neither money nor
food nor house-room; and so he was obliged to enlist himself as a sheriff's man.
He was a shabby stooped little drunkard with a white face and a white moustache and white eyebrows, pencilled above his little eyes, which were pink-
veined and raw; and all day long he sat in the bailiff's room, waiting to be put
on a job. Mrs. Mooney, who had taken what remained of her money out of the
butcher business and set up a boarding house in Hardwicke Street, was a big
imposing woman. Her house had a floating population made up of tourists
from Liverpool and the Isle of Man and, occasionally, *artistes* from the music
halls. Its resident population was made up of clerks from the city. She governed
the house cunningly and firmly, knew when to give credit, when to be stern
and when to let things pass. All the resident young men spoke of her as *The
Madam*.

Mrs. Mooney's young men paid fifteen shillings a week for board and
lodgings (beer or stout at dinner excluded). They shared in common tastes and
occupations and for this reason they were very chummy with one another. They
discussed with one another the chances of favourites and outsiders. Jack
Mooney, the Madam's son, who was clerk to a commission agent in Fleet
Street, had the reputation of being a hard case. He was fond of using soldiers'
obscenities: usually he came home in the small hours. When he met his friends
he had always a good one to tell them and he was always sure to be on to a
good thing—that is to say, a likely horse or a likely *artiste*. He was also handy
with the mits and sang comic songs. On Sunday nights there would often be a
reunion in Mrs. Mooney's front drawing-room. The music-hall *artistes* would
oblige; and Sheridan played waltzes and polkas and vamped accompaniments.
Polly Mooney, the Madam's daughter, would also sing. She sang:

> *I'm a . . . naughty girl.*
> *You needn't sham:*
> *You know I am.*

Polly was a slim girl of nineteen; she had light soft hair and a small full
mouth. Her eyes, which were grey with a shade of green through them, had a
habit of glancing upwards when she spoke with anyone, which made her look
like a little perverse madonna. Mrs. Mooney had first sent her daughter to be a
typist in a corn-factor's office but, as a disreputable sheriff's man used to come
every other day to the office, asking to be allowed to say a word to his daugh-

ter, she had taken her daughter home again and set her to do housework. As Polly was very lively the intention was to give her the run of the young men. Besides, young men like to feel that there is a young woman not very far away. Polly, of course, flirted with the young men but Mrs. Mooney, who was a shrewd judge, knew that the young men were only passing the time away: none of them meant business. Things went on so for a long time and Mrs. Mooney began to think of sending Polly back to typewriting when she noticed that something was going on between Polly and one of the young men. She watched the pair and kept her own counsel.

Polly knew that she was being watched, but still her mother's persistent silence could not be misunderstood. There had been no open complicity between mother and daughter, no open understanding but, though people in the house began to talk of the affair, still Mrs. Mooney did not intervene. Polly began to grow a little strange in her manner and the young man was evidently perturbed. At last, when she judged it to be the right moment, Mrs. Mooney intervened. She dealt with moral problems as a cleaver deals with meat: and in this case she had made up her mind.

It was a bright Sunday morning of early summer, promising heat, but with a fresh breeze blowing. All the windows of the boarding house were open and the lace curtains ballooned gently towards the street beneath the raised sashes. The belfry of George's Church sent out constant peals and worshippers, singly or in groups, traversed the little circus before the church, revealing their purpose by their self-contained demeanour no less than by the little volumes in their gloved hands. Breakfast was over in the boarding house and the table of the breakfast room was covered with plates on which lay yellow streaks of eggs with morsels of bacon-fat and bacon-rind. Mrs. Mooney sat in the straw arm-chair and watched the servant Mary remove the breakfast things. She made Mary collect the crusts and pieces of broken bread to help to make Tuesday's bread-pudding. When the table was cleared, the broken bread collected, the sugar and butter safe under lock and key, she began to reconstruct the interview which she had had the night before with Polly. Things were as she had suspected: she had been frank in her questions and Polly had been frank in her answers. Both had been somewhat awkward, of course. She had been made awkward by her not wishing to receive the news in too cavalier a fashion or to seem to have connived and Polly had been made awkward not merely because allusions of that kind always made her awkward but also because she did not wish it to be thought that in her wise innocence she had divined the intention behind her mother's tolerance.

Mrs. Mooney glanced instinctively at the little gilt clock on the mantel-piece as soon as she had become aware through her revery that the bells of George's Church had stopped ringing. It was seventeen minutes past eleven: she would have lots of time to have the matter out with Mr. Doran and then catch short twelve at Marlborough Street. She was sure she would win. To begin with she had all the weight of social opinion on her side: she was an outraged mother. She had allowed him to live beneath her roof, assuming that he was a man of honour, and he had simply abused her hospitality. He was thirty-four or thirty-five years of age, so that youth could not be pleaded as his excuse; nor could ignorance be his excuse since he was a man who had seen something of the world. He had simply taken advantage of Polly's youth and inexperience: that was evident. The question was: What reparation would he make?

There must be reparation made in such case. It is all very well for the man: he can go his ways as if nothing had happened, having had his moment of pleasure, but the girl has to bear the brunt. Some mothers would be content to patch up such an affair for a sum of money; she had known cases of it. But she would not do so. For her only one reparation could make up for the loss of her daughter's honour: marriage.

She counted all her cards again before sending Mary up to Mr. Doran's room to say that she wished to speak with him. She felt sure she would win. He was a serious young man, not rakish or loud-voiced like the others. If it had been Mr. Sheridan or Mr. Meade or Bantam Lyons her task would have been much harder. She did not think he would face publicity. All the lodgers in the house knew something of the affair; details had been invented by some. Besides, he had been employed for thirteen years in a great Catholic wine-merchant's office and publicity would mean for him, perhaps, the loss of his job. Whereas if he agreed all might be well. She knew he had a good screw for one thing and she suspected he had a bit of stuff put by.

Nearly the half-hour! She stood up and surveyed herself in the pierglass. The decisive expression of her great florid face satisfied her and she thought of some mothers she knew who could not get their daughters off their hands.

Mr. Doran was very anxious indeed this Sunday morning. He had made two attempts to shave but his hand had been so unsteady that he had been obliged to desist. Three days' reddish beard fringed his jaws and every two or three minutes a mist gathered on his glasses so that he had to take them off and polish them with his pocket-handkerchief. The recollection of his confession of the night before was a cause of acute pain to him; the priest had drawn out every ridiculous detail of the affair and in the end had so magnified his sin that he was almost thankful at being afforded a loophole of reparation. The harm was done. What could he do now but marry her or run away? He could not brazen it out. The affair would be sure to be talked of and his employer would be certain to hear of it. Dublin is such a small city: everyone knows everyone else's business. He felt his heart leap warmly in his throat as he heard in his excited imagination old Mr. Leonard calling out in his rasping voice: "Send Mr. Doran here, please."

All his long years of service gone for nothing! All his industry and diligence thrown away! As a young man he had sown his wild oats, of course; he had boasted of his free-thinking and denied the existence of God to his companions in public-houses. But that was all passed and done with . . . nearly. He still bought a copy of *Reynolds's Newspaper* every week but he attended to his religious duties and for nine-tenths of the year lived a regular life. He had money enough to settle down on; it was not that. But the family would look down on her. First of all there was her disreputable father and then her mother's boarding house was beginning to get a certain fame. He had a notion that he was being had. He could imagine his friends talking of the affair and laughing. She *was* a little vulgar; some times she said "I seen" and "If I had've known." But what would grammar matter if he really loved her? He could not make up his mind whether to like her or despise her for what she had done. Of course he had done it too. His instinct urged him to remain free, not to marry. Once you are married you are done for, it said.

While he was sitting helplessly on the side of the bed in shirt and trousers she tapped lightly at his door and entered. She told him all, that she had made a clean breast of it to her mother and that her mother would speak with him that morning. She cried and threw her arms round his neck, saying:

"Oh Bob! Bob! What am I to do? What am I to do at all?"

She would put an end to herself, she said.

He comforted her feebly, telling her not to cry, that it would be all right, never fear. He felt against his shirt the agitation of her bosom.

It was not altogether his fault that it had happened. He remembered well, with the curious patient memory of the celibate, the first casual caresses her dress, her breath, her fingers had given him. Then late one night as he was undressing for bed she had tapped at his door, timidly. She wanted to relight her candle at his for hers had been blown out by a gust. It was her bath night. She wore a loose open combing-jacket of printed flannel. Her white instep shone in the opening of her furry slippers and the blood glowed warmly behind her perfumed skin. From her hands and wrists too as she lit and steadied her candle a faint perfume arose.

On nights when he came in very late it was she who warmed up his dinner. He scarcely knew what he was eating feeling her beside him alone, at night, in the sleeping house. And her thoughtfulness! If the night was anyway cold or wet or windy there was sure to be a little tumbler of punch ready for him. Perhaps they could be happy together. . . .

They used to go upstairs together on tiptoe, each with a candle, and on the third landing exchange reluctant good-nights. They used to kiss. He remembered well her eyes, the touch of her hand and his delirium. . . .

But delirium passes. He echoed her phrase, applying it to himself: *"What am I to do?"* The instinct of the celibate warned him to hold back. But the sin was there; even his sense of honour told him that reparation must be made for such a sin.

While he was sitting with her on the side of the bed Mary came to the door and said that the missus wanted to see him in the parlour. He stood up to put on his coat and waistcoat, more helpless than ever. When he was dressed he went over to her to comfort her. It would be all right, never fear. He left her crying on the bed and moaning softly: *"O my God!"*

Going down the stairs his glasses became so dimmed with moisture that he had to take them off and polish them. He longed to ascend through the roof and fly away to another country where he would never hear again of his trouble, and yet a force pushed him downstairs step by step. The implacable faces of his employer and of the Madam stared upon his discomfiture. On the last flight of stairs he passed Jack Mooney who was coming up from the pantry nursing two bottles of *Bass.* They saluted coldly; and the lover's eyes rested for a second or two on a thick bulldog face and a pair of thick short arms. When he reached the foot of the staircase he glanced up and saw Jack regarding him from the door of the return-room.

Suddenly he remembered the night when one of the music-hall *artistes,* a little blond Londoner, had made a rather free allusion to Polly. The reunion had been almost broken up on account of Jack's violence. Everyone tried to quiet him. The music-hall *artiste,* a little paler than usual, kept smiling and saying that there was no harm meant: but Jack kept shouting at him that if any fellow tried that sort of a game on with his sister he'd bloody well put his teeth down his throat, so he would.

Polly sat for a little time on the side of the bed, crying. Then she dried her eyes and went over to the looking-glass. She dipped the end of the towel in the water-jug and refreshed her eyes with the cool water. She looked at herself in profile and readjusted a hairpin above her ear. Then she went back to the bed again and sat at the foot. She regarded the pillows for a long time and the sight of them awakened in her mind secret, amiable memories. She rested the nape of her neck against the cool iron bed-rail and fell into a reverie. There was no longer any perturbation visible on her face.

She waited on patiently, almost cheerfully, without alarm, her memories gradually giving place to hopes and visions of the future. Her hopes and visions were so intricate that she no longer saw the white pillows on which her gaze was fixed or remembered that she was waiting for anything.

At last she heard her mother calling. She started to her feet and ran to the banisters.

"Polly! Polly!"

"Yes, mamma?"

"Come down, dear. Mr. Doran wants to speak to you." Then she remembered what she had been waiting for.

The Lost Cottage

David Leavitt

The Dempson family had spent the last half of June in a little rented cottage called "Under the Weather," near Hyannis, every summer for twenty-six years, and this year, Lydia Dempson told her son, Mark, was to be no exception. "No matter what's happened," she insisted over two thousand miles of telephone wire, "we're a family. We've always gone, and we'll continue to go." Mark knew from her voice that the matter was closed. They would go again. He called an airline and made a plane reservation. He arranged for someone to take care of his apartment. He purged the four pages of his *Week-at-a-Glance* which covered those two weeks of all appointments and commitment.

A few days later he was there. The cottage still needed a coat of paint. His parents, Lydia and Alex, sat at the kitchen table and shucked ears of corn. Alex had on a white polo shirt and a sun visor, and talked about fishing. Lydia wore a new yellow dress, and over it a fuzzy white sweater. She picked loose hairs from the ears Alex had shucked, which were pearl-white, and would taste sweet. Tomorrow Mark's brother and sister, Douglas and Ellen, and Douglas's girlfriend, Julie, would arrive from the West Coast. It seemed like the opening scene from a play which tells the family's history by zeroing in on a few choice summer reunions, presumably culled from a long and happy series, to give the critical information. Mark had once imagined writing such a play, and casting Colleen Dewhurst as his mother, and Jason Robards as his father. The curtain rises. The lights come up to reveal a couple shucking corn. . . .

Six months before, Alex and Lydia had gathered their children around another kitchen table and announced that they were getting a divorce. "For a long time, your mother and I have been caught up in providing a stable home for you kids," Alex had said. "But since you've been out on your own, we've had to confront certain things about our relationship, certain facts. And we have just decided we'd be happier if we went on from here separately." His words were memorized, as Mark's had been when he told his parents he was gay; hearing them, Mark felt what he imagined they must have felt then: not the shock of surprise, but of the unspoken being spoken, the long-dreaded breaking of a silence. Eight words, four and a half seconds: a life changed, a marriage over, three hearts stopped cold. "I can't believe you're saying this," Ellen said, and Mark knew she was speaking literally.

"For several years now," Alex said, "I've been involved with someone else. There's no point in hiding this. It's Marian Hollister, whom you all know. Your mother has been aware of this. I'm not going to pretend that this fact has nothing to do with why she and I are divorcing, but I will say that with or without Marian, I think this would have been necessary, and I think your mother would agree with me on that."

Lydia said nothing. It was two days before Christmas, and the tree had yet to be decorated. She held in her hand a small gold bulb which she played with, slipping it up her sleeve and opening her fist to reveal an empty palm.

"Years," Ellen said. "You said years."

"We need you to be adults now," said Lydia. "I know this will be hard for you to adjust to, but I've gotten used to the idea, and as hard as it may be to believe, you will, too. Now a lot of work has to be done in a very short time. A lot has to be gone through. You can help by sorting through your closets, picking out what you want to save from what can be thrown away."

"You mean you're selling the house?" Mark said. His voice just barely cracked.

"The sale's already been made," Alex said. "Both your mother and I have decided we'd be happier starting off in new places."

"But how can you just sell it?" Ellen said. "You've lived here all our lives—I mean, all your lives."

"Ellen," Alex said, "you're here two weeks a year at best. I'm sorry, honey. We have to think of ourselves."

As a point of information, Douglas said, "Don't think we haven't seen what's been going on all along. We saw."

"I never thought so," Alex said.

Then Ellen asked, "And what about the cottage?"

Three months later, Alex was living with Marian in a condominium on Nob Hill, where they worked at twin oak desks by the picture window. Lydia had moved into a tiny house in Menlo Park, twenty miles down the peninsula, and had a tan, and was taking classes in pottery design. The house in which Douglas, Mark, and Ellen grew up was emptied and sold, everything that belonged to the children packed neatly in boxes and put in storage at a warehouse somewhere—the stuffed animals, the old school notebooks. But none of them were around for any of that. They had gone back to Los Angeles, Hawaii, New York—their own lives. Mark visited his mother only once, in the spring, and she took him on a tour of her new house, showing him the old dining room table, the familiar pots and pans in the kitchen, the same television set on which he had watched "Speed Racer" after school. But there was also a new wicker sofa, and everywhere the little jars she made in her pottery class. "It's a beautiful house," Mark said. "Harmonious." "That's because only one person lives here," Lydia said, and laughed. "No one to argue about the color of the drapes." She looked out the window at the vegetable garden and said, "I'm trying to become the kind of person who can live in a house like this." Mark imagined it, then; Alex and Lydia in their work clothes, sorting through twenty-six years of accumulated possessions, utility drawers, and packed closets. They had had no choice but to work through this final housecleaning together. And how had it felt? They had been married more years than he has lived.

"Under the Weather" is not the strangest name of a Cape Cod cottage, nor the most depressing. On Nantucket, for instance, there is a house called "Beyond Hope"; another called "Weak Moment"; another called "Seldom Inn." "Under the Weather" is small for such a large group, has lumpy beds and leaky faucets, but stands on a bluff, directly over a shoal where lobstermen pull up their traps. Alex and Lydia spent their honeymoon in the cottage one weekend twenty-six years ago, and loved it so much they vowed to return with their children, should they survive the war. A couple of years later, right after Lydia had Douglas, they persuaded the old woman who owned it to rent it to them for two weeks a year on a regular basis, and since then they have come every summer without fail. They hold onto the cottage as a principle, something which persists even when marriages fail, and other houses crumble. Perhaps for this reason, they have never bothered to ask anyone how it got its name. Such a question of origin interests only Mark, for whom the cottage has always been a tainted place. He remembers, as a child, coming upon his parents before dinner piercing live, writhing sea urchins with their forks, drawing them out and eating them raw. He remembers hearing them knocking about in the room next to his while he lay in bed, trying to guess if they were making love or fighting. And he remembers his own first sexual encounters, which took place near the cottage—assignations with a fisherman's son in a docked rowboat puddled with stagnant seawater. The way he figures it now, those assignations were the closest thing he has known to being in love, and his parents must have been fighting. No noise comes out of their bedroom now. Alex sleeps in the living room. What keeps Mark awake is the humming of his own brain, as he makes up new names for the place: "Desperate Efforts," perhaps, or simply, "The Lost Cottage." And what of "Under the Weather"? Who gave the cottage that name, and why? He has asked some of the lobstermen, and none of them seem to remember.

Since their arrival, Mark's parents have been distant and civil with each other, but Mark knows that no one is happy with the situation. A few weeks after he got back from his visit with his mother, Alex called him. He was in New York on business, with Marian, and they wanted Mark to have dinner with them. Mark met them at an Indian restaurant on the top of a building on Central Park South where there were gold urinals in the men's room. Marian looked fine, welcoming, and Mark remembered that before she was his father's lover, she had been his friend. That was the summer he worked as her research assistant. He also remembered that Alex almost never took Lydia with him on business trips.

"Well," Alex said, halfway through the meal, "I'll be on Cape Cod this June, as usual. Will you?"

"Dad," Mark said. "Of course."

"Of course. But Marian won't be coming, I'm afraid."

"Oh?"

"I wish she could, but your mother won't allow it."

"Really," Mark said, looking sideways at Marian for some hint as to how he should go on. She looked resolute, so he decided to be honest. "Are you really surprised?" he said.

"Nothing surprises me where your mother is concerned," Alex said. Mark supposed Alex had tried to test how far he could trespass the carefully guarded borders of Lydia's tolerance, how much he could get away with, and found he could not get away with that much. Apparently Lydia had panicked, overcome by thoughts of bedroom arrangements, and insisted the children wouldn't be able to bear Marian's presence. "And is that true?" he asked Mark, leaning toward him. "Would the children not be able to bear it?"

Mark felt as if he were being prosecuted. "I don't think Mom could bear it," he said at last—fudging, for the moment, the question of his siblings' feelings, and his own. Still, that remark was brutal enough. "Don't push it, Alex," Marian said, lighting a cigarette. "Anyway, I'm supposed to visit Kerry in Arizona that week. Kerry's living on a ranch." She smiled, retreating into the haven of her own children.

Once, Mark had been very intimate with Marian. He trusted her so much, in fact, that he came out to her before anyone else, and she responded kindly, coaxing him and giving him the strength to tell his parents he was gay. He admires her, and understands easily why his father has fallen in love with her. But since the divorce, he will not talk to Marian, for his mother's sake. Marian is the one obstacle Lydia cannot get around. Lydia never uses Marian's name because it sticks in her throat like a shard of glass and makes her cry out in pain. "Certain loyalties need to be respected" was all she could say to Alex when he suggested bringing Marian to the Cape. And Alex relented, because he agreed with her, and because he realized that two weeks in June was a small enough sacrifice, considering how far she'd stretched, how much she'd given. "Marian and I can survive," he told Mark at the Indian restaurant. "We've survived longer separations." That intimacy scalded him. As if for emphasis, Alex took Marian's hand on top of the table and held it there. "We'll survive this one," he said.

Marian laughed nervously. "Your father and I have been waiting ten years to be together," she said. "What's two weeks?"

Little about the cottage has changed since the Dempson children were children. Though Alex and Lydia talked every year about renovating, the same rotting porch still hangs off the front, the same door creaks on its hinges. The children sleep in the bedrooms they've always slept in, do the chores they've always done. "You may be adults out there," Lydia jokes, "but here you're my kids, and you do what I tell you." Ellen is a lawyer, unmarried. Two days before her scheduled departure she was asked to postpone her vacation in order to help out with an important case which was about to go to trial. She refused, and this (she thinks) might affect her chances to become a partner someday. "Ellen, why?" Mark asked her when she told him. "The family is more important," she said. "Mother is more important." Douglas has brought with him Julie, the woman he's lived with for the past five years. They do oceanographical research in a remote village on Kauai, and hold impressive fellowships. Only Mark has no career and no aspirations. He works at temporary jobs in New York and moves every few months from sublet to sublet, devoting most of his time to exploring the city's homosexual night life. For the last few months he's been working as a word processor at a bank. It was easy for him to get away. He simply quit.

Now, a week into the vacation, things aren't going well. Lydia is angry most of the time, and whenever anyone asks her why, she mentions some triviality: an unwashed pot, an unmade bed. Here is an exemplary afternoon: Douglas, Julie, Mark, and Ellen arrive back from the beach, where they've been swimming and riding waves. Lydia doesn't say hello to them. She sits, knitting, at the kitchen table. She is dressed in a fisherman's sweater and a kilt fastened with a safety pin—an outfit she saves and wears only these few weeks on the Cape. "Are we late?" Douglas asks, bewildered by her silence, out of breath.

"No," Lydia says.

"We had fun at the beach," Julie says, and smiles, unsure of herself, still a stranger in this family. "How was your day?"

"Fine," Lydia says.

Ellen rubs her eyes. "Well, Mom," she says, "would you like me to tell you I nearly drowned today? I wish I had. One less person to make a mess. Too bad Mark saved me."

Lydia puts down her knitting and cradles her face in her hands. "I don't deserve that," she says. "You don't know what it's like trying to keep ahead of the mess in this house. You have no right to make fun of me when all I'm trying to do is keep us from drowning in dirty dishes and dirty clothes."

"Didn't we do the dishes after lunch?" Douglas asks. "We must have done the dishes after lunch."

"If you can call that doing them," Lydia says. "They were soapy *and* greasy."

"I'm sorry, Lydia," says Julie. "We were in such a hurry—"

"It's just that if anything's going to get done right around here, I have to do it, and I'm sick of it. I'm sick of it." She reaches for a pack of sugarless chewing gum, unwraps a stick, and goes to work on it.

"This is ridiculous, Mom," Ellen says. "Dishes are nothing. Dishes are trivial."

"It's that attitude that gets me so riled up," Lydia says. "They're trivial to people like you, so people like me get stuck with them."

"I'm not people. I'm your daughter, Ellen, in case you've forgotten. Excuse me, I have to change."

She storms out of the kitchen, colliding with Alex, whose face and clothes are smeared with mud and sand.

"What are you in such a hurry for?" he asks.

"Ask *her*," Ellen says, and slams the door of her bedroom.

Lydia is rubbing her eyes. "What was that about?" Alex asks.

"Nothing, nothing," she says, in a weary singsong. "Just the usual. Did you fix the pipe yet?"

"No, almost. I need some help. I hoped Doug and Mark might crawl under there with me." All day he's been trying to fix a faulty pipe which has made the bathtub faucet leak for twenty-five years, and created a bluish tail of rust near the spigot. The angrier Lydia gets, the more Alex throws himself into repair work, into tending to the old anachronisms of the house which he has seen fit to ignore in other years. It gives him an excuse to spend most of his days alone, away from Lydia.

"So can you help me?" Alex asks.

"Well," Mark says, "I suppose so. When?"

"I was thinking right now. We have to get out and pick up the lobsters in an hour or so. Henry said we could ride out on the boat with him. I want to get this job done."

"Fine," Douglas says. "I'm game."

Mark hesitates. "Yes," he says. "I'll help you with it. Just let me change first."

He walks out of the kitchen and into his bedroom. It is the smallest in the house, with a tiny child-sized bed, because even though Mark is the tallest member of the family by three inches, he is still the youngest. The bed was fine when he was five, but now most of the springs have broken, and Mark's legs stick a full four inches over the edge. He takes off his bathing suit, dries himself with a towel, and—as he dresses—catches a glimpse of himself in the mirror. It is the same face, as always.

He heads out the door to the hallway, where Alex and Douglas are waiting for him. "All right," he says. "I'm ready."

Of course, it was not this way at first. The day they arrived at the cottage, Lydia seemed exuberant. "Just breathe the air," she said to Mark, her eyes fiery with excitement. "Air doesn't smell like this anywhere else in the world." They had spaghetti with clams for dinner—a huge, decadent, drunken meal. Halfway through Mark fell to the floor in a fit of laughter so severe it almost made him sick. They went to bed at three, slept dreamlessly late into the morning. By the time Mark woke up, Lydia was irritated, and Alex had disappeared, alone, to go fishing. That evening, Ellen and Julie baked a cake, and Lydia got furious at them for not cleaning up immediately afterward. Douglas and Julie rose to the occasion, eager to appease her, and immediately started scrubbing. Douglas was even more intent than his parents on keeping up a pretense of normality over the vacation, partially for Julie's sake, but also because he cherished these two weeks at the cottage even more than his mother did. Ellen chided him for giving in to her whim so readily. "She'll just get angrier if you take away her only outlet," she said. "Leave the dirty dishes. If this house were clean, believe me, we'd get it a lot worse from her than we are now."

"I want to keep things pleasant," Douglas said. He kow-towed to his mother, he claimed, because he pitied her, but Mark knew it was because he feared more than anything seeing her lose control. When he and Douglas were children, he remembers, Lydia had been hit on the head by a softball one afternoon in the park. She had fallen to her knees and burst into tears, and Douglas had shrunk back, terrified, and refused to go near her. Now Douglas seemed determined to make sure his mother never did that to him again, even if it meant she had to suffer in silence.

Lydia is still in the kitchen, leaning against the counter, when Mark emerges from under the cottage. She is not drinking coffee, not reading a recipe; just leaning there. "Dad and Doug told me to pack up and come inside," Mark says. "I was more trouble than help."

"Oh?" Lydia says.

"Yes," Mark says, and sits down at the table. "I have no mechanical aptitude. I can hold things and hand things to other people—sometimes. They knew my heart wasn't in it."

"You never did like that sort of thing," Lydia says.

Mark sits silent for a few seconds. "Daddy's just repairing everything this vacation, isn't he?" he says. "For next summer this place'll be tiptop."

"We won't be here next summer," Lydia says. "I'm sure of it, though it's hard to imagine this is the last time."

"I'm sorry it's such an unhappy time for you," Mark says.

Lydia smiles. "Well," she says, "it's no one's fault but my own. You know, when your father first told me he wanted a divorce, he said things could be hard, or they could be very hard. The choice was up to me. I thought I chose the former of those two. Then again, I also thought, if I go along with him and don't make trouble, at least he'll be fair."

"Mom," Mark says, "give yourself a break. What did you expect?"

"I expected people to act like adults," she says. "I expected people to play fair." She turns to look out the window, her face grim. The table is strewn with gum wrappers.

"Can I help you?" Mark asks.

She laughs. "Your father would be happy to hear you say that," she says. "He told me from the beginning, I'll let them hate me, I'll turn the kids against me. Then they'll be there for you. He was so damn sacrificial. But no. You can't help me because I still have some pride."

There is a clattering of doors in the hallway. Male voices invade the house. Alex and Douglas walk into the kitchen, their clothes even more smeared with mud, their eyes triumphant. "Looks like we fixed that pipe," Alex says. "Now we've got to wash up; Henry's expecting us to pick up those lobsters ten minutes ago."

He and Douglas stand at the kitchen sink and wash their hands and faces. From her room, Julie calls, "You fixed the pipe? That's fantastic!"

"Yes," Douglas says, "we have repaired the evil leak which has plagued this house for centuries."

"We'd better get going, Doug," Alex says. "Does Julie want to come hunt lobsters?"

"Lobsters?" Julie says, entering the room. Her smile is bright, eager. Then she looks at Lydia. "No, you men go," she says. "We womenfolk will stay here and guard the hearth."

Lydia looks at her, and raises her eyebrows.

"O.K., let's go," Alex says. "Mark, you ready?"

He looks questioningly at Lydia. But she is gathering together steel wool and Clorox, preparing to attack the stain on the bathtub.

"Yes, I'm ready," Mark says.

At first, when he was very young, Mark imagined the lobstermen to be literal lobster-men, with big pink pincers and claws. Later, as he was entering puberty, he found that all his early sexual feelings focused on them—the red-faced men and boys with their bellies encased in dirty T-shirts. Here, in a docked boat, Mark made love for the first time with a local boy who had propositioned him in the bathroom of what was then the town's only pizza parlor. "I seen you look at me," said the boy, whose name was Erroll. Mark had wanted to run away, but instead made a date to meet Erroll later that night. Outside, in the pizza parlor, his family was arguing about whether to get anchovies. Mark still feels a wave of nausea run through him when he eats with them at any pizza parlor, remembering Erroll's warm breath on his neck, and the smell of fish which seemed to cling to him for days afterward.

Alex is friends with the local lobstermen, one of whom is his landlord's cousin. Most years, he and Douglas and Mark ride out on a little boat with Henry Traylor and his son, Henry Traylor, and play at being lobstermen themselves, at hauling pots and grabbing the writhing creatures and snapping shut their jaws. The lobsters only turn pink when boiled; live, they're sometimes a bluish color which reminds Mark of the stain on the bathtub. Mark has never much liked these expeditions, nor the inflated caricature of machismo which his father and brother put on for them. He looks at them and sees plump men with pale skin, men no man would ever want. Yet they are loved, fiercely loved by women.

Today Henry Traylor is a year older than the last time they saw him, as is his son. "Graduated from high school last week," he tells Alex.

"That's terrific," Alex says. "What's next?"

"Fixing to get married, I suppose," Henry Traylor says. "Go to work, have kids." He is a round-faced, red-cheeked boy with ratty, bright blond hair. As he talks, he manipulates without effort the outboard rudder of the little boat which is carrying them out into the sound, toward the marked buoys of the planted pots. Out on the ocean, Alex seems to relax considerably. "Your mother seems unhappy," he says to Mark. "I try to talk to her, to help her, but it doesn't do any good. Well, maybe Julie and Ellen can do something." He puts his arm around Mark's shoulder—an uncomplicated, fatherly gesture which seems to say, this love is simple. The love of men is simple. Leave the women behind in the kitchen, in the steam of the cooking pot, the fog of their jealousies and compulsions. We will go hunt.

Henry Traylor has hauled up the ancient lobster trap. Lobster limbs stick out of the barnacle-encrusted woodwork, occasionally moving. "Now you just grab the little bugger like this," Henry Traylor instructs Douglas. "Then you take your rubber band and snap him closed. It's simple."

"O.K.," Douglas says. "Here goes." He stands back and cranes his arm over the trap, holding himself at a distance, then withdraws a single, flailing lobster.

"Oh, God," he says, and nearly drops it.

"Don't do that!" shouts Henry Traylor. "You got him. Now just take the rubber band and fix him tight. Shut him up like he's a woman who's sassing you. That's right. Good. See? It wasn't so hard."

"Do that to your wife," says Henry Traylor the elder, "she'll bite your head off quicker than that lobster."

Out of politeness, all three of the Dempson men laugh. Douglas looks at his handiwork—a single lobster, bound and gagged—and smiles. "I did it," he says. Mark wonders if young Henry Traylor has ever thought of making love to other boys, thinks rudely of propositioning him, having him beneath the boat. "I seen you look at me," he'd say. He thinks of it—little swirls of semen coagulating in the puddles, white as the eddies of foam which are gathering now on the sea in which they float, helpless, five men wrestling with lobsters.

They go back to shore. The Traylors have asked Alex and Douglas to walk up the hill with them and take a look at their new well, so Mark carries the bag of lobsters back to the house. But when he gets to the screen door to the kitchen, he stops in his tracks; Ellen, Lydia, and Julie are sitting at the table, talking in hushed voices, and he steps back, fearful of interrupting them. "It would be all right," Ellen is saying. "Really, it's not that outrageous these days. I met a lot of really decent guys when I did it."

"What could I say?" Lydia asks.

"Just be simple and straightforward. Attractive woman, divorced, mid-fifties, seeks whatever—handsome, mature man for companionship. Who knows? Whatever you want."

"I could never put that down!" Lydia says, her inflection rising. "Besides, it wouldn't be fair. They'd be disappointed when they met me."

"Of course they wouldn't!" Julie says. "You're very attractive."

"I'm an old woman," Lydia says. "There's no need to flatter me. I know that."

"Mom, you don't look half your age," Ellen says. "You're beautiful."

Mark knocks and walks through the door, his arms full of lobsters. "Here I am," he says, "back with the loot. I'm sorry for eavesdropping, but I agree with everything Ellen says."

"Oh, it doesn't matter, Mark," Lydia says. "Alex wouldn't care anyway if he found out."

"Mom, will you stop that?" Ellen says. "Will you just stop that? Don't worry about him anymore, for Christ's sake, he isn't worth it."

"Don't talk about your father that way," Lydia says. "You can tell me whatever you think I need to know, but you're not to speak of your father like that. He's still your father, even if he's not my husband."

"Jesus," Ellen says.

"What did you say?"

"Nothing," Ellen says, more loudly.

Lydia looks her over once, then walks over to the stove, where the water for the lobsters is boiling. "How many did you get, Mark?" she asks.

"Six. Daddy and Douglas went to look at the Traylors' well. They'll be back any minute."

"Good," Lydia says. "Let's put these things in the water." She lifts the top off the huge pot, and steam pours out of it, fogging her reading glasses.

Dinner passes quietly. Alex is in a questioning mood, and his children answer him obediently. Douglas and Julie talk about the strange sleeping habits of sharks, Ellen about her firm, Mark about a play he saw recently Off Broadway. Lydia sits at the head of the table, and occasionally makes a comment or asks a question—just enough to keep them from panicking, or staring at her all through the meal. Mark notices that her eyes keep wandering to Alex.

After dinner is finished, Julie and Lydia carry the dishes into the kitchen, and Douglas says, "O.K., are we getting ice cream tonight, or what?" Every night since their arrival, they have gone to get ice cream after dinner, primarily at the insistence of Douglas and Julie, who thrive on ice cream, but thrive more on ritual. Ellen, who has visited them in Hawaii, revealed to Mark that they feed their cat tea every morning, in bed. "They're daffy," she said, describing to him the way Douglas held the cat and Julie the saucer of tea it licked from. Over the five years they've been together, Mark has noticed, Douglas and Julie have become almost completely absorbed in one another, at the expense of most everything around them, probably as a result of the fact that they've spent so much of that time in remote places, in virtual isolation. They even share a secret language of code words and euphemisms. When Julie asked Douglas, one night, to give her a "floogie," Mark burst out laughing, and then they explained that "floogie" was their private word for backrub.

Tonight, Ellen is peculiarly agreeable. Usually she resists these ice cream expeditions, but now she says, "Oh, what a great idea. Let's go." Mark wonders what led her and Lydia to the conversation he overheard, then decides he'd prefer not to know. "Let's go, let's go," Douglas says. "Mom, are you game?"

But Lydia has her face buried in the steam rising from the sink of dishes, which she has insisted on doing herself. "No," she says. "You go ahead."

Douglas backs away from the sorrow in her voice—sorrow which might at any moment turn into irritation, if he pushes her harder. He knows not to. "How about you, Dad?" he asks Alex.

"No," Alex says, "I'm pooped. But bring me back some chocolate chip."

"Give me money?" Douglas says.

Alex hands him a twenty, and the kids barrel into the car and head off to the ice cream parlor in town. They sit down at a pink booth with high-backed, patent-leather seats which remind Mark of pink flamingos on people's lawns, and a waitress in a pink uniform brings them their menus. The waitress is a local girl with bad teeth, and Mark wonders if she's the one Henry Traylor's going to marry someday. He wouldn't be surprised. She's got a lusty look about her which even he can recognize, and which he imagines Henry Traylor would find attractive. And Douglas is watching her. Julie is watching Douglas watch, but she does not look jealous. She looks fascinated.

Ellen looks jealous.

They order several sundaes, and eat them with a kind of labored dedication. Halfway through the blueberry sundae he is sharing with Ellen, Mark realizes he stopped enjoying this sundae, and this ritual, four days before. Julie looks tired, too—tired of being cheerful and shrieking about fixed faucets. And Mark imagines a time when his brother and Julie will feed their cat tea for no other reason than that they always have, and with no pleasure. He remembers one weekend when Julie and Douglas came to visit him in New York. They had taken the train down from Boston, where they were in school, and they were flying to California the next afternoon. All that day on the train Douglas had been looking forward to eating at a Southern Indian restaurant he had read about, but the train arrived several hours late, and by the time he and Julie had gotten their baggage the restaurant was closed. Douglas fumed like a child until tears came to his eyes. "All that day on the train, looking forward to that dinner," he said on the subway ride back to Mark's apartment. Julie put her arms around him, and kissed him on the forehead, but he turned away. Mark wanted to shake her, then, ask her why she was indulging him this way, but he knew that Douglas had indulged her just as often. That was the basis of their love—mutual self-indulgence so excessive that Mark couldn't live with them for more than a few days without thinking he would go crazy. It wasn't that he wasn't welcome. His presence or absence seemed irrelevent to them; as far as they were concerned, he might as well not have existed. And this was couple-dom, the revered state of marriage? For Mark, the amorous maneuverings of the heterosexual world are deserving of the same bewilderment and distrust that he hears in his sister's voice when she says, "But how can you just go to bed with someone you've hardly met? *I* could never do that." He wants to respond by saying, I would never pretend that I could pledge eternal allegiance to one person, but this isn't really true. What is true is that he's terrified of what he might turn into once he'd made such a pledge.

"So when's the summit conference taking place?" Ellen says now, dropping her blueberry-stained spoon onto the pink table. Everyone looks at her. "What do you mean?" Julie asks.

"I mean I think we should have a talk about what's happening with Mom and Dad. I mean I think we should stop pretending everything's normal when it isn't."

"I'm not pretending," Douglas says.

"Neither am I," says Julie. "We're aware of what's going on."

Mark watches Ellen's blueberry ice cream melt down the sides of her parfait glass. "What has Mama said to you?" he asks.

"Everything and nothing," Ellen says. "I hear her when she's angry and when she wants to cry she does it in my room. One day she's cheerful, the next miserable. I don't know why she decided to make me her confidante, but she did." Ellen pushes the sundae dish away. "Why don't we just face the fact that this is a failure?" she says. "Daddy doesn't want to be here, that's for sure, and I think Mom's beginning to think that she doesn't want to be here. And I, for one, am not so sure I want to be here."

"Mom believes in tradition," Douglas says softly, repeating a phrase they've heard from her a thousand times.

"Tradition can become repetition," Ellen says, "when you end up holding onto something just because you're afraid to let it go." She shakes her head. "I am ready to let it go."

"Let what go?" Douglas says. "The family?"

Ellen is silent.

"Well, I don't think that's fair," Douglas says. "Sure, things are stressful. A lot has happened. But that doesn't mean we should give up. We have to work hard at this. Just because things are different doesn't mean they necessarily have to be bad. I, for one, am determined to make the best of this vacation—for my sake, but also for Mom's. Except for this, without this—"

"She already has nothing," Ellen says.

Douglas stares at her.

"You can face it," Ellen says. "She has. She's said as much. Her whole life went down the tubes when Daddy left her, Cape Cod or no Cape Cod. This vacation doesn't matter a damn. But that's not the end. She could start a new life for herself. Mark, remember the first time Douglas didn't come home for Christmas? I'll bet you never guessed how upset everyone was, Douglas. Christmas just wasn't going to be Christmas without the whole family being there, I said, so why bother having it at all? But then Christmas came, and we did it without you. It wasn't the same. But it was still Christmas. We survived. And maybe we were a little relieved to find we weren't as dependent on your presence as we thought we'd be, relieved to be able to give up some of those old rituals, some of that nostalgia. It was like a rehearsal for other losses we probably all knew we'd have to face someday—for this, maybe."

Douglas has his arm around Julie, his fingers gripping her shoulder. "No one ever told me that," he says. "I figured no one cared."

Ellen laughs. "That's never been a problem in this family," she says. "The problem in this family is that everybody cares."

They get back to the cottage around eleven to find that the lights are still on. "I'm surprised she's still up," Ellen says to Mark as they clamber out of the car.

"It's not so surprising," Mark says. "She's probably having a snack." The gravel of the driveway crunches beneath his feet as he moves toward the screen door to the kitchen. "Hi, Mom," Mark says as he walks through the door, then stops abruptly, the other three behind him.

"What's going on?" Mark asks.

Alex is standing by the ironing board, in his coat, his face red and puffy. He is looking down at Lydia, who sits in her pink bathrobe at the kitchen table, her head resting on her forearms, weeping. In front of her is half a grapefruit on a plate, and a small spoon with serrated edges.

"What happened?" Ellen asks.

"It's nothing, kids," Alex says. "Your mother and I were just having a discussion."

"Oh, shut up," Lydia says, raising her head slightly. Her eyes are red, swollen with tears. "Why don't you just tell them if you're so big on honesty all of a sudden? Your father's girlfriend has arrived. She's at a motel in town. They planned this all along, and your father never saw fit to tell any of us about it, except I happened to see her this morning when I was doing the grocery shopping."

"Oh, God," Mark says, and leans back against the wall of the kitchen. Across from him, his father also draws back.

"All right, let's not get hysterical," Ellen says. "Let's try to talk this through. Daddy, is this true?"

"Yes," Alex says. "I'm sorry I didn't tell any of you but I was afraid of how you'd react. Marian's just here for the weekend, she'll be gone Monday. I thought I could see her during the day, and no one would know. But now that everything's out, I can see that more deception was just a bad idea to begin with. And anyway, am I asking so much? All I'm asking is to spend some time in town with Marian. I'll be home for meals, and during the day, everything for the family. None of you ever has to see her."

"Do you think all this is fair to Marian?" Ellen asks.

"It was her idea."

"I see."

"Fair to Marian, fair to Marian," Lydia mumbles. "All of this has been fair to Marian. These two weeks you were supposed to be fair to me." She takes a Kleenex and rubs at her nose and eyes. Mark's fingers grip the moldings on the walls, while Julie buttons and unbuttons the collar of her sweater.

"Lydia, look," Alex says. "Something isn't clear here. When I agreed to come these weeks, it was as your friend and as a father. Nothing more."

"So go then!" Lydia shouts, standing up and facing him. "You've brought me lower than I ever thought you would, don't stand there and rub it in. Just go." Shaking, she walks over to the counter, picks up a coffee cup, and takes a sip out of it. Coffee splashes over the rim, falls in hot drops on the floor.

"Now I think we have to talk about this," Ellen says. "We can deal with this if we just work on it."

"There's no point," Douglas says, and sits down at the table. "There's nothing left to say." He looks at the table, and Julie reaches for his hand.

"What do you mean there's nothing left to say? There's everything to be said here. The one thing we haven't done is talk about all of this as a family."

"Oh, be quiet, both of you," Lydia says, putting down her cup. "You don't know anything about this. The whole business is so simple it's embarrassing." She puts her hand on her chest and takes a deep, shaky breath. "There is only one thing to be said here, and I'm the one who has to say it. And that is the simple fact that I love your father, and I will always love your father. And he doesn't love me. And never will."

No one answers her. She is right. None of them know anything about *this,* not even Ellen. Lydia's children are as speechless as spectators watching a woman on a high ledge: unable to do any good, they can only stare, waiting to see what she'll do next.

What she does is turn to Alex. "Did you hear me?" she says. "I love you. You can escape me, but you can never escape that."

He keeps his eyes focused on the window above her head, making sure never to look at her. The expression on his face is almost simple, almost sweet: the lips pressed together, though not tightly, the eyes averted. In his mind, he's already left.

Good Advice Is Rarer Than Rubies

SALMAN RUSHDIE

On the last Tuesday of the month, the dawn bus brought Miss Rehana to the gates of the British Embassy. It arrived pushing a cloud of dust, veiling her beauty from the eyes of strangers until she descended. The bus was brightly painted in multicolored arabesques, and on the front it said "MOVE OVER DARLING" in green and gold letters; on the back it added "TATA-BATA" and also "O.K. GOOD-LIFE." Miss Rehana told the driver it was a beautiful bus, and he jumped down and held the door open for her.

Miss Rehana's eyes were large and black and shiny enough not to need the help of antimony, and when the advice expert Muhammad Ali saw them he felt himself becoming young again. He watched her approach the embassy gates and heard her ask the lala who guarded them when they would open. The lala usually enjoyed insulting the embassy's Tuesday-women, but he spoke to Miss Rehana with something approaching courtesy. "Half an hour," he said gruffly. "Maybe two hours. Who knows? The sahibs are eating their breakfast."

The dusty compound between the bus stop and the embassy was already full of Tuesday-women, some veiled, a few barefaced like Miss Rehana. They all looked frightened, and leaned heavily on the arms of uncles or brothers, who were trying to look confident. But Miss Rehana had come on her own, and did not seem at all alarmed. Muhammad Ali, who specialized in advising the most vulnerable-looking of these weekly supplicants, found his feet leading him toward the strange, big-eyed, independent girl.

"Miss," he began. "You have come for permit to London, I think so?" She was standing at a hot-snack stall in the little shantytown by the edge of the compound munching chili-pakoras contentedly. She turned to look at him, and at close range those eyes did bad things to his digestive tract.

"Yes, I have."

"Then please, you allow me to give some advice? Small cost only."

Miss Rehana smiled. "Good advice is rarer than rubies," she said. "But I cannot pay. I am an orphan, not one of your wealthy ladies."

"Trust my gray hairs," Muhammad Ali told her. "My advice is well tempered by experience. You will certainly find it good."

She shook her head. "I tell you I am poor. There are women here with male relatives, all earning good wages. Go to them. Good advice should find good money."

I am going crazy, Muhammad Ali thought, because he heard his voice telling her of its own volition, "Miss, I have been drawn to you. This is fated. I too am a poor man only, but for you my advice comes free."

She smiled again. "Then I must surely listen. When fate sends a gift, one receives good fortune."

He led her to the low wooden desk in his own special corner of the shantytown. She followed, still smiling, eating pakoras from a little newspaper packet. She did not offer him any. He put a cushion on the dusty ground. "Please to sit." She did as he asked. He sat cross-legged across the desk from her, conscious that two or three dozen male eyes were watching him enviously, that all the other shantytown men were ogling the latest young lovely to be charmed by the old grayhair Muhammad Ali. He took a deep breath to settle himself.

"Name, please."

"Miss Rehana," she told him. "Fiancée of Mustafa Dar of Bradford, London."

"Bradford, England," he corrected her gently. "London is a city only, like Multan or Bahawalpur. England is a great nation full of the coldest fish in the world."

"I see," she responded gravely, so that he was unsure if she was making fun of him.

"You have filled application form? Then let me see, please."

She passed him a neatly folded document in a brown envelope.

"Is it O.K.?" For the first time there was a note of anxiety in her voice.

He patted the desk quite near the place where her hand rested. "I am certain," he said. "Wait on and I will check."

She finished her pakoras while he scanned her papers.

"Tip-top," he pronounced finally. "All in order."

"Thank you for your advice," she said. "I'll go now and wait by the gate."

"What are you thinking?" he cried loudly, smiting his forehead. "You consider this is easy business? Just give the form and poof, with a big smile they hand over the permit? Miss Rehana, I tell you you are entering a worse place than any police station."

"Is it so, truly?" His oratory had done the trick. She was a captive audience now, and he would be able to look at her for a few moments longer. Drawing another calming breath, he launched into his speech. He told her that the sahibs thought all the women who came on Tuesdays, claiming to be dependents of bus drivers in Luton or chartered accountants in Manchester, were crooks and liars and thieves.

She protested, "But then I will simply tell them that I, for one, am no such thing!"

Her innocence made him shiver with fear for her. She was a sparrow, he told her, and they were men with hooded eyes, like eagles. He explained that they would ask her questions, personal questions, questions such as a lady's own brother would be shy to ask. They would ask if she was virgin, and, if not, what her fiancé's lovemaking habits were, and what secret nicknames they had invented for one another. Muhammad Ali spoke brutally, on purpose, to lessen the shock she would feel when it actually happened. Her eyes remained steady, but her hands began to flutter at the edges of the desk.

He went on. "They will ask you how many rooms in your family home, and what color are the walls, and what days do you empty the rubbish; they will ask your man's mother's third cousin's aunt's stepdaughter's middle name. And all these things they have already asked your Mustafa Dar in his Bradford. And if you make one mistake, you are finished."

"Yes," she said, and he could hear her disciplining her voice. "And what is your advice, wise old man?"

It was at this point that Muhammad Ali usually began to whisper, to mention that he knew a man, a very good type, who worked in the embassy, and for a fee all the necessary papers could be delivered, with all the proper authentic seals. It was a good business, because the women would often pay him five hundred rupees or give him a gold bracelet for his pains and go away happy. They came from hundreds of miles away—he always checked this before he tricked them—so even when they discovered how they had been swindled they were very unlikely to return. They went away to Sargodha or Lalu Khet and began to pack, and who knows at what point they found out they had been gulled, but it was at a too late point anyway. Life is hard, and an old man must live by his wits. It was not up to Muhammad Ali to have compassion for these Tuesday-women.

But once again his voice betrayed him, and instead of starting his customary speech it began to reveal to her his greatest secret. "Miss Rehana," his voice said, and he listened to it in amazement, "you are a rare person, a jewel, and for you I will do what I would not do for my own daughter, perhaps. One document has come into my possession that can solve your worries at a stroke."

"And what is this sorcerer's paper?" she asked, her eyes unquestionably laughing at him now.

His voice fell low-as-low. "Miss Rehana, it is a British passport. Completely genuine and pukka goods. I have a good friend who will put your name into it and then, hey-presto, England there you come!"

He had said it! Anything was possible now, on this day of his insanity. Probably he would give her the thing free-gratis, and then kick himself for a year afterward. Old fool, he told himself, the oldest fools are bewitched by the youngest girls.

"Let me understand you," she was saying. "You are proposing I should commit a crime, and go to Bradford, London, illegally, and so justify the low opinion the embassy sahibs have of us all. Old babuji, this is not good advice."

"Bradford, *England,*" he corrected her mournfully. "You should not take my gift in such a spirit. I am a poor fellow and I have offered this prize because you are so beautiful. Do not spit on my generosity. Take the thing. Or else don't take, go home, forget England, only do not go in that building and lose your dignity."

But she was on her feet, turning, walking away toward the gates, where the women had begun to cluster and the lala was swearing at them to be patient or none of them would be admitted.

"Be a fool," Muhammad Ali shouted after her. "It is the curse of our people. We are poor, we are ignorant, and we refuse completely to learn."

"Hey, Muhammad Ali," the woman at the betel-nut stall shouted to him. "Too bad, she likes them young."

That day Muhammad Ali did nothing but stand around the embassy gates. Many times he told himself, Go from here, fool, the lady does not wish to speak with you any further. But when she came out, she found him waiting.

She seemed calm, and at peace with him again, and he thought, My God, she has pulled it off. The British sahibs have also been drowning in her eyes, and she has got her passage to England. He smiled at her; she smiled back with no trouble at all.

"Miss Rehana Begum," he said, "felicitations, daughter, on what is obviously your hour of triumph."

Impulsively, she took his forearm in her hand. "Come," she said, "let me buy you a pakora to thank you for your advice and to apologize for my rudeness, too."

They stood in the dust of the afternoon compound near the bus, which was getting ready to leave. Coolies were tying bedding rolls to the roof. A hawker shouted at the passengers, trying to sell them love stories and green medicines. Miss Rehana and happy Muhammad Ali ate their pakoras sitting on the front bumper.

"It was an arranged engagement," Miss Rehana said suddenly. "I was nine years old when my parents fixed it. Mustafa Dar was already thirty then, but my parents knew they were dying and wanted someone who could look after me. Then two months after they died he went to England and said he would send for me. That was many years ago. I have his photo, but I do not know what his voice sounds like. He is like a stranger to me."

The confession took Muhammad Ali by surprise, but he nodded with what he hoped looked like wisdom. "Still and all," he said, "one's parents act in one's best interests. They found you a good honest man who has kept his word and sent for you. And now you have a lifetime to get to know him, and to love."

He was puzzled, now, by the bitterness that had infected her smile.

"But, old man," she asked him, "why have you already packed me and posted me off to England?"

He stood up, shocked. "You looked happy, so I just assumed . . . They turned you down?"

"I got all their questions wrong," she replied. "Distinguishing marks, bathroom décor, all. Now I will go back to Lahore and my job. I work in a great house, as ayah to three good boys. They would be sad to see me leave."

"But this is tragedy!" Muhammad Ali lamented. "Oh, how I pray that you had taken up my offer! Now it is not possible. They have your form on file, cross-check can be made, even the passport will not suffice. It is spoilt, all spoilt, and it could have been so easy."

"I do not think," she told him as she climbed aboard the bus and gave a wave to the driver, "I truly do not think you should be sad."

Her last smile, which he watched from the compound until the bus concealed it in a dust cloud, was the happiest thing he had ever seen in his long, hot, hard, unloving life.

12

The Elements of Drama

THE NATURE OF DRAMA

To write plays you need to do everything you do when you write in other genres—and more. Not only must you keep a journal, read plays, and research, you also must involve yourself *on a working level* in the theater (or film, or television, or radio). It is not enough merely to watch or listen to dramatic works.

In some capacity—acting or moving sets, directing or running a camera—you should become involved in the production of dramatic work so as to experience its freedoms, conventions, energies, and limits. Working in the media, even as a gopher (go-for coffee, go-for a script, go-for a chair) or as a spear carrier, will make you more sensitive to the problems that your collaborators face. These collaborators are the artists who will design your living room, light it, and dress and direct the actors who, in turn, must kiss with convincing passion as if an audience were not watching. Once you have spoken lines that make no sense, or stood about in a scene with nothing to do, or changed a set for the third time in fifteen minutes—once you have been exposed to the *physical reality* of the media—you are more likely to be sensitive to such difficulties and to construct your plays to avoid them. You will begin to think performance.

Of course, you can argue that the reader of a poem or story performs your work mentally; however, the reader's performance does not have to be limited by talent, space, or material. This situation is far different from having a director, sound technician, lighting technician, costumer, set designer, and actors among your host of ultimate collaborators. These other contributors literally and figuratively put on (embody) your words.

Consider the following action: "They walked into the living room and kissed passionately. Then they began to remove their clothes." Think of the difference between your response to this action (1) brought to your mind's eye through print and (2) brought to the range of your senses as it *happens* on stage or screen.

As a reader, you can allow your imagination to build on the writer's material, you can decide to read more quickly to see if they will be interrupted or more slowly to savor the experience, and you can interrupt the experience by putting down the book and then picking it up again. You have some degree of safety and control because you can easily put a distance between yourself and the potential impact of the writer's words. At some level, you are always conscious of holding a book or magazine and looking at the printed page.

In plays and films, the illusion of life-going-on is the result of other people doing something with the writer's words. As a member of an audience, you are confronted by something *happening*. You are a *witness* to the disrobing. Real people as well as characters are undressing before you. The pressure and the pace of the production absorb your attention. Images and voices from outside of you run at someone else's pace and create the particular illusion of life-going-on that is so different from the illusions of fiction.

One way to master the particular illusions of drama (so as to exploit them) is to have hands-on experience with the dramatic media. Another step is to read books intended for the other stage professionals—actors, directors, designers—in order to know their language and concerns. The more familiar you are with their world, the more you can do to ensure that your play will be produced and performed as you have conceived it.

In the sections that follow, we touch only lightly on matters discussed in the fiction chapters. If you have turned to this chapter first, you may want to refer back to those discussions of plot, character, point of attack, scene, and setting. Here we stress how these same elements need to be reconsidered for dramatic presentation. Our discussions refer to Susan Glaspell's *Trifles*, found in Chapter 14, and to some of the short stories in Chapter 11.

Storytelling with People and Things

The "drama" retains the force of its original meaning in Greek—*to do*. You write out your script to communicate with those who will *do* the play for still other persons (the audience). Though your script may end up printed because your play is a success, publication is a by-product of your collaboration. It is best, then, to think of your play as being similar to a musical score: signs placed on paper that show others how to play your work. You can't ask the musician to play notes or make sounds that the instrument can't produce.

Because fiction and drama use many of the same terms, you can easily fall into the trap of thinking that playwriting is simply telling stories on a different instrument. It is certainly true that the story you want your collaborators to present for you contains many of the same elements discussed in the fiction chapters. Like fiction, a play has the following elements.

1. A *plot*
2. in which *characters*
3. are in *conflict*
4. because they individually want their *desires* to dominate about some object and/or idea and/or emotion.

The wants and needs of the characters are based on a structure of beliefs that the author and the audience may or may not share. Willy Loman in *Death of a Salesman* believes that personality—being well liked—can bring success and excuse lying and stealing, and that what people think of you is more important than what you know or what you can do. Arthur Miller's point of view appears to be that this kind of search for outward success—measured by money—can lead to a failure to recognize one's real talents and needs. The struggle to achieve at any cost a materialistic version of the American Dream results in a tragically empty life. (We come to know Miller's point of view because of what happens to Willy Loman.)

Such a combination of (1) controlling ideas in the characters plus (2) a set of circumstances is called the **premise**. The dramatic premise triggers the actions in the play at the point of attack. Because Willy has followed his beliefs, he has—by his lights—failed. He no longer can go on as a salesman either emotionally, mentally, or physically. He is thinking of suicide. At that very moment his son Biff returns. In *Death of a Salesman* the combination of Willy's beliefs, his traits, and the circumstances is the seed from which grow the conflicts, the flashbacks, and all the other actions that, ironically, lead to Willy's suicide. The elements of the premise, then, can be seen as an opportunity, a potential, for something to happen.

Though we might find the basic concept of premise to be useful for any type of storytelling, the *dramatic* premise requires an especially intense combination of triggering forces at the point of attack. For example, it is much more critical in a dramatic presentation for the point of attack to be as close to the climax as possible. At most the playwright has only a few hours of audience attention for showing the story. In effect, most of the events and the development of essential character traits will have happened before the curtain rises. So late a point of attack creates great pressures. In a real hour or two, the play-wright must have the characters (1) reveal all the information necessary for us to understand who they are and what they are doing (the exposition) and (2) do and say the things that will bring on the dramatic conclusion. The pressure of squeezing so much into a limited time has, as we shall see, both advantages and drawbacks.

Playwriting is so linked to the material presence of actual time, spaces, sounds, and people (actors)—life-going-on—that it has unique energies and limits. Many a writer successful in another genre (Henry James, for example) failed in playwriting by ignoring the particular life, effects, and affects of drama. What might be dismissed as merely mechanical differences are quite complex and can cause important changes in the writer's decisions about developing and presenting character and plot.

The following discussions about how one might adapt stories from fiction to drama will begin to illustrate this point. (We suggest you read the pieces of fiction before you read the discussion.)

I. *"Belling the Cat" (pp. 181–82)*

The fable is based on the following simple ideas: (1) If a solution to a problem cannot be put into effect, it is a foolish suggestion, and (2) an inexperienced individual (in this case, a young mouse) is more likely to propose a foolish solu-tion than is an experienced individual. These ideas (whether correct or not) are dramatized through the "plot" which they control. The setting is minimal, as is the characterization. You can read the fable in a minute, absorb the "truth" of the premise (which is stated directly), and move on. It is the idea in the premise that dominates the characters and circumstances.

If you wanted to turn the fable into a dramatic work, keeping the same characters (mice and cat) and circumstances, what problems would you have? (Jot down a few ideas before going on.)

The most obvious problem, though not the most important, is that you would have to teach mice to talk. Solution: make a cartoon and let real human voices substitute. Or: dress human beings in mouse costumes. Or: let the human beings simply think of themselves as mice. Such problems can be solved by dozens of conventional devices (as in *Peter Pan, Equus,* or *Cats).* A good principle to follow when trying to solve such mechanical problems is simply to borrow a convention the audience is used to.

The more difficult "dramatic" problem is how to activate the premise so that it can occupy the stage or screen for more than a minute or two. The typ-ical solution would be to expand the number of scenes and develop the char-acters. For example, to show us the precise nature of the dilemma, the playwright might add a scene in which the Cat decimates a group of the mice as they are raiding the kitchen. Or, perhaps the dramatization will begin with Young Mouse and Old Mouse as father and son. Old Mouse tells Young

Mouse not to make a fool of himself at the meeting. What has caused Old Mouse to do that? Young Mouse is fresh out of Rodent College, where he majored in conflict resolution and felines. He has returned, full of piss and vinegar, to put his academic training to practical and immediate use. Perhaps the first scene will begin just slightly before the meeting. The last scene will show the mice actually trying to bell the cat (as we see in one of the cartoon versions). Somehow, though, in the process of developing the material we have changed a part of the premise. It's not just about wisdom, it has come to involve a conflict between education and experience, new ways and old ways, sons and fathers.

Inexorably, the move from a fictional premise to a dramatic premise will bring changes—additional actions, a reshaping of emphasis, and different ways of developing character. (*Note:* we are by no means suggesting that dramatizing a piece of fiction always requires expansion. It almost always requires contraction of some events and expansion of others.)

In the end, the experience we will receive from "*Belling the Cat*— the Movie" will be different from the experience we get from "*Belling the Cat*—the Fable" because the audience's expectation of the media has been met. We will see and hear the movement rather than imagining it. Also, because the Old Mouse and the Young Mouse will be present to us, we do not expect to be told one is older and one is younger. The director will make sure we can see that. In fact, the characters won't be telling us anything we can see for ourselves. We might, on the other hand, expect to see Young Mouse actually try to *do* the belling.

Ironically, then, it is no praise to say of the dramatic version that it is exactly like the original.

EXERCISE

One might argue that the premise of "Belling the Cat" is all wrong. How would you do so? Now devise a new premise. Can you think of a circumstance around which you could build a plot for your new premise?

II. "Sunday in the Park" (pp. 231–34)

The thematic element of Kaufman's premise is this: at bottom, no matter how much they may praise and encourage the civilized virtues of intellect and gentleness, some women really want a man to protect them (another way of saying to be "manly" or "macho"). Because Bel Kaufman has chosen to tell the story from the wife's point of view, we are as surprised as the wife is to find her more "primitive" nature surfacing after the bully faces down her husband, Morton. The insight—the epiphany—works in the short story because the woman's sudden *conscious* awareness *is the point*. In a way, the premise is not the revelation of her desire for a "manly" man, but the fact that she wasn't aware of the depths of her dissatisfaction.

Taking the same premise for a play, however, would require major changes and expansion. For example, the antagonist (the bully) in the story has a simple function; he forces Morton's choice of whether to fight for his family's right to share the sandbox in peace or to walk away. Once you put the bully into the flesh of an actor and the actor starts walking on stage or through the film, you need something more for him to do during that time than this single action. You might, of course, shape the action so that the bully comes on only toward the end of the scene but, for the purpose of this discussion, let's assume that the bully must be present for a longer period so his action does not appear gratuitous—mere bullying for the sake of showing power.

In order for the character to be present to the audience for a longer period of time, the dramatist will have to increase the bully's active role. What would happen, for example, if instead of separate benches, as in the story, there was only one bench to share and the bully had entered and joined the couple? What kind of byplay would occur among them as they jostled for room? What are the emotions evoked when people have to share territory? Would the bully sit on Morton's *Times?* Might Morton and his wife try to placate the man? Might Morton offer him a section from his *Times?* Would the bully resent this because he senses both Morton's and Morton's wife's condescension? Is the bully (a construction worker) sick and tired of the "college boys" telling him that the concrete isn't mixed properly? Perhaps, after all, he isn't merely a bully; he has a grievance. Are Morton and his wife regentrifying the construction worker's neighborhood and slowly driving out the working class? Notice how the very fact that the bully will be physically present generates questions that begin to affect the premise.

In a ten-minute skit or a comedy show, such elaboration probably would not be needed, but the presence of a character who is more than a functionary increases the playwright's obligation to account for that character.

More important, if the premise has to do with the woman's sudden recognition of her more "primitive" desires, a way has to be found to let the reader directly experience what the narrator only reports: "It was more than just an unpleasant incident, more than defeat of reason by force . . . it had something to do with her and Morton, something acutely personal, familiar, and important." At the very same time the playwright must (1) find ways to reveal how the woman is hiding her true desires beneath what she believes she ought to desire, and (2) convince the spectators to accept that, with the same evidence they have, she can fail to draw the same conclusion until the very end. (For the audience, seeing what she doesn't see increases the dramatic tension. When is she going to find out what is so clear to us?)

It might appear, then, that the playwright needs only to organize and expand the events in preparation for the wife's moment of realization, ignoring (as the narrator of the story can) the husband's wants and presence. Because Bel Kaufman focuses the events through the woman's point of view, the reader is not concerned about the husband. Since a play normally has no narrator to focus the point of view, the husband will be *present to the audience* and his presence must be fulfilled. The playwright shouldn't suddenly throw a spotlight on the wife and filter out his presence. The audience won't forget the husband's reality as quickly as a reader would.

Since the bully creates an occasion for the wife to realize her true feelings but is not directly involved in the important developments in the marriage, the playwright may feel there is no problem getting him off stage. But surely the husband cannot be treated like a functionary. He is directly involved in the conditions that lead to the wife's recognition. To dramatize the wife's dissatisfaction, to put it into action, the playwright is going to have to show us the relationship. The husband's wants will become important, if only to make us interested in the conflict. Perhaps he and the wife will need a scene before the bully enters to give the audience a sense of the prior relationship. And once the husband's prior set of circumstances are revealed, he acquires importance in the dramatic presentation. Inevitably his importance will lead to adjustments in the premise and in the resolution, because he shares the audience's attention with the wife. How is he going to react to her self-realization? Would he say: "I'm signing up for refresher karate lessons. I would have done it long ago if you'd have let me. I should never have let myself get out of shape." In that case, to the premise must be added new ideas and circumstances: sometimes a man's civilized behavior merely reflects a woman's overt desires; given a chance he'll revert to "manliness."

Here is the principle: the playwright must account for *all the characters who have been involved in the conflict that springs from the premise.* Servants, spear carriers, and other beings who function in the plot only as mechanisms do not, of course, need to be accounted for, because they don't have an identity in relationship to the premise. In the process of accounting for the major characters, however, other aspects of the premise will begin to change.

EXERCISE

Since the wife's recognition alone is not likely to suffice for the ending, we will have to create something that gives the husband an "ending" in relationship to her new premise: I want a *man.* He might have a recognition: You got what you created and I'm comfortable being a wimp. Or, he might throw her over his shoulder and take her off the stage. Plan an ending for a dramatic version of "Sunday in the Park." Be sure to work up what the husband *wants.* Try to keep the play to one set.

III. "The Boarding House" (pp. 239–44)

The premise in "The Boarding House" is complex: marriage is seen as a form of "reparation," a payment to the woman for the satisfaction of the male's sexual desire, which the woman may in fact arouse to trap the man. Because men don't want to be married, they must be trapped into it. Manipulation of men through the power of social convention (and their fear of it) is often the way they are brought to heel. The subtle relationships between sex, marriage, family, church, and society are a replay of a very old premise: "In Adam's fall we sinned all," and how ironic it is that we keep on paying for it. It is a rather dreary view that, at best, is lightened by Joyce's wry sense of just how this particular marriage comes to happen.

The unexpressed desires that motivate the major characters (Mrs. Mooney, Mr. Doran, and Polly Mooney) would be difficult to dramatize because Joyce deliberately wants to show the passions as internal and inexpressible. Mrs. Mooney desires for her daughter a good marriage—at least a better one than she had; Polly desires sex and marriage; Doran desires to escape the trap but is too guilty and fearful (of violence, of losing his job, of what others will say) to flee. The technique of the story allows us to see that these desires cannot be expressed to others because one can hardly acknowledge them to oneself.

As a result, a good deal of this story's power comes from what we imagine is floating in the characters' minds. Among the images are the run-down boarding house and Dublin itself—Victorian, morally oppressive, and dreary. These are part of the circumstances in which the characters have developed. We assume that Mrs. Mooney's disappointing marriage is what motivates her—a history told, not shown. Doran's weakness (his mental and physical cowardice) we deduce from many small hints. Even the events that are shown, such as Polly waiting for her proposal, tend to be internal; while she is waiting, Polly's visions of the future are described as amorphous. The scenes not shown—the sex scene, Doran's confession, Mrs. Mooney's confrontation with Doran—have the most potential for action and conflict, the lifeblood of the dramatic genres. Joyce filters out those in order to stress the results. He exploits the possibilities in narrative fiction for *showing* the rich interiority of the characters. He relies on the reader to imagine the scenes and the motives that the dramatist would be sweating to *show* in a different sense of the word—show so that an audience could literally see and hear the action.

For the dramatist, "The Boarding House" contains no end of scenes inviting such showing:

- A scene at Doran's job (to show his fearfulness)
- A scene of women going to mass (including Mrs. Mooney)
- A visit from Mr. Mooney (the former husband)
- A dinner scene with all the boarders
- Doran's confession

And on and on. While the interiority of the story would be lost in the requirement for showing, for example, why Doran is quite right to fear the brutality of Polly's brother, new possibilities emerge. The playwright could show Polly's brother unfiltered through Doran's fearful imagination, exploiting a hint in the narrator's ironic presentation that the brother is a blowhard. Such a comic bully might well create a different sense of Doran's cowardice. Has Mrs. Mooney put her son up to scaring Mr. Doran?

However, to capture Joyce's internal world, the playwright would have to expand on the external world because the emotions that Joyce has rendered subtly could be recreated in the audience only by an accretion of many scenes, if at all.

Here is the principle: *though the ultimate effects may be quite subtle, drama requires presentation to the senses.* Therefore, when the writer imagines a premise requiring an internalized presentation and immense amounts of exposition, the material *as imagined* may not be suitable for a play. The very nature of drama—people witnessing actions and things—requires that the playwright create circumstances in which the motives and emotions of the characters can be swiftly and easily apprehended and felt.

Note: a producer or director might believe it worthwhile to try to recreate the mood of 1890s Dublin. In such a circumstance Joyce's story would be an occasion for a different creative motive, a desire to produce *spectacle*—the pleasure the audience derives from setting and extraordinary action (like acrobatics). Spectacle is one of the arts of the dramatist's collaborators. When the pleasures from spectacle dominate the drama, the playwright's premise becomes subordinate to the pleasures derived from those collaborators' arts. In other words, the play becomes an aspect of the spectacle and not the reverse. Such spectacle for spectacle's sake is outside the concern of this book.

EXERCISES

1. Write Doran's confession scene with the priest so he reveals his inner terrors about marriage (and, of course, his sin of fornicating with Polly). Or write the scene in which Mrs. Mooney gets out of Polly what has happened with Mr. Doran. Is Polly pregnant?

2. Create a **treatment** (a scene-by-scene outline) for a movie version of "The Boarding House." As you select your scenes, keep in mind that you are trying to suggest in another medium the effects of Joyce's short story. For a model, read Joyce's "The Dead" and see John Huston's film rendition of the story.

Adaptation, of course, is but one way to find a subject for a play; often you will start with your own combination of premise, situation, and characters.

The principles will be the same: you will need to develop a premise suitable for the demands of a presentation, not of a printed page. The essential elements of story construction will remain the same as in fiction (see Chapter 9), but the pressures of dramatic presentation will determine how you go about developing the plot.

By this point it should be clear that when you intend to tell stories with real people and things, you must constantly be alert to the impact of the visual. The illumination of characters and plot in dramatic media is more than a matter of transferring your narrative into dialogue and stage directions.

MORE EXERCISES

1. Reread "The Lost Cottage" in Chapter 11. Consider what you would have to do to plot, character, and point of attack to turn it into a play.

2. Choose a popular fairy tale ("Little Red Riding Hood," for example). What is the premise? What is your point of attack? Why? Briefly describe what scenes you would need and list the events in those scenes.

3. Assume that "The Boarding House" characters live today—let us say at an exclusive but small and seedy college dedicated to the arts and overrun with mice, not donors. What kind of premise might you come up with that captures the spirit of the original if Mrs. Mooney runs some kind of off-campus establishment (small apartment house in a former mansion) and Mr. Doran is an assistant professor who is coming up for tenure? Outline your version of the play.

A Final Note

The point of attack in a dramatic presentation, as in fiction (see the discussion in Chapter 9), is generally as close to the climax of the story as the playwright can make it. Try to structure the events so that as much of the story as possible has happened before the curtain rises or credits end. The less that needs to be shown, the less time the production will take and the fewer actors and sets will be required.

CHARACTERS

A character is, as we have already discussed, the sum of "characteristics" that create for an audience some sense that the personages in stories, narrative or dramatic, are present and distinct. (See Chapter 9 for more about this aspect of character.) Just as a fiction writer does, the playwright builds a sense of the characters' reality by having them behave in a manner consistent with their development in the plot. In Ibsen's *Hedda Gabler,* Hedda behaves in a self-centered, independent way, reflecting characteristics attributable to her upbringing as a general's only child. In part, her suicide is understandable as an outcome of (1) that independence and her refusal to allow another man to dominate her, and (2) her fear of public exposure. These characteristics are seen in actions before her suicide.

A flesh-and-blood person will play Hedda. This special condition—actor plus the role the actor plays—creates for the playwright special opportunities and problems. Unless something about a character's physical appearance is extremely important, the playwright need only sketch it in lightly. The director will choose the actors for gross distinctiveness (sex, age, looks) in accordance with the plot. Obviously, except in a radio presentation, the audience will not have to visualize these elements. The actor will provide the accent and the details (makeup, costume, sex, stature, and mannerisms) that a narrator constantly has to supply in fiction. Nor does the dramatist have to provide details to help the spectators visualize actions. The actor (and the other collaborators) present them directly to the senses. On the surface, then, it might appear that since half the job is done, all sensible writers would become playwrights.

The freedoms from some tasks actually create terrible responsibilities because, for most dramatic presentations, the characters have to carry forward in what they say and do almost all the elements of both the premise and the plot. Everything is compressed into the showing—characteristics, relationships, and conflicts. In some ways, condensation for effective dramatic presentation is closer emotionally and artistically to the demands of poetry than to fiction.

In small compass, the following radio advertisement (a playlet) shows how much is compressed into the characters and the situation that unfolds through them, all in a continuous time. We have decided to call it: "The Teeth of the Problem."

(TIME: *The present*
SCENE: *A restaurant. Sounds of dishes clattering and other restaurant noises in the background.*)
    MAN: Hi. Sorry I'm late.
    WOMAN: Oh, that's O.K. This is a nice place.
    MAN: Speaking of nice places—
    WOMAN: Uh-huh?
    MAN: I got the brochures. Here's Jamaica, the Virgin Islands, Martinique.
    WOMAN: I have a [pause] "brochure" for you, too.
    MAN: (*reading*) "When Your Child Needs Braces?" What is this?
    WOMAN: Your child needs braces.
    MAN: Eric?
    WOMAN: That's what Dr. Marshall says.
    MAN: Darn. What's that going to cost?

WOMAN: Oh, the price of a nice cruise.
MAN: Which means—
WOMAN: Right.
MAN: Diane, we need this trip.
WOMAN: Uh-huh.
MAN: We've waited five years for it.
WOMAN: Eric isn't too happy about this either.
MAN: I know. Is there any way we could swing both?
WOMAN: I don't see how, honey.
VOICEOVER: *For anyone who has ever said there isn't enough money, now there is. Sovran has half a billion dollars to lend.*

In traditional terms, we could analyze the elements of the playlet as follows:

Situation: A couple have been planning for a Caribbean cruise for some time and have saved money for it. They have sacrificed to raise their children (or child), and they may need this trip for the health of their marriage and their own mental health. The husband has gone to the travel bureau and picked up information; the wife has taken their son to the dentist. Previously they had planned to meet for lunch and discuss the trip.
Complication: Their son needs braces.
Crisis: They don't have enough money to meet their responsibility and also to take the trip they have worked for.
Conflict: Do they give up their trip or have their son grow up with crooked teeth?
Climax (and resolution): A **deus ex machina**—the bank—arrives to say there is enough money because the bank is willing to make loans.
Premises: (1) You can fulfill your responsibilities to others and yourself if you have enough money. (2) Some pleasures, such as a vacation, may actually be responsibilities. (3) If you are responsible, you are rewarded with pleasures.

It is not fanciful to say that the "plot" of the play we experience here grows from the attributes of the characters. Both are responsible people (they have saved for their trip and take good care of Eric). The husband appears to be the less responsible. He is the one who picks up the brochure and he also seems, at least for a moment, to be the one less willing to give up the trip. So we have a potential dramatic conflict. The wife is the one who takes Eric to the dentist, she arrives on time, and she has apparently already determined that the money is to be spent on Eric. Their need for a vacation comes from the very fact that they are married (rather a stock situation which may reflect the audience's understanding of reality). Their dilemma, paying for the braces, comes from the fact that they have had Eric and are responsible enough to take him to a dentist. "Plot" and "character" are related.

The message from the bank fulfills their needs in terms of their character traits. Anybody as responsible as they have already shown themselves to be can have a slice of the half billion. Such people pay their debts. The principles on which the bank operates—the subtext of the message announced to the audience—is obvious and neatly self-fulfilling.

Note how much of the couple's past, present, and future is condensed into a single minute of presentation, some twenty lines of dialogue. For the playwright to get all this into such short compass requires a sense of how to create for the audience images that it can instantly understand. As we will see, the dramatic presentation does not (usually) contain a narrative point of view to provide additional comments, to filter out accidental impressions, or to focus the audience's attention. Essentially, the whole task of storytelling has to be done with what the characters say and do.

EXERCISE

1. Continue the scene after the bank's message, showing what would happen if the wife decided it would be irresponsible to take out a loan. (Consider what situations and premises would make her decide this and be sure to keep to the characteristics already established, though you may, of course, add to them.)

2. Read Glaspell's *Trifles* (Chapter 14). At what point did you grasp that Mrs. Peters is fearful of her husband and, perhaps, of all men? In what way are her feelings about the men in general and her own past experiences a key to the decision she will finally make to hide the evidence? At the last minute, why is she not able to hide the bird's corpse though she would like to? Is this failure to act with decision typical of her character?

PRESENTING CHARACTER

Beginning playwrights often forget how much the revelation of character traits can be condensed through exploiting opportunities already provided by the chacter's physical presence in the actor. The actor interacts with the environmnent while speaking dialogue. Indeed, the playwright is responsible for preparing conditions that will give the actors opportunities for **stage business**—something to *do*. The stage business need not be spelled out for the actor or director but should be inherent in one or more of the following:

1. The physical habits and condition of the characters.
2. The physical action called for at a particular point.
3. The place in which the characters find themselves.
4. The relationships among the characters.

The more physical the action, the less "business" the actors will have to think up for themselves (and the less they have to say because we see what they are doing). In a screenplay set in Montana, the actors hunting on horseback for wild buffalo will have little difficulty finding things to do when the cameras are rolling.

If your play occurs in a palace, however, and the issue is whether the king will abdicate or not, the actors might find the stage business less obvious. Granted that what the characters say to one another will be a kind of doing, their talking for two hours about the problem is likely to put a strain on the director's and actors' ingenuity for creating visual effects as well as an audience's ability to stay awake. Now give the king a cold (almost too obviously symbolic) and a large briefcase into which he is placing papers from his desk. A servant (let's make him a wise fool) comes and goes bringing handkerchiefs (a king does not use Kleenex), drinks, and news.

> SERVANT: These are the last clean ones, your highness.
> KING: I suppose I should get used to using Kleenex. Bring me the ashtray.
> SERVANT: You should get used to fetching your own.

The king's habit of command is revealed, as is the changing situation to which he must soon become accustomed. The servant's "forgetting" to say "your majesty" in the second speech indicates his realization that the situation is changing. Might not the king's posture stiffen also? Does he touch the crown he is wearing? Suddenly, there are things for the actors to do whether or not they are speaking—objective realities for what are inward attitudes. Remember, though, that these outward manifestations of the plot and character ought not be mechanical. Don't say that the queen pulls at her nose unless you know why she does it and how the other characters might react to it.

Obviously, stage business is most effective when it is the result of clearly thinking through the character's inner cast of mind. In *The Caine Mutiny Court Martial*, Captain Queeg's disturbance is expressed by the business of rolling the two ball bearings in his hand; the same action suggests psychosexual disturbance. His uncontrolled manipulation of the bearings triggers the past for him. Both what he says and what he does reveal to the military jury that Queeg is mentally ill, leading to the acquittal of the mutineers. In this case, stage business that grows from character leads to revelation and resolution.

EXERCISE

1. Create a scene in which a student is trying to get a better grade from a teacher. Let us see within the first five lines of dialogue the student's need (or needs) but not the reasons for it. The teacher does not want to give the student a passing grade but does not wish to *say* so. You may reveal this at any point. Now create things for the characters to handle and do that will indicate their inner natures. Bring us to a point at which the teacher can convincingly tell the student about the "F" because now he or she wishes to.

2. Imagine that you are directing a television version of the radio ad on pages 273–74. Write out directions for how you want the actors to appear and what you want them to do. Include directions for a scene to be shot in a restaurant, their kitchen, or their bedroom. Change the dialogue as necessary (remember we can see what's happening). Try to keep to the same performance time.

STOCK CHARACTERS
AND CHARACTER DEVELOPMENT

Stage business often is what creates the audience's sense of a distinctive trait in what is really a stock character, a stereotype from life or literature. (For more on stock character, see p. 199.) The shy, awkward maid whose role is to serve tea becomes a presence when she invariably spills it. If she is not fired (or put to other activities), the audience makes judgments about the people who pay her salary. One bit of business starts to create a potential for more stage business revealing even more characteristics. The playwright is continually shuttling between the character's business, the internal state that the business indicates, how the other characters react, their internal state, and on and on. In the course of a play's development a stock character, like Shakespeare's Falstaff (the stock bragging soldier), may acquire a sharper identity because while inventing stage business the playwright delves further into the traits behind the visible effects.

In fact, even those characters you originally conceive of as having complex attributes need to be revealed first through their stock attributes, moving from the type to the individual. The actors will be dressed as kings, servants, slatterns, hippies—something that categorizes them. They will be washing dishes, driving a BMW to work, jogging, sleeping, carrying a load of books. In the first few moments the audience will judge the characters by their dress, their looks, what they are doing, what is around them. In the same few moments the audience will be trying to absorb the environment (set) and to figure out what the issues are. Things easily and quickly recognizable—the stock characteristics—orient the audience, just as they would in daily life. The beginning of the play is no time to present the "To be or not to be" soliloquy. The revelations about Hamlet's interior landscape are so complex that they would be lost until we are comfortable with his exterior.

In *Trifles*, for another example, all the characters are seen in their expected roles—sheriff, attorney, farmer, wife. The women mostly stay silent while the men take center stage and discuss the men's business—the murder. The men are courtly and protective of the women. The questioning of Mr. Hale shows the county attorney, George Henderson, as the most educated of the group and clearly in charge. Because the start of a crime investigation is a stock situation, we are quickly oriented to the basic situation. Also, Henderson immediately appears to be a bit of the outsider and a bit of a blowhard, which explains why even the sheriff, Mr. Peters, is uncomfortable with him. Henderson's rather bossy and assured manner is one reason we accept the other characters' defensive attitude toward him. (Later, this attitude will set off Mrs. Hale's annoyance with him, leading her to want to get even with him.) At the beginning, the women appear rather ordinary "wives"—the sheriff's wife and the farmer's wife. In fact, Mr. Henderson even refers to the women as fulfilling "stock" roles in the natural world; in one ironic moment he says that he trusts Mrs. Peters because she is a sheriff's wife. But while the men end up mostly ful- filling their stock roles, it is the women who turn out to be the ones who truly are capable of understanding and action and, in part, the play is intended to point out that their stock characteristics are not all there is to them.

Since the audience has no narrative filter to explain characteristics, nor can it flip back the pages and control the display of information, the playwright has to reveal the characteristics in stages. You might want to think of this grad- ual revelation as similar to how an image slowly emerges on Polaroid film. The image is already there; it must be developed.

Then, as the characters do more, the audience's first impressions may be changed or modified. While the women in *Trifles* appear to be passive and sim- ply accepting of the men's authority at the beginning, when the men are out of the room we see elements of their real attitudes, which include amusement, contempt, and anger. At first Mr. Henderson appears to be the investigator in control as "detective." We may even see his behavior toward the women as acceptable because he is protective of them or because we think men ought to treat women as if they were children and slightly retarded. Then we see him as a bit of an ass. Then we understand that he *is* the one who is the ass and, in the final moment, as the one whose attitudes make him blind to the truth and a bit foolish. The dramatic process is fairly typical; the unfolding of the events cre- ates an opportunity to see more aspects of a character. Putting it another way, we can say that the playwright's plot creates opportunities for the audience's understanding to develop and change.

Of course, the characters may "change" in the sense that events they have experienced will or will not modify their perceptions of past events, the other characters, their own condition, or the decisions they should make. We see that, despite our sense that the sheriff's wife is merely a weak and fearful extension of her husband, Glaspell strongly indicates Mrs. Peters's anger at men's careless brutality when she tells the story of her cat's death. In fact, the latter portion of the play shows that her "change" as a character from mouse to lion is no change at all. This change is a change of behavior, not of characteristics. Shakespeare's King Lear, on the other hand, does appear to undergo a basic change. He appears to soften and become more capable of love and pity. But does he change, or do we see hidden traits revealed? Perhaps the authoritative role Lear has had to play as a king has disguised his loving nature (a softness that his two wicked daughters understand). When the "king" is beaten out of him, Lear's loving side stands revealed.

EXERCISE

Take two of the stock characters in the list on page 199. Put them in a laundromat waiting to use the only working dryer. Both their wash loads are finished at the same time. Problem: who is going to use the dryer first?

1. Create dialogue based on what the audience might expect such characters to do and say.

2. Now assume that after a while one of the characters realizes that he or she is behaving like a stock character. Give that character something to say or do that indicates this realization.

3. Go back to the dialogue you wrote for number 1 and revise it to indicate the character's potential for having such a realization.

Some Final Points

One of the reasons a play appears so raw when you read it, perhaps even emotionally crude, is that the attributes of the characters, like musical notes in a score, can gain timbre—that is, subtlety—only from the player and the context of the presentation. In Ibsen's *A Doll's House,* Nora slamming the door after she leaves her husband appears **melodramatic,** overdone, when we read it. When we experience the actual sound, it almost appears understated. This strange alchemy is in part the result of the fact that we can see her husband react to the sound. The playwright who attempts to show a character with the same narrative subtlety as one would in fiction is attempting to provide what the medium is not intended to carry. In a playscript, the writer needs to paint with a much broader brush.

The playwright should not expect that an important element of character slipped in subtly at the beginning of a play and never reinforced is going to enable the audience to understand another element of character or plot at the end of the play. Remember, the audience does not have the luxury of stopping the film or play to say, "Let's see that again because my attention slipped and I missed what happened." Or, "I see what happened, but what does it mean?" Or, "Now that we've gotten to this point of the play, I appear to have missed something. Let me flip back to see what it was."

Finally, characters on a page will ultimately have to be turned into actors on a stage or in film. As a practical matter, you cannot multiply characters in a play with the same degree of freedom as you can in fiction. The cast of thousands is not possible on the stage and seldom is in film. For one thing, budgets are not likely to be big enough. More important, unless the "characters" are merely part of the scenery, the audience cannot meet too many in such a short period of time and keep them all in mind. (Think of what happens when you meet ten new people at a party.) Certainly it is easier to keep track of four characters than of forty. Many theaters with an interest in new plays suggest that the play require no more than eight to ten actors. While this fact has little to do with the artistic considerations that ideally should concern the writer, in the less than ideal world another character means another actor to pay and costume. Remember, a very late point of attack often avoids the necessity of multiplying characters.

CHARACTERS IN PLACE AND TIME

SHEILA: There are a lot of memories in this room.
BEN: There certainly are. Remember when we bought that?
SHEILA: Oh, Ben, we need to talk now.

For condensation and characterization, a playwright exploits the fact than an actor "puts on" the character and moves in real space and real time. Imagine, for example, a character coming home determined to tell her husband that she is leaving him. She enters the living room that contains all the objects they have collected during six years of marriage. The actor *sees* those objects that the designer has placed on the set. (Remember that to the actor in the role of a character it is a living room, not a set.) If the playwright remembers the small statue the couple bought on their last trip to Stockholm, the actor playing Sheila may have something to pick up and handle lovingly to indicate a state of mind. Her remembrance may well be revealed not in precise terms but as a re*action* that suggests her emotion—and then her immediately conflicting emotions as she replaces the statue on the mantle, turning off Ben's efforts to recreate the past.

The awareness of physical place and objects has to be matched by the playwright's awareness of time. At the simplest level, if an actor goes off to change a costume (to the character it is a change of *clothes)*, the other actors must have something to do that advances the plot or the audience will grow restive in the real time that it takes to make the costume change. A planned silence that the playwright uses to reveal character, advance plot, or create tension is different from silences imposed by the fact that the characters have nothing to do or must cross space without something to say. A real minute can appear to be hours to an audience (or actor) unless the dramatic minute has something in it that advances the plot.

Sometimes the very fact of "real" versus "stage" time can be used for the creation of exciting effects. In the following scene, the climax of Christopher Marlowe's *The Tragicall History of Dr. Faustus,* Faustus is about to pay with his soul for the bargain with the Devil, a bargain that has given Faustus wealth, power, sex, and knowledge. As we pick up the action, his friends are leaving:

> ALL: Faustus, farewell!
> *Exit* Scholars. *The clock strikes eleven.*
> FAUST: Ah, Faustus,
> Now has thou but one bare hour to live,
> And then thou must be damn'd perpetually!
> Stand still, you ever-moving spheres of Heaven,
> That time may cease, and midnight never come;
> Fair Nature's eye, rise, rise again and make
> Perpetual day; or let this hour be but
> A year, a month, a week, a natural day,
> That Faustus may repent and save his soul!
> *O lente, lente, currite noctis equi*
> (Run slowly, slowly steeds of the night.)
> The stars move still, time runs, the clock will strike,
> The Devil will come, and Faustus must be damn'd.

After twenty-one more lines, at most another two to five minutes, we (and Faustus) hear the clock strike again:

> Ah, half the hour is past! 'T will all be past anon!

And, then after another eighteen lines—perhaps one minute of acting—we hear the clock strike midnight. We are told that an hour has gone by, but only ten minutes or so have gone by in real time. The difference creates a sense of speed that fits the situation.

The next part of the action manipulates the opposite effect of time. Keep in mind during the following scene that the clock will be tolling steadily but with greater intervals between each strike than in real time.

> *The Clock striketh twelve.*
> O, it strikes, it strikes! Now, body, turn to air,
> Or Lucifer will bear thee quick to hell!
> > *Thunder and lightning*
> O soul, be chang'd into little water-drops,
> And fall into the ocean—ne're be found!—
> My God, my God, look not so fierce on me!
> > *Enter* Devils
> Adders and serpents, let me breathe awhile!—
> Ugly hell, gape not!—Come not, Lucifer!—
> I'll burn my books!—Ah, Mephistophilis!
> > *Exit* Devil *with him.*

The director will stretch out this speech so it will take as long as possible, dragging out Faustus's final moments.

In a production, the manipulation of the difference between stage time and real time creates tension in the audience that is equivalent to the tension in Faustus. The speeding up of time is an enactment of his desire to hold time back. On the other hand, dragging out the time it would actually take to strike twelve from thirty seconds into two or three minutes increases the tension unbearably. Just as Faustus fearfully waits for Mephistopheles, the great forecloser on souls, so do we.

EXERCISE

Plan a five-minute scene in which the devil is waiting for Faustus. Faustus will come in at the end. The devil's concern is that Faustus will beg God to forgive him and so be saved. Aside from his desire to have Faustus's soul, try to give the devil a personal reason for concern. We will hear the clock that Faustus hears, but we will hear it at a tempo you decide on. You may invent other characters.

BEATS

On stage and in film you can signal the passage of time through a variety of conventional devices. On the stage, the lights or the curtain can be lowered and raised (as between scenes or acts); in film, fades or cuts serve the same purpose.

The breaks in the flow of the action work much as a chapter break might, allowing us to focus on key elements in the plot rather than the transitions. The fact that the audience accepts such devices is useful in two ways: (1) The few minutes of a curtain dropping and raising is accepted as the hours it would take for a character to go from New York to Chicago or the years it takes for a character's hair to grow white; and (2) It allows the writer to account for the time it might take a character's traits to modify. In effect, the audience accepts that, during the break in the time flow signaled by the convention, people have gotten from one place to another and hours, days, or years have gone by. Such devices allow you to compress twenty years of story events into a few hours of performance.

Such conventional devices work as a kind of gravitational force holding scenes and acts, the large conventional units, firmly to the needs of the plot. The **beat,** a smaller unit of stage time, is, from the playwright's point of view, the essential working unit of the play. It is like the line in poetry and the sentence in fiction.

Directors often speak of a play as if it were a piece of music made up of chords or "beats." The sum of the beats is the play. Each beat contains a revelation of a mood, relationship, or an action that advances our understanding of the whole plot. Each beat resolves some tension and leads to another beat until the end. Let us say, for example, that you are writing a car chase scene for a film. The villains are after the heroes, who are trying to rendezvous with a helicopter that will fly them to safety.

> Beat 1. The Blues (the villains) are chasing the Greens (our heroes). The Greens approach a railroad crossing. A train is coming. The Blues are catching up and one of the villains is just raising the M-16. The Greens cross the tracks and The Blues screech to a halt.
> Beat 2. The Greens' car develops a flat. The heroes frantically work to change the tire. The Blues are underway again and rapidly closing the distance. Just as they round the curve, the tire is fixed and the heroes are back on the road.
> Beat 3. The chase continues and the villains are catching up. In the distance we see the helicopter. One of the heroes carefully aims and shoots out the front tires of the villains' car, which overturns. Just ahead now is safety.
> Beat 4. The heroes' car squeals to a halt next to the helicopter. With happy smiles on their faces they start to run to the cabin. In the helicopter we see the boss of the villains raise a submachine gun.
> And so on.

Constructing by beats is equally necessary in less action-filled playscripts, as in the following scene from Harold Pinter's *The Collection*. Note how rapidly the beats follow on one another. The beats are punctuated with a pause.

Situation: Harry enters his apartment and goes to a phone, which we have heard ringing. It is late at night.

HARRY: Hello.
VOICE: Is that you, Bill?
HARRY: No, he's in bed. Who's this?
VOICE: In bed?
HARRY: Who is this?
VOICE: What's he doing in bed?
(*Pause*)
HARRY: Do you know it's four o'clock in the morning?
VOICE: Well, give him a nudge. Tell him I want a word with him.
(*Pause*)
HARRY: Who is this?
VOICE: Go and wake him up, there's a good boy.
(*Pause*)
HARRY: Are you a friend of his?
VOICE: He'll know me when he sees me.
HARRY: Oh yes?
(Pause)
VOICE: Aren't you going to wake him?
HARRY: No, I'm not.
(*Pause*)
VOICE: Tell him I'll be in touch.
(*The telephone cuts off.*)

In the first beat, by not answering Harry, the Voice fails to give Harry what he wants. In the second beat, Harry is forced into the unreasonable position of having to respond to the Voice's questions without having received an answer to his. In a sense, he is defeated. The beat ends when the Voice treats Harry as a servant by asking Harry to wake Bill. Harry, quite understandably, tries to establish equality but is again defeated when the Voice does not answer the question; instead the Voice reasserts his position of authority. Harry is not a "boy." In the next beat Harry again tries to establish his equality, but his question receives an unexpectedly indirect answer—an answer that is almost threatening. Harry's last speech in this beat is a question because he has not really been given an answer. But "Oh yes?" also has in it an assertion of its own—that is, you had better tell me more. In the next to last beat, the Voice refuses to give that information and Harry reestablishes his equality by refusing the Voice's request. In the final beat the Voice wins by cutting Harry off after making a demand that Harry cannot fulfill. Since the Voice has never given his name, who can Harry say called? We end with a feeling that *something* bad is going to happen.

As the Pinter excerpt demonstrates, a beat is like the clenching and unclenching of a hand. Sometimes the struggle between the characters is obvious, ending with violent gestures and actions; sometimes the struggle is simply for a mastery of the situation. Each time the beat unclenches we see a momentary restoration of some type of balance, a relaxation of tension. This relaxation is a small instance of the large resolution we expect at the end of the play. In the Pinter play, the hanging up of the phone literally disconnects the characters and releases the immediate tension. The playwright will, of course, vary the degree of tension in each beat, trying to reach the most intense beat (the climax) as close as possible to the resolution, the final unclenching.

EXERCISE

1. Think of a game whose rules you know well (Trivial Pursuit, Monopoly, chess). Now take two or three characters who are in conflict about something (for example, whether or not to divorce, whether or not to rob a bank, whether or not to sell their business, whether or not to kill their hostage). Write a scene in which your characters are playing the game or kibitzing. You might also have your characters waiting for someone to arrive or waiting for a phone call with important information.

2. Describe the beats—struggle–balance, struggle–balance—between the characters.

3. What would happen in your scene if one of the characters did not know the game or did not play it well?

4. If you haven't done so already, add a third character who is making something (a cake, a house of cards, a bookshelf, a bomb). *Note:* you should know how to make or do whatever you have your character making or doing.

SETTING

We already discussed in Chapter 9 the idea of setting or place for your scenes. You may wish to review that section before continuing here. From your characters' point of view, the setting is not a series of words, it is a real place with real temperatures, light (or dark), furniture or grass, sirens or crickets. The setting in the story becomes a "set" in the play, a work place prepared for the actors who will assume the fictive roles. (Film allows for actual places to become sets.)

In printed versions of plays, you might see the following description of a set.

SCENE: *A court apartment in Los Angeles in the West Adams district. The room is done in white—white ceiling, white walls, white overly elaborate furniture—but a red wall-to-wall carpet covers the floor. A wall bed is raised. Upstairs, two doorless entrances stand on each side of the head of the bed. The right entrance is to the kitchen; the backstage area that represents the kitchen is shielded by a filmy curtain and the actors' dim silhouettes are seen when the area is lighted. The left entrance will be raised and offstage right at the head of a short flight of stairs and a platform which leads into the combination bedroom—dressingroom—closet.*

Ed Bullins, *Goin'a Buffalo*

You may even have seen more elaborate descriptions using words such as "stage left," "curtain," and "scrim." What you are reading in such cases is most likely the playwright's description of the set from the first production of the play. It is unlikely that Ed Bullins had that specific a set in mind when he was first writing the play. Most likely, he thought of his play as happening in a "court apartment." Perhaps he also had in mind that the rooms would be painted totally in white, have a red carpet, and contain ornate furniture.

In many cases, the playwright has a much sketchier notion, a notion more related to a sense of the place in which the action occurs rather than a theatrical set:

Galileo's scantily furnished study. Morning. GALILEO *is washing himself. A barefooted boy,* ANDREA, *son of his housekeeper,* MRS. SARTI, *enters with a big astronomical model.*

Bertolt Brecht, *Galileo*

From this description, a set designer may well build a set just as detailed as the one we see described in Bullins's play.

When you are drafting, you probably are wasting energy if you spend large amounts of time working up a set, though you need to be highly conscious of the place your characters are in because they will be conscious of the place whether it be a mountaintop or their living room. Some playwrights, like some novelists, actually draw out rough designs of the place, but they do so to give themselves a sense of what the character is seeing, not in order to become set designers. Though the matter is not the playwright's primary concern, producers do worry about a play's meeting the needs of the available space and money.

Beth Henley's *Crimes of the Heart* might well have first caught someone's eye because the entire play takes place in an old-fashioned kitchen:

MEG: What's the cot doing in the kitchen?
LENNY [Meg's sister]: Well, I rolled it out when Old Granddaddy got sick. So I could be close and hear him at night if he needed something.

MEG (*glancing toward the door leading to the downstairs bedroom*): Is Old Granddaddy here?

LENNY: Why, no. Old Granddaddy's at the hospital.

The door, of course, actually leads offstage. And, if we are experienced with theatrical reality, we also assume that the cot is in the kitchen to provide a place on which several people can sit at once, saving perhaps a set change to a living room. By the end of the beat, however, from the audience's point of view the door leads to a bedroom and the cot is there for the reason stated. Grandfather's presence is established and so is the cot. (In fact, Grandfather never actually appears in the play.) From a producer's point of view, *Crimes of the Heart* focuses the whole world of the characters in a relatively simple, inexpensive set.

Many theaters specifically request that the plays submitted to them be doable in simple sets. Playwrights who make sets too specific ignore the reality that stages will vary enormously both in shape and size. All these variables suggest that you can waste a good deal of energy being too specific about details of setting that are not absolutely relevant to the particular actions of the characters.

Imagine yourself, for example, as a producer for a local small theater faced with the following description of a set:

> The scene is set in William Hurt's study. At stage left is a small Queen Anne writing table, two by three feet, and next to it is a Chippendale chair with pettipoint seat done in subtle shades of blue and rose. The pattern is a fleur-de-lis in the manner of Rogette. The carpet is a Bengali with dominant mauve colors. Stage right is a large bookcase containing the complete works of Dickens with Dore woodcuts. Upstage is a padded door, the type that one sees in libraries and music halls. It is the only exit from the room. Stage front are two large matching leather chairs with an end table between them. On the table is an ivory chess set with the pieces spread on the inlaid board. The game in progress is a repeat of the famous Spassky/Fisher "Indian Defense" played during the Tunisian challenge. . . .

While one might argue that the playwright needs to think of the setting in such detail, almost as a novelist might, writing it out is largely a waste of time. In any case, the director and set designer will probably ignore the elaborate detail.

The following notation will be sufficient for your purposes:

> SCENE: William Hurt's study. A small antique desk and chair, a bookcase filled with a matched set of books, other bookcases and two large chairs separated by a low table on which a chess game is in progress.

Finally, keep in mind that the setting for the play is more than a visual environment. It influences how the characters are feeling, what they say and do.

Possibilities for characterizing may grow from the fact that the environment may contain smells; it may be hot or cold, light or dark. The playwright can exploit the fact that the characters can react to all the physical elements even when they are not talking about them. (In fiction, the writer has to remind the reader continually that such physical elements are operating.)

EXERCISE

Return to one of the scenes you wrote for the television version of the radio advertisement. Write dialogue for the husband and wife that will be a response to the following facts: it is twelve degrees out and the wife is wearing a new perfume. Remember, these facts are known to them before the scene opens.

13

❖

Dialogue and Its Problems

DIALOGUE: THE ESSENCE OF DRAMA

Most of what you are going to write when you write a play is dialogue. Here is what your dialogue must do:

1. Contain all the necessary exposition, including what happened before the point of attack, between scenes and acts, and offstage (though the audience can be told some things through sounds, such as a gunshot offstage).
2. Reveal everything about the characters' feelings, beliefs, and wants.

In other words, the dialogue is both exposition and action.

From the playwright's point of view dialogue is not "talk," although the actor is, of course, "talking" the character's words. In fact, transcriptions of how people actually talk are difficult to follow because most of our talk lacks shape, that is, purpose in relationship to a plot. While one may suppose there can be idle *talk, dialogue* must be idle only for a purpose. Every line of dialogue must serve (or appear to serve) one or more of the following dramatic purposes:

- to reveal the character's nature
- to reveal the character's needs and intentions
- to have impact on another character or characters

Dialogue means, literally, the *words through;* a stage play will happen mostly through what the characters say. Much of the playwright's work goes into shaping the plot in such a manner that the dialogue is what the characters will *do* to each other. If the dialogue contains information that the audience needs for understanding the situation, that information usually will be a by-product of the interaction among the characters. Even in a screenplay, in which the characters' action can be more physical, the dialogue must be treated as a type of action.

Ideally each speech a character makes will contain both a **text**—an intended message directed at the other character(s)—and a **subtext**—which conveys the characters' real feelings, needs, and attitudes.

> SON: Can I do the dishes after I talk with Joanne about the test tomorrow?
> MOTHER: Do you want to borrow my car on Saturday?

The visible messages—the text—are requests for information. Clearly, however, the son is also trying to put off a task by suggesting that doing the dishes is not as important as doing homework. His real intention (talking with Joanne) is the subtext. The mother's subtext is so clear that it needs no analysis. The questions, as it turns out, are not questions at all.

Even if the other characters do not catch the subtext, the audience will, consciously or unconsciously. As we saw earlier, each character has an agenda and this agenda will be reflected in both text and subtext. Just as the surface of what we say to others is only the window into what we really mean, so too for what characters say to other characters.

The opening scene from a traditionally made play, Noel Coward's *Blithe Spirit,* illustrates the idea. In the play, Charles Condomine, a writer, is talking to his second wife, Ruth, while they have cocktails before guests arrive. Their previous dialogue has been about how Charles got the idea for an interesting character in his last novel. Elvira, Charles's first wife, is dead.

1.   RUTH: Used Elvira to help you—when you were thinking something out, I mean?
2.   CHARLES: Every now and then—when she concentrated—but she didn't concentrate very often.
3.   RUTH: I do wish I'd known her.
4.   CHARLES: I wonder if you'd have liked her.

5.   RUTH: I'm sure I should—as you talk of her she sounds enchanting— yes, I'm sure I should have liked her because you know I have never for an instant felt in the least jealous of her—that's a good sign.

6.   CHARLES: Poor Elvira.

7.   RUTH: Does it still hurt—when you think of her?

Before you go on, think about what this beat is establishing. Of course, the overt purpose (text) is simply that Ruth is asking for information about her predecessor, information that the audience learns also. But we sense other, complex messages. A director and actor preparing the beat for a rehearsal might analyze the subtext as follows:

1. Ruth is really asking if Elvira had the same importance as she does as Charles's creative helper. In a way, Ruth is indicating her concern about something in their relationship. Perhaps she wants to or needs to be told that she is not simply a "second" wife but someone unique.

2. Charles does not catch the subtext at first, and so answers unthinkingly. If he does not modify or correct what he has begun to say, he will have answered "yes" to Ruth's question. That answer would indicate there is nothing unique in their relationship. He realizes immediately that he has been insensitive (does he see a *look* in Ruth's face or a sudden stiffening of her posture?) and in midsentence modifies his statement. The problem is that he can't really correct what has already been said. In any case, he either has to be unfaithful to the memory of his first wife or lie to his second wife.

3. Ruth tries to appear merely inquisitive, as if she is not jealous. Obviously, however, she is thinking about her dead "competition."

4. Charles's question responds to Ruth, but the word "wonder" tells us that something has flashed across his mind about the differences between his wives.

5. Ruth indicates her jealousy precisely because she raises an issue that no one has raised, and the audience will tend to doubt people who deny an emotion no one has accused them of feeling. In short, we don't believe the text of someone who "protesteth too much."

6. Charles appears not to be responding to what Ruth has said but to the train of thought set off by his previous statement. In fact, we might feel that Ruth has started a chain reaction different from the one she expected. (*Note:* Charles responds to what he is thinking, not to the other character's dialogue. He is starting to say what he *has* to say, not what the logic of the dialogue appears to call for.)

7. Ruth has recognized that she has set off a chain of associations in Charles. The text tells us that she is thinking of his well-being. The subtext tells us that she wants some kind of assurance for herself.

Without anyone telling us what they are like, the text and subtext in the speeches between Charles and Ruth allow the audience to see that the characters are debonair, intelligent, and witty. The subtext also creates a sense of mystery revealed rather than stated. Something is going on that has brought Ruth to push the conversation in this direction. The information that is communicated also creates tension because:

1. We wonder what the characters really mean, what they may be hiding in the way of feelings or facts.
2. Or we wonder when another character will catch on to what we know is really being said.
3. Or we wonder when characters will realize something about themselves that we have already figured out.

At one and the same time, the most effective dialogue does all the above. In sum, creating the subtext—suggesting without telling—is a large part of the playwright's work.

EXERCISE

1. Before reading the following passage, review the preceding passage and ask yourself: What is the first word that Charles should say in his answer to Ruth? Now read on:

> CHARLES: No, not really—sometimes I almost wish it did—I feel rather guilty—
> RUTH: I wonder if I died before you'd grown tired of me if you'd forget me so soon?
> CHARLES: What a horrible thing to say. . .
> RUTH: No—I think it's interesting.
> CHARLES: Well, to begin with I *haven't* forgotten Elvira—I *remember* her very distinctly indeed—I remember how fascinating she was, and how maddening—I remember how badly she played all games and how cross she got when she didn't win—I remember her gay charm when she had achieved her own way over something and her extreme acidity when she didn't—I remember her physical attractiveness, which was tremendous—and her spiritual integrity which was nil . . .
> RUTH: You can't remember something that was nil.
> CHARLES: I remember how morally untidy she was . . .
> RUTH: Was she more physically attractive than I am?

CHARLES: That was a very tiresome question, dear, and fully deserves the wrong answer.

RUTH: You really are very sweet.

CHARLES: Thank you.

RUTH: And a little naive, too.

2. Analyze the preceeding speeches as we have done for the previous passage. Note that Ruth's question ("I wonder. . .") really contains two questions. Is Charles's answer a dramatically effective one? Has anything about their emotional relationship been established? Who, if anyone, has "won" points during the beat? How do you know?

3. Assume that Charles says, "Yes, Elvira was more physically attractive." Write a beat for that answer.

4. Take the following situation and write dialogue for the characters. The scene is a dorm room or shared apartment. The situation is that roommate A is trying to get roommate B to leave the room for the evening but does not want to say why.

5. Tape record a real conversation—at the dinner table, for example—and transcribe it (or get a raw transcription of a legislative hearing). As you will see, most of it will be boring and some of it will be incomprehensible and repetitious. Try to carve a dramatic beat from your transcription.

PRINCIPLES AND COMMON ERRORS

Your Exposition Is Showing

The characters should not tell each other expository information simply to transfer that information to the audience. Unless you have a character who has just come into the story and therefore is ignorant of the facts and needs to know them, you must remember that the characters are usually aware of what has happened to them and to each other. Nothing is so absurd as one character telling another:

> John, do you remember when we had our children—Annabelle, Hermes, and Philo?

Nothing destroys an audience's sense of verisimilitude more than characters' telling each other about what they obviously must know. The audience suddenly becomes aware of itself: "Oh, I'm watching a play and the characters are telling me stuff I have to know." Instead of following the characters, as if following real people, the audience becomes conscious of the exposition because the playwright has failed to find a reason in plot and character for slipping in this necessary information. The audience begins to *think about* the play instead of emotionally participating *in* it.

Look at the following scene, for example, in which a couple are having an argument about moving to the town where the wife's parents live.

> JOAN: You are not being fair, Mike.
>
> MIKE: Joan, the issue of fair has nothing to do with it. Your parents do not have a single socially redeeming quality between the two of them.
>
> JOAN: What do you mean my parents do not have any redeeming qualities? Why do you try to hurt my self-esteem like that?
>
> MIKE: That is easy, your father is loud and obnoxious. Your mother, on the other hand, cannot stick to a subject. She comes totally out of the blue with ideas.
>
> JOAN: Mike, you are being totally unreasonable. The last time my parents were over you had a great time.
>
> MIKE: Joan, do you remember the last time we were with your parents? It was at our wedding reception and that was almost six months ago.
>
> JOAN: Is that so?
>
> MIKE: Do you remember how your dad's Polish jokes almost caused my Uncle Joe to throw him through a window? And Uncle Joe had come all the way from New Zealand to be with us. Aunt Sylvia was not any happier.

Aside from any other problems you may have noticed with the dialogue, Mike's speeches are clearly addressed to the audience, since Joan would surely remember the last time they saw her parents. And if she does not, we have to know why.

One way of communicating such expository information naturally is to imbed the information in the dialogue as part of the tension between the characters. Assume Mike and Joan have often talked about the wedding and that it always comes up in their spats.

> MIKE: I still feel like hiding when I think about it.
>
> JOAN: It was six months ago, Mike. I am tired of hearing about it.
>
> MIKE: Your dad had to know my mother was Polish.
>
> JOAN: He was just trying to be friendly.
>
> MIKE: If it was not our wedding, I think my uncle Ted would have thrown him out the window.
>
> JOAN: It was only a Polish joke, Mike.
>
> MIKE: Poles are not dumb. Chopin. Milosc.
>
> JOAN: You tell them yourself.
>
> MIKE: It's different.

JOAN: You just do not like my dad.

MIKE: My uncle did *not* come all the way from New Zealand to be insulted.

JOAN: Do not change the topic.

MIKE: We're not moving to Urbana. I do not like your mother either.

Though the dialogue still needs work, in the rewritten version the audience is beginning to overhear characters who know what their situation is. The information is now within a dramatic beat; it doesn't seem to be directed to the audience but feels like an outgrowth of Joan and Mike's psychological situation.

In short, dialogue must appear to be talk for the characters' purposes, not for the benefit of the audience. When they create dialogue, most playwrights adhere to a primary dramatic convention: *there is a wall between the characters and audience.* The space inside that wall is the real, the only world. Each time the dialogue lapses into obvious exposition, a crack appears in the wall. Too many cracks and the audience will begin to wonder why the playwright didn't try to write a novel instead of promising a play.

Note: the limits of dialogue as a tool for revealing the exposition has led modern dramatists to bring back the chorus as a device for revealing opinions and information. But the chorus in a modern play is usually one person, a kind of "stage manager." If your plot involves long stretches of time (as in a history play) or a great deal of exposition (as in a thriller), you may wish to construct the plot so as to use a narrator. For examples see *A View from a Bridge, Equus,* or *Amadeus.* Such a device appears less clumsy than long stretches in which the characters simply tell the plot to each other. Remember, though, that such stage narrators should not simply provide the narrative bridges for the plot's sake; they should be characters who belong to the play's structure. This convenient device can be a burden since the playwright will also have to account for the narrator. In drama, as in the other genres, there are no free rides.

Contractions and Formality

You do not want your characters to speak as if they are delivering dedications or eulogies. Unless you deliberately intend that your characters demonstrate formal traits, they will elide their speech. In any case, if the playwright doesn't do it for them, the actors will change "it is" to "it's" and "cannot" to "can't," especially if the formality appears merely to be the playwright's adhering slavishly to the absurd rule that one should never use a contraction in writing. In Mike and Joan's dialogue, not using contractions gives their speech a formal quality; it sounds more like a debate than an argument between lovers. Note how stiff even the revised dialogue sounds if you read it aloud.

With the contractions in, their speeches still often sound curiously formal, as if they are reading from a prepared script. Mike's use of the phrase "single socially redeeming quality" (in the first version) is stiff and intellectual, to say nothing of how difficult it is to speak. Though your characters may talk formally because of their natures or because the plot has reached a point that requires a formal address (see "Long Speeches," p. 299), the playwright must prepare the dialogue so it appears to have come from that character at the moment. In other words, the playwright has to plan the dialogue so it seems unplanned.

EXERCISE

Assuming that Joan is not stuffy, rewrite the first version of her dialogue. Now assume that Mike tends to be stuffy and rigid because he thinks that formal speech is a sign of education and class. Rewrite Mike's dialogue to let the audience know that his formality is a bone of contention between them. (You may want to assume that Mike is self-educated.)

Interruptions and Other Ways of Creating Verisimilitude

Dialogue is usually most effective when it follows the *patterns* rather than the content of conversation. Your dialogue is felt as "real" not because it reports what people actually say but because it follows the *way* people talk, the structures of conversation. Just as in actual conversation, your characters' dialogue may be interrupted, may fail to follow from what others have just said, or may appear to be illogical and unreasonable. One reason Mike and Joan sound so stilted is that they are skipping no steps in what they are saying to each other. Notice how one word is echoed in each speech as if they had to prove they were listening. (Go back and circle the repeated words in the first version.)

The devices for achieving an appearance of spontaneity are taken from the conversational patterns of real life:

- ◆ People interrupt each other.
- ◆ People trail off.
- ◆ People do not directly answer the question asked.
- ◆ People say things that are the result of a line of thinking not directly related to the conversation.
- ◆ People use contractions.
- ◆ People use pronouns, that is, they are aware of what is present to them.

Let's apply these principles to part of Mike and Joan's dialogue:

> JOAN: It was six months ago, Mike. I'm tired of hearing—
> MIKE: Your dad had to know my mother was Polish, Joan.
> JOAN: He was just trying to be friendly. He doesn't mean—
> MIKE: If it weren't . . . wasn't our wedding, I think my uncle Ted
> would have thrown him out the window.
> JOAN: It was only a Polish joke, Mike. You know my—
> MIKE: Poles are not dumb. Chopin. Milosc. And . . . and . . .
> hundreds of other people.
> JOAN: You tell them yourself.
> MIKE: Copernicus.

Because interruptions are so typical of our actual conversational habits, they are the most obvious way of creating verisimilitude and of making your dialogue less formal. However, beware of overusing the technique. And be sure that *what* the character was about to say is clear before the next character interrupts.

> ROBIN: What if we get caught?
> THADEUS: That's—
> ROBIN: If the police take me home my father is going—
> THADEUS: Police? What are—
> ROBIN: Are you sure it will be O.K.?

Though it is clear that Robin is frightened, it is never clear to the audience what Thadeus was about to say. In fact, the actor who plays Thadeus will look like a fool if Thadeus's timing is a bit off because he'll have to drag out the word being interrupted. Notice, however, that when Thadeus interrupts Robin, we understand how the rest of the sentence will go: "to give me hell" or some such thing. Be sure to give the character enough words before being interrupted so that the actors playing both the interrupter and interruptee can establish a natural timing.

Beginning playwrights, particularly those who have worked in fiction, often give their characters dialogue that would be used only if the characters were blind. The characters continually use one another's names, mention objects that the audience can see, and name actions as well as respond to them.

> JACK: Here's your martini, Barbara.
> BARBARA: I wanted an onion in the martini, Jack.
> JACK: Try the martini first, Barbara.
> BARBARA (*sips*): Now that I've tried it, what?
> JACK: What do you think, Barbara.
> BARBARA: I still want an onion in my martini.
> JACK (*knocks the martini from her hand*): You ungrateful bitch.
> BARBARA: Why did you knock the martini from my hand?

This dialogue sounds as if it were written for a novel without a narrator (not a particularly good idea) rather than a play with an audience who would see the events. Such dialogue is a sure sign of inexperience with stage or film.

Fake Dialogue or the Dialogue Dummy

Everything that characters say must serve their needs. When a character says a line of dialogue only to break up a long speech or when a character simply sets up another character's speeches, the playwright is committing two fatal errors in one: the poor actor who serves up the gopher ball feels like a fool ("Why am I saying this?"), and the audience begins to wonder whether they are observing a ventriloquist's dummy or a character with needs and wants of his or her own.

Ask yourself why Beth is saying the italicized speeches in the following dialogue.

> BETH: The pitcher has my goldfish in it. You'll have to use a mixing bowl.
> KEVIN: Looks like one of them has gone to paradise.
> BETH: *Paradise?*
> KEVIN: He is a floater.
> BETH: *Floater?*
> KEVIN: Dead.

Not only has the writer taken too long to establish a small point, but Beth appears to be simply feeding Kevin lines. Now add the following to Kevin's last bit of dialogue before the word "dead": "Are you listening to me?" At this point Beth's denseness begins to make sense.

EXERCISE

Go back to Beth's second speech. It also appears to be merely a place holder. Write something for her to say that will give us a sense of her needs and advance the scene. If necessary, rewrite Kevin's speeches.

Designators, or Stealing the Actor's and Director's Jobs

The words the characters say should indicate their emotional state. Being overly elaborate in designating how the speech should be said is an error. The director or actor will ignore the designator unless the playwright's command for a special tone of voice is absolutely necessary. Observe the following.

BARBARA (*concerned*): What do you want to do tonight?

SAM (*only half listening*): How about us going to Seaside tonight, Diane?

BARBARA (*shocked by what she hears*): Diane?

SAM (*embarrassed and placatingly*): I can't believe I said that.

BARBARA (*angry and puzzled*): What can't you believe you said?

SAM (*in a squirming voice*): What I just said.

BARBARA (*questioning*): Who's Diane?

SAM (*whining because he knows he's trapped*): Diane is a friend.

BARBARA (*incredulous*): A friend?

Many of the designators merely sound ridiculous; how does someone say something in an "angry but puzzled" voice?

The rule of thumb is never to use a designator unless the dialogue you write for a character normally would be said in a different tone of voice:

SAM (*softly*): Help.

In fact, a good discipline is to avoid designators altogether, especially when you are creating the playscript. Often writers use elaborate designators to avoid the work needed to ensure that what the characters *say* indicates their emotion. This principle also should be observed in writing dialogue for narrative fiction.

Long Speeches

Usually you will avoid long speeches. There are typical circumstances in which characters may talk on for some time:

1. A character has asked them a question that calls for a long answer.
2. They are making a formal speech as part of the plot (as in a play that contains a trial).
3. Part of their nature is to be long-winded.

Most of the time, however, your characters will be interrupted, challenged, or simply waiting for responses. As a result, most of the individual speeches will be relatively brief. If you find your characters simply giving large blocks of information, it is likely that the dialogue is dialogue only in form.

Grunting and Pausing

Since the actors will create any extra sounds they need (1) for pacing, (2) for transitions, (3) for laughing or crying, or (4) for responding to the action and dialogue, you should avoid indicating grunts and wheezes, conversational place holders. *Uhh, ohhh, ehh, ahh, er, ahhhh* and other self-interrupters are not needed and look absurd on the page. If you wish an actor to pause, write "(*Pause*)" at the proper point; don't try to imitate the pause in the script with blank spaces, periods, or other visual means.

In the following dialogue, the writer appears amateurish, forcing effects on the actor or reader typographically. In this scene, Barbara and Sam are at the beach. Obviously, Sam is horsing around.

> BARBARA: So where, *uhhhhh,* did we, *ha-ha,* decide to go tonight, Mike?
> SAM: *YUK! YUK!* very funny.
> BARBARA: I'm *soooooo* sorry, *ha! ha!* . . . . hey cut that out you, don't you dare throw me in the water. I've got my contacts in! Ok, ok, I love you too, I said I love *yoglogglober glub glub gurgle gurgle!*

It would have been sufficient for the writer simply to let the actors know what is happening and allow them to supply the sounds to fit the action. (*Note:* also avoid representing nonword sounds in fiction; it's a sign of amateurishness.)

Accents, Dialect, and Verbal Tics

The one area in which dialogue should be like conversation is in its imitation of social, regional, or national speech habits. It hardly needs saying that characters should have intonations, accents, grammar, diction, and syntax appropriate to their general background, the circumstances in which they find themselves, and their intentions. A waiter with a seventh-grade education is not likely to speak like a Harvard graduate without a good reason.

When you give a character an accent that is merely a matter of pronunciation, you need only indicate in the description of the character what accent is necessary:

> FORSYTH P. WILLOWBY, a cadaverous looking man of about forty who speaks with a Boston accent.
> PRISCILLA HESTER GARARD, a thirtyish blond who affects a southern accent. Nonetheless one can detect her Brooklyn accent.

Presumably, you have given this information to the director because the characters' particular accents are important. The information will be sufficient and the playwright does not need to indicate the pronunciation through phonetic spelling. In fact, the playwright should not do so. For the following speech, for example, the actor will work out the proper accent according to the playwright's directions about where the character is from (Boston, Alabama, or Russia):

ROSALINDA: After we have finished this game, I intend to leave and never come back.

It is the director's job to cast an actor who can produce the desired accent.

The writer's task becomes more difficult if the character's origins require a dialect. Unlike an accent (how the words are pronounced), a dialect involves different vocabulary, grammar, syntax, and elisions, which will have to be provided for the actor.

Swearing

One way contemporary playwrights create verisimilitude is by reflecting *how* people talk in real life. Words that were once forbidden are now staples for naturalistic plays; in fact, they are almost conventions for creating a feeling of reality. As with all other diction decisions, the type of swearing, if any, your characters will do depends on what they are like and how they would respond verbally to the situations in which they find themselves. You have to take your chances on your audience's reaction. The producer will not choose to do your play if the swearing is inappropriate for the audience. On the other hand, if the audience feels your characters should react to misfortune with contemporary swearing and you have them saying "gee whizzes" when a hammer strikes a finger, then you may unintentionally cause laughter. The audience expects something stronger.

Never have your characters swear because *you* wish to shock or to create the impression that your play is realistic. The audience will hear the author swearing, not the character. A good rule of tongue is to ask yourself why this particular character is swearing at this time. As with accents and dialects, don't use swear words unless you have a feeling for their proper use.

Locker Room Raillery

Though in real life we often chatter at one another in a mocking but friendly way, on paper—and on the stage—this type of wisecracking appears forced, though an individual character may deliver wisecracks as an aspect of his or her personality (as Hawkeye does in *M * A * S * H*). Effective humor occurs when (1) the characters seriously make statements that the audience finds absurd or (2) the character is truly witty, as Algernon is in Oscar Wilde's *The Importance of Being Earnest*.

JACK: I am in love with Gwendolen. I have come up to town expressly to propose to her.
ALGERNON: I thought you had come up for pleasure? . . . I call that business.
JACK: How utterly unromantic you are!

ALGERNON: I really don't see anything romantic in proposing. It is very romantic to be in love. But there is nothing romantic about a definite proposal. Why, one may be accepted. One usually is, I believe. Then the excitement is all over. The very essence of romance is uncertainty. If ever I get married, I'll certainly try to forget the fact.

Algernon intends the humor of his absurd statement as a comment on attitudes toward love. He means to be witty, and his wit is rewarded with our laughter. At the same time, of course, his lightness of character is revealed.

That kind of wit and humor is a far cry from the following rather crude locker room raillery.

KEVIN: Hey, asshole. Have you seen my Kleenex?

SPARKY: Up yours, Kev. You wanna go to Eben's for a couple of brews. The broads are easy.

KEVIN: You're so dumb you can't even get easy.

SPARKY: Who struck out with Lena the Hyena? A nerd can make it with her. Face it, you got the sex appeal of a dustball. . . .

The author of this dialogue might want to argue that the characters are meant to sound embarrassingly crude. As walk-on, walk-off characters, Kevin and Sparky could produce a mild discomfort, the embarrassed laughter characters who are making fools of themselves produce. However, if the audience had to spend much time in their company, they would soon be more irritated than interested or concerned, just as if they met such people in real life.

In any case, the appeal to reality is not convincing. The mere fact that people really speak exactly as you report does not make the fictional or dramatic dialogue effective. A character who is meant to be boring must still be interesting in a way that does not bore the audience.

EXERCISES

1. Read the following dialogue and rewrite it with the basic dialogue principles in mind. Feel free to move lines around and change them. However, you must communicate the essential exposition and keep to the purpose. Keep in mind that both Breck and Atwater have specific wants.

SITUATION: *The following dialogue is from* The Imprisonment of Clarence Atwater, *a student's historical play about a soldier who kept lists of the Union prisoners who died at Andersonville during the Civil War. After he is freed, he sells the rolls to the army because he thinks they will be published to help the prisoners' families receive government compensation more quickly. When the lists are not published, he steals them. The following is from a flashback scene that recounts the events immediately after Atwater steals the lists. Colonel Breck, Atwater's superior, plays the prosecutor role in a scene much like a court martial. However, the "trial" occurs in Breck's office.*

BRECK: So you don t deny Captain Moore's accusation. He's terribly upset that the rolls were misplaced while in his custody. Dereliction of duty is a serious offense and could wreck a good officer's promising career. Did you ever think of that?

ATWATER (*confident*): Moore had nothing to do with the loss of the rolls. It's not his fault that he was given responsibility for items that rightfully belonged to another.

BRECK: You sold your rights to that property. We paid you $300. You give us back the $300 and you can keep the rolls, as far as I'm concerned. This whole affair has been a dirty business from beginning to end. I'm sorry that I ever had anything to do with you. Your behavior has been abominable.

ATWATER: My behavior? You are the one who denied me even a copy of the rolls, after you promised.

BRECK: We did not know then that you were planning to make your fortune publishing the documents. We do not consider ourselves bound by an agreement made before we were in full possession of the facts.

ATWATER (*jubilant*): And now they will be published. Miss Clara Barton has promised to help me. She's already written to Horace Greeley.

BRECK: Don't you realize, you young fool, that you could be charged with conduct to the prejudice of good order and military discipline, not to mention larceny?

ATWATER: I can take my case before General Townsend.

BRECK: General Townsend and I are in complete agreement in this matter.

ATWATER: Then I will have to go further about it. Secretary Stanton—

BRECK: You're not going any further than the Old Capitol prison unless you give up those registers! Mr. Henry! [*Henry enters*] Mr. Henry. Call for the provost Marshal! This man is under arrest.

ATWATER: I'm entitled to appeal to a higher authority. Our government gives every American citizen that privilege. Wasn't that what we fought and suffered for these last four years?

BRECK: This is the army, Mr. Atwater. I don't think it has ever sunk in that you are in the army, not clerking at the local dry goods store.

ATWATER: Oh yes, I forgot for a moment that the soldier who sacrificed his comforts and risked his life to maintain these liberties is the only man in the country who is not allowed to claim their protection!

2. Read the following scene from *The Day They Shot John Lennon.*

The Day They Shot John Lennon

JAMES McLURE

The date is December 9, 1980, the day John Lennon was shot. Shortly after the shooting was announced people began to gather across the street from his apartment house on Seventy-second Street in New York City. Some were fans; some were merely curious. They stood around for hours; they talked to strangers who stood near them; some cried.

One of those gathered that fateful day was Fran Lowenstein, whom the author describes as thirty-five years old, "a native New Yorker and all that implies. Tough, sensitive, a feminist and a member of the Woodstock generation who is also looking for a meaningful relationship." She works as a secretary.

Fran strikes up a conversation with Brian Murphy, who is "in advertising." The author tells us he is "given to quick opinions and stances of self-confidence (though) he is basically a confused individual looking for love." He is thirty-three.

By the time the scene below begins, among the topics Fran and Brian have talked about are Lennon's music, their jobs, the bars they frequent, politics, and modern painting. Their conversation continues:

FRAN: It's like spirals within spirals y'know. I mean I see images tumbling by. I see myself as a little girl on a visit to my grandmother's in Queens and we go to the park. And it's green and beautiful and my father's with me. Big, and young and strong. And whenever I think of that I think of "Penny Lane," it's like, that's the way it felt. *(Pause.)*

BRIAN: I know. It's like background music for our lives. I remember at my first high school dance and I was all sweaty and scared and I was gonna walk across the room to ask Richie Woodall to dance with me. And they started playing "Hey Jude" over the P.A. system. It was a Catholic dance. I think the nuns thought it was about St. Jude. The saint of lost causes.

FRAN: (*Passionately.*) Maybe that's what all this is. A lost cause. The sixties. The peace movement. Look what's happenin' now in the Middle East. El Salvador. Are we any closer? Are we getting there? Take a look at the E.R.A.? Are we getting there? Three-Mile Island. Are we getting there? How can we say we're civilized when we continue to hold people back. Because of sex, because of race. Is that getting us anywhere?

Increased military spending, weapons for defense. *(Laughing.)* And the joke is we're all afraid of the bomb! We blame everything on "They." The Pentagon—"They"! The CIA—"They." But we all have to take responsibility for the society in which we live. All America wants to do is go to the movies! Is that getting us there? Where's the leadership? Where's the dialogue? We're not talking. We're not listening. We're missing the whole point. It's not the sixties. People are just burying their heads in the sand. People will do *anything* rather than be here now. *(Pause.)* Are we getting there? No. People are just going to the office and making money . . . People suck.

BRIAN *(impressed)*: Wow. You know, you're a very passionate woman.

FRAN: Well, what did you expect? Someone dumb?

BRIAN: No, it's just that women—

FRAN: Oh brother, here we go. It's just that women what?

BRIAN: Just that women that you meet in bars—

FRAN: Hey! You didn't meet *me* in a bar! Right? Get it?

BRIAN: But you said you *go* to bars.

FRAN: I go to bars. I wasn't born in a bar. Right?

BRIAN: It's just that I think you're very smart and very passionate and very attractive. And I don't meet women like that.

FRAN: Where do you meet your "woman," Brian?

BRIAN: Bars. I meet my women in bars.

FRAN: Well, then maybe that's *your* problem, Brian. Maybe you're meeting those kind of women—the passionate, attractive, intelligent kind of women but since you're just living for the night, maybe you don't see them for what they are.

BRIAN: Hey. Who're you kidding? You go to bars. You have drinks. You meet guys.

FRAN: That's right, Brian. And I'm the passionate, attractive, intelligent kind. *(He touches her arm.)*

BRIAN: Look babe, I didn't mean to—

FRAN: Don't touch me.

BRIAN: O.k. I won't touch you.

FRAN: Boy I hate your kind.

BRIAN: My *kind*? My *kind*? Boy if that isn't sexual stereotyping I don't know what is.

FRAN: Granted. Sexual stereotyping. But in your case, it works.

BRIAN: Oh yeah? And what is my type?

FRAN: You're—the button-down-collar-junior-executive-climbing-the-ladder-of-success-but-I'm-really-the-sensitive-young-man type. That's your type. I'll bet you haven't been to a museum in a million years.

BRIAN: For your information just last week I went to the Museum of Modern Art.

FRAN: Oh yeah. What did you see?

BRIAN: Paintings.

FRAN: What kind of paintings?

BRIAN: Modern paintings.

FRAN: Oh Jesus. What a fake. What a liar. I bet you weren't even at Woodstock.

BRIAN: I was too!

FRAN: Everybody has their little scheme don't they? Tell me, does this line work a lot? This I-like-art line? Does that work on everybody?

BRIAN: No. Just you.

FRAN: Well, it wasn't working on me. I can assure you of that.

BRIAN: Yeah, come to think of it, now, I've seen you before. Sure yeah. I see you all the time in the bars.

FRAN: You don't see me at bars.

BRIAN: Sure I do.

FRAN: You do not.

BRIAN: The Adams Apple, Michaels, Maxwells, The Meat Place, Martys, The Satyre, Pegasus, sure you're there all the time. You're not special. I thought you were but you're not. You're like all the rest.

FRAN: Fuck you.

BRIAN: My pleasure.

FRAN: One thing though.

BRIAN: Huh.

FRAN: If I'm like all the rest . . . so are you. (*Pause.*)

BRIAN: Look, I'm sorry . . . I don't know what we got so excited about . . . I mean . . . You're a nice girl.

FRAN: Woman.

BRIAN: Woman! Woman! Woman! (*Pause.*) Look . . . wanna smoke . . . I've got some gum . . . spearmint . . . Look I'm not like this . . . maybe I am. I didn't used to be. I don't meet women like you. I felt alive in the sixties. That's why I came here. I wanted . . . I wanted . . . then I met you. I mean. Something. In common. I don't know. Maybe not. I didn't want to go to work. I wanted to talk. (*She accepts cigarette. He lights it.*) I mean. Life goes on.

a. Assume you are the director and that you are discussing the intention behind each speech with the actors who play Fran and Brian. They have asked the following questions that you have to answer.

BRIAN: In the speech beginning "I know" why do I tell Fran who St. Jude is? Since I know who St. Jude is am I only setting up her speech?

Or is something happening that makes me say that? Or should the writer redo the dialogue?

FRAN: In my long speech, do I really know what I'm talking about or am I simply spewing out words that I've heard?

BRIAN: What was Brian going to say when he starts talking about women? When Fran breaks me off and I start again, have I changed what I was going to say the first time?

FRAN: Why is Fran so uptight after her long speech? Up to that time she seems to have been getting along all right with Brian. In fact, Brian appears to be trying hard to please.

BRIAN: When Brian gets angry back starting with "My *kind*," is he serious or is that part of his come-on? And when Fran asks him about the museum, is he putting her on or has she caught him in a lie?

FRAN: Is this attacking and putting down of men one of the reasons that she doesn't get her man? Are her politics always so much up front— perhaps as a defense—that they cut off innocent conversation? Or is there *no* relaxing with her?

BRIAN: When he says he saw her in bars, it's clear that he's striking back because he feels put down. But why does he mention all the bars? And what does he mean when he says "You're like all the rest"?

FRAN: Is she the kind of person who says "fuck you"?

BRIAN: Sure she is, but something more important. His answer just feels like a place holder, a setup. I don't know why he says it from his point of view.

b. In this scene, Fran and Brian have been struggling over something. What is it? How is it resolved?
c. Why is Brian's last speech so chopped up and so illogical?
d. Picking up on Brian's last speech above, write a beat for the time it will take them to smoke the cigarette. Don't forget that they are holding a vigil outside John Lennon's apartment house.

3. A good deal of "The Lost Cottage" (Chapter 11) is actually framed as if it were a play.

a. Take the scene in which Alex brings up the question of Marian sharing the cottage (see p. 247). Expand on his dialogue with Mark.
b. Write a scenario (the word for a play outline) for a one-set adaptation of the short story.

14

Trifles

Introduction

Like a naturalistic landscape of a farmyard painted by a master, Susan Glaspell's *Trifles* appears to be quite simple. But the script contains all the ways of managing technique that one would use in a more complex or experimental work. And while the circumstances may be old-fashioned—few people live on isolated farms any longer—the issues of male brutality and indifference are still with us.

As are almost all plays, *Trifles* is composed of two movements: (1) an exposition of the past (the murder, Mrs. Wright's marriage, bits and pieces of the other characters' histories); and (2) the pressure of the moment (the women's discovery of Mrs. Wright's motive for such anger that she would plan a murder). The plot is deceptively simple. Mrs. Wright has strangled Mr. Wright, a hard and gloomy man, with a rope while he slept. The men—the sheriff, Mr. Hale; the county attorney, George Henderson; and Mr. Peters—search the barn and house looking for clues and a motive for Mrs. Wright to have murdered her husband in this peculiar way. While gathering things to bring to Mrs. Wright who is in the jail, the women—Mrs. Peters and Mrs. Hale—solve the mystery by looking carefully and knowingly at the objects (trifles) the men ignore. The men overlook the clues, the equipment and products of the kitchen and the sewing basket, because they are "women's things."

Through deduction, the women discover that Mrs. Wright strangled Mr. Wright because he twisted the neck of her only companion, a canary—an obvious symbol of the happy and cheerful person she had once been. We imagine that Mr. Wright's mean-spirited action was the final straw and generated the anger that led to Mrs. Wright's action (a premeditated murder). At the end of the play, the audience is to assume that the women will not tell the men about their discovery of the motive in order to give their suffering sister a better chance for acquittal at her trial.

The exposition that occurs throughout the play reveals these additional facts:

♦ Mr. Hale discovered the murder.
♦ Mr. Wright had a reputation as a hard, cheap, unloving man.
♦ Mrs. Wright was a good farm wife, despite appearances.
♦ She did not have children or friends.
♦ She had been a pretty, cheerful but timid girl.

The events that unfold before us contain the revelations (exposition) about Mrs. Wright's life that the women discover from looking through her domain. The unfolding action includes the following:

♦ George Henderson questions Mr. Hale and finds out how the body was discovered.
♦ The men leave to look for clues in the bedroom.
♦ The women look around the kitchen that is not straightened because Mrs. Wright was taken away.
♦ They straighten some things and gather some clothes to take to Mrs. Wright in jail.
♦ The men return and go outside.
♦ They discover that Mrs. Wright was making a quilt but that suddenly her sewing had become careless, as if she were very agitated. Mrs. Hale pulls out the bad stitches and starts resewing, in the process destroying potential evidence of Mrs. Wright's being nervous about something.
♦ The women find the bird cage and then the strangled bird.
♦ The sheriff and county attorney return to the kitchen without Mr. Hale and go upstairs again.
♦ Without saying so directly, the women decide not to tell the men what they have discovered.
♦ The men come downstairs again and Mr. Hale comes in from outside where he has been getting the wagon.
♦ The men exit again and Mrs. Peters starts to steal the box that contains

the dead canary but doesn't have room in her bag and so Mrs. Hale hides the box in her coat.

♦ The sheriff and county attorney return and the play ends.

The women's understanding of Mrs. Wright's life not only leads to the exposition of her hard life but also to the discovery (denouement) and to their implied decision to help her. At the same time, we find out about Mrs. Hale's and Mrs. Peters's hard, lonely lives. Their final decision to hide the clues, which constitutes a possible reversal of fortune (or **peripeteia**), is motivated by their identification with Mrs. Wright and their own anger at the way men treat them.

Glaspell uses some standard devices for gathering her characters and achieving natural exposition. Since Henderson, the county attorney, has been away in Omaha, it is natural that the sheriff wants Mr. Hale at the house to tell about the discovery of the body. When Henderson hears the events, we absorb the exposition. The same device serves Glaspell later in the play when we learn from Mrs. Hale about Mrs. Wright's youth. Glaspell has imagined that Mrs. Peters is not originally from the farm community in Nebraska and so she did not know Mrs. Wright. Therefore, we are overhearing information that Mrs. Hale quite naturally tells Mrs. Peters.

The fire in the stove and the way the characters are dressed show us that it is winter; the sheriff explains to Henderson how the fire got lit. Because she is the sheriff's wife, Mrs. Peters is at the house to gather clothes for Mrs. Wright. We assume that Mrs. Hale came along to keep Mrs. Peters company and that the sheriff stopped to pick up Mr. Hale, though this point is fuzzy. (In her story "A Jury of Her Peers" based on this play, Glaspell opens with Mrs. Hale being picked up.) In fact, we do not learn until quite late the reason for Mrs. Hale being along, and the reason is slipped in while they are examining the bird cage. We learn of all the women's lives—including Mrs. Wright's— through the examination of the props (though, of course, the characters don't think of them as props). Notice that the exposition is not rushed out all at once but parceled out slowly as part of the dramatic action.

The tension in the play is created by the mystery and the conflicts within and between the characters. We want to know, as do the characters, why Mrs. Wright killed her husband in this peculiar manner. Once we discover why, we want to know what the women will do. Additional tension is created by the constant coming and going of the men, particularly as the women begin to realize they have the key information in their hands. The women are tense because they are in the house of a murderer, and Mrs. Hale is particularly tense because she feels guilty for not having been a better neighbor. Once the women solve the mystery, Mrs. Peters's tension increases because she believes that, as a sheriff's wife, she should be loyal to what he represents rather than to the sisterhood of oppressed women. In a way, she does not want to believe a woman capable of murdering a man, a denial which suggests that she has suppressed desires of a similar sort.

The male characters—pretty much of a piece—are only developed sufficiently to distinguish them from one another and to serve the plot: we see them in their roles as officials and husbands. The characteristic we are meant to notice is that they are either condescending to or contemptuous of the women and tend to regard women as handmaidens to serve men. A sheriff's wife can be trusted just because she is a sheriff's wife. Glaspell is economic in exposing their attitudes because the drama of the play turns on revealing that the women are not trivial. A key incident at the beginning foreshadows the fact that they are more aware than the men. Henderson comments on the dirty roller towel in the kitchen and cites it as evidence that Mrs. Wright is a poor housekeeper. Mrs. Hale realizes that the deputy who came out to start the fire probably cleaned his hands on it. The men are, literally, clueless about the meaning of such trifles.

The women are presented in greater detail than the men. Mrs. Peters is hesitant, shy, and fearful—and, we discover, filled with suppressed anger. Obviously she is oppressed within her marriage. Mrs. Hale, on the other hand, is brusque and more likely to challenge men. She is, obviously, a strong and decisive woman and so, when she acts quickly to conceal the strangled canary, we believe she is acting in character.

Notice that the point of attack is well after the discovery and well after Mrs. Wright is in jail. In fact, as is true of so many one-act plays, from the point of attack to curtain takes perhaps a half hour of stage as well as real time. The short time available to the women puts them under tremendous pressure to come to a decision once they know the facts.

Now read the play with special attention to the stage business that Glaspell provides for the actors, the way entrances and exits are used to create tension and reveal conflicts, and the ways in which the basic irony of the play (trifles are not trifles at all) leads us to accept the author's dramatic premise: the discovery that Mr. Wright twisted the neck of the canary is reason enough to make plausible Mrs. Hale and Mrs. Peters hiding the evidence that would convict Mrs. Wright. Consider also how much Mrs. Wright becomes a character in the play though, like Samuel Beckett's title character in *Waiting for Godot*, she never appears.

TRIFLES

Susan Glaspell

SCENE: *The kitchen in the now abandoned farmhouse of* JOHN WRIGHT, *a gloomy kitchen, and left without having been put in order—the walls covered with a faded wall paper.* D. R. *is a door leading to the parlor. On the* R. *wall above this door is a built-in-kitchen cupboard with shelves in the upper portion and drawers below. In the rear wall at* R., *up two steps is a door opening onto stairs leading to the second floor. In the rear wall at* L. *is a door to the shed and from there to the outside. Between these two doors is an old-fashioned black iron stove. Running along the* L. *wall from the shed door is an old iron sink and sink shelf, in which is set a hand pump. Downstage of the sink is an uncurtained window. Near the window is an old wooden rocker. Center stage is an unpainted wooden kitchen table with straight chairs on either side. There is a small chair* D. R. *Unwashed pans under the sink, a loaf of bread outside the breadbox, a dish towel on the table—other signs of incompleted work. At the rear the shed door opens and the* SHERIFF *comes in followed by the* COUNTY ATTORNEY *and* HALE. *The* SHERIFF *and* HALE *are men in middle life, the* COUNTY ATTORNEY *is a young man; all are much bundled up and go at once to the stove. They are followed by the two women—the sheriff's wife,* MRS. PETERS, *first; she is a slight wiry woman, a thin nervous face.* MRS. HALE *is larger and would ordinarily be called more comfortable looking, but she is disturbed now and looks fearfully about as she enters. The women have come in slowly, and stand close together near the door.*

COUNTY ATTORNEY (*at stove rubbing his hands*). This feels good. Come up to the fire, ladies.

MRS. PETERS (*after taking a step forward*). I'm not—cold.

SHERIFF (*unbuttoning his overcoat and stepping away from the stove to right of table as if to mark the beginning of official business*). Now, Mr. Hale, before we move things about, you explain to Mr. Henderson just what you saw when you came here yesterday morning.

COUNTY ATTORNEY (*crossing down to left of the table*). By the way, has anything been moved? Are things just as you left them yesterday?

SHERIFF (*looking about*). It's just the same. When it dropped below zero last night I thought I'd better send Frank out this morning to make a fire for us—(*sits right of center table*) no use getting pneumonia with a big case on, but I told him not to touch anything except the stove—and you know Frank.

COUNTY ATTORNEY. Somebody should have been left here yesterday.

SHERIFF. Oh—yesterday. When I had to send Frank to Morris Center for that man who went crazy—I want you to know I had my hands full yesterday. I knew you could get back from Omaha by today and as long as I went over everything here myself—

COUNTY ATTORNEY. Well, Mr. Hale, tell just what happened when you came here yesterday morning.

HALE (*crossing down to above table*). Harry and I had started to town with a load of potatoes. We came along the road from my place and as I got here I said, "I'm going to see if I can't get John Wright to go in with me on a party telephone." I spoke to Wright about it once before and he put me off, saying folks talked too much anyway, and all he asked was peace and quiet—I guess you know about how much he talked himself; but I thought maybe if I went to the house and talked about it before his wife, though I said to Harry that I didn't know as what his wife wanted made much difference to John—

COUNTY ATTORNEY. Let's talk about that later, Mr. Hale. I do want to talk about that, but tell now just what happened when you got to the house.

HALE. I didn't hear or see anything; I knocked at the door, and still it was all quiet inside. I knew they must be up, it was past eight o'clock. So I knocked again, and I thought I heard somebody say, "Come in." I wasn't sure, I'm not sure yet, but I opened the door—this door (*indicating the door by which the two women are still standing*) and there in that rocker—(*pointing to it*) sat Mrs. Wright. (*They all look at the rocker* D. L.)

COUNTY ATTORNEY. What—was she doing?

HALE. She was rockin' back and forth. She had her apron in her hand and was kind of—pleating it.

COUNTY ATTORNEY. And how did she—look?

HALE. Well, she looked queer.

COUNTY ATTORNEY. How do you mean—queer?

HALE. Well, as if she didn't know what she was going to do next. And kind of done up.

COUNTY ATTORNEY (*takes out notebook and pencil and sits left of center table*). How did she seem to feel about your coming?

HALE. Why, I don't think she minded—one way or other. She didn't pay much attention. I said, "How do, Mrs. Wright, it's cold, ain't it?" And she said, "Is it?"—and went on kind of pleating at her apron. Well, I was surprised; she didn't ask me to come up to the stove, or to set down, but just sat there, not even looking at me, so I said, "I want to see John." And then she—laughed. I guess you would call it a laugh. I thought of Harry and the team outside, so I said a little sharp: "Can't I see John?" "No," she says, kind o' dull like. "Ain't he home?" says I. "Yes," says she, "he's home." "Then why can't I see him?" I asked her, out of patience. "'Cause he's dead," says she. "*Dead?*" says I. She just nodded her head, not getting a bit excited, but rockin' back and forth. "Why—where is he?" says I, not knowing what to say. She just pointed upstairs—like that. (*Himself pointing to the room above*). I started for the stairs, with the idea of going up there. I walked from there to here— then I says, "Why, what did he die of?" "He died of a rope round his neck," says she, and just went on pleatin' at her apron. Well, I went out and called Harry. I thought I might—need help. We went upstairs and there he was lyin'—

COUNTY ATTORNEY. I think I'd rather have you go into that upstairs, where you can point it all out. Just go on now with the rest of the story.

HALE. Well, my first thought was to get that rope off. It looked . . . (*stops, his face twitches*) . . . but Harry, he went up to him, and he said, "No, he's dead all right, and we'd better not touch anything." So we went back downstairs. She was still sitting that same way. "Has anybody been notified?" I asked. "No," says she, unconcerned. "Who did this, Mrs. Wright?" said Harry. He said it business-like—and she stopped pleatin' of her apron. "I don't know," she says. "You don't *know?*" says Harry. "No," says she. "Weren't you sleepin' in the bed with him?" says Harry. "Yes," says she, "but I was on the inside." "Somebody slipped a rope round his neck and strangled him and you didn't wake up?" says Harry. "I didn't wake up," she said after him. We must 'a' looked as if we didn't see how that could be, for after a minute she said, "I sleep sound." Harry was going to ask her more questions but I said maybe we ought to let her tell her story first to the coroner, or the sheriff, so Harry went fast as he could to Rivers' place, where there's a telephone.

COUNTY ATTORNEY. And what did Mrs. Wright do when she knew that you had gone for the coroner?

HALE. She moved from the rocker to that chair over there (*pointing to a small chair in the* D. R. *corner*) and just sat there with her hands held together and looking down. I got a feeling that I ought to make some conversation, so I said I had come in to see if John wanted to put in a telephone, and at that she started to laugh, and then she stopped and looked at me—scared. (*The* COUNTY ATTORNEY, *who has had his notebook out, makes a note*). I dunno, maybe it wasn't scared. I wouldn't like to say it was. Soon Harry got back, and then Dr. Lloyd came, and you, Mr. Peters, and so I guess that's all I know that you don't.

COUNTY ATTORNEY (*rising and looking around*). I guess we'll go upstairs first—and then out to the barn and around there. (*To the* SHERIFF). You're convinced that there was nothing important here—nothing that would point to any motive?

SHERIFF. Nothing here but kitchen things. (*The* COUNTY ATTORNEY, *after again looking around the kitchen, opens the door of a cupboard closet in* R. *wall. He brings a small chair from* R.—*gets up on it and looks on a shelf. Pulls his hand away, sticky.*)

COUNTY ATTORNEY. Here's a nice mess. (*The women draw nearer* U. C.)

MRS. PETERS (*to the other woman*). Oh, her fruit; it did freeze. (*To the* Lawyer). She worried about that when it turned so cold. She said the fire'd go out and her jars would break.

SHERIFF (*rises*). Well, can you beat the women! Held for murder and worryin' about her preserves.

COUNTY ATTORNEY (*getting down from chair*). I guess before we're through she may have something more serious than preserves to worry about. (*Crosses down* R. C.)

HALE. Well, women are used to worrying over trifles. (*The two women move a little closer together.*)

COUNTY ATTORNEY (*with the gallantry of a young politician*). And yet, for all their worries, what would we do without the ladies? (*The women do not unbend. He goes below the center table to the sink, takes a dipperful of water from the pail and pouring it into a basin, washes his hands. While he is doing this the* SHERIFF *and* HALE *cross to cupboard, which they inspect. The* COUNTY ATTORNEY *starts to wipe his hands on the roller towel, turns it for a cleaner place*). Dirty towels! (*Kicks his foot against the pans under the sink*). Not much of a housekeeper, would you say, ladies?

MRS. HALE (*stiffly*). There's a great deal of work to be done on a farm.

COUNTY ATTORNEY. To be sure. And yet (*with a little bow to her*) I know there are some Dickson County farmhouses which do not have such roller towels. (*He gives it a pull to expose its full length again.*)

MRS. HALE. Those towels get dirty awful quick. Men's hands aren't always as clean as they might be.

COUNTY ATTORNEY. Ah, loyal to your sex, I see. But you and Mrs. Wright were neighbors. I suppose you were friends, too.

MRS. HALE (*shaking her head*). I've not seen much of her of late years. I've not been in this house—it's more than a year.

COUNTY ATTORNEY (*crossing to women* U. C.). And why was that? You didn't like her?

MRS. HALE. I liked her all well enough. Farmers' wives have their hands full, Mr. Henderson. And then—

COUNTY ATTORNEY. Yes—?

MRS. HALE (*looking about*). It never seemed a very cheerful place.

COUNTY ATTORNEY. No—it's not cheerful. I shouldn't say she had the homemaking instinct.

MRS. HALE. Well, I don't know as Wright had, either.

COUNTY ATTORNEY. You mean that they didn't get on very well?

MRS. HALE. No, I don't mean anything. But I don't think a place'd be any cheerfuller for John Wright's being in it.

COUNTY ATTORNEY. I'd like to talk more of that a little later. I want to get the lay of things upstairs now. (*He goes past the women to* U. R. *where steps lead to a stair door.*)

SHERIFF. I suppose anything Mrs. Peters does'll be all right. She was to take in some clothes for her, you know, and a few little things. We left in such a hurry yesterday.

COUNTY ATTORNEY. Yes, but I would like to see what you take, Mrs. Peters, and keep an eye out for anything that might be of use to us.

MRS. PETERS. Yes, Mr. Henderson. (*The men leave by* U. R. *door to stairs. The women listen to the men's steps on the stairs, then look about the kitchen.*)

MRS. HALE (*crossing* L. *to sink*). I'd hate to have men coming into my kitchen, snooping around and criticizing. (*She arranges the pans under sink which the* LAWYER *had shoved out of place.*)

MRS. PETERS. Of course it's no more than their duty. (*Crosses to cupboard* D. R.)

MRS. HALE. Duty's all right, but I guess that deputy sheriff that came out to make the fire might have got a little of this on. (*Gives the roller towel a pull*). Wish I'd thought of that sooner. Seems mean to talk about her for not having things slicked up when she had to come away in such a hurry. (*Crosses* R. *to* MRS. PETERS *at cupboard.*)

MRS. PETERS (*who has been looking through cupboard, lifts one end of a towel that covers a pan*). She had bread set. (*Stands still.*)

MRS. HALE (*eyes fixed on a loaf of bread beside the breadbox, which is on a low shelf of the cupboard*). She was going to put this in there. (*Picks up loaf, then abruptly drops it. In a manner of returning to familiar things*). It's a shame about her fruit. I wonder if it's all gone. (*Gets up on the chair and looks*). I think there's some here that's all right, Mrs. Peters. Yes—here; (*holding it toward the window*) this is cherries, too. (*Looking again*). I declare I believe that's the only one. (*Gets down, jar in her hand. Goes to the sink and wipes it off on the outside*). She'll feel awful bad after all her hard work in the hot weather. I remember the afternoon I put up my cherries last summer. (*She puts the jar on the big kitchen table, center of the room. With a sigh, is about to sit down in the rocking chair. Before she is seated realizes what chair it is; with a slow look at it, steps back. The chair which she has touched rocks back and forth.* MRS. PETERS *moves to center table and they both watch the chair rock for a moment or two.*)

MRS. PETERS (*shaking off the mood which the empty rocking chair has evoked. Now in a businesslike manner she speaks*). Well, I must get those things from the front room closet. (*She goes to the door at the* R., *but, after looking into the other room, steps back*). You coming with me, Mrs. Hale? You could help me carry them. (*They go in the other room; reappear,* MRS. PETERS *carrying a dress, petticoat and skirt,* MRS. HALE *following with a pair of shoes*). My, it's cold in there. (*She puts the clothes on the big table, and hurries to the stove.*)

MRS. HALE (*right of center table examining the skirt*). Wright was close. I think maybe that's why she kept so much to herself. She didn't even belong to the Ladies' Aid. I suppose she felt she couldn't do her part, and then you don't enjoy things when you feel shabby. I heard she used to wear pretty clothes and be lively, when she was Minnie Foster, one of the town girls singing in the choir. But that—oh, that was thirty years ago. This all you was to take in?

MRS. PETERS. She said she wanted an apron. Funny thing to want, for there isn't much to get you dirty in jail, goodness knows. But I suppose just to make her feel more natural. (*Crosses to cupboard*). She said they was in the top drawer in this cupboard. Yes, here. And then her little shawl that always hung behind the door. (*Opens stair door and looks*). Yes, here it is. (*Quickly shuts door leading upstairs.*)

MRS. HALE (*abruptly moving toward her*). Mrs. Peters?

MRS. PETERS. Yes, Mrs. Hale? (*At* U. R. *door.*)

MRS. HALE. Do you think she did it?

MRS. PETERS (*in a frightened voice*). Oh, I don't know.

MRS. HALE. Well, I don't think she did. Asking for an apron and her little shawl. Worrying about her fruit.

MRS. PETERS (*starts to speak, glances up, where footsteps are heard in the room above. In a low voice*). Mr. Peters says it looks bad for her. Mr. Henderson is awful sarcastic in a speech and he'll make fun of her saying' she didn't wake up.

MRS. HALE. Well, I guess John Wright didn't wake when they was slipping that rope under his neck.

MRS. PETERS (*crossing slowly to table and placing shawl and apron on table with other clothing*). No, it's strange. It must have been done awful crafty and still. They say it was such a—funny way to kill a man, rigging it all up like that.

MRS. HALE (*crossing to left of* MRS. PETERS *at table*). That's just what Mr. Hale said. There was a gun in the house. He says that's what he can't understand.

MRS. PETERS. Mr. Henderson said coming out that what was needed for the case was a motive; something to show anger, or—sudden feeling.

MRS. HALE (*who is standing by the table*). Well, I don't see any signs of anger around here. (*She puts her hand on the dish towel which lies on the table, stands looking down at table, one-half of which is clean, the other half messy*). It's wiped to here. (*Makes a move as if to finish work, then turns and looks at loaf of bread outside the breadbox. Drops towel. In that voice of coming back to familiar things*). Wonder how they are finding things upstairs. (*Crossing below table to* D. R.) I hope she had it a little more red-up up there. You know, it seems kind of *sneaking*. Locking her up in town and then coming out here and trying to get her own house to turn against her!

MRS. PETERS. But, Mrs. Hale, the law is the law.

MRS. HALE. I s'pose 'tis. (*Unbuttoning her coat*). Better loosen up your things, Mrs. Peters. You won't feel them when you go out. (MRS. PETERS *takes off her fur tippet, goes to hang it on chair back left of table, stands looking at the work basket on floor near* D. L. *window.*)

MRS. PETERS. She was piercing a quilt. (*She brings the large sewing basket to the center table and they look at the bright pieces,* MRS. HALE *above the table and* MRS. PETERS *left of it.*)

MRS. HALE. It's a log cabin pattern. Pretty, isn't it? I wonder if she was goin' to quilt it or just knot it? (*Footsteps have been heard coming down*

the stairs. The SHERIFF *enters followed by* HALE *and the* COUNTY ATTOR-
NEY.)

SHERIFF. They wonder if she was going to quilt it or just knot it! (*The
men laugh, the women look abashed.*)

COUNTY ATTORNEY (*rubbing his hands over the stove*). Frank's fire
didn't do much up there, did it? Well, let's go out to the barn and get
that cleared up. (*The men go outside by* U. L. *door.*)

MRS. HALE (*resentfully*). I don't know as there's anything so strange,
our takin' up our time with little things while we're waiting for them to
get the evidence. (*She sits in chair right of table smoothing out a block with
decision*). I don't see as it's anything to laugh about.

MRS. PETERS (*apologetically*). Of course they've got awful important
things on their minds. (*Pulls up a chair and joins* MRS. HALE *at the left of
the table.*)

MRS. HALE (*examining another block*). Mrs. Peters, look at this one.
Here, this is the one she was working on, and look at the sewing! All
the rest of it has been so nice and even. And look at this! It's all over
the place! Why, it looks as if she didn't know what she was about!
(*After she has said this they look at each other, then start to glance back at
the door. After an instant* MRS. HALE *has pulled at a knot and ripped the
sewing.*)

MRS. PETERS. Oh, what are you doing, Mrs. Hale?

MRS. HALE (*mildly*). Just pulling out a stitch or two that's not sewed
very good. (*Threading a needle*). Bad sewing always made me fidgety.

MRS. PETERS (*with a glance at door, nervously*). I don't think we ought
to touch things.

MRS. HALE. I'll just finish up this end. (*Suddenly stopping and leaning
forward*). Mrs. Peters?

MRS. PETERS. Yes, Mrs. Hale?

MRS. HALE. What do you suppose she was so nervous about?

MRS. PETERS. Oh—I don't know. I don't know as she was nervous. I
sometimes sew awful queer when I'm just tired. (MRS. HALE *starts to say
something, looks at* MRS. PETERS, *then goes on sewing*). Well, I must get
these things wrapped up. They may be through sooner than we think.
(*Putting apron and other things together*). I wonder where I can find a
piece of paper, and string. (*Rises.*)

MRS. HALE. In that cupboard, maybe.

MRS. PETERS (*crosses* R. *looking in cupboard*). Why, here's a bird-cage.
(*Holds it up*). Did she have a bird, Mrs. Hale?

MRS. HALE. Why, I don't know whether she did or not—I've not been
here for so long. There was a man around last year selling canaries
cheap, but I don't know as she took one; maybe she did. She used to
sing real pretty herself.

MRS. PETERS (*glancing around*). Seems funny to think of a bird here. But she must have had one, or why would she have a cage? I wonder what happened to it?

MRS. HALE. I s'pose maybe the cat got it.

MRS. PETERS. No, she didn't have a cat. She's got that feeling some people have about cats—being afraid of them. My cat got in her room and she was real upset and asked me to take it out.

MRS. HALE. My sister Bessie was like that. Queer, ain't it?

MRS. PETERS (*examining the cage*). Why, look at this door. It's broke. One hinge is pulled apart. (*Takes a step down to* MRS. HALE'S *right.*)

MRS. HALE (*looking too*). Looks as if someone must have been rough with it.

MRS. PETERS. Why, yes. (*She brings the cage forward and puts it on the table.*)

MRS. HALE (*glancing toward* U. L. *door*). I wish if they're going to find any evidence they'd be about it. I don't like this place.

MRS. PETERS. But I'm awful glad you came with me, Mrs. Hale. It would be lonesome for me sitting here alone.

MRS. HALE. It would, wouldn't it? (*Dropping her sewing*). But I tell you what I do wish, Mrs. Peters. I wish I had come over sometimes when *she* was here. I—(*looking around the room*)—wish I had.

MRS. PETERS. But of course you were awful busy, Mrs. Hale—your house and your children.

MRS. HALE (*rises and crosses* L.). I could've come. I stayed away because it weren't cheerful—and that's why I ought to have come. I—(*looking out* L. *window*)—I've never liked this place. Maybe because it's down in a hollow and you don't see the road. I dunno what it is, but it's a lonesome place and always was. I wish I had come over to see Minnie Foster sometimes. I can see now—(*Shakes her head.*)

MRS. PETERS (*left of table and above it*). Well, you mustn't reproach yourself, Mrs. Hale. Somehow we just don't see how it is with other folks until—something turns up.

MRS. HALE. Not having children makes less work—but it makes a quiet house, and Wright out to work all day, and no company when he did come in. (*Turning from window*). Did you know John Wright, Mrs. Peters?

MRS. PETERS. Not to know him; I've seen him in town. They say he was a good man.

MRS. HALE. Yes—good; he didn't drink, and kept his word as well as most, I guess, and paid his debts. But he was a hard man, Mrs. Peters. Just to pass the time of day with him—(*Shivers*). Like a raw wind that gets to the bone. (*Pauses, her eye falling on the cage*). I should think she would 'a' wanted a bird. But what do you suppose went with it?

MRS. PETERS. I don't know, unless it got sick and died. (*She reaches over and swings the broken door, swings it again, both women watch it.*)

MRS. HALE. You weren't raised round here, were you? (MRS. PETERS *shakes her head*). You didn't know—her?

MRS. PETERS. Not till they brought her yesterday.

MRS. HALE. She—come to think of it, she was kind of like a bird herself—real sweet and pretty, but kind of timid and—fluttery. How— she—did—change. (*Silence; then as if struck by a happy thought and relieved to get back to everyday things. Crosses* R. *above* MRS. PETERS *to cupboard, replaces small chair used to stand on its original place* D. R.) Tell you what, Mrs. Peters, why don't you take the quilt in with you? It might take up her mind.

MRS. PETERS. Why, I think that's a real nice idea, Mrs. Hale. There couldn't possibly be any objection to it, could there? Now, just what would I take? I wonder if her patches are in here—and her things. (*They look in the sewing basket.*)

MRS. HALE (*crosses to right of table*). Here's some red. I expect this has got sewing things in it. (*Brings out a fancy box*). What a pretty box. Looks like something somebody would give you. Maybe her scissors are in here. (*Opens box. Suddenly puts her hand to her nose*). Why—(MRS. PETERS *bends nearer, then turns her face away*). There's something wrapped up in this piece of silk.

MRS. PETERS. Why, this isn't her scissors.

MRS. HALE (*lifting the silk*). Oh, Mrs. Peters—it's—(MRS. PETERS *bends closer.*)

MRS. PETERS. It's the bird.

MRS. HALE. But, Mrs. Peters—look at it! Its neck! Look at its neck! It's all—other side *to.*

MRS. PETERS. Somebody—wrung—its—neck. (*Their eyes meet. A look of growing comprehension, of horror. Steps are heard outside.* MRS. HALE *slips box under quilt pieces, and sinks into her chair. Enter* SHERIFF *and* COUNTY ATTORNEY. MRS. PETERS *steps* D. L. *and stands looking out of window.*)

COUNTY ATTORNEY (*as one turning from serious things to little pleasantries*). Well, ladies, have you decided whether she was going to quilt it or knot it? (*Crosses to* C. *above table.*)

MRS. PETERS. We think she was going to—knot it. (SHERIFF *crosses to right of stove, lifts stove lid and glances at fire, then stands warming hands at stove.*)

COUNTY ATTORNEY. Well, that's interesting, I'm sure. (*Seeing the birdcage*). Has the bird flown?

MRS. HALE (*putting more quilt pieces over the box*). We think the—cat got it.

COUNTY ATTORNEY (*preoccupied*). Is there a cat? (MRS. HALE *glances in a quick covert way at* MRS. PETERS.)

MRS. PETERS (*turning from window takes a step in*). Well, not *now*. They're superstitious, you know. They leave.

COUNTY ATTORNEY (*to* SHERIFF PETERS, *continuing an interrupted conversation*). No sign at all of anyone having come from the outside. Their own rope. Now let's go up again and go over it piece by piece. (*They start upstairs*). It would have to have been someone who knew just the—(MRS. PETERS *sits down left of table. The two women sit there not looking at one another, but as if peering into something and at the same time holding back. When they talk now it is in the manner of feeling their way over strange ground, as if afraid of what they are saying, but as if they cannot help saying it.*)

MRS. HALE (*hesitatively and in hushed voice*). She liked the bird. She was going to bury it in that pretty box.

MRS. PETERS (*in a whisper*). When I was a girl—my kitten—there was a boy took a hatchet, and before my eyes—and before I could get there—(*Covers her face an instant*). If they hadn't held me back I would have—(*catches herself, looks upstairs where steps are heard, falters weakly*)—hurt him.

MRS. HALE (*with a slow look around her*). I wonder how it would seem never to have had any children around. (*Pause*). No, Wright wouldn't like the bird—a thing that sang. She used to sing. He killed that, too.

MRS. PETERS (*moving uneasily*). We don't know who killed the bird.

MRS. HALE. I knew John Wright.

MRS. PETERS. It was an awful thing was done in this house that night, Mrs. Hale. Killing a man while he slept, slipping a rope around his neck that choked the life out of him.

MRS. HALE. His neck. Choked the life out of him. (*Her hand goes out and rests on the bird-cage.*)

MRS. PETERS (*with rising voice*). We don't know who killed him. We don't *know*.

MRS. HALE (*her own feeling not interrupted*). If there'd been years and years of nothing, then a bird to sing to you, it would be awful—still, after the bird was still.

MRS. PETERS (*something within her speaking*). I know what stillness is. When we homesteaded in Dakota, and my first baby died—after he was two years old, and me with no other then—

MRS. HALE (*moving*). How soon do you suppose they'll be through looking for the evidence?

MRS. PETERS. I know what stillness is. (*Pulling herself back*). The law has got to punish crime, Mrs. Hale.

MRS. HALE (*not as if answering that*). I wish you'd seen Minnie Foster when she wore a white dress with blue ribbons and stood up there in the choir and sang. (*A look around the room*). Oh, I *wish* I'd come over here once in a while! That was a crime! That was a crime! Who's going to punish that?

MRS. PETERS (*looking upstairs*). We mustn't—take on.

MRS. HALE. I might have known she needed help! I know how things can be—for women. I tell you, it's queer, Mrs. Peters. We live close together and we live far apart. We all go through the same things—it's all just a different kind of the same thing. (*Brushes her eyes, noting the jar of fruit, reaches out for it*). If I was you I wouldn't tell her her fruit was gone. Tell her it *ain't*. Tell her it's all right. Take this in to prove it to her. She—she may never know whether it was broke or not.

MRS. PETERS (*takes the jar, looks about for something to wrap it in; takes petticoat from the clothes brought from the other room, very nervously begins winding this around the jar. In a false voice*). My, it's a good thing the men couldn't hear us. Wouldn't they just laugh! Getting all stirred up over a little thing like a—dead canary. As if that could have anything to do with—with—wouldn't they *laugh*! (*The men are heard coming downstairs.*)

MRS. HALE (*under her breath*). Maybe they would—maybe they wouldn't.

COUNTY ATTORNEY. No, Peters, it's all perfectly clear except a reason for doing it. But you know juries when it comes to women. If there was some definite thing. (*Crosses slowly to above table.* SHERIFF *crosses* D. R. MRS. HALE *and* MRS. PETERS *remain seated at either side of table*). Something to show—something to make a story about—a thing that would connect up with this strange way of doing it—(*The women's eyes meet for an instant. Enter* HALE *from outer door.*)

HALE (*remaining* U. L. *by door*). Well, I've got the team around. Pretty cold out there.

COUNTY ATTORNEY. I'm going to stay awhile by myself. (*To the* SHERIFF). You can send Frank out for me, can't you? I want to go over everything. I'm not satisfied that we can't do better.

SHERIFF. Do you want to see what Mrs. Peters is going to take in? (*The* LAWYER *picks up the apron, laughs.*)

COUNTY ATTORNEY. Oh, I guess they're not very dangerous things the ladies have picked out. (*Moves a few things about, disturbing the quilt pieces which cover the box. Steps back*). No, Mrs. Peters doesn't need supervising. For that matter a sheriff's wife is married to the law. Ever think of it that way, Mrs. Peters?

MRS. PETERS. Not—just that way.

SHERIFF (*chuckling*). Married to the law. (*Moves to* D. R. *door to the other room*). I just want you to come in here a minute, George. We ought to take a look at these windows.

COUNTY ATTORNEY (*scoffingly*). Oh, windows!

SHERIFF. We'll be right out, Mr. Hale. (HALE *goes outside. The* SHERIFF *follows the* COUNTY ATTORNEY *into the other room. Then* MRS. HALE *rises, hands tight together, looking intensely at* MRS. PETERS, *whose eyes make a slow turn, finally meeting* MRS. HALE'S. *A moment* MRS.

HALE *holds her, then her own eyes point the way to where the box is con-*
cealed. Suddenly MRS. PETERS *throws back quilt pieces and tries to put the*
box in the bag she is carrying. It is too big. She opens box, starts to take
bird out, cannot touch it, goes to pieces, stands there helpless. Sound of a
knob turning in the other room. MRS. HALE *snatches the box and puts it in*
the pocket of her big coat. Enter COUNTY ATTORNEY *and* SHERIFF, *who*
remains D. R.)

    COUNTY ATTORNEY (*crosses to* U. L. *door facetiously*). Well, Henry, at
least we found out that she was not going to quilt it. She was going to—
what is it you call it, ladies?

    MRS. HALE (*standing* C. *below table facing front, her hand against her*
pocket). We call it—knot it, Mr. Henderson.

CURTAIN

EXERCISE

1. Imagine a version of the play in which Mrs. Wright is brought onstage and
then taken off. What would be the effect?

2. In what ways are the world of a farm community revealed?

3. In what indirect ways—speech habits and actions—are distinctions drawn
among the characters?

4. Write one of the following scenes:

    a. A scene in which Mr. Wright kills the canary. Consider why he might have
        done it. (Perhaps dinner wasn't ready or, perhaps, he had his own problems.)
    b. A scene in which Mrs. Peters takes Mrs. Wright her sewing.
    c. A scene in which the jury tries to come to a decision about the verdict.

5. Write an analysis of one long beat in the play. Use our discussions of *Blithe*
Spirit (Chapter 13) and *The Collection* (Chapter 12) as models.

6. As we have noted, the play is a bit old-fashioned. Using the same basic
premise, try to update it. Surely you will have to put the play in the city or—
perhaps—a trailer park. Might the Wrights run a Seven-Eleven in a small town?
Think through the characters once more. Consider what experiences a woman
might have had in today's world to let her be so brow-beaten by a man as Mrs.
Wright appears to have been.

7. Glaspell's "A Jury of Her Peers," a translation of her play into prose fiction,
appears in many anthologies. Compare and contrast the texts, paying particular
attention to genre-dependent features. Example: in the play, all exposition
must come through dialogue; how does the story's narrator share this task?

A Word on Plays for Film

Learning to write original playscripts for film (whether to be presented in a movie theater or on television) requires that you master special techniques and jargon. You need to read about the media, see the media, and work in the media.

In one sense, of course, the writer has more freedom in film. Whereas theater audiences cannot be moved from place to place, a camera can. Large crowd scenes are possible; underwater scenes are possible; a host of special effects are possible—all growing from the technology that has made the art form possible.

On the other hand, the playwright has to be much more conscious of three conventions inherent in film technology: (1) the audience expects that in *moving* pictures either the people or the camera will be moving all the time; (2) the potential for close camera work increases the requirement for a detailed environment; (3) the camera presents a point of view, a filter for what and how we can see the action. In some ways, this last element brings film closer to narrative fiction than to playwriting.

The effects of the technical elements on playwriting can become too absorbing. Beginning playwrights may get so involved in wide angle shots, pan shots, split screens, zoom-ins, and other camera business that they forget to be playwrights and start to become directors. Since the basic principles of dialogue, character development, premise, and plot are the same for both media, focus your efforts on making a good play that exploits the possibilities of the film medium and, unless you are also a director, keep the technical description simple.

Exploiting the artistic possibilities in film is beyond the scope of this text, but you will want to look at several of the full-length textbooks devoted to film and television that we have listed in Chapter 16.

Summary

A playscript is an occasion for a performance. The most effective playscripts are those written with an appreciation of both the freedoms and limitations of the medium's conventions. On the one hand, the playwright has only to indicate the presence of a chair, not describe it; on the other hand, the detail of the pettipoint will not be visible to most spectators and so it cannot be as important as it might be in a work of fiction. Because a performance is unstoppable, the effects cannot be as subtle as those in poetry and fiction. Character and circumstance must be quickly grasped by the audience. The premise needs to be shaped so that the point of attack is late in the story. Above all, the playwright must master the craft of presenting both text and subtext in dialogue, the primary vehicle of character and plot.

The pleasure of playwriting is that in no other genre can you have so much immediate impact on an audience.

15

❖

From Revision to Submission

REVISION

To **revise** means literally to "see again." To **edit** means to bring into conformity with established standards. Though these two terms are often used interchangeably, they point to different concerns. We will shift back and forth, sometimes focusing on one term, sometimes the other. Paradoxically, taking another look and honoring conventions become part of a single process as the author searches for ways to improve his or her work.

When to Revise

Most writers agree that writing and revising by wholes leads to the best results. This means that it makes sense to begin revising and editing your work only when you have a complete draft in front of you. After all, if a successful literary work is a web of interrelated parts, then changes cannot be made in isolation. A revision in one place almost invariably demands a revision somewhere else. Revising a work that is only partly completed is better than doing nothing at all, but it is an inefficient practice.

    This does not mean that you should completely ignore problems along the way. At the end of each writing session, take informal notes for future revision. Then, when you have in front of you a draft of the whole work, or major portions of it, review those notes and determine what kind of revisions will satisfy your new concerns. For example, if you write your way into a situation that demands "backloading" of information, make yourself a revision note, but don't stop to do the actual revision: push on ahead.

How to Revise

Revising means taking a critical stance toward what you have done. Many writers need to get away from their work for a while in order to see it clearly and objectively. Whether dealing with large-scale structural issues or consistent spelling of a nickname, we see things more clearly when we have reduced the emotional charge that is part of the creative impulse. In a way, you have to take on another personality. You have to become someone who can read and evaluate what you actually wrote, not what you wanted to write or hope you wrote.

We can consider two levels of rewriting:

1. for literary quality
2. for the conventions of mechanics, grammar, and manuscript form

When assessing the literary effectiveness of the work, we consider its impact on the reader, its focus, its handling of the conventions of genre, and its diction. Whatever feeds the aesthetic and conceptual dimensions of the work is considered here—including that elusive thing called **style**. Working with checklists will help you go through the process with greater thoroughness and efficiency than just "looking for things." A checklist is no more than a guide, however. Begin with the lists provided here, and then go on to develop your own based on your experience and work habits.

CHECKLIST FOR POETRY

1. Can the line breaks be justified?
2. Is the speaker's voice consistent?
3. Are the sounds and rhythms of language used expressively?
4. Do figures of speech (or any other devices) call too much attention to themselves at the expense of their function?
5. Have you eliminated stale language—especially clichés and unnecessary trite expressions?
6. Are the parts of the poem subordinated to an overall effect?
7. Are the parts (lines, images, stages, events) in the best possible order?
8. Have you let suggestivity and ambiguity turn into vagueness and unintelligibility?
9. If the poem is in sections, should it be?

10. Do you feel that each section has a proper relationship to the others and to the whole?
11. Do the visual and auditory levels of the poem complement each other?

CHECKLIST FOR FICTION

1. Is your point of attack effective? That is, have you begun the story too early (quite likely) or too late (not likely)? A properly chosen point of attack will allow you to give exactly what the reader needs to follow the story through its climax and resolution.
2. Is the structure effective? Do you have the scenes you need (and only the scenes you need) to develop your material? Are the scenes in the best order? Is there a sense of inevitability about the ending that grows naturally out of the flow of events and information without sending out obvious signals?
3. Are the transitions between scenes clean and clear?
4. Are the sections of summary and exposition adequate? Are they overdone? Have you struck an effective balance between showing and telling?
5. Is the narrator's perspective, the point of view, the best choice for this story? Is the perspective consistently maintained?
6. Are the main characters developed sufficiently? Do they become more than mere types? Do they have sufficient interest as rounded or shaded individuals? Are their actions consistent without being overly predictable?
7. Are minor characters and walk-ons kept to a minimum and kept within the bounds of their functions in the story?
8. Is the dialogue natural? Is it plausible? Does it do more than merely impart information? Are the dialogue tags kept simple? Is it always clear who is speaking?
9. Do you have an energetic mix of the various storytelling elements? Generally, it is wise to avoid long stretches of anything—description, exposition, dialogue. Keep the story moving forward and engage the reader on many levels.
10. Is there an overall unity of effect—a controlling idea, mood, emotion, or thematic thrust that the various ingredients support?

CHECKLIST FOR PLAYS

1. All of the items for fiction, plus . . .
2. Have you given your characters things to do while they are talking (and thereby given your actors something to do)? This is another way of ensuring that the play is visual.
3. Does each beat exist to advance the plot? Even if a beat or moment is interesting in itself, if it does not fit into the plot you must remove it.

4. Have you removed or revised every beat that exists *only* for the purpose of giving exposition?

5. Does each character have an apparent want? Within moments after each character has appeared, something of his or her approach to life should be visible to the audience (even if the judgment will be modified later).

6. Are the character's wants in conflict with the other characters' wants? In most plays, meaningful conflict grows from these personal wants, not from ideas about how best to run the railroad.

7. Have you removed all stretches of dialogue that can be cut without the audience's missing anything of the plot? This type of revision requires line by line effort. If you sense that the dialogue (therefore the plot) is dragging, go back to where the drag began and try deleting until the play begins to feel alive again.

8. Is the environment built into the characters' actions, beliefs, and dialogue? The characters can see, and the audience can see what the characters can see. Exploit the possibilities.

9. Have you eliminated all unnecessary designators and stage directions?

10. Check to see that you have changed or eliminated elements that depended on scenes or characters you excised in the process of developing the script.

MECHANICS

Editing for mechanics requires that you refer to your dictionary and style manual and pay attention to the conventions of manuscript form.

Checking for Correctness

If some of the terms in this checklist cause you to draw a blank, go back to your style manual and give yourself a quick refresher course in mechanics.

Usage: Consult a dictionary whenever in doubt. Trust any anxieties you feel about a word choice or expression and make sure you are in control of your decisions. Check any idiomatic constructions that you're not sure of as well as regionalisms that you have appropriated for your work. Read your work aloud (slowly) to test what you have against your inner ear. If it doesn't "sound" right to your ear, don't let it go just because you are eager to get the manuscript into a publisher's or director's hands.

Spelling: There are no excuses here. Don't guess.

Punctuation: Stick to the conventions whenever you can. Variations for effect can be useful, but they can also be annoying. For example, multiple exclamation points, ampersands instead of "and," & ellipses that leave the reader . . . . . lost in the dots!!!!! In poetry, special conventions adopted for a particular work should be used consistently so the reader can become comfortable with how they are meant to operate. Be careful about what goes inside and what goes outside of quotation marks. Remember that punctuation is an opportunity to shape how the reader sees relationships among words. Don't use punctuation mechanically. On the other hand, don't break conventions of punctuation except for a significant creative purpose.

Grammatical constructions: Avoid the common sins of the dangling modifier, the incomplete comparison, the run-on sentence, or the sentence fragment. Again, break with conventions for a good purpose, not out of ignorance or carelessness.

Agreement/consistency: Check for consistencies in tense and number. Make sure nouns and pronouns clearly agree.

Clarity of pronoun references: Avoid vague uses of "this," "which," "it," "she," "he" and other pronouns. Keep the distance between pronouns and their antecedents minimal. Make sure a pronoun does, in fact, refer to a noun or to a clause or phrase functioning as a noun.

Placement of modifiers: Keep modifiers near what they modify. Avoid "squinters" that point in two directions.

Economy/directness of expression: Choose precise, concrete nouns and verbs that will require minimal modification. Reduce modifying phrases to single words. Avoid circumlocutions.

Sentence style: Don't become a slave to a certain sentence construction or length. Mix complex and simple, long and short. Don't overuse parallelism. Keep your prose moving through sentence variety, and be alert to sounds and rhythms.

Finally, *read the work aloud and have others read it aloud to you.* Doing this gives you new perspective on effectiveness and also gives you the opportunity to catch errors that are often missed in silent reading.

A DESK ON YOUR DISK

Almost every resource that sits on a writer's desk is available in electronic form. Dictionary programs allow you to check individual words or whole textfiles for spelling errors. Since all of these dictionaries are limited, and since they don't list proper names and certain word variations, the programs allow you to compile a personal dictionary so you won't keep being told that "Faulkner" is a possible error. Once you put an entry in the personal dictionary, the program knows that that sequence of letters is legitimate. These dictionaries are not, in fact, really dictionaries at all. They are spelling checkers. Whenever they come across an unknown configuration, the writer is asked to do something: either ignore the signal, change that instance, or change that pattern throughout the document.

These programs are fine for catching typographical errors. However, they do not take the place of your own careful proofreading. No spelling checker will question the word "their" when you mean "there" or "to" when you mean "too." Typographical errors that result in legitimate words—"place" instead of "plate"—will have to be discovered through the diligence of the responsible author.

An electronic thesaurus is available with many word processing packages. When you enter the thesaurus command, you will be given alternatives for the word at the cursor. Given what we have said elsewhere about there being no true synonyms, we won't elaborate here on the dangers of instant word lists. Remember that such a resource is best used to jog your memory. The responsible writer can use this resource wisely and clear the desk of one more reference volume. As with the spelling checker, the range of the computer thesaurus is limited. However, the speed and convenience of these devices is remarkable. No more turning pages to find something. Push one or two keys and what you want to know is on the screen, ready to be automatically placed in your textfile.

Can you put away your style manual? Maybe not. The style analysis programs—RightWriter, Grammatik, and Punctuation & Style, for example—tend to mark as errors too many formulations that are in fact legitimate and intentional. Still, running an analysis with one of these programs may help you catch some blunder you might otherwise miss. We tend to be skeptical about these programs, but see for yourself. And remember, it's *your* job to edit your work properly. There is no sense in blaming your software for your mistakes.

Even without such programs, you can perform basic checks on your work if you are aware of your worst tendencies. Do you tend to overuse forms of "to be" at the expense of active verbs? Use the "find" feature to locate instances of "is" and "are" in your draft, then decide if substitutions are desirable. Do you use coordination when subordination might be appropriate? Run the "find" command for "and" and "but," and then revise accordingly.

You will need to experiment and talk to other writers before deciding which word processing programs and auxiliary programs will be best for you. With experience, you will find the combination that allows you to feel comfortable while taking maximum advantage of computer technology.

Because of the conveniences just described, the word processor can change the way you go about your business. Any writer inhibited by the printed word may find the ephemeral signs on the monitor screen easier to push around than the immovable figures printed on the page. The trial and error process that is essential to composing and revising becomes much less of a trial and more of a game. Word processing, a new form of play, intensifies or even reestablishes the play aspects of creative writing that are so much a part of its delight.

SOME POSSIBLE PROBLEMS

There are some drawbacks to writing with a word processor. The monitor (screen) shows you only a fraction of a page at a time, usually somewhere between a third and a half. This limitation leads to tunnel vision: the tendency to pay too much attention to the limited amount of material glowing before your eyes and not enough to the larger flow of content and style. Even as you flip back and forth among screens full of text, you lose continuity.

To compensate for this difficulty, we recommend that you print out your work often and do much of your revising and editing on the printed copy. It is much easier to work with whole sheets of text, especially since you can then lay three or four next to each other to get a feel for the flow of your work. This practice will cost only a little of the time saved by using a word processor in the first place. With a mildly sophisticated system, you can be printing out one file (or a portion of one) while composing or outlining or revising another. Also, high-speed dot matrix printers crank out draft-quality copy many times faster than anyone can type. Working on printouts of successive revisions allows you to refine your work efficiently and effectively. Remember, you do little retyping; you only enter *changes* on the keyboard.

Some writers get around the tunnel vision problem by single spacing when they draft, so they can see twice as much material. Then, depending on their word processor, they either reformat to double spacing before printing or command the printer to double-space. At best, we find this a partial solution, especially since it is very difficult to read single-spaced material on the screen for a long time. You'll have to discover what works best for you.

Proofreading in particular is best done on printed text. Staring at the monitor—any monitor—is more wearing on the eyes than is scrutinizing printed text. We find that our proofreading is less accurate when we read from the screen. Perhaps it's just a matter of an old habit dying hard, but most writers have had the same experience. Another advantage is the portability of the printed copy: you can work on it wherever you want to.

Frequent printouts are also a safeguard against the vulnerability of electronic text. Materials in memory only (not "saved" to a disk) are susceptible to voltage variations or accidents (such as someone tripping over your power cord and unplugging it). Even saved textfiles can be ruined by keyboard mistakes or electromagnetic damage. Not only should you save and back up your files regularly, you should print out hard copy as a final defense against computer or disk failure. Although these failures are infrequent, it takes only one to make you wish you had taken simple precautions.

Another potential problem is the distraction caused by the very powerful features we have been discussing. Writing and saving textfiles is one thing; editing is another; and page formatting is still another. The gadgetry of the word processor tempts writers to move too quickly to editing or designing the page layout when they should be drafting. Sometimes playing around with margins, typefaces, and various commands affecting the appearance of the finished product substitutes for creative working time in which new ideas and passages are generated. Our advice: stay with the *process* of composition as long as possible. Enjoy the editing features only when you have something to edit. Enjoy the page design features only when everything else is done and you're ready to print out final copy.

Some Words About Proofreading

Technically, **proofreading** means checking galleys or page proofs against the original manuscript from which the typesetting was done. The marking of proofs involves using a standard set of symbols that we illustrate below. Proofing can be done with two people, one reading the "copy" and the other reading the author's original.

One person reads aloud, usually from back to front, including punctuation. (For example, for the preceding sentence, "period/ punctuation/ including/ comma/ front/ to/ back. . . .") Homonyms ("too," "two," "to") are spelled out. The other person reads along silently, searching for discrepancies between what is heard and what is seen. The goal is to ensure that the printed version of a work conforms to the author's intention, as recorded in the typescript, in every way.

In preparing a work for submission to a teacher or an editor, you must take the same kind of care. The copy you present should be as close as possible to your ideal. From your reader's point of view, you are invisible. All the reader sees is the finished page. Errors that interrupt the activity of reading will annoy and confuse the very persons you are trying to reach. From the reader's point of view, a careless error is still an error. Careless copy tends to be carried forward even beyond the most careful copy editor and ends up in print.

Many writers find it helpful to proofread a number of times, concentrating on different potential problems each time through. You might read through

ℓ	delete; take it out out	H	hyphen
⌒	close up; print as o ne word	M	dash
ℯ	delete and close up	⸮	comma
∧	caret; insert here /text	⸴	apostrophe
#	insert aspace	⊙	period
stet	let marked text stand as set	:	colon
tr	transpose; change order the	;	semicolon
/	(used to separate two or more marks)	❝❞	quotation marks
¶	begin a new paragraph	(/)	parentheses
no¶	no paragraph	[/]	brackets
ⓢⓟ	spell out; change 15 to fifteen	Q	? or Q Is this really correct (content or form)
cap	set in capitals		
lc	set in lowerCase		

once using the "checklist for fiction," then again using the "checklist for correctness." A third time through, scan the right margin to check for proper hyphenation. Finally, read each sentence (or line) separately, beginning at the end of the work. By reading things out of order, you are less likely to have your objective examination foiled by anticipating and imagining what comes next.

Use the appropriate proofreading symbols as you prepare a draft for retyping. Familiarity with this system will be useful when your work has been accepted for publication and you are ready to check proofs. On the preceding page are some standard markings that are also useful for editing drafts.

Other marks are used specifically for typesetting problems. You will find a list of these in your dictionary. Also, your publisher will give you a style manual to follow when your manuscript is returned for further revision.

FINDING A HOME FOR YOUR WORK

Like most writers, you will want your work to be published or produced. However, you will discover that finding a proper outlet for your writing is often a frustrating endeavor that requires the skills and energy of a salesperson. The effort appears to be antithetical to the creative process, and it may well be. However, marketing your work is a reality, and you need to get to it rather than moaning about the soul-destroying effort. Even relatively successful writers have to face up to the submission process—and frequently the rejection slip. If that is so for them, then what for writers just starting to submit work for publication?

Many beginning writers have unrealistic expectations. They send their work only to the most prestigious magazines, forgetting that such outlets can publish only a tiny percentage of the thousands of manuscripts they receive. No beginning athlete would expect to go from a college course in golf to making the cut in the U.S. Open; that athlete would first try to make the golf team, then play in local and regional competitions.

In a sense, writing for publication is a form of competition. There are only so many available markets and many more writers seeking homes for their work. Sending manuscripts to inappropriate places only strains the system and lessens your chances of reaching an audience. It is important to send your work to those magazines and journals that are likely to give it a sympathetic reading. Marketing your poems, stories, or plays requires researching the literary or dramatic marketplace and honestly assessing what you have to offer.

At the beginning of this book, we argued that you shouldn't call yourself a writer unless you are a reader. As you become more and more concerned with publishing your work, your reading should also include a survey of the current literary marketplace. Discover the wide range of periodicals that publish literary writing and become familiar with the standards and tastes of the editors. Your starting place can be the entries on "Markets" that we provide in Chapter 16. The short paragraphs that these directories offer tell you what someone else—

the magazine editor or list compiler—thinks you need to know. You can make a somewhat informed decision by carefully studying these lists.

For a more fully informed decision you have to look at the publications. Use the market lists to select periodicals for direct examination. Subscribe to two or three at a time (changing your subscription list from year to year) and write for sample copies of others. Find out if any bookstores in your area stock issues of these periodicals. Most importantly, scour the libraries, especially the college and university libraries. The best place to find literary periodicals is in the library of a university that has a creative writing program. Also pool your resources: exchange copies of magazines with others who are involved in the same search.

The noncommercial literary periodical, privately or institutionally supported, is the most likely place for you or anyone else to publish. These forums are the incubators, hatcheries, and country fairs of literature and literary reputations. They are not interchangeable, however, and some are less distinctive than others. Your task as a writer looking for markets is to read for a match between the editorial character of a periodical and your own work. In a way, you are learning to put yourself in the editor's place: if I were editor of *The Seven Bridges Quarterly,* would my story be considered worthy of publication there?

Your survey efforts will make you familiar with many writers who appear with some regularity in the periodicals you are reading. If your work has something in common with theirs, find out where else they are being published. Contributors' notes often provide such information, as well as a way of gleaning something about the achievement and status of the writers appearing in these pages. Is this periodical *really* open to previously unpublished writers?

Many of the magazines aimed at writers (we list the most important ones in Chapter 16) provide information in a more timely manner than the annual market surveys. Often you can find out about a recently announced contest, a special issue of an established literary magazine, or a call for submissions by a magazine just getting started. This last category is a reasonable place for a beginning writer to send work. You and the magazine have something in common.

(*Note:* beware of contests that charge excessive reading fees or that require the purchase of the "prize anthology" before a final decision can be made on your work. Too often these publishing ventures prey on naive authors who will succumb to their tricks. Your work will appear in print, but no exercise of editorial judgment has taken place: just the exercise of the author writing a check.)

A useful and businesslike way to research the market for your poems and stories is to examine the acknowledgments pages of collections by writers whose work you admire, especially those whose style has some affinity with your own. Here you will find credited those periodicals that first published the individual stories or poems. Now you have a short list of possible markets for your own work. Get your hands on those magazines and target your submissions carefully.

Finally, there is nothing like the company of other writers to help you find your way into print. While literary friendships can be sought and exploited in unhealthy ways, there is something quite natural about being among people who share your interests and goals. Many of them will have that bit of information or that suggestion without which your work either will remain unpublished or will be published in a periodical of lesser merit than it deserves.

We have said nothing about marketing books. In the careers of most writers, publication in periodicals precedes book publication. Writers find their first congenial editors and their first audiences through submission to magazines, especially the noncommercial literary magazines whose main purpose is to nurture writers who have not yet captured a public large enough to warrant investment on the scale of the commercial publishing houses. The publication credits earned in these periodicals can win you the attention of a university or commercial press. What has happened, in effect, is that by meeting the standards and pleasing the tastes of many periodical editors, you have made a case for yourself. Book publishers depend on such credits to help them sift through the thousands of manuscripts that come their way.

Though it is possible to break through with a first novel, most novelists begin by getting "samples" of their work published in periodicals. These samples, presented as short stories, are often relatively self-contained chapters of novels in progress.

Drama presents (if you will excuse the pun) a special case, since "publication" of a play is most often the residual of success in the theater (or on film). Be involved in theater (or with film), even if on a volunteer basis. Work with educational television, small acting groups, experimental theaters, and college and university theaters. Go to conferences and participate in programs at which you might have an opportunity to meet producers and directors. Enter contests for new plays (they'll *have* to read the playscript). The truth is that there is a good deal of "who-do-you-know" in the theater world, though, ultimately, the play has to satisfy also. Look for opportunities to have your play heard—at a staged reading, for example, or in a workshop group.

Just as we recommend that you not look to publish first in those few places in which everyone wants to appear, so we recommend that you have realistic expectations and not search for a Broadway production first time out. When you do submit to a theatrical company, be sure you have researched its requirements. There's no use wasting postage sending a play to a theater that either hasn't the means to produce it or is not interested in the premise. You will notice that many companies now ask for a query letter, a synopsis, and dialogue samples. *Don't send more than they ask for* if you want an unbiased reading.

MANUSCRIPT FORM

The first principle of manuscript presentation is consistency. This is also the second. The third principle is to do everything in your power to make the task of reading and handling your manuscript as simple as possible.

If you take your writing seriously and want others to do so, then you will give your work every chance to succeed with editors. A sloppy manuscript (we really mean typescript) suggests that the author has little regard for the work or for the editor. Your manuscript should have few hand corrections, and these should be done neatly and unobtrusively. (Here is where the word processor is a great boon to writers.) Prose fiction should be double-spaced. Most editors accept single-spaced poetry manuscripts because this format will approximate the printed appearance of the poem, but some prefer that poetry be double-spaced (check market sources). Use standard margins: a 1 1/2-inch margin at top and left, an inch at right and bottom. Use the same margins for successive pages of your manuscript. Make sure that you have a fresh *black* typewriter or printer ribbon and that you use a good quality 8 1/2-by-11-inch bond paper. Avoid glossy or embossed paper as well as anything likely to fade or deteriorate. Avoid so-called erasable paper—it smears. Also, avoid continuous tractor-feed computer paper. Use standard typewriter fonts rather than any of the flashy, but distracting, alternatives.

Always be certain that your work is clearly identified. For multipage works, your name and address should appear at the top left side of the first page. The title of your story is given in capital letters, centered, about one-third of the way down the page. One custom, though it is hardly a requirement, is to provide an approximate word count at the upper right, along with an identification of the kind of work. Thus the first page of your manuscript will begin something like this:

```
Ima Writer
141 Dos Passos Lane                              Short story
Centerville, IA 52240                            3500 Words




[Start your story one-third of the way down]

                    JAGUARS IN THE SNOW

And now the story begins. . . .
```

Number successive pages—the upper right corner is a convenient place—and give a short identifying tag, like your last name, in case the pages of your submission become scattered about the editor's office. For example, "Writer/2." Don't staple the pages together. If you must use a fastener, choose a clip that will hold your pages together securely without defacing the paper.

Poetry manuscripts can be handled more simply, especially since the appearance of the work tells us what kind it is. If the typed poem fits on one page, use the upper left corner for your address only and place your name after the poem, on a separate line and introduced by a dash. Nothing need go in the upper right corner. Do not begin more than one poem on a page. Do not number the page or the successive pages that hold separate works. If you like, a wider left margin—2 inches or even a bit more—can be used to bring the poem closer to the center of the page. Keep the title in caps, centered above the poem or flush with its leftmost margin.

In the case of longer, multipage poems, additional care is needed. Since your byline can't follow the partial poem that appears on the first page, put your name above your address as you would for a fiction submission. Use the upper right corner to indicate how long the poem is *in lines*. Type the word "continued" on the bottom right of the first and successive pages as necessary. At the upper right of the following pages, provide a short title along with page number ("Wheelchair-7"). This system is more useful than your name when you are submitting a number of poems at once. To be even more cautious, you might give your last name at the upper left of successive pages.

If you double-space your poetry manuscript, be sure to quadruple for divisions between sections (stanzas).

Most important, indicate whether the last line on a page does or does not coincide with a stanza break. Don't leave it to the editor or typesetter to guess about this important dimension of your work.

A one-page poetry manuscript might look like the sample shown at the top of page 338.

Since you usually send a play to a producer-director, you need to follow the conventions for production scripts, which differ from the printed appearance of plays in books. Here are some guidelines:

1. Obviously everything that we have mentioned about neatness, paper size and weight, and general professional appearance holds as well for playscripts.
2. Firmly secure your play in some type of binder so pages need to be dynamited before they come loose (this is contrary to the rule for submitting other manuscripts).
3. Send a good copy, not the original.
4. Be sure you send the following with your manuscript:
   a. A brief resume about your experience with the theater and any staged readings or productions the play has had.
   b. A cast page. Producers don't want to be halfway into a play and find out they will need more actors than they have seats for the audience.

14 Stanza Turn
Petrarch, IN 12345

MAKING THINGS FIT

Sonnets are very hard to write.
You shouldn't try one if you're too laid back
Even if you've got the skill--or knack.
It's best if you're a bit up-tight.
Some people write them just for spite!
They don't care if they're out of whack
Just as long as they're on the right track.
These people never see the light.

Me, I've given up on verse
That makes me twist my thoughts around.
My lines and images get worse and worse,
And rhythmic glitches do abound.
Thus I do fume and fret and curse
And swear to seek no more rhyme sounds.

--Wyatt Surrey

c. A plot synopsis (two pages at most) that tells what happens, *not* "what it all means."
d. Contact information *in the lower left of the title page:*
Phyllis Player
7803 Indian Road
Flagstaff, AZ 29073
(777) 652-0839
Copyright or registration information
e. A brief cover letter (see "Cover Letters," p. 342)

The typing format for a playscript is as follows:

1. Single-space, but double-space between speeches.
2. The character speaking is centered on the page. Some playwrights capitalize the name.
3. The speech runs across the page.
4. Stage directions, in parentheses, are indented halfway across the page.
5. At the top right of every page type the act-scene-page.

Theater managers will not reject a manuscript just because it fails to follow exactly this or any other format, but generally speaking they expect a conventional presentation. Remember that manuscript form for playscripts is different from the printed version of the play. See the first pages of *Trifles* for an example of print publication format. The following is a sample playscript prepared for submission to a producer, director, or theater company:

Phyllis Player   I-i-1
The Mouse Bell

CAST :   Young Mouse - in his twenties (days)
         Sweet Mouse - just turning eighteen   (days)
         Grouch Mouse - seventy days if he's one but still spry
         Pal Mouse - in his twenties

Place: A comfortable nest between the walls. Pal Mouse, dressed
in jeans with Sweet Mouse who is laying out some crackers and
cheese.

> Early Morning. Off-stage we hear a
> terrible meeow, a shriek and
> silence.

                          PAL
                 (rises up and sniffs the air.)
I thought they had let him out for the night.

                         SWEET
Who do you think he got?

                          PAL
Hey, not to worry. Young's too smart to be out--

                         SWEET
                  (Bites into the brie)
I know that but he does take chances sometimes. I do wish he'd
be more careful. I start to get nervous and eat too much.

                 (Grouch comes tottering in.)

                          PAL
Good morning, sir.

                         SWEET
Good morning, papa-mouse.

                        GROUCH
You haven't a right to call me that yet. Maybe never. Did you
hear?

                         SWEET
           (Offers Grouch and Pal some crackers and cheese
              but they refuse.)
He told us, papa-mouse that he was only going to scout out the
basement. They keep barrels of wheat in the basement, we heard.

and so on

The format for a screenplay is designed to provide the maximum amount of room for the visual effects. You will see that the dialogue (the heart of a stage play) is squeezed in. This format should tell you something about how much of the plot and characterization have to be "told" through *visualized* action and movement as filtered through the camera.

Here are the basic rules:

1. Type the descriptions and directions (for cameras or actors) across the page.
2. Type dialogue in the middle of the page, each line no more than 3 inches wide. The character's name is centered.
3. Type designators for the speeches in parentheses centered below the character's name.
4. Single-space, but double-space between blocks of dialogue or directions.
5. Divisions of the action (such as FADE or CUT TO) are set apart on their own line, with double-spacing before and after. Some screenwriters put such directions at the right-hand margin.
6. The following elements are always typed in capital letters:
   a. CAMERA SHOTS AND DIRECTIONS
   b. INDICATIONS OF LOCALE AND TIME (when first mentioned)
   c. METHODS OF TRANSITION
   d. NAMES OF CHARACTERS (always capitalize above dialogue, but in descriptions only for first mention)
7. Leave almost 2 inches of margin on both left and right.

You will want to own a good text that gives you information about how to describe camera shots, transitions, and scenes. However, only direct experience will teach you how to avoid merely layering the technical on a story that might better be told in another medium. Or how to remake a story that you have not yet told for the camera.

You can see how screenplay format looks from the sample on page 341.

All work that you send out should be accompanied by a stamped, self-addressed envelope (**SASE**). If you fail to provide one, don't expect to receive your manuscript back. For short stories, short plays, and larger poetry submissions, send your work flat in a large manila envelope (with an *identical* one for return). If you are sending only five or six pages of poetry, a half-sized manila envelope that requires folding the manuscript once is sufficient. ("Thin" manuscripts often get bent and wrinkled in the mail; the double thickness stiffens the manuscript at the expense of one clean fold across the middle.) If you send out just a few pages, you can use a standard letter-size envelope and trifold the manuscript neatly.

If you are fortunate, a carefully prepared manuscript sent in an appropriate envelope with an equally appropriate return envelope will survive both the postal system and the perusal of editors. If the manuscript still looks fresh when returned, you can send it out again. If it is beginning to look worn, then it's time to send out a fresh copy. Put yourself in an editor's place.

Phyllis Player   1
The Mouse Bell

<u>FADE</u> <u>IN</u>:

> INT. KITCHEN
>
> AN OLD FASHIONED KITCHEN. We see a MOUSE
> running across the floor as if we were following
> it.   In the distance looms a hole in a baseboard.
> PANTING and CLAWS SCRATCHING.   The hole
> looms larger.
>
> NEW ANGLE
>
> A HUGE PAW starts to descend.   SLOW MOTION.
>
> > > > > CUT TO:
>
> INT. NEST
>
> It's a typical farm mouse's home--sofa, rocking
> chair, end tables, hooked rug.   PAL is watching
> SWEET MOUSE setting out a spread of crackers and
> cheese. Pal is in his twenties, a pleasant but
> weak-looking mouse, the type you think will be
> a loyal friend but never will go far in life.
> Sweet Mouse bustles about the room straightening,
> putting out refreshments and moving things
> around. MEEOW and SHRIEK. Pal stiffens and
> begins to sniff the air.
>
> CLOSE ANGLE ON SWEET
>
> We see her shudder and then gain control.
>
> > > PAL
> > (His voice is trembling)
> > I would have sworn they had let
> > him out for the night.
>
> TWO SHOTS
>
> > > SWEET
> > Do you think it's anyone we know?
>
> She is immediately sorry she said it and begins
> to bustle around as if she hadn't a care in the
> world. Still, she looks at the hole every once
> in a while. Pal gets off the couch and comes
> toward her.
>
> CLOSE ANGLE ON PAL
>
> > > PAL
> > (He is going to put his paws around

and so on

Most editors no longer mind photocopies, as long as they are crisp, clear reproductions. The old distinction between an "original" or "ribbon copy" and a reproduction has been lost to the technology of the word processor, which allows any number of ribbon copies to be prepared effortlessly. Moreover, a manuscript produced with a laser printer is easily confused with a first-rate photocopy.

For most editors, the concern about "simultaneous submissions" (sending to more than one market at the same time) still exists, in spite of the relaxed stance regarding the nature of the manuscript. Don't send a work to more than one place at a time unless you know that the publisher accepts this practice. Even then, you should always let editors know that a work is being considered elsewhere.

Book-length manuscripts should be sent unbound in a cardboard box, the kind of box that holds typing paper.

Cover Letters

Editors have conflicting things to say about the value of accompanying your submission with a cover letter, though all agree that if you send one it should be brief. Essentially, a cover letter is a letter of transmittal: its job is to call attention to the manuscript as briefly and effectively as possible. A few sentences about yourself, a few about the manuscript, and a few about why you have sent it to this particular publication should do the job. Indeed, finding a way of showing your familiarity with the periodical certainly can't hurt. Don't get cute, abrasive, or overly humble.

Here is a sample cover letter accompanying a playscript:

```
                                        return address
                                        date
    addressee

    Dear _____:
            Please consider my play, "West of East," for production
    by Thespian Theatre.  SASE enclosed.
            Thank you for your time and consideration.

                        Sincerely yours,
                        Phyllis Player
```

You may be tempted to try to use the cover letter to "sell" the play, poem, or story. Not only is this tactic a waste of your writing energy, but it will mark you as an amateur. Let your literary or dramatic work sell itself.

Don't send a manuscript out unless you keep a copy in your files. Editors have been known to lose submissions, and the postal service has been known to fail.

A MISCELLANEOUS CHECKLIST

Here are some additional considerations for you when you submit a work to a publisher or producer.

1. Don't be cute or impolite. Manuscripts with clever drawings (not associated with the story), elegant printing (yes, we know you have a word processor), calligraphy, or any of those other efforts to enhance the words by extraneous means will immediately mark you as an amateur.
2. Don't reverse pages to check out whether your manuscript has been read. If your reader does not get far enough to read the reversed pages, they probably don't deserve reading or are not suitable for the publication (or theater). The reader who does get that far will recognize the trick and be insulted.
3. Check your manuscript to see that all the pages are there. Copy machines do hiccup.
4. Make sure the manuscript will fit the SASE.
5. Don't call the editor(s). If you do, they will be sure to send the manuscript back, since they have better things to do than shepherd a Nervous Nelly.
6. Don't follow your submission with a revised manuscript. You should have sent the revision the first time!
7. Don't sit around waiting for the rejection slip or that beautiful letter saying they loved it. Keep writing.

WHAT ABOUT COPYRIGHT?

"Copyright is a form of protection provided by the laws of the United States . . . to the authors of 'original works of authorship' including literary, dramatic, musical, artistic, and certain other intellectual works. This protection is available to both published and unpublished works." *(Copyright Basics,* Library of Congress Copyright Office, Circular R1.)

Here are the important points for any writer to know:

1. Your work is automatically copyrighted when you get it into a fixed form—on paper, a rock, or a computer disk.

2. You cannot copyright an idea for a work.
3. You cannot copyright a title.

The key thing about copyright is that you have to write something before you can claim copyright. And the minute you write it down (even a letter) you have copyrighted it.

If you want to *register* your copyright as evidence of when you wrote a work, request information and a form from the Copyright Office, Library of Congress, Washington, DC 20559. Read the clearly written brochure, fill out the form, send it in with your check, and you are registered.

In any case, copyright is premature for a beginning writer. Get your work out to publishers and forget copyright. You already have it. Get to work on your next piece.

Good luck.

16

❖

Tools and Resources

This chapter lists books, periodicals, and organizations that will be most helpful to the student of creative writing. The lists are organized according to the plan of this book, so you may think of each subdivision as "supplemental reading" for the individual chapters. Brief annotations follow most of the entries.

KEEPING A JOURNAL

Faber Book of Diaries. Simon Brett. Faber & Faber, 1987. Fourteen hundred entries from four centuries of British diaries arranged in one calendar year. Excerpts from John Wesley and Virginia Woolf, for example, could be juxtaposed. A reading pleasure and useful for those who say, "but what should I put in my journal?"

Keeping Your Personal Journal. George F. Simons. Paulist Press, 1978. A slight religious slant doesn't keep this survey of methods from being filled with practical ideas. Fine exercises and examples.

New Diary. Tristine Rainer. Tarcher/St. Martins, 1978. Aimed at "self-guidance and expanded creativity," this guidebook is rooted in Rainer's appreciation of Anaïs Nin's famous diaries and in various schools of psychoanalysis and art.

Our Private Lives: Journals, Notebooks and Diaries. Daniel Halpern. Ecco, 1988. An excellent sampling of modern and contemporary writers' journals as well as journals by prominent people in other fields.

LANGUAGE IS YOUR MEDIUM

Dictionaries, Unabridged

American Heritage Dictionary of the English Language, 3rd ed. Houghton-Mifflin, 1992. Copiously illustrated. Contains reference material on language history as well as maps and usage notes. Thumb indexed. A good buy for a writer on a budget. Abridged version is called the *College Edition*.

Chambers 20th Century Dictionary. Cambridge University Press, 1983. Perhaps the most comprehensive one-volume dictionary available.

Compact Edition of the Oxford English Dictionary. 3 volumes. Oxford University Press, 1986. This small-type version comes with a magnifying glass at a fraction of the price of the standard set. Earlier editions are sometimes available at considerably lower prices. *Note*: some book clubs offer special rates on this and other useful reference works.

Oxford English Dictionary. 16 volumes. Oxford University Press, 1986. Latest edition of the most comprehensive English language dictionary available, though its price puts it far beyond the means of most writers. And who has space to store it? Make sure you find the closest library that holds this treasure. There is nothing better. The *OED* is notable for providing the historical development of words through usage examples. See description of *Compact Edition*.

Random House Dictionary of the English Language, 2nd ed. Random House, 1987.

Dictionaries, Abridged

American Heritage Dictionary, College Edition, 3rd ed. Houghton Mifflin, 1992.

Random House Webster's College Dictionary. Random House, 1991.

Webster's Ninth New Collegiate Dictionary. G. and C. Merriam Company, 1990. The standard for typesetters, proofreaders and copyeditors, this is the latest desk dictionary based on *Webster's Third New International Dictionary*. Includes excellent auxiliary material. While this popular dictionary has many competitors, we see no reason to prefer any of the others.

Dictionaries, Specialized

Concise Oxford Dictionary of English Etymology. Edited by T. F. Hoad. Oxford University Press, 1986. Based on the comprehensive *Oxford Dictionary of English Etymology*, this handy writer's tool provides "succinct accounts of the origin, history, and development in meaning of a great many basic words and a wide selection of derivatives." A useful partner to your standard desktop dictionary.

Dictionary of American Regional English. Frederick G. Cassidy. Harvard University Press, 1985-(in progress). When completed, this will be the standard reference for regional variations in English usage.

Harper Dictionary of Contemporary Usage, 2nd ed. William and Mary Morris. Harper & Row, 1985. This valuable guide to the state of American English provides quick and authoritative opinions on what goes, what doesn't, and what shouldn't.

NTC's American Idioms Dictionary. Richard A. Spears. National Textbook Co., 1987. This delightful phrase finder has an index to key words in idiomatic constructions.

New Dictionary of American Slang, 2nd ed. Edited by Robert L. Chapman. Harper & Row, 1986. A must for the writer of authentic dialogue. A joy for any writer. This collection has a tolerance for the ephemeral and the vulgar far beyond that of standard compilations.

The Penguin Rhyming Dictionary. Rosalind Feguson. Penguin, 1985.

Words to Rhyme With. Willard Espy. Facts on File, 1986. Better than predecessors and paperback rivals, this poet's tool includes 80,000 words that rhyme as well as examples of various forms and meters. Paperback edition 1988.

Thesauri

Right Word: A Concise Thesaurus. Random House, 1978. This paperback thesaurus is alphabetically arranged and based on the *American Heritage Dictionary.*

Roget's International Thesaurus, 5th ed. Revised by Robert L. Chapman. Harper Collins, 1992. Latest update of the standard work. User begins by looking up word and closest meaning in the index, then turning to the main section entry indicated in the index. The main section is organized by broader and then narrow categories of ideas; that is, the largest headings are broad abstractions under which are found more concrete subdivisions and entries. Useful for zeroing in on the word choices needed to sharpen a general idea or impression.

Roget's 21st Century Thesaurus. Barbara Ann Kipfer. Dell, 1992. This thesaurus uses dictionary format and offers a concept index.

Synonym Finder. J. I Rodale. Warner Books, 1986. An easy-to-use synonym list that is arranged in dictionary form rather than in the classic categories established by Roget. Originally published by Rodale Books (last rev. ed. 1978).

INVENTION AND RESEARCH

Reference

Catalog of Catalogs. Edward Palder. Woodbine House, 1987. An annotated list of free (or almost free) catalogs providing information on almost anything. Though this resource-source is not designed for writers, any writer with imagination can take advantage of this clever volume. Alphabetized by category.

Guide to Reference Books, 10th ed. Edited by Eugene P. Sheehy. American Library Association, 1986. The standard source for annotated entries on reference tools.

Knowing Where to Look: The Ultimate Guide to Research. Lois Horowitz. Writer's Digest, 1984. This detailed research handbook includes question-and-answer examples of research procedures. The same author's *Writer's Guide to Research* (Writer's Digest, 1986) is similar and briefer.

New York Public Library Book of How and Where to Look It Up. Sherwood Harris. Prentice Hall, 1991. An alphabetical subject listing that leads to other references, collections, government agencies, and foundations.

New York Times Guide to Reference Materials. Edited by Mona McCormick. Times Books, 1985. One of the more efficient guides to other reference books, this volume has a valuable discussion of research strategy.

Writer's Resource Guide: A One-Volume Directory of Sources of Information on Practically Any Subject, 2nd ed. Edited by Bernadine Clard. Writer's Digest, 1983. Perhaps more useful to the creative writer than the more standard tools of this type. Includes associations, government agencies, titles and addresses of contact persons.

Facts

Encyclopedia of American Facts and Dates. Edited by Gorton Carruth. Harper & Row, 1987. The ultimate resource for American history trivia, but also a quick way to check the facts alluded to in your historical novel. Organized in chronological columns with categories that include politics, the arts, business, religion, sports, fashion, and folkways. Wonderful suggestions for building "period" scenes and settings. (Aug. 6, 1890. The first electrocution took place at Auburn Prison, Auburn, NY)

Facts on File Yearbook. Facts on File, published annually. Product of the Facts on File news reference service that summarizes, records, and indexes each week's news from major news sources. 52 weekly news digests plus annual index. It's all here. Begun in 1941.

Information Please Almanac. Houghton Mifflin, published annually. This "Atlas and Yearbook" covers a wide range of old and new information under scores of headings including awards, disasters, media, travel, weather and climate. "Countries of the World" section useful for thumbnail sketches of history, geography, politics, demography, and so on.

The New York Public Library Desk Reference. Prentice Hall, 1989. An astonishing one-volume fact resource in twenty-four categories ranging from weights and measures to the arts to health care.

People's Almanac. David Wallechinsky and Irving Wallace. Doubleday, 1975. Later versions by Morrow in hardback and Bantam in paper. Number 3 published in 1981. The best browsing book for idea and fact stimulation. Inspirations for countless creative projects here. A spin-off publication by the same authors plus Amy Wallace is *The Books of Lists.* Morrow/Bantam, #3, 1983.

World Almanac and Book of Facts. Newspaper Enterprises Association, published annually (since 1868). More list oriented than its *Information Please* rival. Similar coverage. Comprehensive index up front.

Quotations

Bartlett's Familiar Quotations, 16th ed. Edited by John Bartlett and Justin Kaplan. Little, Brown, 1992. The classic of quotation books, and well deserving of its reputation. Reasonably priced even in hardback edition. A must for every writer's desktop reference collection. More than 22,500 quotations.

Concise Oxford Dictionary of Quotations. Oxford University Press, 1981. A powerful resource drawn from the larger *Oxford Dictionary of Quotations.* Handy and inexpensive in paperback.

Facts on File Dictionary of Proverbs. Rosiland Fergusson. Facts on File, 1985. Over 7,000 entries. Not only a handy compilation, but entertaining, too.

What They Said. Alan F. Pater and Jason R. Pater. Monitor, published annually. Subtitled "The Yearbook of World Opinion," this reference tool is organized by categories. Representative topics are the military, social welfare, literature, science and technology, and sports.

WRITING POETRY

45 Contemporary Poets. Alberta Turner. Longman, 1985. Each poet responds to a series of questions about the genesis and development of a particular poem. A good survey of poets' writing habits. Many poems are shown in various drafts. Turner's stress on *process* is of great value, and the range of styles and ways of talking about poetry will allow any reader to find congenial suggestions.

Hunting the Snark: A Compendium of New Poetic Terminology. Robert Peters. Paragon House, 1989. This delightful mock dictionary reviews the fashions and follies of contemporary American poetry. High-spirited advice and warnings for readers and writers.

On Being a Poet. Judson Jerome. Writer's Digest Books, 1984. While matters of craft are treated, Jerome is particularly concerned with the calling of poetry in both individual and societal terms. He describes the indispensible features of the poet's personality and the ways in which audiences can be reached. Largely a book about the attitudes and experiences of one who chooses to be a poet.

Patterns of Poetry: An Encyclopedia of Forms. Miller Williams. Louisiana State University Press, 1986. An enchanting and stimulating reference work that will provide the apprentice poet and the experienced one with many new ideas, challenges, and tools.

Poet's Craft. William Packard. Paragon House, 1987. Interviews with major poets from *New York Quarterly.* Updates Packard's earlier collection, *The Craft of Poetry* (1974). Intriguing representations of contemporary poetic thought and practice.

Poetic Meter and Poetic Form, rev. ed. Paul Fussell. Random House, 1979. The very best discussion of the ways in which form communicates. Though not written for writers, every poet should be thoroughly familiar with this book. Relatively sketchy on free verse, Fussell's treatment of the older conventions is unparalleled.

The Practice of Poetry. Robin Behn and Chase Twitchell. HarperCollins, 1993. A collection of exercises gathered from master poet-teachers that covers everything from inspiration to form to revision.

Rhyme's Reason, rev. ed. John Hollander. Yale University Press, 1989. A witty, engaging, and most competent review of poetic conventions. The book contains many poems written by Hollander to illustrate his definitions.

To Make a Poem. Alberta Turner. Longman, 1982. The strength of this book is in Turner's ability to stimulate the writer's imagination through exercises, examples, and discussion. She is best at helping writers generate the raw material for poems, less useful at showing how to shape and polish that material. "Freeing the Felt Idea," the title of her second chapter, is indicative of her approach.

Writing Poems, 3rd ed. Robert Wallace. HarperCollins, 1991. Copiously illustrated and very thorough on all aspects of poetic conventions, elements, and approaches to composition. A useful chapter on submitting poetry for publication. Always solid, rarely inspiring.

Writing Poetry. Barbara Drake. Harcourt Brace Jovanovich, 1983. A good mix of prescriptions, examples, and exercises, Drake's book moves from sources (memory, lists, observation) through kinds of poems, means of revision, and some key elements of poetry. Solid treatment of voice and tone.

WRITING FICTION

The Art of Fiction: Notes on Craft for Young Writers. John Gardner. Knopf, 1984. Reprint Vintage, 1991. An excellent craft book, but with a valuable theoretical underpinning.

Aspects of the Novel. E. M. Forster. Harcourt Brace Jovanovich, 1985. Reissue of 1927 classic based on Forster's Cambridge University lectures. Designed for readers rather than writers, but still an essential exploration of how fiction works.

Creating Short Fiction. Damon Knight. Writer's Digest, 1985. Oriented around exercises. Deals with discovering and correcting weaknesses.

Making Shapely Fiction. Jerome Stern. Norton, 1991. Fascinating, conversational cook's tour of the possibilities and hazards of prose fiction. Always practical and always engaging.

On Becoming a Novelist. John Gardner. Harper & Row, 1983. Focuses on a writer's nature, education, and habits of mind. Not a craft book (thus unlike his *The Art of Fiction*), but an effective discussion of writerly attitudes.

On Writing the Short Story. Hallie Burnett. Harper & Row, 1983. A classic in the field.

The Passionate, Accurate Story. Carol Bly. Milkwee Editions, 1990. One of the most readable discussions, with important suggestions on how the successful writer must approach first drafts differently from later drafts.

Technique in Fiction, 2nd ed. Robie Macauley and George Lanning. St. Martin's, 1987. This major revision of the 1964 classic is thorough, clear, and well illustrated. The chapter on "Narrative Style: Time and Pace in Fiction" provides excellent coverage of material we have had no room to include. An expert enumeration of problems and how to avoid them, with examples from published work.

Writing a Novel. John Braine. McGraw-Hill, 1975. Highly personalized and anecdotal, much of Braine's advice won't fit the working needs of other writers. Still, attractively written and not to be ignored.

Writing Fiction, 2nd ed. R. V. Cassill. Prentice-Hall, 1975. A classic by one of the foremost teachers of creative writing, this book has sage, succinct advice but little technical detail and almost no exercises.

Writing Fiction: A Guide to Narrative Craft, 3rd ed. Janet Burroway. HarperCollins, 1992. Conceptually rich and generous treatment. Copious examples, including student work. Good on underscoring the many ways in which fiction is *not* like life.

Writing the Novel: From Plot to Print. Lawrence Block. Writer's Digest, 1985. Organized around the kinds of questions beginning novelists ask. Good notes on researching and marketing, as well as aspects of craft.

WRITING PLAYS

Art of Dramatic Writing. Lajos Egri. Simon & Schuster, 1960. This classic text works from character out to the other elements of drama. Explorations of characters' natures, motives, and relationships lead to the focusing of conflicts on which to build plays. Useful for fiction as well.

Art of Screenwriting. William Packard. Paragon House, 1987. Not only screenplay techniques, but also fundamental aspects of plotting and storytelling are covered. Includes a handy "Screenplay Format Glossary" that is illustrated with an actual screenplay.

Complete Book of Scriptwriting. J. Michael Straczynski. Writer's Digest, 1982. Covers radio, film and theater with discussions of both the mechanics and the marketing of dramatic scripts.

How to Write a Play. Raymond Hull. Writer's Digest, 1983. Useful for its practice exercises and its concern with what is, in fact, performable.

Playwriting: How to Write for the Theatre. Bernard Grebanier. Harper & Row, 1979. A comprehensive step-by-step guide that includes exercises. Includes material on one-act plays and writing for television.

The Screenwriter's Workbook. Syd Field. Dell, 1984. This master teacher of screenwriting provides practical exercises and clear, systematic instruction for getting the job done.

Script into Performance: A Structuralist Approach. Richard Hornby. Paragon House, 1987. Reprint of 1979 edition. Useful on the relationship between the playwright's art and the work of the director.

Writing Your First Play. Roger A. Hall. Focal Press, 1991. Exercises in action, dialogue, character, and conflict lead to the shaping of a brief three- or four-character play.

ADDITIONAL TEXTS ON CREATIVE WRITING

The College Handbook of Creative Writing. Robert DeMaria. Harcourt Brace Jovanovich, 1991. A handy guide, with number/letter codes for various issues as in your freshman composition text.

Three Genres, 5th ed. Stephen Minot. Prentice Hall, 1993. Like the present volume, an attempt to cover all areas. Insightful throughout, Minot does not provide as many exercises.

Working Words: The Process of Creative Writing. Wendy Bishop. Mayfield, 1992. A powerful mix of suggestions, exercises, and readings that stresses the interrelatedness of the reading and writing processes and the shared concerns of all good writing. Our second favorite textbook.

The Writer's Handbook. Sylvia K. Burack. The Writer, 1993. Comprehensive compendium of writing tips (in the form of short essays by various hands), marketing advice, and market lists covering all major genres and subgenres.

A Writer's Time: A Guide to the Creative Process, from Vision Through Revision. Kenneth Atchity. Norton, 1986. An excellent application of time management principles for writers. Overcoming writer's anxieties, exploiting dreamwork, and working toward economies of effort are key issues.

Writing Down the Bones. Natalie Goldberg. Shambhala, 1986. Focused on freeing imagination and creativity. Not a craft or technique book, but a discussion of how to tap inner resources.

Writing in a Convertible with the Top Down. Christi Killien and Sheila Bender. Warner Books, 1992. Shaped as correspondence, this lively discussion of the creative writing process stresses getting started, keeping going, and making your writing vivid.

Writing with a Word Processor. William Zinsser. Harper & Row, 1983. The author of *Writing Well*, an excellent book on personal style, examines the impact of word processing on writing. Zinsser provides ways to use the new technology to improve your writing.

FROM REVISION TO SUBMISSION

Revising Fiction: A Handbook for Writers. David Madden. Penguin/Plume, 1988. Contains 185 questions against which to measure your story or novel draft. Concrete illustrated suggestions for finding flaws and making improvements.

Chicago Manual of Style. University of Chicago Press, revised regularly (use most recent edition). This is the standard manual for manuscript form. Conventions for capitalization, hyphenation, and anything else you can think of are found here.

Marketing and General Market Lists

Directory of Literary Magazines. Moyer Bell Limited. Prepared annually by the Council of Literary Magazines and Presses. Promotes member publications. Offers pertinent data on editorial requirements.

The Indispensable Writer's Guide. Scott Edelstein. Harper & Row, 1989. More elaborate than *Lit Biz 101*, this one puts greater emphasis on free-lance work and writing for hire. Both are useful on finding homes for your work, negotiating contracts, developing proposals.

International Directory of Little Magazines and Small Presses. Dustbooks, published annually. If you get no other market directory, get this one. It is the bible for marketing literary writing, though it excludes the commercial presses and periodicals that few beginning writers can hope to find space in. Of course, you know about these already: they're on every magazine stand.

International Literary Market Place. Bowker, published annually. Comprehensive list of book-related business and organizations including publishers, distributors, agents, libraries, and associations. Expanded version of *Literary Market Place* at slightly higher price.

Lit Biz 101: How to Get Happily, Successfully Published. Dell, 1988. Despite his over-reaching title, Mungo gives sound advice on what to do once you have the finished manuscript.

Literary Market Place: The Directory of American Book Publishing. Bowker, published annually. Detailed lists of publishers, distributors, agents, prizes, journals, printers, designers, associations—just about anything connected with publishing. Good on contact persons. Presented more from the publisher's perspective than from the writer's. Useful tool for those who can afford it or get a nearby library to purchase it.

Writer's Market: Where and How to Sell What You Write. Mark Kissling. Writer's Digest, published annually. Thorough coverage of the paying markets in all genres, but not as useful for the beginner or noncommercial writer as Dustbooks' *International Directory.* Includes information on greeting card companies and syndication publishers as well as the usual outlets for creative writing. Over 4,000 entries in 1992–93 edition. Some writers' profiles are included.

Markets, Poetry

Directory of Poetry Publishers. Len Fulton and Ellen Ferber. Dustbooks, published annually. A subset of Fulton's remarkable *International Directory of Little Magazines and Small Presses*, this volume is well indexed and has detailed information on each of the listed markets. Gives data on submission policies, rights purchased, and so on.

Poet's Market: Where and How to Publish Your Poetry. Michael Begeja and Christine Martin. Writer's Digest, published annually. Formerly prepared by Judson Jerome. Lists 1,700 poetry publishers with information about publishers' needs, audience, remuneration, and so forth.

Poet's Marketplace: The Definitive Sourcebook on Where to Get Your Poems Published. John Kelly. Running Press, 1985. Submission guidelines for both periodicals and book publishers. Also includes information on grants, contests, and organizations for poets.

Markets, Fiction

Novel & Short Story Writer's Market. Robin Gee. Writer's Digest, published annually (replaces *Fiction Writer's Market*). The latest edition contains 1,900 listings of magazines and book publishers hospitable to fiction. Articles on fiction writing as well as interviews with editors and authors are also included.

Writer's Guide to Magazine Markets: Fiction. Karen Krieger and Helen R. Freedman. Plume/New American Library, 1983.

Markets, Plays

Dramatist's Bible. International Society of Dramatists, published annually. Script requirements and submission procedures of theaters and other producing organizations in the English-speaking world. Complete and essential.

Dramatist's Sourcebook. M. Elizabeth Osborn. Theatre Communications Group, annual. Where to send scripts for prize competitions, production, and publication. The latest volume includes material on adaptation as well as information about fellowships, residencies, and service organizations.

GLOSSARIES

A Handbook to Literature, 4th ed. C. Hugh Holman. Bobbs-Merrill, 1980. One of the clearest and most complete handbooks of literary terms. This book, or something like it, should be in any writer's library.

The Concise Oxford Dictionary of Literary Terms. Chris Baldick. Oxford University Press, 1990. A fine reference, especially good on the terminology associated with modern literary theory.

PERIODICALS

AWP Newsletter. Associated Writing Programs. Old Dominion University, Norfolk, VA 23508. Articles and information for writers. Published four times a year. One or two solid pieces per issue, especially on the teaching of creative writing.

Poets & Writers Magazine. 201 W. 54th Street, New York, NY 10019. This is the flagship publication of Poets & Writers, Inc. (see Organizations section). Published six times a year, this is our favorite way of keeping up with what's going on in the literary community. Highlights include provocative interviews and reports on regional literary activity. Articles are not craft oriented, but nonetheless valuable to any writer. Good market information on small and university press needs.

Small Press Review. Dustbooks. P.O. Box EE, Paradise, CA 95969. This monthly effort of the Dustbooks family includes news about small presses, notices from presses and magazines soliciting material, and reviews of small press books. A good way to find a sympathetic reading for your first book.

Writer. 120 Boylston Street, Boston, MA 02116. This monthly magazine features advice columns on craft and marketing in the various genres as well as updated market news.

Writers Digest. 205 West Center Street, Marion, OH 43305. Content similar to *The Writer*, but this one has, in recent years, given readers more for their money. The status of contributors continues to be impressive. Published monthly.

ORGANIZATIONS

What follows is a small sampling of the many national, regional, and local literary arts organizations. Your state arts council should be able to help you find a group in your area.

Associated Writing Programs. Old Dominion University. Norfolk, VA 23508. (804) 440-3839. AWP is an umbrella organization serving undergraduate and graduate creative writing programs, their faculties, and their students. One can be a member through affiliation with a member institution or as an individual. AWP holds an annual meeting at which sessions are conducted on various aspects of creative writing and pedagogy. The organization runs a placement service for writers; publishes award series in poetry, short fiction, the novel, and creative nonfiction; and updates regularly its *Official Guide to Writing Programs*, the best guide for anyone seeking to enter a creative writing degree program. This reference also offers information on conferences, colonies, and writers' centers. See also the *AWP Newsletter* in Periodicals section.

Poets & Writers Inc. 201 W. 54th Street, New York, NY 10019. (212) 757-1766. A full-scale service organization for writers and the literary community, Poets & Writers is primarily an information source. Its various publications include pamphlets on copyright, lists of organizations that sponsor readings, and the invaluable *Directory of American Poets and Fiction Writers*, which is updated regularly. The *Directory* lists qualified (published) writers along with their key publications and special interests, thereby making available to prospective employers or hosts a comprehensive list of writers whose credentials have undergone some degree of screening. The *Directory* is arranged by state and indexed. Listed writers receive publication discounts. See also *Poets & Writers Magazine* in Periodicals section.

Beyond Baroque Literary/Arts Center, 681 Venice Boulevard, Venice, CA 90291. (310) 822-3006.

Just Buffalo, 111 Elmwood Avenue, Buffalo, NY 14201. (716) 885-6400.

Lane Literary Guild, Lane Regional Arts Council, 411 High Street, Eugene, OR 97401. (503) 485-2278.

The Literary Center, Box 85116, Seattle, WA 98145-1116.

The Loft, Pratt Community Center, 66 Malcolm Avenue S.E., Minneapolis, MN 55414. (612) 379-8999.

Maine Writers and Publishers Alliance, 12 Pleasant Street, Brunswick, ME 04011. (207) 729-6333.

North Carolina Writers' Network, P.O. Box 954, Carrboro, NC 27510. (919) 967-9540.

PEN American Center, 568 Broadway, New York, NY 10012. (212) 334-1660.

The Poetry Project, St. Mark's Church in the Bowery, 10th Street and 2nd Avenue, New York, NY 10003. (212) 674-0910.

The Poetry Society of America, 15 Gramercy Park South, New York, NY 10003. (212) 254-9628.

The Thurber House, 77 Jefferson Avenue, Columbus, OH 43215. (614) 464-1082.

The Unterberg Poetry Center, The 92nd Street Y, 1395 Lexington Avenue, New York, NY 10128. (212) 996-1100.

Walt Whitman International Poetry Center, 2nd and Cooper Streets, Camden, NJ 08102. (609) 757-7276.

Woodland Pattern Book Center, P.O. Box 92081, 720 East Locust Street, Milwaukee, WI 53212. (414) 263-5001.

Writers and Books, 740 University Avenue, Rochester, NY 14607. (716) 473-2590.

The Writer's Center, 4508 Walsh Street, Bethesda, MD 20815. (301) 654-8664.

Glossary of Key Terms

ABSTRACT: Language is abstract when it refers to intangible attributes or qualities—love, freedom, ideas. Abstract does not point to the material, physical bases of experience. Abstractions appeal to the intellect rather than to the senses. See **concrete.**

ACCENT: In poetry, equivalent to *stress*. Accent occurs when a syllable receives greater emphasis in pronunciation than those around it.

ACCENTUAL-SYLLABIC VERSE: Equivalent to *metrical verse*. Poetic lines based on counting units that in themselves systematically alternate stressed and unstressed syllables. See **meter.**

ACCENTUAL VERSE: Verse in which lines are defined by the number of stressed syllables, as in "iambic pentameter." See **meter.**

ACT: Major unit of a play containing a major division of the dramatic action. Acts are often marked by intermissions or a lowering of the curtain. Act divisions punctuate the emotional or logical development of the play. See **scene.**

ACTION: "What happens" in a literary or dramatic work. The events that constitute the **plot.**

ALLITERATION: Proximate repetition of identical consonant sounds at the beginning of words or emphasized syllables. Use with great care to avoid unintentionally comic effects and to avoid calling so much attention to the sound that the sense becomes submerged in the lilting lyrical lullabies of labial liquidities.

ALLUSION: **Figure of speech** making an implied reference to something, real or fictitious, outside of the work. Effective allusions bring useful associations to the reader's mind. "She didn't exactly have his head brought in on a platter, but she might as well have," evokes in a short space a complex story from the Bible.

AMBIGUITY: In a word, passage, or complete text, ambiguity allows for multiple interpretations, none of which is allowed to prevail over the others. *Unintentional* ambiguity can result in confusion and distraction because the meaning is merely obscure. Purposeful ambiguity allows one meaning to enrich another or all plausible meanings to complicate an issue or observation. Ambiguity should arise because the subject and emotions are complex, not because the writer has failed to think deeply about the subject or express it well.

ANALOGY: Comparison, often figurative, that explains or describes an unfamiliar object or idea through characteristics it shares with a more familiar object or idea. "A dictator is like the captain of a ship who thinks his crew has no other purpose than to obey his commands."

ANAPEST: See **meter**.

ANAPHORA: Repetition of a word or phrase at the beginning of successive lines.

ANTAGONIST: Character representing an obstacle or blocking force to the **protagonist** or hero. Often the rival or adversary of the protagonist. Satan to God in *Paradise Lost*.

ANTICLIMAX: Sudden drop in dramatic tension or seriousness in a fiction or drama. Usually a falling off after the **climax**, allowing for a serene concluding note. Sometimes an unintentional failure to sustain interest, relevance, or power. It usually occurs because the writer wants to spell out what happened, leaving nothing to the reader's or viewer's imagination.

ARCHAIC: Diction that is filled with obsolete words or word usage: "yore," "go thee hence." Archaisms in contemporary poetry are rarely tolerated, since they most often suggest the wish to receive unearned poetic status by a liberal sprinkling of terms and phrases from revered works of the past. Archaisms can be used successfully for special purposes, such as to capture the flavor of the past in a historical or fantasy narrative.

ARCHETYPE: Psychic strain or pattern, believed to be universal and stored in the unconscious mind, based on the typical experiences of humankind. An image, plot element, character type, or descriptive detail can be archetypal. These primordial patterns are found in dreams, fantasies, and folklore as well as in conscious artworks. See also **myth**.

ASSONANCE: Repetition of identical or similar vowel sounds in close proximity, as in "f*e*tch the m*e*ssage."

ATMOSPHERE: Figuratively, the "air" or essential **mood** of a literary work: creepy, peaceful, gloomy, cheery. Related to the less tangible aspects of **setting.**

AWKWARD: The stylistic mistake without a better name. A clumsy relation of **diction** or **syntax**.

BALLAD STANZA: Popular quatrain in folk songs and poetry, in which the first and third lines are iambic tetrameter and the second and fourth iambic trimeter. The usual rhyme scheme is *abcb*.

BATHOS: Insincere or excessive **pathos**; a falling away from the sublime to the ridiculous or from the elevated to the banal or commonplace. Also, a miscalculation in which intended elevation is not attained.

BEAT: Working unit of dialogue in which a shift in the emotional dynamic between characters occurs.

BLANK VERSE: Unrhymed iambic pentameter. See **meter.**

CAESURA: Pause, usually punctuated, *within* a line of verse.

CATASTROPHE: See **denouement.**

CHARACTER: Imagined personage in a literary or dramatic work.

CHARACTERIZATION: Means used to create a **character**. Includes what the character says and does as well as what the narrator or another character is given to say (or think) about the character. Presentation of a character's thoughts, fancies, and dreams are also means of characterization.

CHRONOLOGY: Relating of facts or events in the order of their occurrence. The temporal order of events, as distinguished from their rearrangement in memory or in a **plot.**

CLICHÉ: Stale phrase, usually figurative, that reveals the writer's unwillingness to work hard for something fresh. Such borrowed formulas of expression as "it takes two to tango" have lost their original strength through overuse (and even misuse). See also **dead metaphor.**

CLIMAX: Moment of greatest tension in a dramatic or narrative work; it is most often also the major turning point. The moment at which the reader or audience is moved to its highest pitch of excitement. See **crisis.**

CONCEIT: Particularly elaborate or striking **figure of speech**. Usually characterized by its quality of wit or intellectual sophistication.

CONCRETE: Concrete diction points to particulars, and most often to material objects, their qualities, and their motions. The concrete fastens upon palpable experience. See **abstract.**

CONFIDANT(E): In drama, a character designed to receive the confidences of another (major) character. This device allows the pressured character to unburden his or her feelings, thoughts, and secrets—which now also reach the eavesdropping audience. Though to the same end, this device is thought to be more natural than the **soliloquy.**

CONFLICT: Actions and tensions resulting from opposing forces set loose in a **plot.** These forces may be external or internal. For example: Jill and Beth want the same man. Arthur is torn between honor and greed. The shipmates pit themselves against the storm.

CONNOTATION: Suggestions or associations provoked by a word. Though connotations are subjective, totally private ones cannot be communicated. Even though you may associate "pain" with ice cream on a hot day, it is unlikely your reader will. It is because of connotation that there are no synonyms. If "rug" and "carpet" mean the same thing (see your dictionary), how come no one advertises "wall-to-wall rugging"? Contrast with **denotation.**

CONSONANCE: Loosely, the echoing of terminal consonants in end words. More narrowly, a kind of *slant* **rhyme** in which patterns of consonants surround contrasting vowels: *blood/blade.*

CONVENTION: Literary or dramatic convention is any recognized and accepted means of expression within a particular form—or the form itself. When we speak of *convention,* we are usually addressing those features or devices that are particularly unrealistic: for example, Shakespeare's characters speaking in **blank verse,** or a first-person narrator remembering a conversation word for word that happened twenty years before. The public's acceptance and expectation is what matters here. Often, conventions embody "rules": the conventions of the **sonnet,** of the well-made play, of indicating a change of speakers (in fiction dialogue) by beginning a new paragraph. The language system itself is a body of conventions dealing with how words and phrases may be related, spelled, and punctuated. Informational and artistic communication depends on the conventions shared by artist and audience, writer and reader.

CONVENTIONAL: According to **convention.** Sometimes used pejoratively to suggest a lack of inventiveness, but most often meaning the tried and true way of doing something.

COUPLET: In poetry, a two-line unit of composition (sometimes a **stanza**). Couplet lines are usually matched in length, meter, and rhyme.

CRISIS: See **climax.** That moment after which things must change for better or worse.

DACTYL: See **meter.**

DEAD METAPHOR: Overworked **metaphor** that has lost its figurative vividness and its image content. When we say "the constitution is the *bulwark* of the nation," we are using a dead metaphor because the meaning is now merely denotative. What was once concrete is in the process of becoming an abstraction. We no longer envision a wall or the side of a ship in a battle scene. A dead metaphor is often a **cliché.**

DENOTATION: Direct, specific meaning. Often called the "dictionary" meaning of a word, in contrast with **connotation.**

DENOUEMENT: Outcome of a dramatic work; the trailing or falling action that follows the climax and ties up loose ends. In tragic plays, the denouement is called the **catastrophe.**

DESIGNATOR: See **dialogue tag.**

DEUS EX MACHINA: Literally, a god out of a machine. The abrupt and improbable appearance of a solution to a problem. The use of such devices (as a miracle cure that saves the young wife because the story must end happily) almost always reveals a deficiency in plotting.

DIALECT: Regional or cultural variation (in pronunciation, **idiom,** grammar, or **syntax**) within a language: for example, the Yorkshire dialect in England or the Cajun dialect in Louisiana.

DIALOGUE: Representation of speech in a literary or dramatic work. More strictly, the representation of conversation between two or more characters.

DIALOGUE TAG: In fiction dialogue, the terminology that identifies the speaker and (sometimes) describes the tone of the speech. For example, "William said," "she screamed," "Jim answered haughtily." Avoid the excessive and unnecessary, as in the last two.

DICTION: Refers to the choice of words in a particular work. Writers must consider the aptness of their word choices to the occasion. Conventionally, there are four levels of diction: formal, informal, colloquial, and slang. We have argued that diction should be accurate, precise, concrete, appropriate, and idiomatic. How words are characteristically chosen and combined by an author constitutes that author's **style.**

DONNÉE: Literally, "the given," the raw material—**premise, character, theme, setting,** or idea—on which the writer works toward the development of the finished work. Also, the assumption, not necessarily made explicit, out of which the work develops.

DRAFT: Unless prefaced by "final," an early version or state of a work in progress. The preliminary work, in writing, that will be revised and edited into the completed and "finished" work. As a verb: to compose; to write tentatively; to explore in writing without stopping for refinements.

DRAMATIC MONOLOGUE: In poetry, a speech by a single character, usually to an implied listener or audience, that reveals the speaker's personality. The speaker is an imagined character, clearly distinguished from the poet.

DRAMATIS PERSONAE: Characters in a drama, usually as listed and described in the bill or program for a performance and in the printed version of the play.

DRAMATIZE: To create a **drama.** In **fiction,** to render a scene in detail, stressing what the characters are saying and doing. *Showing* in contrast to *telling* or *summarizing.*

EDIT: To refine a piece of writing by (1) bringing it into conformity with accepted standards **(conventions)** of usage and genre, and (2) making adjustments of the relationships between parts. See **revise.**

ELEGANT VARIATION: Comes from fear of repetition and often results in elaborate searches for another word when the best choice has already been made. Usually, the attempt is to impress the reader with the range of one's vocabulary rather than to communicate. "Scribe" or "maker" for "author."

END RHYME: **Rhyme** that occurs at the end of lines.

END-STOPPED LINES: Lines that terminate with some degree of grammatical completeness and with punctuation, causing a definite pause or break when read aloud or "heard" silently.

ENJAMBEMENT: Also, *ejambment* and **run-on** line. No pause at the end of a line. The grammatical structure (and sense) "runs on" from one line to the next.

EPIPHANY: Sudden insight or moment of illumination in which an important truth is understood by a character (or, additionally, by the reader). Often, the epiphany is the climactic moment of a short story.

EPISTOLARY: Poem that takes the form and tone of a letter. It is a cousin of the **dramatic monologue.** An epistolary novel is one in which the narrative is developed through an exchange of letters between characters.

EUPHONY: Pleasant combination of sounds.

EXPOSITION: Explanation. Presentation (by the narrator in fiction, through dialogue in drama) of essential information, especially what has happened prior to the ongoing present of the literary or dramatic work.

FABLE: Brief **narrative,** in prose or verse, composed to make a moral point. Fables often involve improbable or supernatural events and sometimes use animals as characters.

FARCE: In drama, a low form of comedy that depends on fast-paced, surprising twists of plot, physical frenzy, and misunderstandings. Farce aims at broad, unsubtle effects.

FICTION: Imagined happenings presented in the guise of history or biography—thus **narrative**—and usually in prose. The two principal types of fiction are the novel and the short story.

FIGURES OF SPEECH (FIGURATIVE LANGUAGE): Expressing one thing in terms of something else. Figurative language exploits words for more than their literal meanings. Major figures of speech include **metaphor, simile, personification,** and **allusion.**

FIXED FORM: Poem whose structure is defined by a set pattern of meter, rhyme, and sometimes repetition of line or phrase. The **sonnet, villanelle,** sestina, rondeau, triolet, and limerick are among the more popular fixed forms.

FLASHBACK: **Scene** that interrupts ongoing action with prior action, usually triggered by a present event that jogs a character's memory.

FOIL: A **character,** set in similar circumstances to the **protagonist,** whose nature or behavior is in sharp contrast to that of the protagonist. Thus a foil is used to **characterize** the primary personage.

FOOT: In metrical poetry, a unit combining stressed and unstressed syllables in a set pattern. See **meter. Lines** are measured by the number of feet they contain.

FORESHADOWING: Manipulation of events and access to information so as to anticipate, without predicting, future events. Frequently the reader does not know that something has been foreshadowed until the events themselves happen. Foreshadowing is one way of creating **verisimilitude. Mood** is often used to foreshadow.

FORM: See **genre.** Also, the arrangement of component parts in a literary or dramatic work so as to ensure unity and coherence.

FORMAL: Following established custom, usage, or **convention.** Respecting decorums, especially of ceremonial occasions. Following the principles of the literary or dramatic type. In **diction,** serious or dignified.

FORMAT: General structure or plan; more specifically, the conventions of manuscript presentation or the layout of a page or book: the typographical design.

FREE VERSE: Lines that follow no fixed metrical pattern, though they are often loosely rhythmical. Free verse often employs parallel grammatical phrasing, verbal repetition, and typographical patterning as means of expression.

GENRE: Literary kind, species, or form. Each genre is defined and recognized by its **conventions. Novel, short story, poem,** and **play** are all such categories, as are subdivisions such as **sonnet** and **farce.**

HERO: Major character around whom the events occur. Loosely, a character held up for emulation because of his or her superior traits. See **protagonist.**

HEROIC COUPLET: Iambic pentameter rhymed **couplets.**

HYPERBOLE: **Figure of speech** in which exaggeration is used to make a point. Calling a prose style "hyperbolic" is usually a negative comment.

IAMB: See **meter.**

IDIOM: Particular usage peculiar to a language (or to a subgroup of a language) whose meaning does not logically grow out of the meanings of its parts. For example, when we say "the kettle is boiling," we are using an idiom we understand but that would not translate literally into another language. Indeed, the kettle is *not* boiling, though the water is. Most idioms have their roots in **metaphor.**

IDIOMATIC: Usage in accord with an **idiom.** Natural, vernacular, a normal expression of native speakers that may violate the school rules of the language. Write idiomatically.

IMAGE: **Concrete** representation of sensory reality. Thing or quality that can be experienced by one or more of the senses.

IMAGERY: Collective character of the **images** in a particular work: its sensory content and the suggestive nature of that content.

INDIRECT DISCOURSE: Paraphrase of dialogue without actually quoting.

IN MEDIAS RES: "In the middle of things." The strategy of beginning a literary or dramatic work in the midst of the action rather than at the beginning of the chronological sequence. See **point of attack.**

INTERIOR MONOLOGUE: Expression of a flow of thoughts through the mind of a single character, usually limited to a single event or occasion. A reproduction of interior experience. See also **stream of consciousness.**

INTERNAL RHYME: **Rhyme** words occurring *within* consecutive or proximate lines, rather than at the beginning (head rhyme) or at the end **(end rhyme).**

IRONY: Most forms of irony involve a contradiction (often only apparent) for what is at first taken to be true and then is discovered to be otherwise. *Verbal irony* contrasts statement and suggestion: Hemingway has Jake say "Isn't it pretty to think so," at the end of *The Sun Also Rises,* but it's really rather painful to think so. This form of irony fades into **sarcasm.** *Dramatic irony* involves a situation in which the truth is the tragic opposite of what the characters think it is, and the audience knows this truth before the character does. It is thought to be ironic when fate or luck pushes someone's life in an unexpected, undeserved direction *(cosmic irony).* Irony always involves an incongruity of some sort. It can be comic or tragic. Swift's *Modest Proposal* is ironic: his real intention is to make it clear that the English landlords are already, in effect, eating Irish children. The apparent prescription for a problem is really a description of the problem.

LINE: Unit of composition in poetry. Line as an expressive concern is one of the few absolute distinctions between poetry and prose.

LINE BREAK: Convention of how lines end in a particular poem or how a particular line ends. Line breaks may coincide with or counterpoint sense and syntax. They may be preset or unpredictable. They may or may not be reinforced by repeated sounds.

LITERAL: **Denotative,** without **figurative** suggestion or embellishment. "Jane looks like Mary" is a literal comparison; "Jane looks like a goddess" is figurative (a **simile**). In translation, a capturing of the exact meaning of the original: "Word for word."

LYRIC: Poem, usually brief, expressing subjective reality. Most often cast in the **first person,** lyric poetry is called the poetry of emotion.

MASK: See **persona.**

MEASURE: See **meter.**

MELODRAMA: Form of **drama** in which sensational incident and audience thrills dominate over characterization. Melodrama disdains probability and **motivation** while insisting on cheaply won justice for one-dimensional heroes, heroines, and villains. Thus, *melodramatic* is often used as a pejorative term.

METAPHOR: **Figure of speech** that depends on an unexpected area of likeness between two unlike things which are said to be identical. Metaphors tend to be literally impossible assertions: "The moon is a gold doubloon."

METER: In poetry, the recurrence of a pattern of syllables **(syllabic verse),** stressed syllables **(accentual verse),** or feet **(accentual-syllabic verse).** Most often used to describe the latter, in which **lines** are defined by type and number of feet. There are four basic feet in English meter. The **iamb** is an unstressed syllable followed by a stressed (˘/), the **trochee** is a stressed syllable followed by an unstressed (/˘), the **anapest** is two unstressed syllables followed by a stressed (˘˘/), and the **dactyl** is one stressed syllable followed by two unstressed (/˘˘). Two other feet are used only for variation within lines. These are the **pyrrhic,** of two unstressed syllables (˘˘), and the **spondee,** of two stressed syllables (//). Line length is labeled as follows: monometer, dimeter, trimeter, tetrameter, pentameter, hexameter, and heptameter. Thus a line of four dactyls would be called "dactylic tetrameter." *Meter* means **measure.** See **prosody** and **scansion.**

METONYMY: **Figure of speech** in which the name of one thing is substituted for another with which it is associated in some way. When we read "The White House announced," we know that, in fact, the White House represents a spokesman for the president or the administrative branch of government.

MISE-EN-SCÈNE: (1) The scenery and properties used in a play to represent the **setting** (lights, costume, sound, and special effects), along with the positioning and gestures of the actors. Whatever is needed to stage a scene. (2) By extension, the surroundings in which something happens.

MIXED METAPHOR: **Metaphor** in which the terms of comparison are shifted, usually unintentionally. "I smell a rat, and I shall nip it in the bud."

MOOD: Emotional atmosphere of a literary or dramatic work. The state of mind produced in the reader or audience. See **tone** and **atmosphere.**

MOTIVATE/MOTIVATION: Causes, within a **character** and the circumstances surrounding the character, for the ensuing action. Literally, the character is *moved* to seek revenge because of some prior event or need. Without adequate motivation, the **action** will seem arbitrary and unconvincing.

MYTH: **Narrative,** usually communally developed and transmitted, often involving supernatural events and gods. Myths tend to be stories of origination: of the universe, of a river, of the seasons, of an animal, of a royal family, of a nation, of a ceremony. Myths are grounded in the folk beliefs and ritual practices of tribes, nations, and races.

NARRATE: Act of reporting a story or a scene in a story. The result is the **narrative.**

NARRATIVE: See **narrate.**

NARRATOR: Person who tells the story to the audience. The narrator may be a character in the story (first person) or someone the author makes up to tell the story more objectively (third person). To speak of the story's "narrator" or "speaker" allows us to speak about the manner in which the story is being told without confusing that manner with the author's. A "naive narrator," for example, may take quite a bit of sophistication to create.

OBJECTIVE NARRATOR: See **point of view**.

ODE: **Lyric** poem generally celebrating a person, place, or event and usually employing a complex stanzaic pattern (see **stanza).** More loosely, any poem of commemoration.

OFF-RHYME: See **rhyme.**

OMNISCIENT NARRATOR: See **point of view**.

ONE-DIMENSIONAL CHARACTER: Character who is presented without an explanation of the reasons for his or her behavior and who behaves in a relatively predictable way (see **stock character**). The term is often used negatively. However, a good deal of comic writing relies on one-dimensional characters, and even in noncomic writing many of the characters who have simple tasks in the plot need only to be one dimensional.

ONOMATOPOEIA: Imitation in the sound of a word (or word combination) of the sound connected to the action or thing named or described. "Slap," "swish," and "ping-pong" are examples, as is Poe's invention "*tintinabulation* of the bells. . . ."

ORGANIC (FORM): Idea that a work of art should be seamless. Ideally, the work would be so integrated that no word, scene, character, line—not a period—could be changed or deleted without destroying the effect of the work. When form is organic, it seems to grow out of its content, that is, to be inseparable from it. This is an ideal that the writer should aim for—though, ultimately, the work may be submitted without having reached the promised land.

OVERWRITING: Usually caused by excessive use of adjectives and adverbs in an attempt to impress the reader.

OXYMORON: Compressed **paradox** in which an apparent contradiction makes sense when one of the terms is reinterpreted, as in "the sound of silence." Most often an adjective-noun combination: "terrible beauty" or "fortunate fall" or (humorously) "jumbo shrimp."

PACE: Tempo of the unfolding action as it is felt by the reader. The writer controls pace through a careful blending of dialogue, narration, description, exposition, and other elements. Long, unbroken stretches of one or another method destroy pace in fiction. In plays, pace refers to the timing of emotional ebbs and flows.

PARADOX: Contradiction, as in "paradoxically Mary's humor, the virtue that attracted people to her, kept her in hot water with her friends." Paradox creates tension in a work because the human mind wants to resolve the contradiction. For example, in the **oxymoron** "hateful love," the contradiction leads us to see that love (a good) is hateful (a bad) when it is unrequited. Paradox is not necessarily effective *unless you have provided a resolution or potential for a resolution* of that paradox.

PARODY: Imitation of the **style** of a literary or dramatic work, usually treating a contrasting subject.

PASSIVE: Grammatical constructions in which the action is not given an immediate actor or agent: the verb has no subject (in the expected place). For example, "The ball was hit out of the park." Who hit it? "It was discovered that. . . ." Who discovered it? Passive constructions are often called weak because the energizing link of actor and action is either missing or weakly made: "The pail of water was fetched by Jack and Jill." Though legitimate for some purposes, passive constructions often give the impression of indecision, fuzzy thinking or imagining, or downright deceitfulness, as in bureaucratic and academic prose.

PATHOS: Evocation of pity and sympathy, particularly by the sufferings of blameless or helpless characters.

PERIPETEIA: Sudden, usually unexpected, change of circumstances or fortune.

PERSONA: In poetry and prose fiction, the speaker or **narrator** of a literary work, especially as distinguished from the author. A figurative *mask* the author wears in order to tell a story. In drama, more simply a **character**.

PERSONIFICATION: Giving human characteristics to inanimate objects: "the sleeping sea." In contemporary writing this figure of speech is used sparingly and with great care.

PETRARCHAN SONNET: See **sonnet.**

PLOT: Sequence in which an author arranges (narrates, dramatizes) events (actions). The order in which the reader or spectator receives information. Only when this sequence is chronological is plot equivalent to story. A *story* stresses the temporal connections among events; a *plot* stresses the causal connections, often by introducing causes after their effects (as in a **flashback**).

PLOT LINE: Metaphorical way of talking about a plot as if it were, for example, a clothesline on which the author hangs scenes.

POETIC DICTION: Refers to the belief that poetry is, in part, characterized by a special type of language composed of archaic grammar and diction ("thou," "erst," "yore," "finny prey") and the avoidance of common, unpoetic words ("fish," "toes," "sit," "crap"). Modern poetic practice is to avoid poetic diction as artificial and, therefore, unable to communicate real emotions.

POINT OF ATTACK: Moment in a literary or dramatic work at which the plot, but not necessarily the story, begins. See *in medias res.*

POINT OF VIEW: Vantage point from which the materials of a story are presented. See Chapter 3.

PREMISE: Combination of **character, setting,** and situation at the **point of attack**.

PROOF(READ): To check your manuscript for grammatical, punctuation, and spelling errors. A manuscript with many proofing errors is unlikely to receive a favorable reading because the editor's attention is drawn to the manner rather than the matter.

PROSODY: Principle(s) of organization in a poem, especially those dealing with the **conventions** of **versification:** sound patterns, **rhyme, meter,** and **stanzas.** Also, the study of such principles. See also **scansion.**

PROTAGONIST: Main character in a work from whose destiny the plot develops. See **antagonist.**

PURPLE PROSE: Elaborately adjectival and adverbial descriptions torturing the reader's patience with high-sounding but often hollow verbiage. See **overwriting** and **hyperbole.**

PYRRHIC FOOT: See **meter.**

QUATRAIN: **Stanza** of four lines.

RESOLUTION: Moment at which the work's conflicting elements come together. See **denouement.**

REVISE/REVISION: To look at again. Of course, the idea is not to look at it but to make changes in what you look at. "Revision" is not the same as "proofing" or "editing." The word is meant to suggest a more radical act in which the author rearranges, eliminates, and adds elements to the work.

RHYME: *True* rhyme is the agreement in the last vowel and final consonant (if there is one) of two or more words: "Terence this is stupid st*uff*/You eat your victuals fast en*ough*" (A.E. Housman). Rhyme is no longer considered a sure sign that you are in the presence of poetry. Contemporary poets tend to avoid the blatancy of true rhyme in favor of less intense echoes, known collectively as off rhyme or slant rhyme. These include consonant echoes ("leaf/chaff") and even the more subdued mating of similar but not identical sounds ("meat/lad"). For some poets, the occurrence of the same sound(s) anywhere in the last syllable (or word) represents a rhyme ("lass/slip"). One special kind of off rhyme is **consonance,** in which a pattern of identical consonant sounds surrounds any vowel: "kiss/case."

RHYTHM: Flow of stressed and unstressed syllables, pauses, line breaks, and other devices the writer can control for musical effects. While we most frequently speak of "rhythm" or the lack thereof when considering poetry, prose also has rhythms that can add to or detract from your work. "Rhythm" can also be used more loosely to refer to how the parts of a work are patterned.

RUN-ON: See **enjambement.**

SARCASM: Type of bitter **irony** or cutting remark. It means literally "to tear flesh." A sarcastic tone in a character or narrator should be used with great care since it can easily be mistaken for mere nastiness.

SASE: Self-addressed, stamped envelope. To be included with all submissions to publishers.

SATIRE: Refers to those works (or parts of works) in which the actions or the statements of the characters ridicule contemporary behavior or fashion. Satiric writing relies for its effects on **irony.** Mishandled, satire falls off into mere **sarcasm.**

SCANSION: Analysis of the metrical features of a poem (accented and unaccented syllables, **feet, caesuras**). When we *scan,* we use graphic symbols to indicate and highlight the essential features. Scansion does not create these features, it only indicates what they are by conventional markings. Stressed syllables are indicated by slashes (/) placed over the syllables, unstressed syllables by hyphens (-) or macrons (˘) over the syllables, feet by vertical lines between the syllables (|) and caesuras by doubled vertical lines (||) at the pauses. **Rhyme** schemes are described by equating the rhymed syllables to letter symbols. Thus a poem in rhymed **couplets:** *aa bb cc,* etc.; a poem in **terza rima:** *aba bcb cdc ded,* etc.

SCENARIO: In playwriting and screenwriting, an extended outline of the play's **action** used to convey (to a producer) what the completed script will contain. Less formal than **treatment.**

SCENE: Dramatic subdivision of a work, identified by a change of place or time. See **act.**

SENTIMENTAL (SENTIMENTALITY): Not to be confused with "sentiment" (feeling), *sentimental* refers to the expression of inappropriately excessive emotions. One writes sentimentally when the language demands from the reader more intense responses than the occasion really demands. Unless meant humorously or to reveal the self-indulgence of a character, the writer of the following is sentimental: "Did my itty bitty kitty hurt its poor sweet tail?" A mature audience is likely to laugh at or throw aside sentimental writing.

SET (SETTING): Physical place (and all the things in it) created for a play or film or parts of them in which the scene happens. It is the place the author mentions or describes in a story. See *mise-en-scène.*

SHIFTS: Normally, a work is told in one tense (past or present) and from a single **point of view.** Avoid unexplained, casual, or hectic changes from one tense or point of view to another.

SIMILE: Usually described as a comparison using "like" or "as," the simile is a type of analogy in which the quality of one thing is used to identify it with what is essentially a different thing: A state is like a ship; She is as beautiful as a rose. Effective similes give us a sense of an unknown through a known. See **figure of speech** and **metaphor.**

SLANT RHYME: See **rhyme.**

SOLILOQUY: Related to the **dramatic monologue,** this kind of poem or (in a play) speech represents the reflections or thoughts of a character, addressed to no one in particular. A speech to one's self.

SONNET: Poem in fourteen lines, usually iambic pentameter, rhyming in one or another of the major sonnet traditions or a variation thereof. The **Petrarchan** (Italian) sonnet rhymes *abbaabba/cdcdcd.* The first eight lines (octave) always use envelope rhymes on the same two sounds. The final six lines (sestet) have various schemes, including *cdecde* and *cddcdd.* The Shakespearean (English) sonnet has three **quatrains** of alternating rhyme followed by a **couplet:** *ababcdcdefefgg.*

SPONDEE: See **meter.**

SPRUNG RHYTHM: System developed by Gerard Manley Hopkins in which a **foot** has one accented syllable followed by either no or varying numbers of unaccented syllables. Sprung rhythm forces an accumulation of stressed syllables, as in these lines from "The Windhover" by Hopkins:

> Brute beauty and valour and act, oh, air, pride, plume, here
> Buckle! AND the fire that breaks from thee then, a billion
> Times told lovelier, more dangerous, O my chevalier!

STAGE BUSINESS: Refers to the actions of an actor that are usually *suggested* by the script rather than *stated* in it. For example, if coffee is being served, the actor may sip from the cup for a needed pause or in order to do something while another character is speaking.

STANZA: Group of lines defined by a space break from another, usually equivalent, group of lines. Stanzas are frequently organized around metrical (see **meter**) and **end rhyme** patterns that are repeated from stanza to stanza. See **strophe**. Though both *stanza* and *paragraph* are divisions that assume there is some type of internal organization, we do not use the word "paragraph" when speaking of a stanza.

STEREOTYPE: From the process that printers use to produce many copies from a casting, by analogy this refers to a character type continued or repeated without change from one work to another. Though the word is often used with a negative connotation, writers often rely on stereotypes. See **stock character** and **one-dimensional character.**

STICHIC: Continuous, unbroken poem. Browning's "My Last Duchess" is stichic.

STOCK CHARACTER: Such characters lack a unique set of traits, but they are immediately recognizable from their past appearances: "the good-hearted whore," "the wise-cracking Brooklyn street kid," "the deaf but spry grandmother."

STOCK SITUATION: Conventional situations found frequently in fiction and drama. Examples are (1) a boarding house (dorm, boat, hotel) filled with quirky people and managed by one relatively sane person, and (2) two girls—best friends—falling in love with the same guy.

STORY: See **plot.**

STREAM OF CONSCIOUSNESS: Type of **interior monologue** that pretends to imitate the unselected, chaotic, unorganized flow of real thought. Useful for writing works that invoke psychological realism.

STROPHE/STROPHIC: A strophe is a major division of a poem. A strophic poem is one that is divided into distinct, though not necessarily equivalent, units rather than being continuous **(stichic).** See **stanza.**

STYLE: Manner of expression typical of a writer or artist. Distinctive styles result from identifiable habits of **diction** and **syntax.** "Style" can also refer to typical choices of material or point of view. Everyone, of course, has a style, but that style may be dull or ineffective because the language is trite or inappropriate for poetry or storytelling.

SUBPLOT: Secondary series of actions that reflects and heightens the concerns of the main **plot.** Within a narrative that presents a group's struggle to survive a storm, a romance may spring up between two of the characters. The romance, as it complicates the survival plot, adds interest and point.

SUBTEXT: What is implied rather than stated in a communication. Whatever the words say on the surface, like an iceberg, most of the message lies beneath. At the simplest level, for example, "How did you like my poem?" contains a request for affirmation, a concern about your opinion, and an indication of insecurity (otherwise why ask?). It *is not* a request for an honest opinion, and the asker would be hurt if you gave a negative one. See **text.**

SYLLABIC VERSE: Verse in which lines are defined by the number of syllables.

SYMBOL: Concrete objects (or evocations of concrete objects through words) that stand for or evoke images of ideas, stories, or other things. *Natural symbols,* like water, may literally be life-giving and purifying, as well as suggesting spiritual purification. Both natural symbols and cultural symbols (the cross) or signs (a traffic light or these very words) can communicate relatively simple ideas (stop or you'll get a ticket) and extremely complex relationships (sacrifice, redemption, and salvation). Everyone, including writers, uses symbols for communication. For the most part it is a mistake to work consciously to create symbols for your works. In the process of creating precise images, symbols will naturally emerge. Usually people do not read or go to the theater for the symbolism.

SYNECDOCHE: Figure of speech in which a part refers to the whole: "Can I borrow your wheels tonight?"

SYNOPSIS: Summary of the plot. If you are asked for a synopsis, don't tell what the work is supposed to mean; tell what happens.

SYNTAX: *Order* in which you place the words. For example, in English syntax you normally place the modifier before the noun and the subject before the verb. (*Grammar* refers to how a word is changed to indicate number, time, and gender.) Unusual syntax in poetry or awkward syntax in prose tends to call attention to the order of the words and draws attention from their meaning.

TERCET: **Stanza** of three lines. A *triplet* rhymes *aaa.*

TERZA RIMA: Three-line stanza interlocked with adjoining **tercets** rhyming *aba bcb cdc* and so forth, as in Shelley's "Ode to the West Wind":

> Make me thy lyre, even as the forest is:
> What if my leaves are falling like its own!
> The tumult of thy mighty harmonies
>
> Will take from both a deep, autumnal tone,
> Sweet though in sadness. Be thou, Spirit fierce,
> My spirit! Be thou me, impetuous one!

TEXT: Either the written material under discussion ("Let's look at the text") or the surface meaning of the material. *Text* often refers to the **denotative** meaning, the vehicle for the **subtext.**

THEME: Paraphraseable *message* in a work. Literally "a proposition," the theme of a work is likely to involve the writer's view about society, nature, or some other system of relationships. A writer who has studied and thought most deeply about a subject and who has felt it most intensely is likely to have the most interesting things to say about it. Even if your wish to communicate a theme is the reason you start writing, your job is to write the work well. Don't push the theme; it will get in.

TONE: Refers to the narrator's (or speaker's) attitude toward the subject and/or the reader: haughty, playful, somber, nasty, or ironic, for example. Tone is related to **point of view** and **subtext** in that it results from choices in content and technique: images, symbols, rhythms, sentence structure, and so on. Metaphorically, "tone of voice." See also **mood.**

TREATMENT: Technical term for an extended synopsis that presents your idea for a film or television program. There are quite specific rules for doing a treatment and you should read several treatments before trying your own. Compare **scenario.**

TRITE: Word for a figure of speech that no longer surprises because it is shopworn. Do not confuse trite ("that's the way the ball bounces") with idiomatic ("shopworn").

TROCHEE: See **meter.**

VERISIMILITUDE: *Like* reality. Distinguish between reporting real events and making up events that appear to be real. The creative writer's task is the latter, not the former.

VERSE/VERSIFICATION: Metrical aspect of poetry. Sometimes used synonymously for **line** or metrical, rhymed passages; for example, "in the following verses. . . ." Also used pejoratively, as in "that's merely verse," suggesting the work in question only wears the costume of poetry.

VILLANELLE: Nineteen-line poem in which the first and third lines of the first **tercet** are alternately the last lines of the following four tercets and also form the couplet that ends the concluding **quatrain:** A_1bA_2 abA_1 abA_2 abA_1 abA_2 abA_1A_2. Thus there are only two rhyme sounds. Most often in iambic pentameter.

Acknowledgments

We wish to thank the following authors and publishers for permission to reprint or publish for the first time the following:

The Morning Watch by James Agee. Copyright 1959 by James Agee. Copyright © renewed 1979 by Mia Fritsch Agee. Excerpt reprinted by permission of Houghton Mifflin Company.

Lines from poetry exercise "Hope" by Wilma A. Alcala used by permission of the author.

"World's Fair Proposal" by Thomas Allen and Allan B. Lefcowitz, printed by permission of the authors.

"The Poem Queen" from *Dame* by Susan Astor. Copyright © 1980 University of Georgia Press. Reprinted by permission of the University of Georgia Press.

"Small Explosion" by Elizabeth Bennett first appeared in *Poet Lore* (Fall 1986). Reprinted, along with earlier draft, by permission of the author.

Excerpt from "The Last of the Gold Star Mothers" by Carol Bly. Copyright © 1979 by Carol Bly. First published in *The New Yorker*. Reprinted from *Backbone* by permission of George Borchardt, Inc. on behalf of the author.

Excerpts from *The Heart of Boswell* by James Boswell, edited by Mark Harris and published by McGraw-Hill Book Company. Copyright © 1981. Reprinted by permission of the publisher and the Editorial Committee of the Boswell Papers, Yale University.

Excerpt from *Galileo* by Bertolt Brecht translated by Charles Laughton published by Grove Press, 1966, reprinted by permission of Grove Press.

"Figure Eights" from *Letters from the Floating World* by Siv Cedering. Copyright © 1984 by Siv Cedering. Reprinted by permission of the University of Pittsburgh Press.

From *The Journals of John Cheever* by John Cheever. Copyright © 1990 by Mary Cheever, Susan Cheever, Benjamin Cheever, and Federico Cheever. Reprinted by permisson of Alfred A. Knopf, Inc.

Poetry exercise "January Thunder" by Sally Cheney used by permission of the author.

Passenger to Frankfurt, by Agatha Christie. Copyright © 1970 by Agatha Christie Limited. Excerpt from the Introduction reprinted by permission of Dodd, Mead & Company, Inc.

"At My Father's Grave" by John Ciardi. Copyright © 1966, the Estate of John Ciardi. Excerpt used by permission of the Literary Executor of the Estate.

Excerpts from *Blithe Spirit* by Noel Coward. Copyright © by the Estate of Noel Coward. Reprinted by permission of Michael Imison Playwrights Ltd.

"Inside Out" by Sandy Daniels reprinted by permission of the author.

Excerpt from *What's Bred in the Bone* by Robertson Davies. Copyright © 1985 Robertson Davies. All rights reserved. Reprinted by permission of Viking Penguin Inc.

"Dreams" by James J. Dorbin is reprinted by permission of the author.

Excerpt from "Sunday at the Zoo" reprinted from *Brass Knuckles* by Stuart Dybek, University of Pittsburgh Press, 1979, by permission of the author.

"The Dance" from *Victims of the Latest Dance Craze* by Cornelius Eady. Copyright © 1985 by Cornelius Eady. Reprinted by permission of Omnation Press.

"Anatomy of Melancholy" by Denise Edson reprinted by permission of author.

Excerpt from *The Great Gatsby* by F. Scott Fitzgerald. Copyright © 1925 Charles Scribner's Sons; copyright © renewed 1955 Frances Scott Fitzgerald Lanahan. Reprinted with the permission of Charles Scribner's Sons, an imprint of Macmillan Publishing Company.

Poetry exercises beginning "Summer came on slow" and "Kirk burned for a while" by Bruce Fleming. Used by permission of author.

"August from My Desk" and "Earthworm" from *Resuming Green* by Roland Flint. Copyright 1965, 1968, 1972, 1973, 1974, 1975, 1976, 1978, 1980, 1983 by Roland Flint. Reprinted by permission of Doubleday, a division of Bantam, Doubleday, Dell Publishing Group.

"Fog Township," reprinted from *Seals in the Inner Harbor* by Brendan Galvin. Copyright © 1986 by Brendan Galvin. Used by permission of the author.

"An Alabama August," by Charles Ghigna, first appeared in *Southern Poetry Review*, Fall 1983, vol. 23, no. 2. Copyright © by Charles Ghinga. Reprinted by permission of the author.

"Affirmations" from *Long Walks in the Afternoon* by Margaret Gibson. Copyright © 1983 by Margaret Gibson. Excerpt reprinted by permission of Louisiana State University Press.

Trifles by Susan Glaspell. Copyright © 1920, renewed 1948 by Susan Glaspell. Reprinted from *Plays* by Susan Glaspell published by Dodd, Mead & Company.

"Rhody's Path," by William Goyen, copyright © 1960 by William Goyen, renewed 1988 Doris Roberts and Curtis William Goyen Family Trust. Reprinted from *The Collected Stories of William Goyen*, (Doubleday, 1975), by permission of Weiner & Weiner, Inc., New York.

Lines from poetry exercise "Island" by Kirsten Benson Hampton used by permission of the author.

"Actor's Blood," by Ben Hecht, excerpt reprinted from *The Collected Stories of Ben Hecht* Copyright © 1945 by Ben Hecht, copyright renewed 1973 by Rose Hecht. Used by permission of Crown Publishers, Inc.

"A Very Short Story" from *In Our Time* by Ernest Hemingway. Copyright 1925 Charles Scribner's Sons; copyright © renewed 1953 Ernest Hemingway. Reprinted with the permission of Charles Scribner's Sons, an imprint of Macmillan Publishing Company.

Excerpt from "In Another Country" from *The Snows of Kilimanjaro and Other Stories*. Copyright 1927 Charles Scribner's Sons; copyright renewed 1955 Ernest Hemingway. Reprinted with the permission of Charles Scribner's Sons, an imprint of Macmillan Publishing Company.

Poetry exercise beginning "Early one morning" by Jim Henley used by permission of the author.

"The Return" from *Long Island Light: Poems and a Memoir* by William Heyen. Published by Vanguard Press. Copyright © 1977 William Heyen. Reprinted by permission of the author.

Excerpts from *The Imprisonment of Clarence Atwater* by Ann M. Heyneman used by permission of the author.

"From the wash the laundress sends," by A. E. Housman. Copyright 1936 by Barclays Bank, Ltd. Copyright © 1964 by Robert E. Symons. Reprinted from *The Collected Poems of A. E. Housman* by permission of Henry Holt and Company, Inc.

Excerpt from "Thank You, M'am" by Langston Hughes from *The Langston Hughes Reader*. Copyright © 1958 by Langston Hughes. Copyright renewed 1986 by George Houston Bass. Reprinted by permission of Harold Ober Associates, Incorporated.

The lines from "Letter to Kathy from Wisdom" are reprinted from *Selected Poems* by Richard Hugo, by permission of W. W. Norton & Company, Inc. Copyright © 1979, 1977, 1975, 1973 by W. W. Norton & Co., Inc.

"Criminal Career," by Josephine Jacobsen, excerpt reprinted from *Adios, Mr. Moxley: Thirteen Stories*, published by Jackpine Press, copyright © 1986 by Josephine Jacobsen. Used by permission of author.

Poetry exercise "Desert Rain Poem" by Alice S. James used by permission of the author.

"Meeting the Day" from *Sleeping Near the Fire* by Philip K. Jason. Copyright © 1983 by Philip K. Jason. Published by Dryad Press. Reprinted, along with early drafts, by permission of the author.

"Because I Never Learned the Names of Flowers," by Rod Jellema, reprinted from *The Eighth Day: New & Selected Poems.* Copyright 1984 by Rod Jellema. Used by permission of Dryad Press.

"The Boarding House" and excerpt from "The Dead" from *Dubliners* by James Joyce. Copyright 1916 by B. W. Huebsch. Definitive text. Copyright © 1967 by the Estate of James Joyce. All rights reserved. Reprinted by permission of Viking Penguin Inc.

"Sunday in the Park" by Bel Kaufman from The Available Press *PEN Short Story Collection.* Copyright © 1985 by the PEN American Center. Reprinted by permission of the author.

"Balancing Act" from *Nothing to Do with Love* by Joyce Reiser Kornblatt. Copyright © 1975, 1978, 1979, 1981 by Joyce Reiser Kornblatt. All rights reserved. Reprinted by permission of Viking Penguin Inc.

"Stopped Time in Blue and Yellow," from *Our Ground Time Here Will Be Brief* by Maxine Kumin. Copyright © 1975 by Maxine Kumin. All rights reserved. Reprinted by permission of Viking Penguin Inc.

"The Lost Cottage" from *Family Dancing* by David Leavitt. Copyright © 1983, 1984 by David Leavitt. Reprinted by permission of Alfred A. Knopf, Inc.

"For Fran" from *On the Edge* (originally published by The Stone Wall Press copyright © 1963) in *Selected Poems* by Philip Levine. Copyright © 1984 by Philip Levine. Excerpt reprinted with the permission of Atheneum Publishers.

Poetry exercise "Teen Mall Rats Die in Suicide Pact" by Rose MacMurray used by permission of the author.

"Bagged Air" by Karen Malloy reprinted by permission of the author.

Excerpt from short story exercise "GP" by Jerome Marr used by permission of author.

"Hope," from *Forseeable Futures* by William Matthews. Copyright © 1987 by William Matthews. Reprinted by permission of Houghton Mifflin Company.

"Discipline Is the Write Way," by Colman McCarthy appeared in the *Washington Post,* January 2, 1987. © 1987, Washington Post Writers Group, reprinted with permission.

Excerpt from *The Plain Princess* by Phyllis McGinley. Copyright © 1945 by Phyllis McGinley, renewed 1973 by Phyllis McGinley and Helen Stone. Reprinted by permission of Curtis Brown, Ltd.

Excerpt from *The Day They Shot John Lennon* by James McLure. Copyright James McLure. Used by permission of Bret Adams Ltd. Artists Agency.

"The Fish," by Marianne Moore, from *Collected Poems.* Copyright 1935 by Marianne Moore, renewed 1963 by Marianne Moore and T. S. Eliot. Excerpt reprinted with permission of Macmillan Publishing Company.

Vowel and consonant charts adapted from *Western Wind: An Introduction to Poetry* by John Frederick Nims. Used by permission of Random House, Inc.

The Diary of Anais Nin, Volume I, copyright © 1966 by Anais Nin. Excerpt reprinted by permission of Harcourt Brace Jovanovich.

"Gloves" from *A Language of Hands* by Jean Nordhaus. Copyright © 1982 by SCOP Publications, Inc. Reprinted by permission of the author.

Excerpt from *Going After Cacciato* by Tim O'Brien. Copyright © 1975 by Tim O'Brien. Reprinted by arrangement with Delacorte Press/Seymour Lawrence. All rights reserved.

"The Waves" from *Dream Work* by Mary Oliver. Copyright © 1986 by Mary Oliver. Reprinted by permission of The Atlantic Monthly Press.

Excerpt from *The Cannibal Galaxy* by Cynthia Ozick. Copyright © 1983 by Cynthia Ozick. Reprinted by permission of Alfred A. Knopf, Inc.

"Written in Pencil in the Sealed Railway-Car" from *Variable Directions* by Dan Pagis. Translated by Stephen Mitchell. Copyright © 1989 by permission of North Point Press.

Excerpt from "The Collection" from *Complete Works: Two* by Harold Pinter. Copyright © 1963, 1964 by H. Pinter Ltd. Reprinted by permission of Grove Press.

"What Doesn't Go Away," from *What Women Know, What Men Believe,* by Wyatt Prunty. Copyright © 1986 by The Johns Hopkins University Press, Baltimore and London. Excerpt reprinted by permission of the publisher.

Poetry exercise beginning "The old man sits" by Linda Replogle used by permission of the author.

"Lifeguards" by John M. Richardson reprinted by permission of the author.

"Murder Mystery 1" and "Murder Mystery 2" by Jay Rogoff from *Shaping: New Poems in Traditional Prosodies,* edited by Philip K. Jason, published by Dryad Press. Copyright © 1978 Jay Rogoff. Reprinted by permission of the author.

"Good Advice Is Rarer Than Rubies" by Salman Rushdie first appeared in *The New Yorker*. Copyright © 1987 by Salman Rushdie. Reprinted by permission of Wylie, Aitken & Stone, Inc.

Poetry exercise "Departure" by Pedro J. Saavedra used by permission of the author.

Poetry exercise "Sunday Evening Matisse," by Lisa A. Schenkel, used by permission of the author.

"Jazz Sundae" by Peter M. Scheufele reprinted by permission of the author.

A Poet's Journal: Days of 1945–1951, by George Seferis, Cambridge, Massachusetts: Harvard University Press, Copyright © 1974 by the President and Fellows of Harvard College, excerpt reprinted by permission of the author.

Excerpt from *The Killing Ground* by Mary Lee Settle. Copyright © 1982 by Mary Lee Settle. Reprinted by permission of Farrar, Straus, and Giroux, Inc.

"A Cut Flower" by Karl Shapiro. Copyright © 1942 and renewed 1970 by Karl Shapiro. Reprinted from *Collected Poems, 1940–1972* by permission of Wieser & Wieser, Inc.

"French Movie" by Pat Shelley was originally published in *Bogg* #56 (1986). Reprinted with permission of the author.

"Leaving," reprinted from *The Science of Goodbyes* by Myra Sklarew, © 1982 the University of Georgia Press. Reprinted by permission of the author.

"Night Fishing for Blues" reprinted from *Cumberland Station* by Dave Smith. Copyright © 1971, 1973, 1974, 1975, 1976 by Dave Smith. Excerpt used by permission of the author and University of Illinois Press.

Ellis Island: Then and Now. Text by Sharon Spencer. Photographs by Dennis Toner. Copyright © 1988. Published by Lincoln Springs Press, Franklin Lakes, N.J. Material reprinted as it originally appeared in *Paintbrush* 11/12 (1984–1985). Used by permission of Sharon Spencer and Dennis Toner.

"A Woman Disappears Inside Her Own Life" from *Deception Pass* by Sue Standing. Copyright © 1984 by Alice James Books, Cambridge, Mass. Reprinted by permission of the publisher.

From *Working Days: The Journals of the Grapes of Wrath* by John Steinbeck, Introduction by Robert DeMott. Copyright © 1989 by Elaine Steinbeck. Introduction copyright © 1989 by Robert DeMott. Used by permission of Viking Penguin, a division of Penguin Books USA Inc.

"Costume Book" section of "A Short History of the Fur Trade," from *Land of Superior Mirages* by Adrien Stoutenburg. Copyright © 1986 by The Johns Hopkins University Press. Reprinted by permission of the publisher.

"The Blindman" from *New & Selected: Things Taking Place* by May Swenson, published by Atlantic Monthly Press. Copyright © 1965 by May Swenson. Reprinted by permission of the author.

Adaptation of "Gun and Bible: Ritual Poem" exercise from *Creative Writing Exercises* by Ross Talarico, Associated Creative Writers, Publisher, 1982. Used by permission of the author.

Excerpt from "In the Miro District" by Peter Taylor from *In the Miro District and Other Stories*. Copyright 1974, 1975, 1976, 1977 by Peter Taylor. Reprinted with permission of Alfred A. Knopf, Inc.

"Do Not Go Gentle Into That Good Night" and "The Hand That Signed the Paper" from *The Poems of Dylan Thomas*. Copyright 1939 by New Directions Publishing Corporation, 1952 by Dylan Thomas. Excerpts used by permission of New Directions Publishing Corporation.

Poetry exercise "Land Lord Dharma" by Jerry Webster used by permission of the author.

"The Dance" by William Carlos Williams from *Later Collected Poems*. Copyright © 1944 by William Carlos Williams. Reprinted by permission of New Directions Publishing Corporation.

"Friends" from *The Snow Prince* by Harold Witt. Copyright © 1982 by Harold Witt. Originally published in *The Hudson Review*. Reprinted with permission of Blue Unicorn and the author.

"Soap Opera," from *Good Trembling* by Baron Wormser. Copyright © 1985 by Baron Wormser. Reprinted by permission of Houghton Mifflin Company.

"Eli and the Coal Strippers" from *With Wanda: Town and Country Poems* by Paul Zimmer. Copyright © 1980 by Paul Zimmer. Reprinted by permission of Dryad Press.

"Beaufort Scale" is used by permission. From *Webster's Ninth New Collegiate Dictionary*, © 1987 by Merriam-Webster Inc., publisher of the Merriam-Webster® dictionaries.

"Florida Bog Reveals 8,000-Year-Old Secret," reprinted in shortened form from *The Washington Post*, October 26, 1986. Copyright © 1986 The Washington Post. Headline and Daylight-Saving Time graphic, along with article, used by permission of the publisher.

"Sovran Bank Advertisement," Copyright © Sovran Financial Corporation and Lawlor Ballard Advertising Used by permission of Sovran Financial Corporation.

Other quotations:

From "The Grasshopper" and "Rothschild's Fiddle" collected in *Anton Chekhov's Short Stories*. Edited by Ralph E. Matlaw. New York: W. W. Norton & Company, 1979.

From "Goin'a Buffalo" by Ed Bullins. Collected in *New Black Playwrights*. New York: Avon Books, 1970.

From *Writing Fiction* by Janet Burroway. 2nd edition. Boston: Little, Brown and Company, 1987.

From *Writing Fiction* by R. V. Cassill. 2nd edition. Englewood Cliffs, New Jersey: Prentice-Hall, Inc., 1975.

From *Crimes of the Heart* by Beth Henley. New York: Viking Penguin Inc., 1982.

From "Innovation and Redemption: What Literature Means," included in *Art & Ardor* by Cynthia Ozick. New York: E. P. Dutton, 1984.

We would also like to thank our students and colleagues at The Writer's Center in Bethesda, Maryland for their many valuable suggestions during the preparation of this book.

Index